THE EARLY
BIOGRAPHIES OF

SAMUEL JOHNSON

THE EARLY
BIOGRAPHIES OF

SAMUEL JOHNSON

Edited by

O M Brack, Jr.
Robert E. Kelley

UNIVERSITY OF IOWA PRESS

IOWA CITY

Library of Congress Catalog Card Number:73–77385
University of Iowa Press, Iowa City, Iowa 52242
© *1974 by The University of Iowa. All rights reserved*
Printed in the United States of America
ISBN 87745–038–2

Contents

Preface

Biography, for the purposes of this collection, has been rather loosely defined as any account that begins with the phrase, "Samuel Johnson was born," or some rough equivalent, and makes some attempt, no matter how haphazard, to survey his life or his career in chronological order. Readers of this volume will be quick to note how repetitious these early biographies are. But we have included all of the early lives of Johnson in the belief that the integrity of each biography — and the rather full account of his standing in the eyes of his contemporaries that these lives offer, taken together — is a concern that overrides the problem of frequent repetitiousness. The texts of the biographies have been reproduced, to the extent possible, just as they appeared. Documents (such as the Walmesley and Gower letters) and long quotations from printed material (such as "Ad Urbanum") have been omitted after their first appearance, with the omission recorded in the text. Admittedly there are some minor variations, but most of these can be accounted for by the cavalier attitude of the writers of the period toward quotations, and this sacrifice of completeness seemed worthwhile in the interest of conserving forests. Misprints have been corrected and only minimal changes in the spelling or punctuation have been made when they seemed necessary for the sake of clarity and consistency. Except for proper names, there has been no attempt at normalization. We have not preserved the typographical peculiarities of the eighteenth-century text; the long "s," the quotation marks lacing the margin, the ornamental capitals, and so forth, have all been brought into conformity with modern usage.

We have exercised what we hope is sensible rigor in annotation, keeping the footnotes as few in number and as brief as possible. All notes are placed at the back of the book. Since these biographies are so derivative, annotating each one as if it were an entity unto itself would have resulted in apparatus more repetitious and unwieldy than useful. Our editorial procedures in this regard were also determined by the assumption that the audience for which this volume is intended is comprised of readers who will bring to it a knowledge of and interest in Johnson and biography. At the same time, we recognize that even scholars cannot remember everything — for example, first ascriptions to the Johnson canon, the date of Johnson's first meeting with Garrick, and so on. We have tried in each case to annotate Johnson and not the learning of the biographer. This is a particularly crucial distinction with a writer like Tyers, who draws on a large body of classical and contemporary literature to illustrate his observations on Johnson's life and character. To have identified all of these quotations and allusions would have swelled the volume without adding to our knowledge of Johnson. If the author identified a quotation or clarified an allusion in a footnote, we have brought it into conformity with modern scholarship. The footnotes which were supplied by the biographer are indicated thus: [A]. We have allowed the biographers' opinions to stand without comment unless based on factual misinformation. On the assumption that this collection will be used in conjunction with the three major contemporary sources of Johnsonian biography — Boswell, Hawkins, and Piozzi — we have heavily cross-referenced our materials to their works. For convenience, and because of the inaccuracy in quoting from Johnson, we have made citations to the standard editions of his writings. We have tried to correct the errors in the biographies but have not always done so when an error persists because of the use of a common source. In the case of such persistent errors we have corrected them only the first time they appear. It is hoped that the index will serve as a useful cross-reference here. We have corrected a number of wrong dates in square brackets in the text, particularly to keep the chronology straight, when practical. Occasional names have also, when practical, been supplied in square brackets if there was any possibility of confusion or if a footnote would otherwise have been necessary. In the use of bracketed material our aim has been to impede the flow of the text as little as possible. Persons named in the passages are normally identified from the *DNB* or the Hill-Powell edition of Boswell's *Life* without acknowledgement. Several quotations and paraphrased passages we have not identified, either because we could not locate the printed source or because we assumed that the material was transmitted orally to the biographers, especially to those who knew Johnson personally.

Our *Samuel Johnson's Early Biographers* is intended to serve as an introduction to this material.

Our first and greatest debt is to Herman W. Liebert, who first suggested that we undertake this project and has provided generous assistance through all of its phases. We are grateful to James L. Clifford, Donald J. Greene, William Kupersmith, John C. Riely, and the late Curt A. Zimansky for giving of their time and energies to further our researches, especially in the difficult later stages of the work. For assistance of various kinds we are indebted to Lois Fields, Terry Firkins, Vince Heinrichs, Leonard Kallio, Cindy Kuhn, Donald Stefanson, Robert and Catherine Ward, and Evan Watkins. Particular thanks must go to Sharon Graves and Linda Schuppener for their good-humored and excellent assistance. Our researches have been greatly facilitated by the cooperation and assistance of the staffs of the Yale University Library, particularly Kenneth Nesheim, the University of Illinois Library and the University of Iowa Library. To our wives we are grateful for their continued patience during an association with the early biographers of Johnson which has persisted longer than either would care to remember.

$$\boxed{I}$$

(1762)

Mr. Johnson

William Rider

Samuel Johnson, M.A. after having studied at *Oxford*, kept for some Time
a private Academy at *Lichfield*, but being by Nature endowed with a
Genius which shews him to have been born to instruct Mankind, and
not teach Boys, he came to *London*, where he soon acquired a distinguished Character in the Republic of Letters. That excellent Collection
of Essays, which he published in periodical Papers, under the Title of
The Rambler, would be sufficient to immortalize his Name. It is by many
(and in my Opinion not without Reason) preferred to the *Spectator*;
and indeed, if it was only equal to it (which it is universally allowed
to be) it would reflect the highest Honour upon its Author; for he
that alone has composed a Work equal in Merit to one produced by
a Coalition of the brightest Geniuses, is doubtless worthy of the highest
Encomiums. Mr. *Johnson* has likewise composed another Work of the
same Kind, entitled, *The Idler*. This, though superior to most of the
Productions of other modern Essay Writers, does not equal the *Rambler*,
and several of the Papers, which turn upon Subjects before treated
in the latter, though in different Words, give Room to think, that the
Author had almost exhausted his Stock of Subjects in the first Work.
But Mr. *Johnson*'s Genius is as various as prolific; he does not derive
his Reputation as an Author from one Species of Composition. His
Tragedy of *Irene*, though it was played without Success, discovers the
true Spirit of Poetry, and is allowed by all judicious Critics to be the
best that has been wrote these last twenty Years. As this Piece is not

now generally known,[1] I shall beg Leave to cite one Passage of it, as a Proof of the Truth of what I have advanced, and a Specimen of this Author's Genius for Poetry. At a Meeting of Conspirators, one of which is known to be deeply in Love with a certain Lady, an old Visir reproaches the Lover with proposing a Measure favourable to the Interest of his Passion, though it ran counter to the Dictates of Reason; whereupon the amorous Conspirator makes the following spirited Reply.[2]

> Hast thou grown old amidst the Wiles of Courts,
> And turn'd the instructive Page of human Life,
> To cant at last of Reason to a Lover?
> Know'st thou not yet, when Love invades the Soul,
> That all her Faculties receive its Chains?
> That Reason yields Submission to its Empire,
> Or else but struggles to be more enslav'd?

A little lower he speaks of Reason in the following Terms.

> Reason, the hoary Dotard, that to shun
> The Rocks of Life, must ever miss the Port.

Nothing can be more strong and pathetic than the Exclamations made by the Emperor upon being informed that *Irene*, whom he passionately loved, had been put to Death, particularly the following.

> Such Beauty, Sweetness, Worth were cheaply bought
> With half the groveling Slaves that load the Earth.

Besides this Tragedy Mr. *Johnson* has wrote a Poem entitled *London,* which gave high Satisfaction to all Persons of Taste. About three Years ago he published *Rasselas, Prince of Abyssinia*, a Novel in the oriental Way, a Species of Writing, which is near of Kin to Poetry, and in which Mr. *Johnson* is allowed to surpass all *English* Authors. The *Life of Savage,* wrote by him, is looked upon as a Masterpiece of Biography, and shews that he is possessed of considerable Talents for writing History, though he has not thought proper to attach himself to that Branche of Literature. To conclude Mr. *Johnson*'s Character as an Author, he is endowed with a Genius at once both penetrating and sublime: The Sagacity of his Criticisms sufficiently proves his Penetration; the noble Enthusiasm that runs through his allegorical and oriental Compositions equally demonstrates his Turn to the sublime. From these two Qualities united, we may reasonably expect that his Commentary upon *Shakespeare* will do Justice to that great Author, who has hitherto suffered so much

by Editors. With Regard to Mr. *Johnson*'s private Character, he seems
to be entirely of Mr. *Pope*'s Opinion, that

> All Praise is foreign but of true Desert,
> Plays round the Head, but comes not to the Heart.

Not contented with surpassing other Men in Genius, he makes it his
Study to surpass them in Virtue, and all that Humanity and that sincere
Attachment to Religion, which shine through his Writings, are equally
conspicuous in his Life. Though by no Means in Affluence, he is always
ready to assist the indigent; and being of a truly philosophical Disposition, he is satisfied with a Competency, though by the Superiority of
his Talents, he might have long since made a Fortune.

(1764)

Mr. Samuel Johnson, M.A.

David Erskine Baker

This excellent Writer, who is no less the Glory of the present Age and Nation, than he will be the Admiration of all succeeding ones, received his Education and took his Degrees at the University of *Oxford,*[1] after quitting which Place I have been informed he for some Time was Master of a private Academy at *Lichfield.* A Genius like his, however, could not long content itself with that most disagreeable of all Drudgery, the mere classical Instruction of Youth, nor suffer its Brightness to be concealed in the dull Obscurity of a Country Academy. He came up therefore to *London,* where he immediately gave Proofs how high a Rank in the World of Letters he deserved to hold. Having conceived the Design of one of the noblest and most useful, though at the same Time the most laborious Works that could be possibly undertaken, *viz.* A compleat *Grammar* and *Dictionary* of our hitherto unsettled Language; he drew up a Plan of the said Design, in a Letter to the Right Honourable the Earl of *Chesterfield,* which being published, gave the strongest Proof, in its own Composition, how great a Degree of grammatical Perfection and classical Elegance the *English* Tongue was capable of being brought to. The Execution of this Plan cost him the Labour of many Years; but the Manner in which it was at last executed made ample Amends for all the Expectations of the Public in Regard to it for so long a Time; and the Honours paid him on the Occasion of its Publication by several of the foreign Academies, particularly by the *Academia della Crusca,* leave all Encomium on the Work in this Place entirely unnecessary. During some Intervals of Recess necessary to the Fatigue of this stupendous Undertaking, Mr. *Johnson* published many other Pieces which are most truly capital in their Kind; among which the *Rambler,* a Series of periodical Essays which came out twice a Week for two Years successively, stood in the foremost Rank. In the Course of so great a Number of these Papers as this long Period demanded, the Number which the Undertaker of them was favoured with by others, was inconsiderable;[2] and yet, on the whole, the Product of this single Genius, thus perpetually employed, proved at least equal, if not superior, to that of the Club of first-rate Wits, who were concerned in those celebrated Works the *Spectator* and *Tatler.* Mr. *Johnson*'s Stile in Prose is nervous and classically correct; in Verse his Numbers are harmonious and musical, yet bold and poignant, and on the whole approach nearer to Mr. *Pope*'s Manner of Versification than that of any other Writer; and though he has favoured the World with but little in *absolute Verse* (for all his *Prose* is *Poetry*) yet that little, like Diamonds of the first Water, will ever be held in the highest Estimation, whilst Gems of larger Bulk, with less intrinsic Worth, are scarcely looked upon. In short, while the Name of *Juvenal* shall be remembered, this Gentleman's improved Imitations of him, in his two Poems, entitled *London,* and *The Vanity of Human Wishes,* must be read with Delight. His Imagination is amazingly extensive, and his Knowledge of Men and Manners unbounded, as may be plainly traced in his *Eastern* Stories in the *Rambler,* in which he has not only supported to the utmost the Sublimity of the Eastern manner of Expression, but even greatly excelled any of the Oriental Writers in the Fertility of his Invention, the Conduct of his Plots, and the Justice and Strength of his Sentiments.[3] His capital Work of that Kind, however, is a Novel, entitled *Rasselas, Prince of Abyssinia,* too well known and universally read to need any Comment here, and in which, as he does at present, so he probably ever will, stand without an equal.

Our Author has wrote only one dramatic Piece, the Success of which was not equal to its Merit, owing entirely to his having too strictly adhered to the Aristotelian Rules of the Drama to render his Piece agreeable to the Taste of our present theatrical Audiences, who look for little more than Plot and Incident, without paying any great Regard either to Character, Language, or Sentiment; it was performed at *Drury-Lane* Theatre, and entitled,

Irene. Trag.

It would, however, be the highest Injustice, after bestowing these undeniable Encomiums on his Genius, were I not to observe, that nothing *but* that Genius can possibly exceed the Extent of his Erudition, and it would be adding a greater Injury to his still more valuable Qualities, were we to stop here, since, together with the *ablest Head,* he seems possessed of the very *best Heart* at present existing. Every Line, every Sentiment, that issues from his Pen, tends to the great Centre of all his Views, the Promotion of Virtue, Religion, and Humanity; nor are his Actions less pointed towards the same great End. Benevolence, Charity and Piety are the most striking Features in his Character, and while his Writings point out to us what a good Man *ought to be,* his own Conduct sets us an Example of what he *is.*

IRENE. Trag. by *Sam. Johnson,* 8vo. 1749. This is the only dramatic Piece among all the Writings of this celebrated Author. It is founded on the same Story with the foregoing;[4] the Author, however, has taken some trifling Liberties with the History, *Irene* being here made to be strangled by Order of the Emperor, instead of dying by his own Hand. The Unities of Time, Place and Action are most rigidly kept up, the whole coming within the Time of Performance, and the Scene, which is a Garden of the Seraglio, remaining unmoved through the whole Play. The Language of it is like all the rest of Mr. *Johnson*'s Writings, nervous, sentimental and poetical. Yet, notwithstanding all these Perfections, assisted by the united powers of Mr. *Garrick,* Mr. *Barry,* Mrs. *Pritchard,* and Mrs. *Cibber* all together in one Play, it did not meet with the Success it merited, and might therefore justly have expected.

3

(1774)

An Account of the Life, and Writings of Dr. Samuel Johnson

James Tytler (?)

This excellent writer, who is no less the glory of the present age and nation, than he will be the admiration of all succeeding ones, received his education, and took his degrees at the university of Oxford; after quitting which place, he, for some time, was master of a private academy at Lichfield. A genius like his, however, could not long content itself with that most disagreeable of all drudgery, the mere classical instruction of youth, nor suffer its brightness to be concealed in the dull obscurity of a country academy. He came up therefore to London; and what is worthy of observation, in the same stage-coach[1] with Mr GARRICK: So that both these geniuses started into the great world at the same time; both alike stimulated by ambition; and both the good fortune to have it amply gratified in being at the head of their respective professions.

Mr JOHNSON immediately gave proofs, how high a rank in the world of letters he deserved to hold; for having conceived the design of one of the noblest, and most useful, though at the same time the most laborious works that could possibly be undertaken, viz. a complete GRAMMAR and DICTIONARY of our hitherto unsettled language; he drew up a plan of the said design, in a letter to the right honourable the Earl of CHESTERFIELD, which being published, gave the strongest proof in its own composition, how great a degree of grammatical perfection, and classical elegance, the English tongue was capable of being brought to. The execution of this plan cost him the labour of many years; but the manner in which it was at last executed, made ample amends for all the expectations of the public in regard to it for so long a time; and the honours paid him on the occasion of its publication by most of the foreign academies, particularly by the *Academia della Crusca*. During some intervals of recess necessary to the fatigue of this stupendous undertaking, Mr JOHNSON published many other pieces which are most truly capital in their kind; among which, the RAMBLER, a series of periodical essays which came out twice a week for two years successively, stood in the foremost rank. In the course of so great a number of these papers as this long period demanded the number which the undertaker of them was favoured with by others was inconsiderable; and yet, on the whole, the product of this single genius, thus perpetually employed, proved at least equal, if not superior, to that of the club of first rate wits, who were concerned in those celebrated works, the SPECTATOR and TATLER. While the name of JUVENAL shall be remembered, this gentleman's improved imitations of him in his two poems, entitled LONDON, and THE VANITY OF HUMAN WISHES, must ever be read with delight. His stile in prose is nervous and classically correct: In verse his numbers are harmonious and musical, yet bold and poignant; and on the whole, approach nearer to Mr POPE'S manner of versification, than that of any other writer: And though he has favoured the world but with little in verse, yet that little, like diamonds of the first water, will ever be held in the highest estimation; whilst gems of larger bulk, with less intrinsic worth, are scarcely looked upon. He is the author of three prologues which are scarcely to be equalled in the English language; one spoken before a play performed for the benefit of MILTON'S grand-daughter, one to Dr GOLDSMITH'S comedy of the *Good-natured Man*, [2] and one spoken by Mr GARRICK when he purchased the property of Drury-Lane Theatre, with the renovation of that patent, and which may be no unwelcome offering to our readers, to serve as a specimen of his versification. [Omitted.] [3]

Mr JOHNSON'S imagination is amazingly extensive, and his knowledge of men and manners unbounded, as may be plainly traced in his *Eastern* stories in the *Rambler,* in which he has not only supported to the utmost the sublimity of the *Eastern* manner of expression, but even greatly excelled any of the oriental writers in the fertility of his invention, the conduct of his plots and the justice and strength of his sentiments.

His capital work of that kind however is a novel, entitled *Rasselas Prince of Abyssinia*, too well known and universally read to need any comment; and in which, as he does at present, so he probably ever will stand without an equal. He is the author of the tragedy of *Irene*, the language of which is nervous, sentimental, and poetical; yet its success, although considerable, was not equal to its merit. He has likewise written the *Idler*, a periodical paper in two volumes; the lives of Richard Savage, Sir Francis Blacke, and Admiral Drake, published together in one volume;[4] several other lives in the Gentleman's Magazine, where a number of miscellaneous compositions of his are to be found; in particular, an elegant Latin translation of Pope's Messiah. Mr JOHNSON has also written two very capital political pamphlets, *The false alarm*, and *Thoughts on the transactions concerning Falklands islands*. The *preface* to his edition of Shakespeare's works is a master-piece of its kind, and must be ever esteemed by the judicious as a standard of Dramatic Criticism. His small pieces are very numerous, many of them are prefaces and dedications to the works of his friends, or of poor authors to whom he gave them out of charity.

The world are in expectation, that he will soon publish an account of the *Tour* made by him and the celebrated Mr Boswell through Scotland and the western isles in Autumn last; and surely a performance of this kind, executed by a man of his genius and observation, cannot fail in giving the highest satisfaction to every person of curiosity and taste.

Mr JOHNSON has the honour to be esteemed by almost every author of reputation, foreigners as well as natives, and to whose judgment, in all literary points, they are ever ready to submit; indeed, his knowledge is so great in every branch of literature, that we should be apt to imagine each had been the sole study of his life. By his writings he has raised himself to that state of ease, affluence and independence, which must be agreeable to every one who respects distinguished abilities. However, after bestowing these undeniable encomiums on his genius, were we to stop here, it would be an injury to his still more valuable qualities, since, together with the *ablest head*, he seems possessed of the very *best heart* at present existing. Every line, every sentiment that issues from his pen, tends to the great center of all his views, the promotion of virtue, religion, and humanity: Nor are his actions less pointed towards the same great end. Benevolence, charity, and piety, are the most striking features in his character; and while his writings point out to us what a good man *ought to be,* his own conduct sets an example of what he *is.*

4

(1774)

An Impartial Account of the Life, Character, Genius, and Writings, of Dr. Samuel Johnson

Isaac Reed (?)

This excellent writer is generally said to have received his birth at Lichfield, in Staffordshire; but however positive some are in favour of this assertion, we find none who have favoured the world with an account of his parentage. Their silence upon so very interesting a head, would naturally lead many to doubt the truth of their assertion in respect to the place of his nativity. However, be that as it may, it is undeniable that he received his education at Oxford, at which University he took his degrees; after quitting which, being somewhat straitened in his circumstances, he opened a private academy at Lichfield. A genius like his, however, could not long content itself with the disagreeable task of superintending the mere classical instruction of youth, and burying those talents in obscurity that are the glory of the present Age, and will be the admiration of all succeeding ones.

Having, therefore, established an intimacy with Mr. Garrick, about the year 1736[1] they conjointly agreed to come to London; the one to try his abilities on the Stage, and the other to commence Author. How they have succeeded, let the world declare.

After having experienced the various hardships inseparable from the drudgery of compiling and translating for the Booksellers, the first work of any consequence we find the Doctor engaged in was his *Dictionary,* where he has at once successfully extended the bounds, improved the elegance, and elucidated the genius, of our very unsettled and difficult language. Notwithstanding the attention and uncommon erudition requisite to insure success in a work so amazingly complicate, we nevertheless find, from *his* labour alone, what our forefathers would have despaired of acquiring from an exertion of the associated abilities of numbers. In this immense work, the variety of readings is so numerous, the investigation of language is so precise, the definitions are so conclusive, and so many operations, traced through a variety of sources, are contrived so artfully to combine for the completion of one great purpose, that we are at a loss which most to admire, the learning or genius of a man, who alone and unassisted was equal to so arduous a study.

During those intervals of recess necessary to the fatigue of so stupendous an undertaking, we find him commenced Moralist, and presenting to the world divers series of periodical essays, amongst which *The Rambler* possesses the first claim to the attention of the judicious; and although the Doctor cannot be said to have much extended the system of moral philosophy, he may nevertheless be justly said to have improved it.

He has been too frequently charged with sacrificing the simple beauties of Nature to the studied decorations of Art; that he is sonorous without melody, and aspiring without sublimity; and that the pompous parade of his periods, though it may awhile excite the admiration of the vulgar, will in the man of taste create only disgust. How far such observations may be just, we shall leave to the consideration of the critical reader; only on the other hand, to balance the scale, we shall present him with the opinion of the late Dr. Goldsmith, who says, "In every sentence produced by the pen of that very able writer (Dr. Johnson), we see to how great a degree of grammatical perfection, and classical elegance, the English tongue is capable of being brought."

His abilities as a Novelist and an Allegorist, are too well known to need a recital. His *Eastern* stories, many of which are interspersed in *The Rambler,* possess not only the sublimity and spirit of the manner of expression peculiar to the people of the *East,* but even greatly excel any of the Oriental writings, whether we consider them for fertility of invention, the conduct of their plots, or the justice and strength of their sentiments. His most capital work of that kind, however, is a Novel, intitled, *Rasselas, Prince of Abyssinia;* which, as it does at present, probably will ever stand *without an equal.*

As a Poet, he possesses many happy qualities; his numbers are harmonious and musical, yet bold and poignant, and on the whole approach nearer to Mr. Pope's manner of versification than those of any other writer. His poetical productions, however, are few; which is the more to be regretted, as, like diamonds of the first water, they will ever be held in the highest estimation, whilst gems of larger bulk, with less intrinsic worth, are scarcely looked upon. In short, while the name of Juvenal shall be remembered, his much improved imitations of him, in his two Poems, entitled, *London,* and *The Vanity of Human Wishes,* cannot fail of being read with delight.

The only Dramatic Piece Dr. Johnson ever wrote was *Irene,* a tragedy, the success of which was not equal to its merit, owning entirely to his having too strictly adhered to the *Aristotelian* rules of the Drama. In the present Age, an audience looks for little more in a Play than plot and incident, without paying any regard either to character, diction, or sentiment. No wonder, then, that the Doctor should grow disgusted at the little encouragement given to the efforts of real genius, from a Public which would prefer noise and bustle even to the most finished work of classical perfection!

As a Biographer, his *Life of Savage* may justly be pronounced a standard for such species of literature. He, however, has been accused of partiality in the character of that unfortunate man, and that his friendship and intimacy with him led the Doctor to throw a veil over his miscarriages, and to paint his virtues in too strong a light. However just this remark may be, the morality inculcated in this little work sufficiently atones for such a fault, which at worst can only be termed the error of friendship.

After having so many years boasted of, and preserved his independence, every friend to his country must lament, that the Doctor in his declining age should venture into the field of Politics. His *False Alarm,* and his *Falkland Island,* both of which are pamphlets written with a professed view of justifying the conduct and measures of those in power, and for each of which he received a pension from the unpopular party he so particularly served,[2] will tend to throw a blemish upon his moral character, which even his uncommon abilities will never be able sufficiently to efface.

At a time when every one expected that he had entirely relinquished all further literary pursuits, we find him lately returned from making the Tour of Scotland; which journey he undertook, it is said, with a view of collecting authentic materials for presenting the world with a genuine history of the escape of the Young Chevalier after the battle of Culloden. The observations he collected in the above Tour, are now in the press, will shortly be published, and will doubtless prove an acceptable present to the Literary World. Perhaps it may be curious to learn the Doctor's opinion of a people of whom he in general had conceived but an indifferent idea. Being asked how he liked his entertainment in the Highlands, he said, "The sauce to every thing was the benevolence of the inhabitants, which cannot be too much commended: I love the people better than their country." When he was at St. Andrew's, somebody happened to ask where John Knox was buried? The Doctor, whose High Church principles are well known, and who never disguises them, said, "I hope in the *highway;* I have been seeing some effects of his reformation."

When in the Isle of Sky, he paid a visit to the celebrated Lady so well known by the name of Miss Flora Macdonald, whose heroic adventures, in 1745, have rendered her fame immortal with the Generous of all parties. She is now the wife of Mr. Macdonald of Kingsburgh, at whose house the Doctor staid a night. — He was at great pains to enquire into the authenticity of the Poems published to the World as the Works of Ossian, an ancient Highland Bard; but it is said, he is confirmed in his disbelief.

As a Wit, the Doctor has long been celebrated; but it is generally observed, that his witticisms seldom partake of so much justice as ill-nature. However, he is fully blessed in that happy combination of ideas, which is more dependent upon the judgment, than upon any other faculty. Hence his readiness of reply will amply counter-balance that cynical severity he too often evidences in these flights of fancy.

There is a story told of him, that being once in a Bookseller's shop, a certain would-be Critic, who was possessed of more vanity than judgment, and who wanted to impress the Doctor with a notion of his taste, began to pass some remarks upon a Poem that had been lately published; out of which he repeated several lines, and amongst the rest the following:

Who rules o'er *Freemen,* should himself be *free.*

"There, Doctor," says the Coxcomb, "I call That Poetry — What do you call it?" "Stark nonsense, Sir," replied Johnson; "it contains an *assertion without a proof.* The Blockhead might as well have said,

Who drives *fat oxen,* should himself be *fat.*[3]

His intimacy with Lord Chesterfield was well known, which he gained by drawing up the original plan of his Dictionary, in a Letter to that

Nobleman, who not only assisted him with hints for the Work, but also published two very elegant and friendly letters in a periodical Paper called *The World*, recommending the Doctor to the attention of the Public with great warmth. And here it will be necessary to mention an anecdote, which, if true, will serve as a proof how little the Doctor was inclined to return his Lordship's friendship. — A Gentleman of Dr. Johnson's acquaintance, on the first publication of his Dictionary, asked him, whether he was not in some respect indebted to Lord Chesterfield for assisting him in the Work? "Not at all, Sir (replied Johnson); the fact was only this: I had been sailing round the World of Learning for many years, and just as I got up to the Downs, my Lord Chesterfield sends out two little cock-boats to conduct me up the Thames.[4] My Lord Chesterfield! No, no; he may be a Wit amongst Lords, but I fancy he is no more than a Lord amongst Wits."[5]

The Doctor has ever affected a singularity in his manners, and to contemn the social rules which are established in the intercourse of civil life. This habit he has indulged so far, as to subject himself to the charge of a morose, ill-natured pedant. Indeed, however partial we may be to the Doctor's abilities, we cannot help acknowledging there is but too much justice in the remark. A confirmed haughtiness of temper, and a dogmatical manner of decision, acquired by long-established literary reputation, has so far possessed him, that his opinion often savours more of caprice than candour or judgment. Perhaps, as a proof of the singular manners of the Doctor, it will not here be amiss to present the Reader with his character, as drawn up by the very elegant pen of the noble Peer, and judge of mankind, before mentioned: In a letter to his Son, he says,

There is a man, whose moral character, deep learning, and superior parts, I acknowledge, admire, and respect; but whom it is so impossible for me to love, that I am almost in a fever whenever I am in his company. His figure (without being deformed) seems made to disgrace or ridicule the common structure of the human body. His legs and arms are never in the position which, according to the situation of his body, they ought to be in, but continually employed in committing hostilities upon the graces. He throws any where, but down his throat, whatever he means to drink, and only mangles what he means to carve. Inattentive to all the regards of social life, he mis-times or mis-places every thing. He disputes with heat, and indiscriminately. Mindless of the rank, character, and situation of those with whom he disputes, absolutely ignorant of the several gradations of familiarity or respect, he is exactly the same to his superiors, his equals, and his inferiors; and therefore, by a necessary consequence, absurd to two of the three. Is it possible to love such a man? No. The utmost I can do for him, is to consider him as a respectable Hottentot.[6]

Notwithstanding we mean not to dispute the justice of his Lordship's remarks, yet we would beg leave to observe, that though an affectation of so extravagant a humour be undoubtedly a fault, yet if it has been acquired by the habitudes of his temper, and by his indolence, it scarcely merits censure. Genius has ever its peculiarities; and to a man who can so far soar above the multitude, some indulgence is requisite, to allow him sometimes to descend into himself.

To shew how closely we have adhered to the impartiality we professed to observe, we shall conclude the life of this great Man with the following character of him by the Author of the *Companion to the Play-house*.

Nothing but his genius can possibly exceed the extent of his erudition: with the ablest head, he seems at present possessed of the very best heart existing. Every line, every sentiment that issues from his pen, tends to the great center of all his views, the promotion of virtue, religion, and humanity; nor are his actions less pointed towards the same noble end. Benevolence, charity, and piety, are the most striking features in his character; and while his writings point out to us what a good Man *ought to be,* his own conduct sets us an example of what he *is.* [7]

$\boxed{5}$

(1782)

Samuel Johnson

David Erskine Baker,
with Additions by Isaac Reed

This excellent writer, who is no less the glory of the present age and nation than he will be the admiration of all succeeding ones, was the son of a bookseller at Lichfield, in the county of Warwick [*sic*]. He was entered of Pembroke College, Oxford, on the 31st of October, 1728, but left the University without taking any degree. On his return to his native county, he appears to have devoted his attention to the education of youth; and Mr. Davies, in his *Life of Garrick,* p. 7, fixes the beginning of the year 1735 as the period when he undertook, as a private tutor, to instruct Mr. Garrick and some other youths in the *Belles Lettres.*[1] This mode of instruction, however, could not have lasted long; for, in the succeeding year, 1736, we find him advertising to board and teach young gentlemen in general the Latin and Greek languages at Edial near Lichfield. Yet his last scheme perhaps not answering his expectation, he left the country in March 1737, and, what will be thought remarkable, in company with Mr. Garrick, who at the same time first launched into active life. At London again our author appears to have met with disappointments which disgusted him with the town; for in August 1737, we find him desirous of returning again into his native county to take upon himself the office of master of a charity-school in his neighbourhood then vacant, the salary of which was sixty pounds a year. But the statutes of the school requiring the person who should be elected to be a master of arts, this attempt seems to have been frustrated.[2] Having conceived the design of one of the noblest and most useful, though at the same time the most laborious works that could be possibly undertaken, viz. a compleat Grammar and Dictionary of our hitherto unsettled language; he drew up a plan of the said design, in a letter to the right honourable the earl of Chesterfield, which being published, gave the strongest proof, in its own composition, how great a degree of grammatical perfection and classical elegance the English tongue was capable of being brought to. The execution of this plan cost him the labour of many years; but the manner in which it was at last executed made ample amends for all the expectations of the public in regard to it for so long a time; and the honours paid him on the occasion of its publication by several of the foreign academies, particularly by the Academia della Crusca, leave all encomium on the work in this place entirely superfluous. During some intervals of recess, necessary to the fatigue of this stupendous undertaking, Mr. Johnson published many other pieces, which are most truly capital in their kind; among which the *Rambler,* a series of periodical essays, which came out twice a week for two years successively, stood in the foremost rank. In the course of so great a number of these papers as this long period demanded, those which the undertaker of them was favoured with by others, was inconsiderable; and yet, on the whole, the product of this single genius, thus perpetually employed, proved at least equal, if not superior, to that of the club of first-rate wits, who were concerned in those celebrated works the *Spectator* and *Tatler.* Dr. Johnson's stile in prose is nervous and classically correct; in verse his numbers are harmonious and musical, yet bold and poignant, and, on the whole, approach nearer to Mr. Pope's manner of versification than that of any other writer; and though he has favoured the world with but little in absolute verse (for all his Prose is Poetry), yet that little, like diamonds of the first water, will ever be held in the highest estimation, whilst gems of larger bulk, with less intrinsic worth, are scarcely looked upon. When Mr. Pope had read his *London,* and received no satisfactory answer to repeated enquiries concerning its author, his observation was, "It cannot be long before my curiosity will be gratified; the writer of this poem will soon be *deterré.*" In short, while the name of Juvenal shall be remembered, this gentleman's improved imitations of him, in his two satires, entitled *London,* and *The Vanity of Human Wishes,* must be read with delight. His imagination is amazingly extensive, and his knowledge of men and manners unbounded, as may be plainly traced in his Eastern stories in the *Rambler,* in which he has not only supported to the utmost the sublimity of the Eastern manner of expression, but even greatly excelled any of the oriental writers in the fertility of his invention, the conduct of his plots, and the justice and strength of his sentiments. His capital work of that kind, however, is a novel, entitled *Rasselas, Prince of Abyssinia,* too well known and universally read to need any comment here, and in which, as he does at present, so he probably ever will, stand without an equal.

Our author indeed was formed to sustain the character of an exalted moralist; and never was known to descend from himself till he became a political writer. When talents designed for the support of religion and truth are prostituted to the defence of royal and ministerial errors, who is not ready to exclaim with Pistol — *Then did the sun on dunghill shine!*

Dr. Johnson has written only one dramatic piece, the success of which was not equal to its merit, owing entirely to his having too strictly adhered to the Aristotelian rules of the drama to render his piece agreeable to the taste of our present theatrical audiences, who look for little more than plot and incident, without paying any great regard either to character, language, or sentiment; it was performed at Drury-lane Theatre, and is entitled,

Irene. Trag. 8vo. 1749.

It would, however, be the highest injustice, after bestowing these undeniable encomiums on his genius, were I not to observe, that nothing but that genius can possibly exceed the extent of his erudition, and it would be adding a greater injury to his still more valuable qualities, were we to stop here, since, together with the ablest Head, he seems possessed of the very best Heart at present existing. Every line, every sentiment, that issues from his pen, tends to the great centre of all his views, the promotion of virtue, religion, and humanity; nor are his actions less pointed towards the same great end. Benevolence, charity, and piety, are the most striking features in his character; and while his writings point out to us what a good man ought to be, his own conduct sets us an example of what he is.

His last undertaking, *The Lives of the Poets,* would alone have been sufficient to immortalize his name among his countrymen. The excellence of this work is powerful enough to extinguish even the indignation which his political tenets (so frequently incorporated with his critical remarks) may sometimes have excited in those of an opposite way of thinking.

Within a few years past, the Universities of Oxford and Dublin have presented him with the honorary degrees of master of arts, and doctor of laws, as their testimonials of his public merits.[3] May it be long before he seeks the place which only can supply a reward adequate to his private virtues!

6

(1782)

Memoirs of the Life and Writings of Dr. Samuel Johnson

William Cooke (?)

Though there may be some general exceptions against writing the Memoirs of a *living* Author, on the principle of his not having *finished his course*, and consequently leaving his character undecided, yet whoever is in the least acquainted with Dr. Johnson, either as a *man*, or as a *writer*, will think his Biographer runs very little chance of temerity, in supposing that both are too fully established to be forfeited by any subsequent action of his life; but that as he has long lived an honour to our nation, he will carry down that honour pure and unsullied to the grave.

Dr. Samuel Johnson was born about the year 1709, at Lichfield, in the county of Warwick [*sic*], and as appears by a passage in his lives of the British Poets, was the son of a Bookseller in that town.[1] He was entered of Pembroke College, Oxford, on the 31st October 1728, and left the University without taking any degree. The use he made of his academical education when he returned to Lichfield, was devoting his attention to the education of youth, and Mr. Davies, in his late history of the stage, fixes the beginning of the year 1735, as the period when he undertook as a private tutor to instruct Garrick, and some other youths of the same county, in the *Belles Lettres*.

This occupation however could not have lasted long, for in the succeeding year 1736, we find him advertising to board and teach young gentlemen in general, the Latin and Greek languages, at Edial, near Lichfield; but whether from the disappointment of this last scheme, or from what other cause, the following year he came up to London, determined to bring his abilities to a scene where as they would be sooner and more accurately discovered, would of course be sooner, and more liberally rewarded.

Though the circumstance of Dr. Johnson's coming up to London, may be recorded as a particular event in favour of the literary world; yet it is still rendered more particular by that of his fellow traveller, who was no less than the late Mr. Garrick. Both these remarkable geniuses left Lichfield together, on the recommendation of Mr. Walmesley, Register of the Ecclesiastical Court of Lichfield, to a Mr. Colson, a celebrated Mathematician.[2] This letter Mr. Davies gives in the life of Garrick; it is dated March 2d, 1737, and the part relative to Dr. Johnson is as follows:

He (meaning Garrick) and another neighbour of mine, one Mr. Samuel Johnson, set out this morning for London together; Johnson is to try his fate with a tragedy, and to see to get himself employed in some translation either from the Latin, or the French; Johnson is a very good scholar and Poet, and I have great hopes will turn out a fine tragedy writer. If it should any ways lay in your way, [I] doubt not but you would be ready to recommend and assist your countryman.[3]

Soon after Dr. Johnson arrived in London, what from the competition of rival interests in which his modesty was perhaps his greatest enemy, and the ignorant avarice of some Booksellers who measured his writings more by the *quantity,* than the *quality,* he felt himself disgusted with the town, and seemed determined on returning again to his native country, in order to take upon himself the office of master of a charity school in his neighbourhood then vacant; the salary of which was but sixty pounds *per* year. But the statutes of the school requiring the person so elected to be a *master of arts,* which Mr. Johnson was not, the late Earl Gower,[4] who seems to have been his Patron, wrote the following letter in his favour to a friend of Dean Swift's then in Dublin.

Sir,

Mr Samuel Johnson (author of London, a satire, and some other poetical pieces) is a native of this county, and much respected by some worthy gentlemen in his neighbourhood, who are trustees of a charity school now vacant, the certain salary of which is sixty pounds *per* year, of which they are desirous to make him master; but unfortunately he is not capable of receiving their bounty, which would make him happy for life, by not being a *master of arts,* which by the statutes of this school the master of it must be. Now those gentlemen do me the honour to think, that I have interest enough in you to prevail upon you to write to Dean Swift to persuade the University of Dublin to send a diploma to me, constituting this poor man master of arts in their University. They highly extol the man's learning and probity, and will not be persuaded that the University will make any difficulty of conferring such a favour upon a stranger, if he is recommended by the Dean. They say he is not afraid of the strictest examination, though he is of so long a journey, and will venture it, if the Dean thinks it necessary, choosing rather to die upon the road, *than be starved to death in translating for Booksellers,* which has been his only subsistance for some time past.

I fear there is more difficulty in this affair than those Good-natured gentlemen apprehend, especially as their election cannot be delayed longer than the 11th of next month. If you see this matter in the same light that it appears to me, I hope you will burn this, and pardon me for giving you so much trouble about an impracticable thing; but if you think there is a probability of obtaining the favour asked, I am sure your humanity and propensity to relieve merit in distress, will incline you to serve the poor man, without my adding any more to the trouble I have already given you, than assuring you that I am, with great truth,

Sir,

Your most faithful humble servant,

Trentham, August 1st, 1737. Gower.

Fortunately for the public, this application was unsuccessful, otherwise the world would have lost many of those excellent works which they have been since indebted to him for, and for which all those are bound to thank him who have any respect either for the purity of their language, or the cause of morality.

From a passage in the above letter we are warranted to think, that the first publication of Dr. Johnson's works were his *London* and other poetical pieces, which were so well received, at least, by the judicious part of the public, that when Mr. Pope read the former, and received no satisfactory answer to repeated enquiries concerning its author, his observation was "it cannot be long before my curiosity will be gratified, the writer of this poem will soon be *deterré*" — his remark was soon verified, and whilst the name of Juvenal shall be remembered, those two highly improved imitations of him, *London,* and the *Vanity of Human Wishes,* must be read with delight and improvement. Soon after this we find Dr. Johnson employed in translations, memoir-writing, &c. most of which have been since collected by Mr. Davies, and published in three volumes under the title of *Fugitive Pieces.* To this species of lighter writing, we may add his *Rasselas, Prince of Abyssinia,* a little work abounding with such elegance of sentiment, and moral instructions, as would be in itself sufficient to support the character of *Novel writing* in this country.

But the great work which he produced about this period, was a complete grammar and dictionary of our hitherto unsettled language. He previously drew up a plan of his design, in a letter to the late Right Hon. the Earl of Chesterfield, which gave the strongest proof, in its own composition, to how great a degree of grammatical perfection, and classical elegance the English tongue was capable of being brought. The execution of this plan cost him the labour of many years, but the manner in which it was at last executed made ample amends. — His countrymen received it as the standard of their language, whilst the foreign Academies, particularly the *Academia Della Crusca,* paid him such honours on the occasion, as leave all encomium in this place entirely superfluous.

During the intervals of recess, necessary to the fatigues of this great undertaking, he published a series of periodical Essays, which came out twice a-week for two years successively, under the title of the *Rambler,* and though in the course of so many papers as this long period demanded, the number he was favoured with by others was very inconsiderable, yet the product of this single genius, thus perpetually employed, proved at least equal to that of the club of first rate wits, who were concerned in those celebrated works the *Spectator* and *Tatler;* as a moralist, he has no doubt exceeded them, as his genius seems to rise with a fervour peculiar to itself, whenever he discusses the great duties of Religion and Virtue.

Dr. Johnson has written only one dramatic piece, which is called "Irene" a tragedy, brought with him from Lichfield, and to introduce which on the stage, was probably his first inducement to come up to town. It appeared in the year 1749, a little after his friend Garrick came to the management of Drury Lane Theatre, but the success was not equal to its merit, owing it is thought to his having too strictly adhered to the Aristotelian rules of the Drama, or according to the opinion of others, not having been explicative enough to his audience in unravelling the plot. From which of these causes, or from what, we do not pretend at this distance of time, to say, yet, though it did not succeed on the stage, it is still read in the closet with delight and improvement.

Of his political pieces, the subjects are too recent, and the opinions too much in litigation for us to decide upon. — We are warranted to think however from the general integrity of his character, as well of his writings, that he has delivered his opinions upon these subjects with freedom and candour; and that they are supported in many parts with his usual imagination and intelligence, nothing but the voice of party will deny.

We are now come to his last undertaking the *Lives of the British Poets.* In which he has confirmed his own observation in the life of Waller, "that the mind does not grow old with the body," [5] as in this work he has displayed not only the full maturity of his judgment, but of his imagination; and if he had never written any thing before, this masterly performance alone would be sufficient to celebrate his name as a writer and a critic. It is true those who look for nothing short of perfection may object to the dogmatism of some political opinions — but who is entirely free from prejudices? or what is it, that is *wholly excellent* which comes out of the hands of man? "it is not by comparing line with line that the merit of great works is to be estimated, but by their general effects and ultimate result." An imperial crown cannot be one continued diamond, the gems must be held together by some less valuable matter. [6]

As a writer Dr. Johnson has long since, even by cotemporary authors, been allowed to stand at least in the first line. — His prose is nervous and classically correct, and though upon the first publication of his Ramblers, his style was thought too turgid, the novelty gradually wearing off, it is now pretty generally confessed, that he has not only established our language by his dictionary, but given a copiousness and energy to it by his writings. In verse his numbers are so harmonious and musical, yet so bold and poignant, that we have only to regret he had not given a greater indulgence to his muse, as perhaps he might have succeeded Pope with better pretensions than any other poet since his time.

It would be unjust, after bestowing these merited encomiums on his genius, not to remark that this genius is accompanied with a most extensive erudition, and it would be still adding a greater injury to his fame, not to declare with one of the best heads, he possesses one of the most amiable and benevolent hearts. Every effort of his pen has been exerted in the promotion of virtue, religion and humanity, and whilst his writings point out in theory what a *good man* ought to be — his life has given us the *example.*

As some public acknowledgement to such established merit, the universities of Oxford and Dublin have long since presented him with the honorary degrees of Master of Arts and Doctor of Laws, and the Crown has followed up those distinctions with a pension which, contrary to the opinion generally entertained of those pecuniary grants, is approved of by the people, because they know it to be the just reward of merit. He is now at a very advanced age, enjoying his fame with moderation, and the fruits of his honest earnings with health, cheerfulness and content; may it be long before he seeks that place which can only supply a reward, equal to his many private and public virtues!

7

(1784)

Memoirs of the Life and Writings of Dr. Samuel Johnson

"L"

Great and generous minds, while they aspire to superior attainments, are fond to contemplate the characters, which have already risen to eminence and fame. Emulation, when once awakened, is animated to ardour and perseverance, in beholding the various means by which men, like ourselves, have been distinguished for the acquisitions of science, or honoured as the instructors of mankind. We are taught, from their examples, that the heights of honour, however steep, are not inaccessible; and we reproach with pusillanimity the man, who, panting after fame, would despair to scale the precipices, by which Virtue and Learning conduct their votaries. Genius, indeed, may be the privilege of a favoured few; but to Application all may be indebted: for, while inactive Genius is content to loiter in the vale below, obscure and unobserved, laborious Application may overcome all the difficulties of ascent, demand the honours of Victory, and triumph in the consciousness of conspicuous worth.

Hence, in all ages, from the sagacious Plutarch to the illustrious Johnson, the writers of Biography have been the delight of every class of readers. 'As the greater part of human kind speak and act wholly by imitation, most of those who aspire to honour and applause, propose to themselves some example, which serves as the model of their conduct, and the limit of their hopes; and, when the original is well chosen and judiciously copied, the imitator often arrives at excellence, which he never could have attained without direction: for few are formed with abilities to discover new possibilities of excellence, and to distinguish themselves by means never tried before.'[1]

Biography, in this instructive view of it, has some peculiar characteristics, which are not often discerned but by acute and discriminating minds. History, from a thousand obvious sources, can collect the memorable actions of the statesman and the soldier; like the industrious bee, that in every common field can find the flowers from which it extracts its sweets. Biography, on the contrary, when the subject of narration has ceased to exist, is doomed to wander in the obscure and intricate recesses of domestic life, for wisdom of which few memorials now remain, or for virtues which cannot now be discovered; like him who would explore some gloomy ruins of antiquity, for treasures of learning and art, now defaced by Time, or long mouldered into dust.

While wars, conquests, and revolutions fill the Historian's page; while he describes the dawn, and progress, and maturity of civilization; or traces the first symptoms of decay, and gradual declension of empires; the Philosopher, indeed, may find themes of melancholy speculation, and the Patriot, of instructive retrospect and comparison: but such general narratives do not interest the mass of readers, who find no similitude between the calamities of private life and the elevated woes of royalty; between the humble felicity of a cottage and the captivating grandeur of a palace.

In the Lives of particular persons every man has an interest; provided, that in these narrations, the Writer devote his attention, not so much to extrinsic and adventitious distinctions of rank, or power, or other concomitants of greatness, but to those less obvious traits, which are most likely to elucidate a character; which display the man without decoration or disguise; and, in the momentary sallies of mirth or passion, afford to all some incidents of amusement, or some topics of instruction.

Various, indeed, are the excellencies of Biography, when cultivated with this necessary view to whatever can most interest and amuse, and to what may be most useful and instructive. But such is the vanity of all terrestrial aims, that what is thus beautiful in theory cannot often be accomplished. In quest of the more minute details of life and manners, the Biographer will meet with a thousand difficulties which retard his progress, and a thousand obstructions which he can never overcome. No Writer, perhaps, was ever more sensible of these difficulties, nor more harassed by these impediments, than the great man who is the subject of this article, and who is one of the most judicious and entertaining Biographers of any age or nation.

'There are,' says he, 'some natural reasons, why most accounts of particular persons are barren and useless. If a Life be delayed till interest and envy be at an end, we may hope for impartiality, but can expect little intelligence; for the incidents, which give excellence to Biography, are of a volatile and evanescent kind, such as soon escape the memory, and are rarely transmitted by tradition.'[2]

This, one would think, is an irrefragable argument, to enforce the propriety, and even necessity, of communicating Memoirs and Characters during the life-time of their subject. Were such Lives often undertaken, and judiciously compiled from the liberal communications of friends, the advantages to society would be innumerable. They would tend to inspire a generous passion for the sciences, an ardour for glory, and the practice of all the virtues. They would excite a noble emulation among those who devote their talents and labours to the happiness of mankind. Nor is it a circumstance which the Philosopher could perceive without pleasure, nor the good Citizen estimate too much, that Memoirs, or even Sketches of a living Character, powerfully impel him, as it were, to justify the suffrages which he has already obtained from his compatriots, by new virtues, new exploits, or new exertions in literature and science.

But it is useless to display the advantages of what is not likely to be attained. Of the observation just quoted Dr. Johnson himself felt the whole force, when he attempted his great Biographical Work, 'The Lives of the Poets'; nor can we doubt that he deplored, in secret, the real or affected delicacy, and obstinate uncommunicativeness of friends, that had left him to seek a thousand essential circumstances, which once might have been told, but for which it is now in vain to enquire. 'The necessity of complying with times,' he elsewhere complains,[3] 'and of sparing persons, is the great impediment of Biography. History may be formed from permanent monuments and records; but Lives can only be written from personal knowledge, which is every day growing less, and in a short time is lost for ever. What is known can seldom be immediately told; and when it might be told, it is no longer known. The delicate features of the mind, the nice discriminations of character, and the minute peculiarities of conduct, are soon obliterated.'[4]

Of Dryden, for instance, he says, that 'his contemporaries have left his Life unwritten; and nothing, therefore, can be known, beyond what casual mention and uncertain tradition have supplied.'[5] Mr. Croft,[6] his excellent coadjutor in the Life of Young, remarks, that 'of the great author of the Night Thoughts much has been told, of which there never could have been proofs; and that little care has been taken to tell that, of which proofs, with little trouble, might have been procured': in other words, that no communications were sought for during the life-time of Dr. Young, who having survived all his friends, except his house-keeper, nothing could be obtained at last, but what she, in a state of decrepitude, perhaps, might be able to relate. He then observes, that 'of the domestic manners and petty habits of the Author of the Night Thoughts he had hoped to give an account from the best authority: but who shall dare to say, *To-morrow I will be wise or virtuous, or to-morrow I will do a particular thing?* Upon enquiring for his housekeeper, he learned that she was buried two days before he reached the town of her abode.'[7] — It may be a question, to whom a reluctance to solicit information, or a refusal to communicate it, be most injurious; whether to mankind in general, to whom such Lives might afford the most excellent lessons, or to the venerable subjects themselves, who are certainly entitled to every kind of posthumous distinction? The 'petty habits' of a man whose piety was so sublime, that over a deception in his garden he inscribed, *Invisibilia non decipiunt,* must have been replete with peculiar instruction.[8] But delicate attentions were to be observed; solicitations for materials were to be postponed till solicitations were useless; what might have edified and instructed is now lost for ever; and all the consolation we have for this fatal neglect, is a philosophical reflection on the folly of procrastination, which had been before repeated by a thousand others.

Indeed, in many of these admirable Lives, we observe an extreme scantiness of information, which might have induced a writer of less excellence to abandon his work as impracticable. Yet Lives were to be written, 'where no minute knowledge of familiar manners could be obtained.'[9] Such, however, is the splendour of decorations; such the profusion of the richest sentiment, and commanding Criticism, that we read as *Lives* the pages where no transactions are recorded, nor one peculiarity described. Curiosity, while in quest only of incidents and events, chases in vain a beautiful butterfly, and returns to the chase with pleasure. With Promethean skill, the inimitable artist exerts creative powers; steals, as it were, celestial fire; and gives form, and substance, and animation, to a shadow.

All, however, have not this fascinating power. The paucity of materials will still continue to be lamented by future Biographers. But imperfection is the common characteristic of all human efforts; and, as of that which cannot be remedied, it is useless to complain much, it may be

hoped that attention and candour in the following Memoirs will sufficiently compensate for the want of abundance and variety.

DR. SAMUEL JOHNSON, now the first name in the literary world, was
born at Lichfield, in Staffordshire, about the year 1710. His father
was a bookseller, of whom all we can learn is from his son, who informs·
us, that 'he was an old man, who had been no careless observer of
the passages of the times' in which he lived.[10] Of his youth, before
he was sent to the university, of indications of dulness or prognostics
of future fame, of propensities to pleasure or examples of discretion,
we have no anecdotes on record. But a mind endued with prodigious
powers, cultivated with laborious assiduity, and enriched with all the
stores of ancient and modern learning, with a life ever distinguished
by a zealous attachment to the interests of piety and virtue, is the best
demonstration, that his early years were unsullied by any sallies of folly
or habits of dissipation.

He was entered of Pembroke College, in Oxford, on the 31st of
October 1728; but left the University without taking any degree. On
his return to his native county, he appears to have devoted his attention
to the education of youth. For an account of his first undertaking we
are indebted to Mr. Davies, who, in his 'Memoirs of the Life of Garrick,'
(a rich and various treasure of entertaining anecdotes and judicious
criticism) informs us, that about the beginning of the year 1735, Mr.
Johnson undertook the instruction of some young gentlemen of
Lichfield in the Belles Lettres; and that David Garrick, then turned of
eighteen, became one of his scholars, or, to speak more properly, his
friend and companion. — As this is an interesting incident in the Lives
of two celebrated men, it may be deemed no unpleasing digression to
observe, that, notwithstanding the brilliancy of his parts, the classic
authors appeared to have no charms for Mr. Garrick. His thoughts
were incessantly upon the stage. When his master, Mr. Johnson,
expected from him some exercise or composition upon a theme, he
shewed him several scenes of a new comedy which had engrossed his
time; and these, he told him, were the produce of his third attempt
in dramatic poetry. — To Mr. Davies' account we may add, that one of
Mr. Johnson's pupils was the Author of 'The Adventurer.'[11] Few men,
perhaps, who have been singly engaged in the honourable employment
of cultivating the human mind, can boast the felicity of having contributed to form two such distinguished characters as a Hawkesworth
and a Garrick.

This mode of instruction, however, could not have lasted long: for,
in the succeeding year, we find him advertising to board, and teach

young gentlemen the Latin and Greek languages, at Edial, a village on the west side of Lichfield.[12] Perhaps the success of this new undertaking did not correspond with his expectations: for, some time after, Mr. Garrick and he agreed to try their fortunes in the metropolis, and actually left Lichfield together, on the 2d of March 1737. This singular circumstance is authenticated by two Letters from Mr. Gilbert Walmesley, then Register of the Ecclesiastical Court at Lichfield, to the Rev. Mr. Colson, a celebrated mathematician, at Rochester. These two letters are preserved by Mr. Davies, in the Memoirs before quoted; and, from the second, which bears the above date, we give the following extract, which more immediately relates to Mr. Johnson. [Omitted.]

It appears by these letters, that Mr. Walmesley had a very particular regard for Mr. Johnson and Mr. Garrick. The former, in his Life of Edmund Smith, has embraced the opportunity to shew his gratitude to the memory of this his earliest patron.[13]

London, however, did not seem, at first, to encourage any sanguine expectations. Some months afterwards, he appeared desirous of returning to his native county. His ambition was even confined to the desire of obtaining the office of master of a charity-school, then vacant in the vicinity of Lichfield, the salary of which was sixty pounds a year. But the statutes of the school requiring that the candidate for this office should be a Master of Arts, this attempt was frustrated. Those whom the writings of Dr. Johnson have delighted or informed, may have reason to rejoice, perhaps, that his views met with such an effectual obstruction. Whether, in this humble station,

> ———— where oft resides
> Unboastful worth, above fastidious pomp,

he would have risen to the illustrious heights to which he has since attained, may be a subject of curious, if not useful speculation.

> Full many a gem of purest ray serene,
> The dark unfathomed caves of ocean bear:
> Full many a flower is born to blush unseen,
> And waste its sweetness on the desert air.

But a genius so exalted, we cannot imagine would have been obscure even in the bosom of retirement. His high descent, his kindred to the Muses, could not have been concealed; and if he had not been destined to figure as the great Dictator in the Republic of Letters, he must yet have been the gentle Apollo in exile, who sung the felicity of rural life, and taught the shepherds the love of knowledge and virtue, of industry and good order.[14]

In London, however, he remained, and was engaged by Mr. Edward Cave, as an assistant in the compilation of the Gentleman's Magazine.

In 1738, he began a Translation of the famous Father Paul's History of the Council of Trent.[15] But no great progress was made in this translation; although some sheets of it were actually printed. These have been long converted into waste paper. Such an excellent writer, translated by such a master, would have been a literary treasure.

The same year he published 'London, a Poem, in imitation of the third Satire of Juvenal'; which, it will be easily imagined, was directed against the vices and follies of the capital. Our limits will not allow us to enter into a minute examination of any of his Works. But the merit of this Poem will appear as conspicuous in the following charming lines, as in the most copious extracts.[16] [Omitted.]

Of the publication of this Poem a remarkable circumstance is related. The copy was offered to Cave, who did not choose to purchase it, but proposed to print it on the author's account. The latter accepted the proposal, and was entitled, in course, to whatever profits might accrue. The Poem had a rapid sale. A first edition was bought up; a second was printed and sold; and a third was preparing. In the mean time, the author was entirely ignorant of a success, which Cave had not only been careful to conceal himself, but had given directions to his servants not to mention. By some inadvertency, however, a discovery ensued; and the author soon found an opportunity to call his publisher to account, without betraying the person from whom he had received his information. The profits of this Poem were not more acceptable than unexpected; and, in the sequel, its merit introduced him to the acquaintance of the late ingenious Mr. Robert Dodsley, in whom he found a man of honour and generosity.[17]

There are degrees of moral obliquity which a good mind would be unwilling to construe into absolute turpitude. This incident might have created some momentary disgust, but the connection was not dissolved; nor did the subsequent conduct of the author bespeak any permanent resentment. In the Rambler we even find quotations from the poetry of Edward Cave;[18] who, when he could no longer be sensible of the honour, received, moreover, a tribute of regard, which would have dignified the greatest names. Mr. Johnson wrote his Life, from which, if much amusement cannot be expected, some instruction may be gathered. While it inculcates in the aspiring mind the happy effects of patient and persevering industry, it exhibits a salutary warning in the restlessness of desultory contrivance and incessant enterprise. — Cave, when he employed his literary dependent, in investing our parliamentary orators with Roman names,[19] could not be supposed to divine, that he himself was one day to be enrolled by him, among the greatest and most venerable characters of the British nation.[20]

In January 1749, Mr. Johnson published 'The Vanity of Human Wishes,' an imitation of the 10th Satire of Juvenal. An extract from its beautiful conclusion will preclude the necessity of a single observation on its merit.[21] [Omitted.]

This excellent Poem, was followed, in the same year, by 'Irene,' the Tragedy alluded to by Mr. Walmesley. This was founded on the cele-brated story of the Sultan Mahomet II, who, being reproved by his cour-tiers for the inconsiderate indulgence of his passion for a beautiful Greek, named Irene, to the neglect of his state-affairs, and the prejudice of the empire, immediately affected the hero, while he acted the mon-ster, and, in the presence of the whole court, struck off the head of his enchanting mistress. Mr. Johnson, however, has taken some liberties with the history; for he represents Irene as strangled by order of the Emperor, instead of being sacrificed by his own hand. The unities of time, and place, and action, he has most rigidly preserved. The language is nervous, sentimental, and poetical: yet with all these perfections, assisted by the united powers of Mr. Garrick, Mr. Barry, Mrs. Pritchard, and Mrs. Cibber, this tragedy did not meet with the success which might have been expected from its intrinsic excellence. This has been imputed to his too strict adherence to the Aristotelian rules of dramatic com-position. — Irene was acted from the 8th to the 20th of February inclusive.[22] The part of Demetrius was performed by Mr. Garrick.

'London,' 'The Vanity of Human Wishes,' and 'Irene,' were the only poems of any length, that Mr. Johnson ever published; but, although he favoured the world with but little in absolute verse (for his prose is often the most exquisite poetry) 'yet that little, like diamonds of the first water, will ever be held in the highest estimation, while gems of larger size, but less intrinsic worth, are scarcely noticed.' — When Pope had read his 'London,' and received no satisfactory answer to his repeated enquiries concerning the author, his observation was, 'It cannot be long before my curiosity is gratified: the writer of this poem will soon be *deterré*.'[23]

On the 20th of March 1750, he published the first Number of that celebrated periodical paper, 'The Rambler,' which was continued twice a week, for two years successively. His principal design appears to be to inculcate wisdom and piety. There are, however, many noble excur-sions of Fancy, particularly in his Eastern Tales, with many excellent disquisitions of criticism, and pictures of real life. A sprightly, and not uninstructive writer, gives him this well-merited praise: 'Were morality only to be considered, Horace is to be preferred to Virgil, and the Author of the Rambler to both together.'[24]

The style of the Rambler, though nervous and classically correct, has not, perhaps, commanded the *unanimous* suffrages of those who may be esteemed judges of fine writing. But that we may escape the imputation of fastidious criticism, we shall lay before our readers the sentiments of a writer, who has long enjoyed the approbation of the public.

With respect to the Rambler, if I have prejudices concerning it, they are all in its favour. I read it at an early age with delight, and, I hope, with improvement. Every thing laudable and useful in the conduct of life is recommended in it, often in a new manner, and always with energy, and with a dignity which commands attention. When I consider it with a view to its effects on the generality of the people, on those who stand most in need of this mode of instruction, it appears greatly inferior to the easy and natural Spectator. Those elegant and expressive words derived from the Latin, which are called by common readers hard words, and which abound in the Rambler, will prevent the greater number from entering on the perusal. And indeed, with all my prepossessions in favour of this writer, I cannot but agree with the opinion of the public, which has condemned in his style an affected appearance of pomposity. The constant recurrence of sentences in the form of what have been called triplets, is disgusting to all readers. But I will remind his censurers, that Cicero himself, in several of his works, fatigues the ear by a close of his periods almost uniformly similar. Not only the numbers, but the very words are frequently repeated in a few pages. I will also take the liberty to add in his defence, that the introduction of so many unusual and well-sounding words will gradually improve the English language, though it must necessarily circumscribe the writer's popularity. It seems, however, as if he himself recognised the fault of perpetual triplets in his style, since they are by no means frequent in his last productions.[25]

But whoever would compare the Rambler with any preceding or subsequent work, ought to be previously informed, that of 208 numbers, seven only are not entirely by the hand of Dr. Johnson.[26] When the Rambler was terminated, 'The Adventurer' was begun by Dr. Hawkesworth. To this work, which is an imitation of the former, Dr. Johnson contributed all the papers with the signature T, besides the History of the admirable Crichton.[27]

He had long conceived the design of one of the noblest and most useful, and at the same time, one of the most laborious works, that could be undertaken by one man. This was a complete Grammar and Dictionary of the English Language; of the want of which Foreigners had universally complained. Of this design he drew up a plan in a letter to the Earl of Chesterfield. This very letter exhibits a beautiful proof, to what a degree of grammatical perfection, and classical elegance our language was capable of being brought. The execution of this plan cost him the labour of many years; but when it was published, in 1755, the sanguine expectations of the public were amply justified; and several foreign Academies, particularly the Academia della Crusca, honoured the Author with their approbation. 'Such is its merits,' says the learned Mr. Harris, 'that our language does not possess a more copious, learned, and valuable work.'[28] But the excellence of this great work will rise in the estimation of all who are informed, that 'it was written,' as its Author declares 'with little assistance of the Learned, and without any patronage of the Great; not in the soft obscurities of retirement, or under the shelter of academic bowers, but amidst inconvenience and distraction, in sickness and in sorrow.'[29]

Chesterfield, at that time, was universally esteemed the Mecænas of the age; and it was in that character, no doubt, that Dr. Johnson addressed to him the letter before-mentioned. His Lordship endeavoured to be grateful, by recommending that valuable work in two Essays,[30] which, among others, he published in a paper entitled 'The World,' conducted by Mr. Edward Moore, and his literary friends. Some time after, however, the Doctor took great offence at being refused admittance to Lord Chesterfield; a circumstance, which has been imputed to the mistake of a porter. Just before the Dictionary was published, Mr. Moore expressed his surprise to the great Lexicographer, that he did not intend to dedicate the book to his Lordship. Mr. Johnson answered, that he was under no obligation to any great man whatever, and therefore he should not make him his patron. 'Pardon me, Sir,' said Moore, 'you are certainly obliged to his Lordship, for two elegant papers he has written in favour of your performance.' — 'You quite mistake the thing,' replied the other; 'I confess no obligation; I feel my own dignity, Sir; I have made a Commodore Anson's voyage round the whole world of the English language, and, while I am coming into port, with a fair wind, on a fine sun-shining day, my Lord Chesterfield sends out two little cockboats to tow me in. I am very sensible of the favour, Mr. Moore, and should be heartily sorry to say an ill-natured thing of that Nobleman; but I cannot help thinking he is a Lord amongst Wits, and a Wit amongst Lords.'

The severity of this remark seems never to have been forgotten by the Earl, who, in one of his Letters to his son, thus delineates the Doctor. [The "respectable Hottentot" sketch has been omitted.]

In this portrait there is certainly too much of the distortion of caricatura, and too much of the malignity of resentment. In real excellence there can be no comparison between this celebrated Nobleman and our illustrious author. The one seems to confine all his instructions to arts in which the most profligate might excel. The incessant aim of the other is to promote the cultivation of all that is great and excellent. The benefit to be derived from the lessons of the first is confined to the poor extent of a few years, which, in the common course of things, must soon cease to be numbered. The labours of the other will tend to perpetuate felicity, when the glittering vanities of mortality are no more. In this noble point of comparison he might have exclaimed:

> A celebrated wretch when I behold;
> When I behold a genius bright and base,
> Of tow'ring talents and terrestrial aims,
> Methinks I see, as thrown from her high sphere,
> The glorious fragments of a soul immortal,
> With rubbish mixt, and glitt'ring in the dust.

In 1758, Dr. Johnson began a new series of periodical papers, entitled 'The Idler,' which, in 1761, were collected into two volumes 12mo.

In the Eastern tales, inserted in 'The Rambler,' he had displayed a wonderful extent of imagination, with an unbounded knowledge of men and manners. He had not only supported the sublimity of the Eastern manner of expression, but even greatly excelled the Oriental writers in fertility of invention, in the conduct of his plots, and in the justness and solidity of his sentiments. This superiority was to appear more conspicuous still, in that admirable romance 'Rasselas, Prince of Abysinnia.' Nothing can exceed the richness and luxuriance of the descriptions, nor the purity and excellence of the morality which is here inculcated. In a word, it is impossible for any one to read this book, without being wiser in the only essential of life — the knowledge how to be happy in what he is. But let us not be censured, if in the superior understanding of Dr. Johnson, we lament some tincture of superstition. There are prejudices in the noblest minds, for the origin of which it is in vain to enquire, and which can never be overcome. To a slavery more deplorable still was the great Pascal subject, whose mind, like Johnson's, was vast and wonderful; and of Dryden, whom to praise is superfluous, he himself observes, as a blemish in his character, that there is little doubt that he put confidence in the prognostications of judicial astrology.[31] It is to be suspected that Dr. Johnson does not wholly disbelieve the exploded doctrine of the reality of apparitions. In Rasselas, when the Prince ridicules the terrors of Pekuah, at the entrance of the pyramids, and asserts that 'He that is once buried will be seen no more,' Imlac, the philosopher, urges reasons to prove the actual appearance of spectres.[32] The silence of the Prince, which is at least an acquiescence in his reasons, appears to bespeak the author's opinion. This seems confirmed by an attention which he afterwards paid to the celebrated story of the Cock-lane ghost, which was unworthy of the dignity of his character; and which furnished a popular satirist of the time, with an opportunity of invective, which he did not neglect. In one of his poems, entitled, 'The Ghost,' a description is given of Pomposo, descending into a vault of St. Sepulchre's church, to summon the spirit of Fanny. But the writings of Johnson will be read with universal admiration, when the temporary satires of Churchill are forgotten.[33]

It would have been a national disgrace, if such talents, distinguished by such writings, had met with no other recompense than the empty consciousness of fame. In 1762, his Majesty was pleased to bestow upon him a pension of 300£.

He had been for some time past employing his great critical abilities in preparing a new edition of Shakespeare. This appeared in 1765, in eight volumes 8vo. with an elegant preface, in which he enters into a general disquisition of the beauties and blemishes of that immortal bard, and into a discussion of the dramatic laws respecting the unities of time and place. In a subsequent edition, in 10 volumes 8vo.[34] the ingenious Mr. George Steevens, nephew of a distinguished Admiral of that name, appeared as a coadjutor, for whom the most celebrated critic need not blush.

He had now attained to the most exalted height of reputation; and little discretion was requisite to maintain an enviable character of dignity, independence, and superiority. He thought proper, however, to descend from his splendid elevation (the object of literary reverence, if not of literary adoration) to become the partisan of administration, and to mingle with the mob of political pamphleteers; as if the Jupiter of ancient fable were to desert the heights of Olympus, leave his thunder and his eagle, and stoop to combat in the amphitheatre with contending gladiators. — In 1770, he published 'The False Alarm,' in which he discusses the great question of the Middlesex Election. In 1771, the dispute with Spain attracted his attention; and he published 'Thoughts on the late Transactions at Falkland's Islands.' This was intended to justify the conciliatory measures, that had been adopted by the Ministry then in being. A third pamphlet, 'The Patriot,' appeared in 1774, addressed to the Electors of Great Britain, on the calling of a new Parliament; and a fourth, 'Taxation no Tyranny,' was published in 1775, in answer to the Resolutions and Address of the American Congress.[35]

As, in all these pamphlets, Dr. Johnson was professedly the champion of Administration, this circumstance did not contribute to augment the number of his admirers. His pension, in course, became a subject of reproach in all the diurnal publications.[36] But if it appears that he did not desert one single political principle, no one can charge him with unbecoming motives. If the sentiments predominant in these pamphlets be ever so obnoxious, it should be recollected, at the same time, that he had uniformly professed them. His early prejudices had never taught him to be the demagogue of democracy, nor to investigate with virulence the measures of Ministers and Monarchs.

In 1775, he published his 'Journey to the Western Islands of Scotland,' which he had undertaken in company with Mr. Boswell, the Gentleman to whom the world is indebted for an Account of Corsica, and of the once celebrated Paoli. This may be regarded as a valuable Supplement to Mr. Pennant's Account of his Northern Expeditions.[37] But the latter explores the country in the characters of a naturalist and antiquary; while Dr. Johnson travels as the moralist and observer of men and manners.

His last work, 'The Lives of the Poets,' first appeared in 1779, as Prefaces, in six small volumes, to a beautiful edition of the English Poets in sixty-eight; and they were afterwards separately printed in four volumes 8vo.[38] These have been already mentioned in the introduction to this article. But, notwithstanding their various excellencies, the decisions of this great Critic have been frequently disputed. The greatest blemish, however, is the frequent recurrence of certain political opinions, which are far from enhancing the value of a work, the sole object of which should have been literary instruction and amusement. It was stepping out of his way to call the immortal Hampden, 'The Zealot of Rebellion.'[39] The veneration, moreover, due from every man of genius to the Author of Paradise Lost, might have taught him to forgive much political heresy in the Latin Secretary of Oliver Cromwell; especially when, in respect to his own political tenets, many of the best judges of the Constitution are of opinion, that he himself has much to be forgiven. Sentiments, which do not discriminate the essential difference between resistance and rebellion, which have a tendency to revive the exploded doctrine of passive obedience, and which are inimical, in course, to the glorious principles of the revolution, or in other words, to the dearest privileges of Englishmen; sentiments like these might be read in the pages of a Sacheverell or a Filmer with calm contempt.[40] Their writings, as they can never reach, can have no tendency to enslave posterity. But when we anticipate the lustre with which the name of

Johnson will shine amongst our descendants, it is impossible to read such sentiments without a regret not absolutely devoid of indignation.

Besides the writings we have enumerated, several occasional Verses, some Prologues, and some other pieces of Biography, have dropped from this superior pen. The latter, consist of the Lives of Barretier, Sydenham, Sir Francis Drake, Roger Ascham, Sir Thomas Browne, Peter Burman, Herman Boerhaave, and Edward Cave. These, with the Plan of his Dictionary, some Prefaces, &c. appear in 'Miscellaneous and Fugitive Pieces,' in 3 volumes.[41]

Dr. Johnson was married in 1740, to Mrs. Porter, a widow Lady of Lichfield, who died about ten years afterwards, leaving an only daughter, by her former marriage.[42] She was long lamented by a husband, whose conjugal tenderness had been uniformly exemplary. Before her death, he had received into his house, Mrs. Anna Williams, the daughter of Dr. Zachariah Williams. This Lady, who had the misfortune to be blind, was endued with such intellectual accomplishments, and cheerfulness of disposition, as rendered her a very amiable companion to her benefactor. She died about a year ago.[43] In 1746, she translated the life of the Emperor Julian, from the French of Father La Bleterie. In this she was assisted by two sisters of the name of Wilkinson.[44] In 1736, by the kind assistance of Dr. Johnson, who wrote several of the Pieces, she published a quarto volume of 'Miscellanies in Prose and Verse.'[45]

A few years ago the Universities of Oxford and Dublin presented Mr. Johnson with the honorary degrees of Master of Arts and Doctor of Laws. This was a tribute, not more due to his celebrity in the world of letters, than to the exalted virtues by which he was equally distinguished. His writings, indeed, have ever been devoted to instructions in piety, benevolence, and virtue; and of these instructions his life has been one uniform example. The noblest gifts of genius, with respect to the possessor, are accidental, and can only command the secondary praise of diligence, in the pursuit of acquisitions, which when attained, may terminate in *self* alone; but he who is animated by Piety, to the practice of all the social virtues, and who delights to inculcate them by precepts, can claim a praise that is pure and undiminished; for, although his views, when successful, may eventually secure his own felicity, yet the highest enjoyment of his generous bosom is the felicity of others.

(1784–1785)

An Account of the Writings of Dr. Samuel Johnson, Including Some Incidents of His Life

Isaac Reed *and/or* George Steevens

The Death of an Author who has been so long known to the Publick, and so justly celebrated as Dr. Johnson, will naturally draw the notice of mankind to the History of his Life, and an enquiry after his Writings. Of his Life many narratives are already promised from various quarters; and we imagine that many anecdotes will now come to light, as the partiality of friendship, or the suggestions of malice, may prompt the several writers. The character of a man of letters will, however, be best known by his Writings. Leaving, therefore, the petty peculiarities of this admirable writer to those who are better acquainted with them, and to that discretion which candour, we hope, will dictate to them on a subject of so much delicacy; we shall proceed to give an account of such of his Writings as have come to our knowledge. If it should not be perfect, it will, at least, serve to assist some of his future biographers in a more full and complete account of his life.

Dr. SAMUEL JOHNSON was born in the month of September 1709, at Lichfield, in the county of Stafford, where his father,[1] an old book-seller, then resided, and afterwards died.[2] He received his education at the free-school of his native town, which at that time flourished[3] greatly under the direction of Mr. Hunter; and which, among other eminent men, had produced Bishop Smalridge, Mr. Wollaston, author of *The Religion of Nature Delineated*, Bishop Newton, Chief-Justice Willes, &c. It is generally believed, that his early proficiency in literature induced some persons belonging to the Cathedral to send him to Oxford, and to undertake the expence of finishing his education there. Certain it is he was admitted of Pembroke College on the 19th October 1728,[4] under the tuition of Dr. Adams, the present Master of that Seminary. He was then 19 years of age, and is supposed to have remained there not more than two years, as we find he quitted the University without taking any Degree.

Whether an inability to continue the expence of a College life, or a disinclination towards it, occasioned his quitting Oxford so soon, we are not informed, but the former is generally supposed to have been the case. The first employment we find him in afterwards was the very useful, but ignoble one, of Usher to the Free-School at Market Bosworth, in Leicestershire.

Those who can feel for the depression of genius will naturally lament that the person who was fitted to instruct mankind should be confined to so limited a sphere. — Here, however, he had leisure to devote himself to literary pursuits; and here, it is believed, he laid in those stores of information which afterwards enabled him to inform, to entertain, and improve the world.

In the year 1735 he resided at Birmingham, in the house of one Warren, a printer, and wrote various essays now irrecoverably lost, which were printed in a news-paper published by his landlord.[5] It was here also he translated "A Voyage to Abyssinia, by Father Jerome Lobo, a Portuguese Jesuit, with a Continuation of the History of Abyssinia down to the Beginning of the Eighteenth Century"; and "Fifteen Dissertations on various Subjects, relating to the History, Antiquities, Government, Religion, Manners, and Natural History of Abyssinia and other Countries mentioned by Father Jerome Lobo. By Mr. Le Grand. 8vo."[6] While he lived in this town, he wrote the "Verses on a Lady's presenting a Sprig of Myrtle to a Gentleman," which have been printed in several Miscellanies, under the name of Mr. Hammond.[7] They were, as the Author very late in life declared, written for a friend who was desirous of the reputation of a Poet with his Mistress.[8]

About the beginning of the year 1735, Mr. Davies[9] fixes upon as the time when our Author undertook the instruction of some young gentlemen of Lichfield in the belles lettres, and, amongst others, of Mr. Garrick. This plan did not succeed; for we find him, in July 1736, advertising a boarding-school at Edial, near Lichfield.[10] This was also as unsuccessful as the former scheme; and the beginning of the year following, our Author abandoned the country, and came to seek his fortune in London.

It was at this juncture Mr. Garrick was by his friend Mr. Walmesley [11] recommended to the care of Mr. Colson, at Rochester; and in company with our Roscius Dr. Johnson came to London in March 1736-7. On this occasion Mr. Walmesley sent the following letter, which we shall give at length. [The letter of 2 March has been omitted.]

What immediate employment Dr. Johnson obtained as a translator, is unknown. That his tragedy was not produced until many years afterwards, is certain. It is probable at this period he became acquainted with the celebrated Richard Savage; and if the malignity of party deserved any notice, it seems not unlikely that he shared the distresses of that ingenious, unfortunate, and contemptible being. [12]

By Savage, who was a writer in monthly publications, it may be conjectured Dr. Johnson was introduced to Mr. Cave, the proprietor of the Gentleman's Magazine, who became his patron and employer. [13] The first performance we find in that miscellany is the following, [14] which the author has been heard to say first occasioned his being noticed. [*Ad Urbanum* has been omitted.]

In the next month he complimented his friend Savage in these lines:

Ad RICARDUM SAVAGE, *Arm. Humani Amatorem.*

Humani studium generis cui pectore fervet
O! colat humanum te foveatque genus! [15]

In May appeared "LONDON, a Poem, in Imitation of the Third Satire of Juvenal." This admirable composition was received with the applause that its merits entitled it to. It was praised by Mr. Pope, and passed to a second edition in the course of a week. This latter circumstance is mentioned in the Gentleman's Magazine of the month in which it was published, and is a sufficient refutation of an impudent calumny inserted in some late Newspapers, [16] of Mr. Cave's attempting to keep the author in ignorance of his success after *two* editions had been sold. Had such a fact existed, Mr. Cave would have been little entitled to the eulogium of Dr. Johnson.

The trade (if such an expression may be allowed) of writing was however so little profitable, that notwithstanding the success of his Poem, Dr. Johnson soon afterwards meditated a return into the country. In this year a settlement as a Schoolmaster in Staffordshire [17] offered itself; and could the qualification required by the Statutes have been obtained, it is probable he would have sunk into obscurity, and passed the rest of his life merely as the Head of a Provincial Academy. On this occasion Lord Gower applied to a friend in Ireland in the following letter. [This letter, here dated 1738, has been omitted.][18]

The failure of Lord Gower's application in Dr. Johnson's behalf, for the degree, seems to have fixed him as an Author in London. In August 1738, he had engaged to translate Father Paul's History of the Council of Trent; and from that time to the 21st of April 1739, received of Mr. Cave forty-seven guineas[19] on that account. In the *Gentleman's Magazine* November 1738,[20] the design was announced to the Public, and the Life of Father Paul published as a specimen of the Translator's abilities. Part of this work was printed; but another version, under the patronage of Dr. afterwards Bishop Pearce, being undertaken at the same time,[21] Mr. Cave was afraid of compleating his edition; and, in the end, both the translations remained unfinished. In May this year, he began the Apotheosis of Milton, which was continued through several Magazines.[22] In November, he is believed to have published a translation of An Examination of Mr. Pope's Essay on Man, by M. Crousaz, Professor of Philosophy and Mathematics at Lausanne, 12mo. whose Commentary on Pope's Principles of Morality, or Essay on Man, we can ascribe to him with confidence.

We find, in January 1739, the Life of Dr. Boerhaave begun in the Gentleman's Magazine, and concluded in April. In May 1739 appeared a performance which its author afterwards wished to suppress.[23] It was called *"Marmor Norfolciense; or, An Essay on a Prophetical Inscription[24] in Monkish Rhyme, lately discovered near Lynn, in Norfolk. By Probus Britannicus."* 8vo. This piece might very properly pass unnoticed in a list of the author's works, if it had not been a few years since republished (1775), with some severe censures on the principles contained in it.[25] In the same year he published another pamphlet called, *"A complete Vindication of the Licensers of the Stage from the malicious and scandalous Aspersions of Mr. Brooke, Author of Gustavus Vasa; with a Proposal for making the Office of Licensers more extensive and effectual. By an impartial Hand."* 4to.[26] This is an ironical defence of the persons who occasioned the suppression of Mr. Brooke's play.

The following year (1740) he is supposed to have commenced writer of the Political Debates for Mr. Cave, and from circumstances it may be conjectured, that the characters in the month of March were his first essays. We know not of any successor that he had in this employment, and therefore conclude, that he continued the Compiler as long as they were published in the Magazine.[27] In the month of December 1745, they were omitted on account of the alarm occasioned by the

Rebellion, and, except for two months in 1746, never afterwards resumed.[28] His performances, this year, besides were the Preface to the Gentleman's Magazine; the Life of Admiral Blake, p. 301; the Life of Admiral Drake, p. 389; and, probably, an Essay on Epitaphs, p. 593. He also began the Life of John Philip Barretier.[29]

Of his works published the succeeding year, we know only of the Life of Dr. Morin (Gentleman's Magazine 1741, p. 375), and that is rather imputed to him on conjecture than any certainty.[30]

In the following year, 1742, he published the Life of Peter Burman (Gentleman's Magazine, 207) and the Life of Dr. Sydenham (ibid., 633), which was also prefixed to Dr. Swan's Translation of that Author.[31] On the 16th of June, 1741, died Edward Earl of Oxford, whose library being purchased by Tom Osborne, celebrated in the Dunciad for his modesty, our Author was some time employed in arranging and compiling the Catalogue. During his intercourse with this Bookseller, the disagreement happened between them which ended in the extraordinary correction which the latter received from his Author, and which probably put an end to the connection between them.[32] About the conclusion of this year, the Account of the Harleian Library by Dr. Johnson, prefixed to the first Volume of the Catalogue, was made public.[33] He also wrote the Preface to the Harleian Miscellany, though the selection of the Pamphlets was made by Mr. Oldys.[34]

The death of Richard Savage, August 1, 1743, gave Dr. Johnson an opportunity of shewing his regard for the memory of an unfortunate man, with whom he had lived in intimacy, by writing his Life. When Savage left London, in July 1739, "he took leave (says his Biographer) of his friends with great tenderness, and of the author of this narrative (i.e. his Life) with tears in his eyes." [35] Whether any correspondence subsisted between them while absent, we are not informed; but from many facts mentioned in the Life, it may be presumed there did.[36] In February 1744, the work appeared, and on the 21st of that month was noticed in *The Champion,* a periodical paper, which had been, and perhaps then was, under the direction of Henry Fielding,[37] in the following terms:

This pamphlet is, without flattery to its Author, as just and well written a piece as of its kind I ever saw; so that at the same time that it highly deserves, it certainly stands very little in need of this recommendation. As to the History of the unfortunate person whose Memoirs compose this work, it is certainly penned with equal accuracy and spirit, of which I am so much the better judge, as I know many of the facts mentioned in it to be strictly true, and very fairly related. Besides, it is not only the story of Mr. Savage, but innumerable incidents relating to other persons and other affairs, which render this a very amusing, and withal a very instructive and valuable performance. The Author's observations are short, significant, and just, as his narrative is remarkably smooth and well disposed. His reflections open to us all the recesses of the human heart; and, in a word, a more just or pleasant, a more engaging or a more improving treatise on the excellencies and defects of human nature is scarce to be found in our own, or, perhaps, in any other language.

In April his Life of John Philip Barretier was published in a pamphlet.

His next undertaking was an edition of Shakespeare, which at this time failed of success. In April 1745, he published a pamphlet, entitled, "Miscellaneous Observations on the Tragedy of Macbeth, with Remarks on Sir T.H.'s (Sir Thomas Hanmer's) edition of Shakespeare. To which is affixed, Proposals for a new edition of Shakespeare, with a Specimen." This edition was designed to have been printed in ten small volumes at the price of one pound five shillings. In the Postscript to the pamphlet, he was extremely severe on Sir Thomas Hanmer's edition, which he condemned without reserve. On the publication of his own edition, twenty-one years afterwards, he altered his opinion of the merits of his predecessor's work, and bestowed on it, at least, as much praise as it was fairly intitled to.[38] As Dr. Warburton at this period had his edition of Shakespeare in contemplation, it will appear the less extraordinary, that the Proposals of an anonymous writer, whose reputation was unsettled, should be neglected. In the Preface[39] to his edition, Dr. Warburton had the candour to exempt Dr. Johnson's pamphlet from the general censure which he threw out on the Writers of Essays, Remarks, Observations, &c. on his Author, and spoke of it as the work of a man of parts and genius. This obligation Dr. Johnson always acknowledged in terms of gratitude.

The small encouragement his Proposals for Shakespeare met with, probably induced him to turn his thoughts to the most laborious and important of his works, his Dictionary of the English Language. This might then be esteemed one of the desiderata of English literature; and, when it is considered as the performance of one man, will ever remain a monument of consummate genius, application, taste, and judgment. Mr. Addison had once entertained a like design, and we are told was offered three thousand pounds by Jacob Tonson to compleat it.[40] Dr. Johnson says he was furnished by Mr. Locker with a collection of examples, selected from Tillotson's works by Mr. Addison, for this undertaking, but that it came too late to be of use; he therefore inspected it but slightly, and, from an indistinct remembrance, thought the passages too short.[41] In the year 1746, we find no performance of Dr.

Johnson published. The Life of Nicholas Rienzi, in the Gentleman's Magazine of that year, has been pointed out, but with no degree of certainty.[42]

Having formed and digested the plan of his English Dictionary, he communicated it to the Public (in 1747) in a pamphlet, intitled, "The Plan of a Dictionary of the English Language: addressed to the Right Honourable Philip Dormer, Earl of Chesterfield, one of His Majesty's Principal Secretaries of State." 4to. From a passage in this pamphlet, it may be presumed that he was not unknown to Mr. Pope, by whom he says many of the writers whose testimonies will be alledged, were selected; and of whom he adds, "I may be justified in asserting, that were he still alive, solicitous as he was for the success of this work, he would not be displeased that I have undertaken it."[43] In September this year, Mr. Garrick commenced Manager of Drury-Lane Theatre, and opened his house with the excellent Prologue, which may be considered as the most perfect performance in that species of composition.[44] The Gentleman's Magazine this year (p. 239), furnishes an Epitaph on Sir Thomas Hanmer, and a few detached poems.[45]

In 1748, *The Preceptor* was published by Mr. [Robert] Dodsley, to which Dr. Johnson contributed the Preface, and "The Vision of Theodore the Hermit of Teneriffe, found in his Cell." In January 1749, "The Vanity of Human Wishes, imitated from Juvenal," was published; and on the 6th of February, the tragedy of Irene, under the title of "Mahomet and Irene," was first acted at Drury-Lane Theatre. Though the principal characters were supported by Garrick, Barry, Pritchard, and Cibber, it was not successful. It, however, was performed nine nights, at the end of which it was laid aside; and with it the Author gave up all further views of emolument from the stage. In November this year, Lauder's extraordinary attack on Milton was published in "An Essay on the imitation of the Moderns in the Paradise Lost"; and Dr. Johnson was imposed upon so much by the Author, that he wrote for him the Preface and Postscript to his work.[46] In Dr. Douglas's Answer, printed the next year, that writer says, "It is to be hoped, nay it is expected, that the elegant and nervous writer whose judicious sentiments and inimitable style point out the Author of Lauder's Preface and Postcript, will no longer allow one to plume himself with his feathers who appears so little to have deserved his assistance; an assistance which, I am persuaded, would never have been communicated, had there been the least suspicion of those facts which I have been the instrument of conveying to the world."[47] Dr. Douglas's expectation was not without foundation. Dr. Johnson not only disclaimed the fraud, but insisted

on the imposter confessing his offence; which he accordingly did, in
a pamphlet written for him by Dr. Johnson, whose hand is plainly discoverable in it, intitled, "A Letter to the Reverend Mr. Douglas,
occasioned by his Vindication of Milton. By William Lauder, M.A." 4to.
1751.[48] On the 20th of March 1750, he began "The Rambler," and
continued it twice a-week without intermission, until the 17th [14th]
of March 1752. On the 5th of April 1750, Comus was acted at Drury-
Lane, for the benefit of Milton's grand-daughter. A Prologue, written
by Dr. Johnson, who greatly interested himself on this occasion, was
spoken by Mr. Garrick. On the day preceding the performance, the
following Letter was published by Dr. Johnson in *The General Advertiser;*
which, being little known, and liable to be lost in a news-paper, we
shall here reprint.

Sir,
That a certain degree of reputation is acquired merely by approving the
works of genius, and testifying a regard to the memory of authors, is a truth
too evident to be denied; and therefore to ensure a participation of fame with
a celebrated Poet, many who would perhaps have contributed to starve him
when alive, have heaped expensive pageants upon his grave.

It must, indeed, be confessed, that this method of becoming known to posterity with honour is peculiar to the great, or at least to the wealthy; but an opportunity now offers for almost every individual to secure the praise of paying
a just regard to the illustrious dead, united with the pleasure of doing good
to the living. To assist industrious indigence, struggling with distress and
debilitated by age, is a display of virtue, and an acquisition of happiness and
honour.

Whoever, then, would be thought capable of pleasure in reading the works
of our incomparable Milton, and not so destitute of gratitude as to refuse to
lay out a trifle in a rational and elegant entertainment for the benefit of his
living remains, for the exercise of their own virtue, the encrease of their reputation, and the pleasing consciousness of doing good, should appear at Drury-
Lane Theatre tomorrow, April 5, when Comus will be performed for the benefit
of Mrs. Elizabeth Foster, grand-daughter to the author, and the only surviving
branch of his family.

N.B. There will be a new prologue on the occasion, written by the author
of Irene, and spoken by Mr. Garrick; and, by particular desire, there will be
added to the masque a dramatic satire, called Lethe, in which Mr. Garrick will
perform.

We shall just observe, that though Mr. Tonson gave 20£ and Dr.
Newton brought a large contribution, yet all their efforts, joined to
the allurements of Dr. Johnson's pen and Mr. Garrick's performance,
could produce only 130£.[49]

By a Letter to Dr. Birch, now in the British Museum, dated March 12, 1750, Dr. Johnson informed him of a manuscript written by Sir Walter Raleigh, and begged his recommendation of it to the Booksellers for the benefit of the owner, who is described as a person afflicted with blindness.[50] The title of the work does not appear; but as in the same year a pamphlet was published, called "The Interest of England with Regard to Foreign Alliances Explained," in two Discourses, 8vo. from a manuscript by Sir Walter Raleigh, we may presume it was the piece offered to Dr. Birch.[51] Prefixed to it is a Preface, which we should, without much hesitation, ascribe to Dr. Johnson, had not the present reigning family been spoken of in more respectful terms than he would at that time have expressed himself concerning it.

In 1751, he printed the Life of Dr. Francis Cheynel, in three numbers of The Student;[52] and in 1752, republished his translation of Mr. Pope's Messiah, in the Gentleman's Magazine, p. 184. This was one of his first productions, and was originally printed in the year 1730,[53] in a Collection of Poems by John Husbands, Fellow of Pembroke College, who says it was delivered as an exercise by Mr. Johnson, whom he stiles a Commoner of that Society, to his tutor. In 1753, he wrote for Mrs. Lennox, the Dedication to Shakespeare Illustrated, in 2 vols. 12mo; and in the month of March, in the same year, he lost his wife.[54]

The death of Mr. Cave, Jan. 10, 1754, gave him opportunity of shewing his regard for his early patron, by writing his life. This seems to have been the only new performance of that year.

His great work the Dictionary of the English Language had the finishing hand put to it in 1755, and it was published in the month of May [15 April]. Previous to the appearance of this excellent and useful performance, the University of Oxford conferred on him the degree of Master of Arts, Feb. 28 [20]. Contrary to the expectation of the world, it came out without any dedication. Lord Chesterfield, who was considered as the patron of the work, had offended the author by some neglect; and, from the character which he gave of Dr. Johnson in one of the letters to his son,[55] joined to the difference in the manners of the Peer and the Author, little union or friendship could be looked for between them. In the Preface to the Dictionary, Dr. Johnson says, "It was written with little assistance of the learned, and without any patronage of the great, not in the soft obscurities of retirement, or under the shelter of academic bowers, but amidst inconvenience and distraction, in sickness and in sorrow."[56] Lord Chesterfield, however, wrote some papers in *The World* in praise of it, and Mr. Garrick the following lines:

Talk of war with a Briton, he'll boldly advance,
That one English soldier will beat ten of France;
Would we alter the boast from the sword to the pen,
Our odds are still greater, still greater our men:
In the deep mines of science though Frenchmen may toil
Can their strength be compared to Locke, Newton, and Boyle?
Let them rally their heroes, send forth all their pow'rs,
Their verse-men and prose-men; then match them with ours!
First Shakespeare and Milton, like gods in the fight,
Have put their whole drama and epic to flight;
In satires, epistles, and odes, would they cope,
Their numbers retreat before Dryden and Pope;
And Johnson, well arm'd like a hero of yore,
Has beat forty French, and will beat forty more.[57]

As though he had foreseen some of the circumstances which would attend this publication, he observes, "A few wild blunders and risible absurdities, from which no work of such multiplicity was ever free, may for a time furnish Folly with Laughter, and harden Ignorance into contempt; but useful Diligence will at last prevail, and there never can be wanting some who distinguish desert."[58] Among those who amused themselves and the public on this occasion, perhaps Mr. Wilkes[59] is the only one who deserves to be remembered. Dr. Kenrick's threatened attack several years after never saw the light;[60] and the Author of *Lexiphanes* is scarce worthy of notice.[61]

In this year (1755) he afforded his assistance to Mrs. Williams's father, Mr. Zachariah Williams,[62] and wrote for him "An Account of an Attempt to ascertain the Longitude at Sea, by an exact Theory of the Variation of the Magnetical Needle; with a Table of the Variations at the most remarkable Cities in Europe, from the Year 1660 to 1860." 4to. This was published in English and Italian, the translation being the work, as it is supposed, of Signior Baretti.

Having disengaged himself from a work which had so long been the object of his attention, he again turned his thoughts to Shakespeare, and put forth proposals for printing an edition of that author, which were dated June 1, 1756. By these the work was promised on or before Christmas 1757. Since his former proposals Dr. Warburton's edition had been published, and had universally disappointed the expectations of the world. The Reader who peruses Dr. Johnson's plan of his edition, will lament that he could not, or at least did not, execute his own design. "The editor, says he, will endeavour to read the books which the author read, to trace his knowledge to the source, and compare his copies with their originals. Again: he hopes, that by comparing the works of Shakespeare with those of writers who lived at the same time, immediately preceded, or immediately followed him, he shall be able to ascertain his ambiguities, disentangle his intricacies, and recover the meaning of words now lost in the darkness of antiquity." [63] In the Museum is a letter to Dr. Birch, dated June 22, 1756, in which he solicits the assistance of that gentleman to furnish him with the books which would be useful to him. [64] That he did not procure them is evident, and would have been a circumstance still more to be regretted, had not the plan been pursued, and the want supplied by the assistance of several gentlemen, whose labours have left little to add to the commentaries on Shakespeare. The principal of these are, Mr. Steevens, Dr. Farmer, Mr. Tyrwhitt, Mr. Malone, Dr. Percy, Mr. Warton, Mr. Tollet, and many others who have contributed in an inferior degree. [65]

In 1756, a new periodical publication was undertaken to be published in the middle of the month: It was entitled, *The Literary Magazine,* and the first number appeared on the 15th of May. The entire superintendance of this performance during 15 numbers, fell to the share of Dr. Johnson, who wrote the Criticisms on Books, during that period. He also wrote the Address to the Public; the Introduction to the Political State of Great-Britain, in No. 1. Observations on the Treaties, in No. 3. Observations on the Present State of Affairs, in No. 4. Memoirs of the King of Prussia, and the Reply to Jonas Hanway, Esq; republished in our last Magazine. He also wrote the Life of Sir Thomas Browne, prefixed to a new edition of *Christian Morals,* by that author. In this year also he contributed to *The Universal Visiter, or Monthly Memorialist,* a periodical work by Christopher Smart and Richard Rolt, the following pieces, as appears by the signatures, viz. in No. 1. The Life of Chaucer, (which as Dr. Johnson's sentiments on this poet will be new to most of our Readers we shall reprint in our Magazine of next month). No. 2. Reflections on the State of Portugal. No. 3. Thoughts on Agriculture. No. 4. Dissertations on Authors. No. 5. Dissertations on Pope's Epitaphs. No. 6. The Rise, Progress and Perfection of Architecture among the Ancients, with some account of its declension among the Goths, and revival among the Moderns. [66]

In April 1758, he began The Idler, which was originally published in a News-Paper, called *The Universal Chronicle,* or *Weekly Gazette.* In 1759, appeared *Rasselas, Prince of Abyssinia,* in 2 vols. It was in this year his mother died, at a very advanced age. For both his parents he some years afterwards wrote the following Epitaph:

H.S.E.

MICHAEL JOHNSON:

Vir impavidus, constans, animosus, periculorum, immemor, laborum patien-
tissimus; fiduciâ Christianâ fortis fervidusque; Paterfamilias apprimé strenuus;
Bibliopola admodum peritus; mente et libris et negotiis excultâ; animo ita firmo,
ut, rebus adversis diu conflictatus, nec sibi nec suis defuerit: Lingua sic tempera-
ta, ut ei nihil quod aures vel pias vel castas laesisset, aut dolor vel voluptas
unquam expresserit. Natus Cubleiae in agro Derbiensi, anno MDCLVI, obiit
MDCCXXXI.

Apposita est SARA Conjux,

Antiqua FORDORUM gente oriunda; quam domi sedulam, foris paucis notam;
nulli molestam, mentis acumine et judicii subtilitate præcellentem; aliis multum,
sibi parum indulgentem: Æternitati semper attentam, omne fere Virtutis nomen
commendavit.

Nata Nortoniæ Regis, in agro Varvicensi anno MDCLXIX, obiit MDCCLIX.
Cum NATHANELE illorum filio, qui natus MDCCXII, cum vires et animi et
corporis multa pollicerentur, anno MDCCXXXVII, vitam brevem piâ morte
finivit.

The fidelity and attachment of Dr. Johnson's servant Francis Barber,
and the notice taken of him in his master's will, it is presumed will
excuse our mentioning, that in March this year (1759) our author found
himself obliged to solicit the interposition of his friends to obtain the
release of his domestic out of the hands of an officer who had pressed
him into his Majesty's service. On this occasion he applied to Dr. Smollett, who wrote the following letter to Mr. Wilkes, which had the wished-
for effect:

Dear Sir,   *Chelsea, March* 16, 1759
    I am again your Petitioner in behalf of that great cham [67] of literature Samuel
Johnson. His black servant, whose name is Francis Barber, has been pressed
on board the Stag frigate, Capt. Angel and our lexicographer is in great distress.
He says the boy is a sickly lad, of a delicate frame, and particularly subject
to a malady in his throat, which renders him very unfit for his Majesty's service.
You know what matter of animosity the said Johnson has against you, and
I dare say you desire no other opportunity of resenting it than that of laying
him under an obligation. He was humble enough to desire my assistance on
this occasion, tho' he and I were never cater cousins; and I gave him to understand that I would make application to my friend Mr. Wilkes, who, perhaps,
by his interest with Dr. Hay and Mr. Elliott, might be able to procure the discharge of his lacquey. It would be superfluous to say more on the subject,

which I leave to your own consideration; but I cannot let slip this opportunity of declaring that I am, with the most inviolable esteem and attachment,

Dear Sir,

Your affectionate obliged humble Servant,

T. Smollett.

In the same year, he translated for Mrs. Lennox a Dissertation upon the Greek Comedy, and the General Conclusion to Brumoy's Greek Theatre.

The quarrel between Dr. Francklin and Mr. Murphy, which has already been mentioned in our account of the former,[68] occasioned Mr. Murphy to address a poetical epistle to Dr. Johnson, in 1760, which he introduced with the following lines:

> Transcendant genius, whose prolific vein
> Ne'er knew the frigid Poet's toil and pain;
> To whom Apollo opens all his store,
> And ev'ry Muse presents her sacred lore;
> Say, pow'rful Johnson, whence thy verse is fraught
> With so much grace, such energy of thought;
> Whether thy Juvenal instructs the age
> In chaster numbers, and new points his rage;
> Or fair Irene sees, alas! too late
> Her innocence exchang'd for guilty state:
> Whate'er you write, in ev'ry golden line
> Sublimity and elegance combine;
> Thy nervous phrase impresses ev'ry soul,
> While harmony gives rapture to the whole.

For some years after this period, it may be presumed, Dr. Johnson almost entirely devoted his attention to Shakespeare, as no work of importance was published by him until the year 1765, when his edition of that author appeared. Fortune, however, who had left him hitherto to struggle with the inconveniencies of a slender and precarious subsistence, entirely arising from his own labours, in the year 1762 gave him that independence which his talents and virtues long before ought to have obtained for him. In July in that year, his Majesty settled upon him a pension of 300£ a-year, which was afterwards encreased to 400£ [69] and released him from the drudgery of literature, and dependence on his only former patrons the Booksellers, whose liberality he, however, frequently mentioned in terms of respect. For this independence he paid the usual tax. Envy and resentment soon made him the mark to shoot their arrows at. Some appeared to think themselves more entitled to Royal favour, and others recollected his political opinions and sentiments of the reigning family. By some he was censured as an apostate; and by others ridiculed for becoming a pensioner. His own definition of a pension was quoted against him, and much obloquy was heaped upon him. The North Briton supplied himself with arguments against the Minister for rewarding a Tory and a Jacobite; and Churchill drew his character in the *Ghost* under the name of Pomposo.[70] Dr. Johnson never condescended to reply to any of the invectives against him, and, with the trash of the day, they will be in a few years forgotten.

In 1763, he wrote the Life of his friend Collins, which he presented to Mess. Fawkes and Woty, the Editors of *The Poetical Calendar,* where it appeared in the month of December.[71] He had on many occasions assisted his friends in their literary pursuits; and it has been surmised, that the Dedication to *The Reliques of Ancient Poetry* was either wholly or in part the production of his pen.[72]

In 1765, the Edition of Shakespeare was published, which, as far as it fell short of affording that complete satisfaction which was expected from it, may be ascribed to the circumstance we have already mentioned. It was treated with great illiberality by Dr. Kenrick in the first part of a review of it, which was never completed. The snarling of this malignant writer seems to have had but little effect, as two editions of the author were soon sold. The Preface, which will be allowed one of the first compositions in the English Language, is said to have been written in less than a week.[73] In July this year, the University of Dublin conferred on him the degree of Doctor of Laws.

Two Prefaces, one to Mrs. Williams's Miscellanies, and another to Adams's Book on the Globes,[74] seem to be the only publications of Dr. Johnson in 1766.[75] In the next year, he furnished Mr. Bennet with all the new materials introduced into his edition of Roger Ascham's Works.[76]

In 1768 he supplied his friend Dr. Goldsmith with a Prologue to his comedy of The Good-Natured Man;[77] and on the establishment of the Royal Academy in 1769, he accepted the title of Professor of Ancient Literature.

The political feuds of this period soon afterwards tempted him to become the champion of that government which, in some measure, had furnished him with the independence he possessed. In 1770 he published *The False Alarm,* a defence of the then administration respecting the clamour excited by the determination of the House of Commons relative to the expulsion of Mr. Wilkes. The next year he defended the measures adopted by the Ministry in the dispute with the Court of Spain, in a pamphlet called *Thoughts on the late Transactions respecting Falkland's Islands.* It is supposed that for these services an addition was made to his pension.

In the Autumn of 1773, he gratified a wish which he so long entertained, that he scarcely remembered how it was originally excited, of visiting the Hebrides, or Western Islands of Scotland. He was accompanied by Mr. Boswell, whose acuteness, he after observed, would help his enquiry, and whose gaiety of conversation, and civility of manners, were sufficient to counteract the inconveniences of travel in countries less hospitable than those they were to pass.

On the 18th of August they left Edinburgh, and continued on their travels through several parts of Scotland and the Hebrides until the month of November. Of this journey Dr. Johnson wrote a narrative, published in 8vo. 1775. The public will soon be entertained with a new relation of it by the Doctor's friend and fellow-traveller, Mr. Boswell, who regularly committed to writing the conversations and incidents of each day. Many parts of this performance were, we are assured, perused and approved of by Dr. Johnson.

In the course of this Journey, our author made some enquiries relative to the authenticity of the Poems published under the name of Ossian; but not finding evidence to satisfy him of their genuineness, he declared his conviction of their being spurious in the following terms:

I believe they never existed in any other form than that which we have seen. The Editor, or Author, never could shew the original; nor can it be shewn by any other. To revenge reasonable incredulity by refusing evidence, is a degree of insolence with which the world is not yet acquainted; and stubborn audacity is the last refuge of guilt. It would be easy to shew it if he had it; but whence could it be had? It is too long to be remembered, and the language formerly had nothing written. He has doubtless inserted names that circulate in popular stories, and may have translated some wandering ballads, if any can be found; and the names and some of the images being recollected, make an inaccurate auditor imagine, by the help of Caledonian bigotry, that he has formerly heard the whole.[78]

This paragraph did not pass without notice. The Editor is said to have insisted on a recantation of it, not without some threats of revenge, if that satisfaction was refused. These menaces are reported to have had no other effect than producing the following reply, which, together with the whole conduct of both parties, may be now numbered amongst the follies of the wise.

Mr. James Macpherson,

I received your foolish and impudent letter. Any violence that shall be attempted upon me I will do my best to repel; and what I cannot do for myself, the law shall do for me; for I will not be hindered from exposing what I think a cheat, by the menaces of a ruffian. What would you have me retract? I thought your work an imposture; I think so still; and for my opinion, I have given reasons which I here dare you to refute. Your abilities since your Homer are not so formidable; and what I hear of your morality, inclines me to credit rather what you shall prove, than what you shall say.

S. Johnson.[79]

In 1774 he published *"The Patriot,"* addressed to the Electors of Great Britain, 8vo. and in the succeeding year he received the honour of a degree of Doctor of Laws from the University of Oxford. About the same period he published his Journey to the Western Islands. It was this year also he gave the public the last of his political writings, viz. *"Taxation no Tyranny."*

From this period until the year 1777, he seems to have produced no literary performance.[80] On the death of Mr. Kelly he called forth his Muse for the service of the family of that gentleman, and wrote a Prologue, spoken at Covent-Garden by Mr. Hull, before a play acted there the 29th May for their benefit.[81] He was at the same time exerting himself in behalf of Dr. Dodd, for whom he wrote the *Convict's Address,* his speech on receiving sentence, and various petitions and letters soliciting a remission or alteration in his sentence.

A short time afterwards a plan being proposed of publishing a compleat collection of the Works of the English Poets, Dr. Johnson was prevailed upon to write a short account of each poet in the manner of some French collections of the like kind. In executing this work he found his attention so much engaged, that he enlarged his scheme, and entered more fully into the merits and failures of the principal writers. In 1779 the first four volumes appeared, and in 1781 the remaining five. They have been since republished in four volumes in 8vo. and, if a conjecture may be hazarded of their effects, are very likely to form the judgment and settle the opinions of the rising generation with respect to English Poetry.

On the completion of this work, he was requested to engage in some other, and at times appeared to be willing to resume his pen. The life of Spenser was suggested from very high authority.[82] Application was also made to him to write the life of Captain Cook from authentic materials to be procured for him. To both these proposals he expressed no objection; and the latter, though it never proceeded further, had his direct assent. He also received into his hands some papers in order to compile an account of his friend John Scott, Esq; of Amwell, to be prefixed to a volume of criticism, which that gentleman left unpublished. In this last undertaking he engaged with alacrity, but the state of his health never permitted him to execute his intention; and the materials have since been put into the possession of another gentleman, who is every way capable of performing the task to the credit of himself and his deceased friend.[83]

In 1781 he lost Mr. Thrale, with whom he had many years lived in terms of the most unreserved friendship and intimacy, and for whom he wrote an Epitaph. In January, 1782, died Mr. Levet of whom an account has been already given; and in September, 1783, Mrs. Williams, who had resided in his house almost since he had possessed one, departed this life. In June preceding, he had felt a stroke of the palsy, from which, however, he recovered so far, as to enjoy the company of his friends in a small degree. This happiness continued but a short time. In the summer of 1784, he visited his native country. The state of his health was then very unsettled, and he returned to London in October, worse than when he left it. From this time his illness increased. He continued to linger with short intermissions, until the 13th December, 1784, when he expired at 7 o'clock in the evening, in the 75th year of his age, and was buried in Westminster Abbey on the 20th of the same month.

9

(1785)

A Biographical Sketch of Dr. Samuel Johnson

Thomas Tyers

"Much may be right, yet much be wanting." Prior.

When Charles the Second was informed of the death of Cowley, he pronounced, "that he had not left a better man behind him in England." It may be affirmed with truth, that this was the case when Dr. Johnson breathed his last. Those who observed his declining state of health during the last winter, and heard his complaints of painful days and sleepless nights, for which he took large quantities of opium, had no reason to expect that he could survive another season of frost and snow. His constitution was totally broken, and no art of the physician or surgeon could protract his existence beyond the 13th of December. At the request of Mr. Cruikshank, the executors permitted his body to be opened, on the suggestion that his internals might be uncommonly affected, which was the case on inspection.[1] The dead may sometimes give instruction to the living. The Cyrus of Xenophon ordered his breathless body to fertilize the earth that had given it nourishment. Johnson's inside had not the soundness of that of old Parr (as related by Harvey), not far from whom he is now deposited. One of his kidneys was found to be decayed. He never complained of disorder in that region (which was mortal to his friend Mr. Garrick); and probably it was not the immediate cause of his dissolution. Perhaps "of no disease he died," like the character from the Tragedian; for who can tell wherein vitality consists? Johnson could hear, perhaps, with ambitious satisfaction, that he was to be buried in Westminster Abbey; for the love of fame is the last infirmity of noble minds; and, to continue quotation in the words of Dr. Young, "Nor ends with life, but nods on sable plumes, / Adorns our hearse, and flatters on our tombs." Possibly the thought of talk of the incisions of anatomy would have disturbed his imagination. But, in this case, what was not prohibited was permitted. For it may be easily asked, in the words of the soldier to the Ephesian Matron, in Petronius, "Id cinerem aut manes credis curare sepultos?" It might be thought that so strong and muscular a body might have lasted many years longer; for Johnson drank nothing but water, and lemonade (by way of indulgence) for many years, almost uninterruptedly, without the taste of any fermented liquor; and he was often abstinent from animal food, and kept down feverish symptoms by dietetic management. Of Addison and Pope he used to observe, perhaps to remind himself, that they ate and drank too much, and thus shortened their days.[2] It was thought by many who dined at the same table, that he had too great an appetite. This might now and then be the case, but not till he had subdued his enemy by famine. But his bulk seemed sometimes to require to be repaired by kitchen physic. To great old age not one in a thousand arrives. How few were the years of Johnson in comparison of those of Jenkins and Parr? But perhaps Johnson had more of life by his intenseness of living. Jenkins, as it is expressed on his memorial in Bolton church (in which parish he lived, and died, at the antediluvian age of one hundred and sixty-nine) was happy, if not in the variety, yet in the duration of his enjoyments, which were probably of fishing and of drinking. His diet was coarse and sober, says Cheyne. Johnson's time is to be dated from the number of his ideas. He was old in mind, though not comparatively in years. Most people die of disease. He was all his life preparing himself for death; but particularly in the last stage of his asthma and dropsy. "Take care of your soul — don't live such a life as I have done — don't let your business or dissipation make you neglect your sabbath" — were now his constant inculcations. Private and public prayer, when his visitors were his audience, were his constant exercises. He cannot be said to be weary of the weight of existence, for he declared, that to prolong it only for one year, but not for the comfortless sensations he had lately felt, he would suffer the amputation of a limb. He was willing to endure positive pain for possible pleasure. But he had no expectation that nature could last much longer; and therefore, for his last week, he undoubtedly abandoned every hope of his recovery or duration, and committed his soul to God. Whether he felt the instant stroke of death, and met the king of terrors face to face, cannot be known; for "death and the sun cannot be looked upon," says Rochefaucault. But the writer of this has reason to imagine that when he thought he had made his peace with his Maker, he had nothing to fear. He has talked of submitting to a violent death, in a good cause, without apprehensions. On one of the last visits from his surgeon, who, on performing the puncture on his legs, had assured him that he was better, he declared, "he felt himself not so, and that he did not desire to be treated like a woman or a child, for that he had made up his mind." He had travelled through the vale of this world for more than seventy-five years. It probably was a wilderness to him for more than half his time. But he was in possession of rest and comfort and plenty, for the last twenty years. Yet the blessings of fortune and reputation could not compensate to him the want of health, which pursued him through his pilgrimage on earth. *Post equitem sedet atra cura.* "For when we mount the flying steed, / Sits gloomy Care behind." Of the hundred sublunary things bestowed on mortals, health is ninety-nine. He was born with a scrophulous habit, for which he was touched, as he acknowledged, by good queen Anne, whose piece of gold he carefully preserved. But even a Stuart could not expel that enemy to his frame, by a touch. For it would have been even beyond the stroaking power of Greatrix in all his glory, to charm it away. Though he seemed to be as athletic as Milo himself, and in his younger days performed several feats of activity, he was to the last a convulsionary. He has often stept aside, to let nature do what she would with him. His gestures, which were a degree of St. Vitus's dance, in the street, attracted the notice of many; the stare of the vulgar, but the compassion of the better sort. This writer has often looked another way, as the companions of Peter the Great were used to do, while he was under the short paroxysm. He was perpetually taking aperient medicines. He could only keep his ailments from gaining ground. He thought he was worse for the agitation of active exercise. He was afraid of his disorder's seizing his head, and took all possible care that his understanding should not be deranged. *Orandum est, ut sit mens sana in corpore sano.* When his knowledge from books, and he knew all that books could tell him, is considered; when his compositions in verse and prose are enumerated to the reader, (and a complete list of them, wherever dispersed, is desirable) it must appear extraordinary he could abstract himself so much from his feelings, and that he could pursue with ardour the plan he laid down of establishing a great reputation. Accumulating learning (and the example of Barretier, whose life he wrote) shewed him how to arrive at all science. His imagination often appeared to be too mighty for the controul of his reason. In the preface to his Dictionary, he says, that his work was composed "amidst inconvenience and distraction, in sickness and in sorrow." "I never read this preface," says Mr. Horne, "but it makes me shed tears."[3]

If this memoir-writer possessed the pen of a Plutarch, and the subject is worthy of that great biographer, he would begin his account from his youth, and continue it to the last period of his life, in the due order of an historian. What he knows and can recollect, he will perform. His father (called "gentleman" in the parish register) he says himself, and it is also within memory, was an old bookseller at Lichfield, and a whig in principle.[4] The father of Socrates was not of higher extraction, nor of a more honourable profession. Our author was born in that city; and the house of his birth was a few months ago visited by a learned acquaintance, the information of which was grateful to the doctor. It may probably be engraved for some monthly repository. The print and the original dwelling may become as eminent as the mansion of Shakespeare at Stratford, or of Erasmus at Rotterdam: the house at Coltersworth, where Newton was born: the birth house of Milton, in Bread street: Pope's Villa at Twickenham: or the porch house at Chertsey, where Cowley breathed his last. He composed a poetical stanza, at five years old, on his treading on a duck.[5] If it is to be given to the public, it ought to be with authentication. He was Hercules in his cradle. Could Lopez del Vega, or Cowley, or Milton, or even Pope, have asserted more truly, "they lisped in numbers"? It is said of some men, they hardly had a childhood, but arrived to early ripeness, just as the Russian winter turns into summer without passing through the spring. He certainly must have had a good school education. He was entered of Pembroke college, Oxford, Oct. 31, 1728, and continued there for several terms. By whose bounty he was supported, may be known to enquiry.[6] While he was there, he was negligent of the college rules and hours, and absented himself from some of the lectures, for which when he was reprimanded and interrogated, he replied with great rudeness and contempt of the lecturer. Indeed he displayed an overbearing disposition that would not brook controul, and shewed that, like Caesar, he was fitter to command than to obey.[7] This dictatorial spirit was the leading feature in his deportment to his contemporaries. His college themes and declamations are still remembered; and his elegant translation of Pope's Messiah into Latin verse found its way into a volume of poems published by one Husbands. In 1735, after having been some time an usher to Anthony Blackwall,[8] his friends assisted him to set up an academy near

Lichfield. Here he formed an acquaintance with the late bishop Green, then an usher at Lichfield, and with Mr. Hawkins Browne.[9] As the school probably did not answer his expectation, (for who does not grow tired of teaching others, especially if he wants to teach himself?), he resolved to come up to London, where every thing is to be had for wit and for money *(Roma omnia venalia)*, and to seek his fortune. He was accompanied by his pupil Mr. Garrick, and travelled on horseback to the metropolis in March, 1737.

The time and business of this journey are before the public in some letters from Mr. Walmesley, who recommends Johnson as a writer of tragedy, as a translator from the French language, and as a good scholar. He brought with him his tragedy of Irene, which afterwards took its chance on Drury-Lane theatre. Luckily he did not throw it into the fire, by design or otherwise, as Parson Adams did his Æschylus by mistake. He offered himself for the service of the booksellers; "for he was born for nothing but to write," — "And from the jest obscene reclaim our youth, / And set our passions on the side of truth."

The hurry of this pen prevents the recollection of his first performances. But he used to call [Robert] Dodsley his patron, because he made him, if not first, yet best known, by printing and publishing, upon his own judgment, his satire, called "London," which was an imitation of one of Juvenal, whose gravity and severity of expression he possessed. He there and then discovered how able he was "to catch the manners living as they rise." The poem had a great sale, was applauded by the public, and praised by Mr. Pope, who, not being able to discover the author, said, "he will soon be *deterré*." In 1738 he luckily fell into the hands of his other early patron Cave. His speeches for the senate of Lilliput were begun in 1740, and continued for several sessions. They passed for original with many till very lately. But Johnson, who detested all injurious imposition, took a great deal of pains to acknowlege the innocent deception. He gave Smollett notice of their unoriginality, while he was going over his historical ground, and to be upon his guard in quoting from the Lilliput Debates.[10] It is within recollection, that an animated speech he put into the mouth of Pitt, in answer to the parliamentary veteran Horace Walpole, was much talked of, and considered as genuine.[11] Members of parliament acknowledge that they reckon themselves much obliged for the printed accounts of debates of both houses, because they are made to speak better than they do in the senate. Within these few years, a gentleman in a high employment under government was at breakfast in Gray's inn, where Johnson was present, and was commending the excellent preservation of the speeches of both houses, in the Lilliput Debates. He declared, he knew how to appropriate every speech without a signature; for that every person spoke in character, and was as certainly and as easily known as a speaker in Homer or in Shakespeare. "Very likely, Sir," said Johnson, ashamed of having deceived him, "but I wrote them in the garret where I then lived." [12] His predecessor in this oratorial fabrication was Guthrie; his successor in the Magazine was Hawkesworth. It is said, that to prove himself equal to this employment (but there is not leisure for the adjustment of chronology) in the judgment of Cave, he undertook the life of Savage, which he asserted (not incredible of him), and valued himself upon it, that he wrote in six and thirty hours.[13] In one night he also composed, after finishing an evening in Holborn, his Hermit of Teneriffe. He sat up a whole night to compose the preface to the Preceptor.

His eye-sight was not good; but he never wore spectacles; not on account of such a ridiculous vow as Swift made not to use them, but because he was assured they would be of no service to him. He once declared, that he "never saw the human face divine." He saw better with one eye than the other, which however was not like that of Camoens, the Portuguese poet, as expressed on his medal. He chose to say to an observer and inquirer after the apparent blemish of his left eye, that "he had not seen out of that little scoundrel for a great many years." "It is inconceivable," he used to observe, "how little light or sight are necessary for the purpose of reading." Latterly, perhaps, he meant to save his eyes, and did not read so much as he otherwise would. He preferred conversation to books; but when driven to the refuge of reading, by being left alone, he then attached himself to that amusement. "Till this year," said he to an intimate, "I have done tolerably well without sleep, for I have been able to read like Hercules." But he picked and culled his companions for his midnight hours, "and chose his author as he chose his friend." The mind is as fastidious about its intellectual meal as the appetite is as to its culinary one; and it is observable, that the dish or the book that palls at one time is a banquet at an other. By his innumerable quotations you would suppose, with a great personage, that he must have read more books than any man in England, and have been a mere book-worm; but he acknowledged that supposition was a mistake in his favour. He owned he had hardly ever read a book through. The posthumous volumes of Mr. Harris of Salisbury[14] (which treated of subjects that were congenial with his own professional studies) had attractions that engaged him to the end. Churchill used to say, having heard perhaps of his own confession, as a boast, that "if Johnson had only read a few books, he could not be the author of his own works." His opinion, however, was, that he who reads most, has the chance of knowing most; but he declared, that the perpetual task of reading was as bad as the slavery in the mine, or the labour at the oar. He did not always give his opinion unconditionally of the pieces he had even perused, and was competent to decide upon. He did not choose to have his sentiments generally known; for there was a great eagerness, especially in those who had not the pole-star of judgment to direct them, to be taught what to think or to say on literary performances. "What does Johnson say of such a book?" was the question of every day. Besides, he did not want to increase the number of his enemies, which his decisions and criticisms had created him; for he was generally willing to retain his friends, to whom, and their works, he bestowed sometimes too much praise, and recommended beyond their worth, or perhaps his own esteem. But affection knows no bounds. Shall this pen find a place in the present page to mention, that a shameless Aristophanes had an intention of taking him off upon the stage, as the Rehearsal does the great Dryden?[15] When it came to the notice of our exasperated man of learning, he conveyed such threats of vengeance and personal punishment to the mimic, that he was glad to proceed no farther. The reverence of the public for his character afterwards, which was increasing every year, would not have suffered him to be the object of theatrical ridicule. Like Fame, in Virgil, *vires acquirit cundo.* In the year 1738 he wrote the Life of Father Paul, and published proposals for a translation of his History of the Council of Trent by subscription; but it did not go on. Mr. Urban even yet hopes to recover some sheets of this translation, that were in a box under St. John's Gate; more certainly once placed there, than Rowley's poems were in the chest in a tower of the church of Bristol.

Night was his time for composition. Indeed he literally turned night into day, *noctes vigilabat ad ipsum mane,* but not like Tigellius in Horace. Perhaps he never was a good sleeper, and (while all the rest of the world was in bed) he chose his lamp, in the words of Milton, "In midnight hour, / Were seen in some high lonely tower."

He wrote and lived perhaps at one time only from sheet to sheet, and (according to vulgar expression) from day to day. Dr. Cheyne reprobates the practice of turning night into day, as pernicious to mind and body. Jortin has something to say on the vigils of a learned man, in his Life of Erasmus. As he would not sleep when he could, nothing but opium could procure him repose. There is cause to believe he would not have written unless under the pressure of necessity. *Magister artis ingenique largitor venter,* says Persius. He wrote to live, and luckily for mankind lived a great many years to write. All his pieces are promised for a new edition of his works, under the inspection of sir John Hawkins, one of his executors, who has undertaken to be his biographer. Johnson's high tory principles in church and state were well known. But neither his Prophecy of the Hanover House, lately maliciously reprinted, nor his political principles or conversations, got him into any personal difficulties, nor prevented the offer of a pension, nor his acceptance.[16] *Rara temporum felicitas, ubi sentire quae velis, et quae sentias, dicere licet.* The present royal family are winning the hearts of all the friends of the house of Stuart. There is here neither room nor leisure to ascertain the progress of his publications, though, in the idea of Shenstone, it would exhibit the history of his mind and thoughts.

He was employed by Osborne to make a catalogue of the Harleian library. Perhaps, like those who stay too long on an errand, he did not make the expedition his employer expected, from whom he might deserve a gentle reprimand. The fact was, when he opened a book he liked, he could not refrain from reading it. The bookseller upbraided him in a gross manner, and, as tradition goes, gave him the lie direct, though our catalogue-maker offered at an excuse. Johnson turned the volume into a weapon, and knocked him down, and told him, "not to be in a hurry to rise, for when he did, he proposed kicking him down stairs." Perhaps the lie direct may be punished *ad modum recipientis,* as the law gives no satisfaction. His account of the collection, and the tracts that are printed in quarto volumes, were well received by the public. Of his folio labours in his English Dictionary, a word must be said; but there is not room for much. This writer has sufficient proof that [Robert] Dodsley suggested the first idea of this great collection. Johnson wanted a long and a large literary employment. The proposal rather took him by surprize. *Tantæ molis erat!* The pecuniary bargain was necessary to him, and the engagement for time and payment was concluded. But the work went on but slowly. The money was all gone (for time and money are the most wastable things in the world) before the task was completed. Illness, weariness, or dissipation, clogged the wheels of this machine. A refreshing fee was perpetually necessary; or, to use classical instead of legal allusion, golden showers were to be thrown into the lap of this literary Danae, to the amount of three hundred additional pounds. It required the purses of five eminent booksellers to be opened to pay for the labours of this Hercules.[17] When Johnson came to settle with his employers, said Andrew Millar, they produced their receipts for the money they had advanced, most of which were for small sums. He was confounded to find the balance against himself, for he kept no account, and that he had been working nine years for nothing. The creditor instantly became the debtor.[18] The book-sellers generously made him a present of the difference, and paid his reckoning for him. Dodsley wished for an alphabetical list of the books quoted for this dictionary to be prefixed to the work; but he was not gratified. The delineation of his plan, which was esteemed a beautiful one, was inscribed to lord Chesterfield, no doubt with permission, whilst he was secretary of state. It was at this time, he said, he aimed at elegance of writing, and set for his emulation the preface of Chambers to his Cyclopedia.[19] Johnson undoubtedly expected beneficial patronage. It should seem that he was in the acquaintance of his lordship, and that he had dined at his table, by an allusion to him in a letter to his son, printed by Mrs. Stanhope, and which he himself would have been afraid to publish. Whilst he was ineffectually hallooing the Graces in the ear of his son, he set before him the slovenly behaviour of our author at his table, whom he acknowledges as a great genius, but points him out as a rock to avoid, and considers him only as "a respectable Hottentot." When the book came out, Johnson took his revenge, by saying of it, "that the instructions to his son inculcated the manners of a dancing-master, and the morals of a prostitute." Within this year or two he observed (for anger is a short-lived passion) that, bating some impro-prieties, it contained good directions, and was not a bad system of educa-tion. But Johnson probably did not think so highly of his own appear-ance as of his morals; for, on being asked if Mr. Spence had not paid him a visit![20] "Yes," says he, "and he probably may think he visited a bear." He has nothing of a bear, but his skin, said Goldsmith. "Johnson," says the author of the Life of Socrates, "is a literary Caliban."[21] "Very likely," replied Johnson, "and Cooper (who was as thick as long) is a liter-ary Punchinello."

It does not appear that Lord Chesterfield shewed any substantial proofs of approbation to our philologer, for that was the professional title he chose. A small present he would have disdained.[22] Johnson was not of a temper to put up with the affront of disappointment. He revenged himself in a letter to his lordship, written with great acrimony, and renouncing all acceptance of favour. It was handed about, and probably will be published, for *litera scripta manet*. He used to say, he was mistaken in his choice of a patron, for he had simply been endeavouring to gild a rotten post. An endeavour has been made to procure a copy of it, in order to afford an abstract to the reader, but without success. Mr. Langton, when applied to, thought he could not grant it without a breach of trust.[23] It is in more hands than one; and, perhaps, where secrecy was not enjoined. Johnson took care to send his letter by a safe hand to lord Chesterfield, who shewed it to [Robert] Dodsley. His lordship defended himself very plausibly against the mis-statements of the writer, and candidly pointed out some beautiful sentences and happy expressions. It was a long letter *(grandis epistola)* and written with great asperity. It prevented, as Dodsley reported, the patronage of his lordship, and the benefit from a dedication, which he said would have been the promotion of the sale. One of Johnson's acquaintance, who in conversation probably made lord Chesterfield to be in the wrong, said before him, that his lordship, though the politest, was the proudest man alive; "Except one person," said an acquaintance.[24] "That," said Johnson, "I take to myself; but my pride is defensive." But nothing that is here said is meant as an arraignment of lord Chesterfield.

Lord Chesterfield indeed commends and recommends Mr. Johnson's dictionary in two or three numbers of the World. Not words alone pleased him. "When I had undergone," says the compiler, "a long and fatiguing voyage, and was just getting into port, this lord sent out a small cock-boat to pilot me in." The agreement for this great work was for sixteen hundred pounds.[25] This was a large bookseller's venture at that time: and it is in many shares. Robertson, Gibbon, and a few more, have raised the price of manuscript copies. In the course of fifteen years, two and twenty thousand pounds have been paid to four authors. Johnson's world of words demands frequent editions. His titles of Doctor of Laws from Dublin and from Oxford, (both of which came to him unasked and unknown, and only not unmerited) his pension from the king, which is to be considered as a reward for his pioneering services in the English language, and by no means as a bribe, gave him consequence, and made the dictionary and its author more extensively known. It is a royal satisfaction to have made the life of a learned man more comfortable to him. "These are imperial works, and worthy kings."

Lord Corke, who would have been kinder to him than a Stanhope, (if he could) as soon as it came out, presented the dictionary to the Academy della Crusca at Florence in 1755.[26] Even for the abridgement in octavo, which puts it into every body's hands, he was paid to his satisfaction, by the liberality of his booksellers.[27] His reputation is as great for compiling, digesting, and ascertaining the English language, as if he had invented it. His grammar in the beginning of the work, was the best in our language, in the opinion of Goldsmith. During the printing of his dictionary, the Ramblers came out periodically; for he could do more than one thing at a time. He declared that he wrote them by way of relief from his application to his Dictionary, and for the reward. He has told this writer that he had no expectation they would have met with so much success, and been so much read and admired. It is said he was paid two guineas for each paper. What was amusement to him, is instruction to others. Goldsmith declared that a system of morals might be drawn from these essays: this idea is taken up and executed by a publication in an alphabetical series of moral maxims.[28] Indeed he seems to be the great lay-preacher of morality to the nation.

The Rambler is a great task for one person to accomplish, single-handed. For he was assisted only in two essays by Richardson, two by Mrs. Carter, and one by Miss Talbot.[29] His Idlers had more hands.[30] The World, the Connoisseur, (the Gray's Inn Journal an exception) the Mirror, the Adventurer, the Old Maid, all had help-mates. The toilet, as well as the shelf and table, have these volumes, lately republished with decorations. Shenstone, his fellow collegian, calls his style a learned one.[31] There is, indeed, too much Latin in his English. He seems to have caught the infectious language of sir Thomas Browne, whose works he read, in order to write his life. Though it cannot be said, as [John] Campbell did of his own last work, that there is not a hard word in it, nor words of learned length, in the poetical phrase of the Deserted Village, yet he does not rattle through hard words and stalk through polysyllables, to use an expression of Addison, as in his earlier productions. His style, (the banter and ridicule of Lexiphanes) as he says of Pope, became smoothed by the scythe, and levelled by the roller.[32] It pleased him to be told by Dr. Robertson, that he had read his dictionary twice over. If he had some enemies beyond and even on this side of the Tweed, he had more friends. Only he preferred England to Scotland. It were to be wished, he had not pronounced, in his Hebridian Tour, whatever particular provocation was before him, that "a Scotchman must be a sturdy moralist who does not prefer Scotland to truth." [33] An inadvertent expression in the house of lords, on the imputed cowardice of the Americans, accelerated them into enemies and heroes. If Johnson's accusation had been more confined, a Caledonian, like Wotton's Embassador, might have been permitted to exaggerate for the honour of his country.[34] But it was taken for a national reflection, never to be forgiven nor forgotten: and it is considered as a breach of the union, at least between Johnson and Scotland. The dead cannot send a negociator in their cause. To say the truth, Johnson confessed at last, that the Scotch would never forgive him for publishing that book. But he never wished he had not written it. As it is cowardly to insult a dead lion, it is hoped, that as death extinguishes envy, it also does ill-will: "for British vengeance wars not with the dead." [35]

The well known short epigram of Cleveland, against our sister kingdom, is more malignant than all that Johnson has said or written. But that shall have no place here. It may be admitted of Johnson, at least by his enemies, as it was said of South by Tillotson, "that he wrote like a man, but bit like a dog." This may be applicable to the epic poem of Fingal, and to the personality of the translator. It puts the writer in mind of the complaint and expression of sir Isaac Newton, on the controversy of Hare and Bentley about Terence, that "it was a shame two such great men should be fighting about a play-book!" The particulars of the dispute here alluded to must be trusted to future biographers. *Non nostrum inter vos tantas componere lites.* But for the injunction of lord Chesterfield, "not to seem to be ignorant, (especially as an historiographer) of any fact," this literary and personal altercation would not have been referred to.

He gave himself very much to companionable friends for the last years of his life, (for he was delivered from the daily labour of the pen, and he wanted relaxation) and they were eager for the advantage and reputation of his conversation. Therefore he frequently left his own home, (for his houshold gods were not numerous or splendid enough for the reception of his great acquaintance) and visited them both in town and country. This was particularly the case with Mr. and Mrs. Thrale *(ex uno disce omnes),* who were the most obliging and obliged of all within his intimacy, and to whom he was introduced by his friend Murphy. He lived with them a great part of every year. He formed at Streatham a room for a library, and increased by his recommendation the number of books. Here he was to be found (himself a library) when a friend called upon him; and by him the friend was sure to be introduced to the dinner-table, which Mrs. Thrale knew how to spread with the utmost plenty and elegance; and which was often adorned with such guests, that to dine there was, *epulis accumbere divum.* Of Mrs. Thrale, if mentioned at all, less cannot be said, than that in one of the latest opinions of Johnson, "if she was not the wisest woman in the world, she was undoubtedly one of the wittiest." She took or caused such care to be taken of him, during an illness of continuance, that Goldsmith told her, "he owed his recovery to her attention." She taught him to lay up something of his income every year. Besides a natural vivacity in conversation, she had reading enough, and the gods had made her poetical. The Three Warnings, (the subject she owned not to be original) are highly interesting and serious, and literally come home to every body's breast and bosom. The writer of this would not be sorry if this mention could follow the lady to Milan. At Streatham, where our philologer was also guide, philosopher, and friend, he passed much time. His inclinations here were consulted, and his will was a law. [36] With this family he made excursions into Wales and to Brighthelmstone. Change of air and of place were grateful to him, for he loved vicissitude. But he could not long endure the illiteracy and rusticity of the country; for woods and groves, and hill and dale, were not his scenes — "Tower'd cities please us then, / And the busy hum of men."

On hearing that this literary lady (one of the joys of his own life) was likely to be courted into matrimony a second time, Johnson set himself to prevent it, and wrote her a letter, as full of friendship as her heart was of affection; to which, or to a second letter of the objurgatory kind, it is said, she made a spirited reply. He offered, ill as he was, to travel to her to Bath, with all possible expedition, to expostulate with her, and to obtain only an hour's conversation, with the hope of dissuading her from her inclinations. "Can Love be controuled by advice?" Hardly ever. Then, "Let Cupid and Hymen agree!" Johnson was asked about the letter in print, that is addressed to her and signed with his name; which occasions the present extravagance of this pen. He said, it exhibited his opinion, but had not two sentences together as he wrote them. He said, "it was an adumbration of his letter." [37]

But the greatest honour of his life was from a visit that he received from a great personage in the library of the queen's palace — only it was not from a king of his own making. Johnson, on his return, repeated the conversation, which was much to the honour of the great person, and was as well supported as Lewis the XIVth could have continued with Voltaire. He said, he only wanted to be more known, to be more loved. They parted, much pleased with each other. If it is not an impertinent stroke of this pen, it were to be wished that one more person had conveyed an enquiry about him during his last illness. "Every body has left their names, or wanted to know how I do," says he; "but ———." [38] In his younger days he had a great many enemies, of whom he was not afraid. "Ask you what provocation I have had? / The strong antipathy of good to bad."

Churchill, the puissant satirist, challenged Johnson to combat: satire the weapon. Johnson never took up the gauntlet or replied, for he thought it unbecoming him to defend himself against an author who might be resolved to have the last word. He was content to let his enemies feed upon him as long as they could. This writer has heard Churchill declare, "that he thought the poems of London, and The

Vanity of Human Wishes, full of admirable verses, and that all his compositions were diamonds of the first water." But he wanted a subject for his pen and for raillery, and so introduced Pomposo into his descriptions. "For, with other wise folks, he sat up with the ghost." Our author, who had too implicit a confidence in human testimony, followed the newspaper invitation to Cock-lane, in order to detect the impostor, or, if it proved a being of an higher order, and appeared in a questionable shape, to talk with it. Posterity must be permitted to smile at the credulity of that period. Johnson had otherwise a vulnerable side; for he was one of the few non-jurors that were left,[39] and it was supposed he would never bow the knee to the Baal of whiggism. This reign, which disdained proscription, began with granting pensions (without requiring their pens) to learned men.

Johnson was unconditionally offered one; but such a turn was given to it by the last mentioned satirical poet, that it might have made him angry or odious, or both. Says Churchill, amongst other passages very entertaining to a neutral reader — "He damns the pension that he takes, / And loves the Stuart he forsakes." [40]

Not so fast, great satirist — for he had now no friends at Rome. In the sport of conversation, he would sometimes take the wrong side of a question, to try his hearers, or for his own exertions. But this may do mischief sometimes. "For, without aiming at ludicrous quotation, he could dispute on both sides, and confute." Among those he could trust himself with, he would enter into imaginary combat with the whigs, and has now and then shaken the principles of a sturdy revolutionist. All ingenious men can find arguments for and against every thing: and if their hearts are not good, they may do mischief with their heads. On all occasions he pressed his antagonist with so strong a front of argument, that he generally prevented his retreat. "Every body," said an eminent detector of imposters,[41] "must be cautious how they enter the lists with Dr. Johnson." He wrote many political tracts since his pension. Perhaps he would not have written at all, unless impelled by gratitude. But he wrote his genuine thoughts, and imagined himself contending on the right side. A great parliamentary character[42] seems to resolve all his American notions into the vain expectation of rocking a man in the cradle of a child. Johnson recounted the number of his opponents with indifference. He wrote for that government which had been generous to him. He was too proud to call upon lord Bute, or leave his name at his house, though he was told it would be agreeable to his lordship; for he said he had performed the greater difficulty, for he had taken the pension.

The last popular work, to him an easy and a pleasing one, was the writing the Lives of our Poets, now reprinted in four octavo volumes. He finished this business so much to the satisfaction of the booksellers, that they presented him a gratuity of one hundred pounds, having paid him three hundred pounds as his price. The Knaptons made Tindal a large present on the success of his translation of Rapin's history. But an unwritten space must be found for what Johnson did respecting Shakespeare; for the writer and reader observe a disorder of time in this page. He took so many years to publish his edition, that his subscribers grew displeased and clamorous for their books, which he might have prevented; for he was able to do a great deal in a little time. Though for collation he was not fit. He could not pore long on a text. It was Columbus at the oar. It was on most literary points difficult to get himself into a willingness to work. He was idle, or unwell, or loth to act upon compulsion. But at last he tried to awake his faculties, and, like the lethargic porter of the Castle of Indolence, "to rouse himself as much as rouse himself he can." He confessed that the publication of his Shakespeare answered to him in every respect. He had a very large subscription.

Dr. Campbell, then alive in Queen-Square, who had a volume in his hand, pronounced, that the preface and notes were worth the whole subscription money.[43] You would think the text not approved or adjusted by the past or present editions, and requiring to be settled by the future. It is hoped that the next editors will have read all the books that Shakespeare read: a promise our Johnson gave, but was not able to perform.

The reader is apprized, that this memoir is only a sketch of life, manners, and writings — "In every work regard the writer's end: / For none can compass more than they intend."

It looks forwards and backwards almost at the same time. Like the nightingale in Strada, "it hits imperfect accents here and there." Hawkesworth, one of the Johnsonian school, upon being asked, whether Johnson was an happy man, by a gentleman who had been just introduced to him, and wanted to know every thing about him, confessed, that he looked upon him as a most miserable being. The moment of enquiry was probably about the time he lost his wife, and sent for Hawkesworth, in the most earnest manner, to come and give him consolation and his company. — "And screen me from the ills of life!" is the conclusion of his sombrous poem on November.[44] In happier moments (for who is not subject to every skyey influence, and the evil of the hour?) he would argue, and prove it in a sort of disseration (his conversation was generally a dissertation, said Smollett), that there was, generally and individually, more of natural and moral good than of the contrary. He asserted, that no man could pronounce he did not feel more pleasure than misery. Every body would not answer in the affirmative; for an ounce of pain outweighs a pound of pleasure. There are people who wish they had never been born — to whom life is a disease — and whose apprehensions of dying pains and of futurity embitter every thing. The reader must not think it impertinent to remark, that Johnson did not choose to pass his whole life in celibacy. Perhaps the raising up a posterity may be a debt and duty all men owe to those who have lived before them. Johnson had a daughter, who died before its mother, if this pen is not mistaken. [The supposition of his having had a daughter was groundless. Mrs. Johnson never had a child after her marriage with the doctor, nor, from her advanced age, was such an event probable.] [45]

When these were gone, he lost his hold on life, for he never married again. He has expressed a surprize that sir Isaac Newton continued totally unacquainted with the female sex, which is asserted by Voltaire, from the information of Cheselden, and is admitted to be true. For curiosity, the first and most durable of the passions, might have led him to have overcome that inexperience. This pen may as well finish this last point in the words of Fontenelle, that sir Isaac never was married, and perhaps never had time to think of it. Whether the sunshine of the world upon our author raised his drooping spirits, or that the lenient hand of time removed something from him, or that his health meliorated by mingling more with the croud of mankind, or not, he, however, apparently acquired more chearfulness, and became more fit for the labours of life and his literary functions. But he certainly did not communicate to every intruder every uneasy sensation of mind and body. Who, it may be asked, can determine of the pleasure and the pain of others? True and solemn are the lines of Prior, in his Solomon — "Who breathes must suffer, and who thinks must mourn; / And he alone is blest, who ne'er was born."

Johnson thought he had no right to complain of his lot in life, or of having been disappointed: the world had not used him ill; it had not broken its word with him; it had promised him nothing; he aspired to no elevation; he had fallen from no height. Lord Gower endeavoured to obtain for him, by the interest of Swift, the mastership of a grammar-school of small income, for which Johnson was not qualified by the statutes to become a candidate. [46] His lordship's letter, published some years ago, is to the honour of the subject; in praise of his abilities and integrity, and in commiseration of his distressed situation. The younger Warton,[47] by his influence, procured for him the honorary degree of Master of Arts at Oxford, on the conclusion of his Dictionary. Johnson wished, for a moment, to fill the chair of a professor, at Oxford, then become vacant, but he never applied for it. He was offered a good living by Mr. Langton, if he would accept it, and take orders; but he chose not to put off his lay habit.[48] He would have made an admirable library-keeper; like Casaubon, Magliabechi, or Bentley. But he belonged to the world at large. He was nominated to be professor of ancient literature, amongst the royal society of artists at Somerset-place, as was the late Dr. Francklin of history. A post of honour, but of nothing else. No suit, nor service to be performed. Their names did not appear in the Red Book, or Court Calendar, amongst the other professors. Johnson had done that state some service, during their incorporation, and they knew it. Talking on the topick of what his inclinations or faculties might have led him to have been, had he been bred to the profession of the law, he has said he should have wished for the office of master of the rolls. He gave into this idea in table-talk, partly serious and partly jocose; for it was only a manner he had of describing himself to his friends without vanity of his parts (for he was above being vain) or envy of the honourable stations enjoyed by other men of merit. He would correct any compositions of his friends (*habes confitentem*) and dictate on any subject on which they wanted information. He could have been an orator, if he would. On account of his occasional connexion with Dr. Dodd, for whom he made a bargain with the booksellers for his edition of the Bible,[49] he wrote a petition to the crown for mercy, after his condemnation. To comply with the request in a letter which he received during divine service at Streatham church, he retired to Mr. Thrale's "relinquishing, as he said, for the first time, the worship of his Creator to serve a fellow-creature." The letter he composed for the translator of Ariosto, that was sent to Mr. Hastings in Bengal, is esteemed a master-piece.[50] Dr. Warton,[51] of Winchester, talked of it as the very best he ever read. He could have been eminent, if he chose it, in letter-writing; a faculty in which, according to Sprat, his Cowley excelled. His epistolary and confidential correspondence would make an agreeable publication, but the world will never be trusted with it.[52] He wrote as well in verse as in prose. Though he composed so harmoniously in Latin and English, he had no ear for music; and though he lived in such habits of intimacy with sir Joshua Reynolds, and once intended to have written the lives of the painters, he had no eye, nor perhaps taste, for a picture, nor a landscape. He renewed his Greek some years ago, for which he found no occasion for twenty years. He owned that many knew more Greek than himself; but that his Grammar would shew he had once taken pains. Sir William Jones,[53] one of the most enlightened of the sons of men, as Johnson described him, has often said he knew a great deal of Greek. He amused himself, very lately, with translating into Latin verse, many of the Greek epigrams; and had read over the Expedition of Xenophon, and the Iliad of Homer. He took care to keep up all his stock of learning of all sorts, and, in the words of queen Elizabeth, "to rummage up his old Greek." With French authors he was familiar. He had lately read over the works of Boileau. He passed a judgment on Sherlock's French and English letters,[54] and told him there was more French in his English, than English in his French. His curiosity would have led him to read Italian, even if Baretti had not been his acquaintance.[55] Latin was as natural to him as English. He seemed to know the readiest roads to knowledge, and to languages their conductors. He possessed himself enough of the Saxon tongue, for the purpose of his work, and had always the assistance of Mr. Lye, when he wanted it.[56] He made such progress in the Hebrew, in a few lessons, that surprised his guide in that tongue.[57] In company with Dr. Barnard[58] and the fellows at Eton, he astonished them all with the display of his critical, classical, and prosodical treasures, and also himself, for he protested, on his return, he did not know he was so rich.

Christopher Smart was at first well received by Johnson. This writer owed his acquaintance with our author, which lasted thirty years, to the introduction of that bard.[59] Johnson, whose hearing was not always good, understood he called him by the name of Thyer, that eminent scholar, librarian of Manchester, and a non-juror. This mistake was rather beneficial than otherwise to the person introduced. Johnson had been much indisposed all that day, and repeated a Psalm he had just translated, during his affliction, into Latin verse, and did not commit to paper; for so retentive was the memory of this man, that he could always recover whatever he lent to that faculty. Smart in return recited some of his own Latin compositions. He had translated with success, and to Mr. Pope's approbation, his St. Cecilian Ode. Come when you would, early or late, for he desired to be called from bed, when a visitor was at the door, the tea-table was sure to be spread, *te veniente dic, te decedente.* — With tea he cheered himself in the morning, with tea he solaced himself in the evening; for in these, or in equivalent words, he expressed himself in a printed letter to Jonas Hanway, who had just told the public, that tea was the ruin of the nation, and of the nerves of every one who drank it.[60] The pun upon his favourite liquor he heard with a smile. Though his time seemed to be bespoke, and quite engrossed, it is certain his house was open to all his acquaintance, new and old. His amanuensis has given up his pen, the printer's devil has waited on the stairs for a proof-sheet, and the press has often stood still. His visitors were delighted and instructed. No subject ever came amiss to him. He could transfer his thoughts from one thing to another with the most accommodating facility. He had the art, for which Locke was famous, of leading people to talk on their favourite subjects, and on what they knew best. By this he acquired a great deal of information. What he once heard he rarely forgot. They gave him their best conversation, and he generally made them pleased with themselves, for endeavouring to please him. Poet Smart used to relate, "that the first conversation with him was of such variety and length, that it began with poetry, and ended at fluxions." He always talked as if he was talking upon oath. He was the wisest person, and had the most knowledge in ready cash, this writer had the honour to be acquainted with. — Here a little pause must be endured. The poor hand that holds the pen is benumbed by the frost as much as by a torpedo. It is cold within, even by the fire-side, and a white world abroad. His reader has a moment's leisure to censure or commend the harvest of anecdote that is brought in, for his sake; and if he has more reading than usual, may remark for or against it in the manner of the Cardinal to Ariosto, "All this may be true, extraordinary, and entertaining; but where the deuce did you pick it all up?" The writer perhaps comes within the proverbial observation, that the inquisitive person ends often in the character of the tell-tale. — Johnson's advice was consulted on all occasions. He was known to be a good casuist, and therefore had many cases for his judgment. It is notorious, that some men had the wickedness to over-reach him, and to injure him, till they were found out. Lauder was of the number, who made, at the time, all the friends of Milton his enemies. For this Johnson expiated, by composing a prologue to Comus, for the benefit of his great- [sic] grand-daughter, and by praising Milton. There is nobody so likely to be imposed upon as a good man. "In the business of Lauder" (says Johnson, in a letter) "I was deceived, partly, by thinking the man too frantic to be fraudulent." [61] His conversation, in the judgment of several, was thought to be equal to his correct writings. Perhaps the tongue will throw out more animated expressions than the pen. He said the most common things in the newest manner. He always commanded attention and regard. If he wrote for money, he talked for reputation. His person, though unadorned with dress, and even deformed by neglect, made you expect something, and you was hardly ever disappointed. His manner was interesting; the tone of his voice, and the sincerity of his expressions, even when they did not captivate your affections, or carry conviction, prevented contempt. "No wonder he talks with more sense than any of us," said Goldsmith, "for it is discharged from a larger caliber." If the line, by Pope, on his father, can be applied to Johnson, it is characteristic of him, who never swore, nor told a lie. If the first part is not confined to the oath of allegiance, it will be useful to insert it. "Nor dar'd an oath, nor hazarded a lie."

It must be owned, his countenance, on some occasions, resembled too much the medallic likeness of Magliabechi, as exhibited before the printed account of him by Mr. Spence. No man dared to take liberties with him, nor flatly contradict him; for he could repel any attack, having always about him the weapons of ridicule, of wit, and of argument. No man was prophane or obscene in his company; and no one could leave his conversation without being wiser or better. It must be owned, that some who had the desire to be admitted to him, thought him too dogmatical, and as exacting too much homage to his opinions, and came no more. For they said, while he presided in his library, surrounded by his admirers, he would, "like Cato, give his little senate laws." He had great knowledge in the science of human nature, and of the fashions and customs of life, and knew the world well. He had often in his mouth this line of Pope, "The proper study of mankind is man." He was desirous of surveying life in all its modes and forms, and in all climates. Twenty years ago he offered to attend his friend Vansittart to India, who was invited there to make a fortune; but it did not take place.[62] He talked much of travelling into Poland, to observe the life of the Palatines, the account of which struck his curiosity very much. His Rasselas, it is reported, he wrote to raise a purse of pecuniary assistance to his aged mother at Lichfield. The first title of his manuscript was, "Prince of Ethiopia"; but, as he had erected a history of Seged, king of Ethiopia, in his Ramblers, he changed it to Abyssinia.[63] He had formerly translated an account of those countries, written by a French [*sic*] Jesuit. Mr. Bruce is expected to give us a history of both these countries. The happy valley he would hardly be able to find in Abyssinia. Dr. Young used to say, "that Rasselas was a lamp of wisdom." [64] He there displays an uncommon capacity for remark, and makes the best use of the descriptions of travellers. It is an excellent romance. But his journey into the Western Islands is an original thing. He hoped, as he said, when he came back, that no Scotchman had any right to be angry with what he wrote. It is a book written without the assistance of books. He said, "it was his wish and endeavour not to make a single quotation." His curiosity must have been excessive, and his strength undecayed, to accomplish a journey of such length, and subject to such inconvenience. His book was eagerly read. One of the first men of the age (lord Camden) told Mr. Garrick, "that he would forgive Johnson all his wrong notions respecting America, on account of his writing that book." [65] He thought himself the hardier for travelling. He took a tour into France, and meditated another into Italy or Portugal, for the sake of the climate. But Dr. Brocklesby, his friend and physician, (and who that knows him can wish for more companionable and professional knowledge?) conjured him, by every argument in his power, not to go abroad in the state of his health; but that if he was resolved on the first, and wished for something additional to his income, he desired he would permit him to accommodate him out of his fortune with one hundred pounds a year, during his travels, to be paid by instalments. "Ye little stars, hide your diminish'd heads." The reply to this generosity was to this effect, "That he would not be obliged to any person's liberality, but to his king's." [66] The continuance of this design to go abroad, occasioned the application for an increase of pension, that is so honourable to those who applied for it, and to the lord chancellor, who gave him leave to draw on his banker for any sum. It is just come to the knowledge of this narrator, that Mr. Gerard Hamilton offered Johnson his purse of one hundred guineas *(honos erit huic quoque);* but it was not accepted, [67] "for," said Johnson, "I am worth fifteen hundred pounds!" A sum of money that would last longer than the whole half-guinea that Parson Adams boasted was sufficient for all his charges and expences. The reader, if he is in a good humour, may not dislike the comparative allusion. Adams, for the moment, was richer than Johnson. With the courage of a man, Johnson demanded to know of Brocklesby, if his recovery was impossible? Being answered in the affirmative; "then," says he, "I will take no more opium, and give up my physicians."

At last he said, "If I am worse, I cannot go; if I am better, I need not go; but if I continue neither better nor worse, I am as well where I am." The writer of this Sketch could wish to have committed to memory or paper all the wise and sensible things that dropped from his lips. If the one could have been Xenophon, the other was a Socrates. His benevolence to mankind was known to all who knew him. Though so declared a friend to the church of England, and even a friend to the Convocation, it assuredly was not in his wish to persecute for speculative notions. He used to say, he had no quarrel with any order of men, unless they disbelieved in revelation and a future state. This writer has permission, from Dr. Dunbar, [68] to publish this specimen of his pertinacious opinion: for which Mr. Hume would have put him into his chapter of bigots. "That prominent feature in Johnson's character was strongly marked in a conversation one morning with me *tête à tête*. He reproached me in a very serious, though amicable strain, for commending Mr. Hume as I had done in my Essays on the History of Mankind. I vindicated myself from the imputation as well as I was able — But he remained dissatisfied; still condemned my praise of Hume; and added: 'For my part, sir, I should as soon have praised a *mad dog*.'"

Another morning when he expostulated with me on the same offence, I answered, that I had, indeed, commended Mr. Hume for talents which really belonged to him; but, by no means for his Scepticism, his Infidelity, or Irreligion. "I could not, sir," said Johnson, "on any account, have been the instrument of his praise. When I published my Dictionary, I might have quoted *Hobbes* as an authority in language, as well as many other writers of his time: but I scorned, sir, to quote him at all; because I did not like his principles." He would indeed have sided with Sacheverell against Daniel Burgess, if he thought the church was in danger.[69] His hand and his heart were always open to charity. The objects under his own roof were only a few of the subjects for relief. He was at the head of subscription in cases of distress. His guinea, as he said of another man of a bountiful disposition, was always ready. He wrote an exhortation to public bounty. He drew up a paper to recommend the French prisoners, in the last war but one, to the English benevolence; which was of service.[70] He implored the hand of benevolence for others, even when he almost seemed a proper object of it himself.

Like his hero Savage, while in company with him, he is supposed to have formerly strolled about the streets almost houseless, and as if he was obliged to go without the chearful meal of the day, or to wander about for one, as is reported of Homer. If this were true, it is no wonder if he was unknown, or uninquired after, for a long time: "Slow rises worth by poverty depress'd." [71] When once distinguished, as he observes of Ascham,[72] he gained admirers. He was fitted by nature for a critic. His Lives of the Poets (like all his biographical pieces) are well written. He gives us the pulp without the husks. He has told their personal history very well. But every thing is not new. Perhaps what Mr. Steevens helped him to, has increased the number of the best anecdotes.[73] But his criticisms of their works are of the most worth, and the greatest novelty. His perspicacity was very extraordinary. He was able to take measure of every intellectual object; and to see all round it. If he chose

to plume himself as an author, he might on account of the gift of intui-
tion. "The brightest feather in the Eagle's wing." He has been censured
for want of taste or good nature, in what he says of Prior, Gray, Lyttelton, Hammond, and others, and to have praised some pieces that
nobody thought highly of. It was a fault in our critic too often to take
occasion to shew himself superior to his subject, and also to trample
upon it. There is no talking about taste. Perhaps Johnson, who spoke
from his last feelings, forgot those of his youth. The love verses of
Waller and others have no charms for old age. Even Prior's Henry
and Emma, which pleased the old and surly Dennis, had no attractions
for him.[74] Of Gray, he always spoke as he wrote, and called his poetry
artificial. If word and thought go together, the odes of Gray were not
to the satisfaction of our critic.[75] But what composition can stand before
the porcupine pen of criticism? Mr. Potter,[76] the elegant translator of
Æschylus, has ably defended the ode and ode-writing of Gray against
the opinion of Johnson: so has a Scotch professor,[77] in an entertaining
but sarcastical imitation of his language and criticism. Lyttelton, Akenside, and Hammond, have also found friends in their defence against
Johnson's accusation.[78] He made some fresh observations on Milton,
by placing him in a new point of view; and if he has shewn more of
his excellencies than Addison does, he accompanies them with more
defects. He took no critic from the shelf, neither Aristotle, Bossu, nor
Boileau. He hardly liked to quote, much more to steal. He drew his
judgments from the principles of human nature, of which the Rambler
is full, before the Elements of Criticism by Lord Kames made their
appearance.[79]

It may be inserted here, that Johnson, soon after his coming to London, had thought of writing a History of the Revival of Learning. The
booksellers had other service to offer him. But he never undertook
it. The proprietors of the Universal History wished him to take any
part in that voluminous work. But he declined their offer. His last
employers wanted him to undertake the life of Spenser. But he said,
Warton had left little or nothing for him to do.[80] He said, he could
not read enough, for the purpose and, that no body could read for
him. A system of morals next was proposed. But perhaps he chose
to promise nothing more. He thought, as, like the running horse in
Horace, he had done his best, he should give up the race and the chace.
His character for learning lifted him into so much consequence, that
it occasioned several respectable writers to dedicate their works to him.
This was to receive more reverence than he paid. Murphy (to whom
he was obliged, as he often said, for many social happinesses) addressed

to him an imitation of a satire of Boileau: the last line of which has this injunctive wish, "Write not at all, or else to write like thee!" and Goldsmith dedicated a comedy to him, and praised him for what, as he explained it, Johnson would like to be praised — "his piety, and his wit." [81] Francklin, (as a sincere admirer of his respectable character) inscribed his translation to Lucian's Demonax to him, and terms him the Demonax of the present age.[82] His dependent Levet died suddenly under his roof. He preserved his name from oblivion, by writing an elegiac epitaph for him, which shews that his poetical fire was not extinguished, and is so appropriate, that it could belong to no other person in the world. Johnson said, that the remark of appropriation, was just criticism: his friend was induced to pronounce, that he would not have so good an epitaph written for himself. Pope has nothing equal to it in his sepulchral poetry. When he dined with Mr. Wilkes, at a private table in the city, their mutal altercations were forgot, at least for that day. Johnson did not remember the North Briton, nor the sharpness of a paper against his description or definition of an alphabetical point animadverted upon in his Dictionary by that man of acuteness; who, in his turn, forgot the severity of a pamphlet of Johnson's.[83] All was, during this meal, a reciprocation of wit and good humour. During the annual contest in the city, Johnson confessed, that Wilkes would make a very good chamberlain. When Johnson (who had said that he would as soon dine with Jack Ketch as with Jack Wilkes) could sit at the same table with this patriot, it may be concluded he did not write his animosities in marble. — Johnson was famous for saying what are called *good things*. Mr. Boswell, who listened to him for so many years, has probably remembered many. He mentioned many of them to Paoli, who paid him the last tribute of a visit to his grave. If Johnson had had as good eyes as Boswell, he might have seen more trees in Scotland, perhaps, than he mentions.

This is not the record-office for his sayings: but a few must be recollected here. For Plutarch has not thought it beneath his dignity to relate some things of this sort, of some of his heroes. "Pray, Dr. Johnson" (said somebody), "is the master of the mansion at Streatham a man of much conversation, or is he only wise and silent?" "He strikes," says Johnson, "once an hour, and I suppose strikes right." Mr. Thrale left him a legacy, and made him an executor. It came to Johnson's ears, that the great bookseller[84] in the Strand, on receiving the last manuscript sheet of his Dictionary, had said, "Give Johnson his money, for I thank God I have done with him." The philologer took care that he should receive his compliments, and be informed, "he was extremely glad he returned

thanks to God for any thing." Well known is the rude reproof he gave
to a talker, who asserted, that every individual in Scotland had literature.
(By the by, modern statesmen do not wish that every one in the king's
dominions should be able to write and read.) "The general learning
of the Scotch nation (said he, in a bad humour) resembles the condition
of a ship's crew, condemned to short allowance of provisions: every
one has a mouthful, and nobody a bellyful." [85] Mr. Garrick used to relate
an incident, with great humour, but without personal mimickry (of
which perhaps he was the inventor, and the inheritance went to Foote),
says the communicator, who desired it might have a place here, that
made a good story, as he told it. Johnson was once beset with questions,
by somebody, about the merits of the tragedy of Douglas, that had
just made its public appearance. After submitting to hear some favourite
descriptive passage, which the reciter praised to the skies, ignorantly
or hypocritically, he was asked, if there ever had been written lines
so transcendently excellent by any other poet? To get rid of the impor-
tunity, Johnson impetuously replied; "Yes, by many a man — by many
a woman — and by many a child." — This answer immediately checked
the enthusiasm of the querist. On reporting this decision at a table it
was asserted in company, that Johnson took an opportunity of saying
this again, to a very eminent scholar at Edinburgh, whom he made
an enemy by it. [86]

This opinion of our critic was not meant as a severity against Douglas;
for he had said, "he thought it as good a first play as he had read."
Gray commended it excessively. It accordingly holds its rank at the
theatre. Its merits, and the great performance of the character of lady
Randolph by Mrs. Siddons, who is above praise, bring it into frequent
representation, and occasion clapping hands and weeping eyes. Johnson
received, in the course of the last year, a long and agreeable visit from
this actress. On his being asked afterwards, if he could not wish to compose a part in a new tragedy (Euripides and Voltaire wrote plays when
they were older than Johnson) to display her powers? He replied, "Mrs.
Siddons excels in the pathetic, for which I have no talent." Then, says
his friend, imperial tragedy must belong to you (alluding to his Irene).
Johnson smiled. Of this enough. His size has been described to be large:
his mind and person both in a large scale. His face and features are
happily preserved by Reynolds and by Nollekens. [87] His face and shoul-
ders were moulded and taken off since his death, (alas! how changed
from him!) by Hoskins, of St. Martin's-lane, from which a bust is made. [88]
His elocution was energetic, and, in the words of a great scholar in
the North, who did not like him, he spoke in the Lincolnshire dialect. [89]

His articulation became worse, by some dental losses. But he never was silent on that account, nor unwilling to talk. It may be said of him, that he was never overtaken with liquor, a declaration bishop Hoadly makes of himself. He owned that he drank his bottle at a certain time of life. Lions, and the fiercest of the wild creation, said he, drink nothing but water. Like Solomon, who tried so many things for curiosity and delight, he renounced strong liquors, (strong liquors, according to Fenton, of all kinds, were the aversion of Milton); and he might have said, as that king is made to do by Prior, "I drank, I lik'd it not, 'twas rage, 'twas noise, / An airy scene of transitory joys." His temper was not naturally smooth, but seldom boiled over. It was worth while to find out the *mollia tempora fandi*. The words *nugarum contemptor* fell often from him in a reverie. When asked about them, he said, he appropriated them from a preface of Dr. Hody.[90] He was desirous of seeing every thing that was extraordinary in art or nature; and to resemble his Imlac in his moral romance of Rasselas. It was the fault of fortune that he did not animadvert on every thing at home or abroad. He had been upon the salt-water, and observed something of a sea-life: of the uniformity of the scene, and of the sickness and turbulence belonging to that element, he had felt enough. He had seen a little of the military life and discipline, by having passed whole days and nights in the camp, and in the tents, at Warley Common. He was able to make himself entertaining in his description of what he had seen. A spark was enough to illuminate him. The giant and the Corsican fairy were objects of attention to him.[91] The riding-horses in Astley's amphitheatre (no new public amusement, for Homer alludes to it) he went to see; and on the fireworks of Toiri he wrote a Latin poem.[92]

The study of humanity, as was injuriously said of the great Bentley, had not made him inhuman. He never wantonly brandished his formidable weapon. He intended to keep his enemies off. He did not mean, as in the advice of Radcliffe to Mead, "to bully the world, lest the world should bully him." He seemed to be endowed with great clemency to all subordinate beings. He said, "he would not sit at table, where a lobster that had been roasted alive was one of the dishes." His charities were many; only not so extensive as his pity, for that was universal. He frequently remarked, that every year took something from him of life, and robbed him of a companion or an acquaintance. He had said in his Preface to his Dictionary, that he had outlived all he wished to please.[93] However fond he was of existence, and afraid of death, he would have thought the lot contained in the wish and punishment of the ancients, *ultimus suorum moriatur!* intolerable. An evening convivial club, for three nights in every week, was contrived to amuse him, in Essex-street, founded, according to his own words, "in frequency and parsimony"; to which he gave a set of rules, as Ben Jonson did his *leges convivales* at the Devil tavern. — Johnson asked one of his executors, a few days before his death (which, according to his will, he expected every day) "where do you intend to bury me?" [94] He answered, "In Westminister Abbey." "Then," continued he, "place a stone over my grave (probably to notify the spot) that my remains may not be disturbed." This direction is executed. His expectations of death were so immediate, that he had not time to bequeath his house at Lichfield, to maintain an exhibition at Pembroke-College, as he had resolved.[95] For he was desirous of paying that tributary respect, and of taking that method of making himself remembered by that society. He gave a copy of his works very lately to Dr. Adams, the present master, who had been his tutor. Tutor and pupil had a meeting in the way to London from Derbyshire, which furnished a conversation, the former thinks, (though old in years and in wisdom), he shall be the better for as long as he lives, and which, if Johnson had lived longer, the world also might have been the better for. He intended to compose and publish a volume of Devotions, says Dr. Adams. Who will come forth with an inscription for him in the Poet's-Corner? Who should have thought that Garrick and Johnson would have their last sleep together? It were to be wished he could have written his own epitaph with propriety. None of the lapidary inscriptions by Dr. Freind have more merit than what Johnson wrote on Thrale, on Goldsmith, and Mrs. Salusbury.[96] By the way, one of these was criticised, by some men of learning and taste, from the table of sir Joshua Reynolds, and conveyed to him in a round robin. Maty, in his Review, praises his Latin epitaphs very highly.[97] This son of study and of indigence died worth above seventeen hundred pounds; Milton died worth fifteen hundred.[98] His legacy to his black servant Frank is noble and exemplary. Milton left in his hand-writing the titles of some future subjects for his pen; so did Johnson. The booksellers gave it out, as a piece of literary news, that he had an inclination to translate the lives of Plutarch from the Greek. It appears from his literary memorandum-book, that this was one of the tasks he assigned to himself. He had cut out so much for himself, that many more years of life would not have concluded these Herculean labours. In one sense of the sentimental expression, he lived, as if he was never to die. The winter before he died, he talked seriously of a translation of Thuanus, one volume of which is already translated in folio, by Dr. Wilson of Newark.

Johnson died *by a quiet and silent expiration*, to use his own words on Milton:[99] and his funeral was respectably and numerously attended. The friends of the doctor were happy on his easy departure, for they apprehended he might have died hard. It must be told, that a dissatisfaction was expressed in the public papers, that he was not buried with all possible funeral rites and honours. In all processions and solemnities something will be forgotten or omitted. Here no disrespect was intended. The executors did not think themselves justified in doing more than they did. For only a little cathedral service, accompanied with lights and music, would have raised the price of interment. In this matter, fees run high: they could not be excused; and the expences were to be paid from the property of the deceased. His funeral expences amounted to more than two hundred pounds.[100] Future monumental charges may be defrayed by the generosity of subscription: the whole cost will be more than the last mentioned sum. At the end of this Sketch, it may be hinted (sooner might have been prepossession) that Johnson told this writer, for he saw he always had his eye and his ear upon him, that at some time or other he might be called upon to assist a posthumous account of him. Hawkesworth, and Goldsmith were now no more, who could have written his Life, as he led it.

A hint was given to our author, many years ago, by this rhapsodist, to write his own life, lest somebody should write it for him. He has reason to believe, he has left a manuscript biography behind him.[101] His executors, all honourable men, will sit in judgment upon his papers. Thuanus, Buchanan, Huetius, Bayle, and others, have been their own historians, or journalists.

It was forgot to be told, that twenty years ago he gave an abstract in the Gentleman's Magazine, of Mr. Tytler's book, in vindication of Mary queen of Scots, at the instigation of an old acquaintance.[102] Probably he thought her innocent of the charge of writing the letters to Bothwell.

But he confessed, that her letting Bothwell run away with her, and the marrying him afterwards, was very profligate and indefensible. This writer cannot avoid giving the classical reader, Dryden's Virgil lying upon his table, a parallel adventure (for, says Voltaire, there are examples of every thing in this world) of Dido the queen of Carthage, who was ruined by love (as much as the desiring and the desirable Mary of Scotland), and followed her paramour Æneas into the cave, where and when, says poetical history, "She call'd it marriage, by that specious name / To veil the crime, and sanctify the shame."

"That the ceremonies were short, we may believe," says Dryden, "for Dido was not only amorous, but a widow."

He wrote the plan for the Literary Magazine, and furnished it with some excellent essays and criticisms. He composed the Preface to the Poems of Miss Williams, the Preface to Sully's Memoirs, to Macbean's Classical Geography, and to Adams on the Globes.[103] Mr. Davies collected most of his Fugitive Pieces into three handsome volumes.

He had a large, but not a splendid library, near 5000 volumes. Many authors, not in hostility with him, presented him with their works. But his study did not contain half his books. He possessed the chair that belonged to the Ciceronian Dr. King of Oxford, which was given him by his friend Vansittart. It answers the purposes of reading and writing, by night or by day; and is as valuable in all respects as the chair of Ariosto, as delineated in the Preface to Hoole's liberal translation of that poet. Since the rounding of this period, intelligence is brought, that this literary chair is purchased by Mr. Hoole. Relicks are venerable things, and are only not to be worshipped. On the reading-chair of Mr. Speaker Onslow a part of this historical sketch was written.

"The memory of some people," says Mably very lately, "is their understanding." This may be thought, by some readers, to be the case in point. Whatever anecdotes were furnished by memory, this pen did not choose to part with to any compiler. His little bit of gold he has worked into as much gold-leaf as he could.

The following ADDITIONS came too late to be inserted in their proper Places.

In 1750, we find Johnson at Oxford, (which he visited almost every year) during the instalment of lord Westmorland, the chancellor of the university: on which occasion he wore his academical gown in the theatre, "where," says he, "I have clapped my hands, till they are sore, at Dr. King's speech." From hence he transmitted a periodical Idler, during the Idler season, and whilst his visits were at this place.[104] Like Erasmus, he carried his powers of composition with him wherever he went. University college was frequently his home; and he often expressed his wishes for an apartment in Pembroke college, which were rather discouraged, for whatever reasons. That college might have had, till they were weary of each other, this most respectable layman to itself, where, like father Paul, in his monastic cell, he might have enjoyed his meditations, and been consulted, like that Venetian oracle, on all points and cases whatsoever.

In 1765, Johnson was at Cambridge, with Mr. Beauclerk, "where he drank his large potations of tea, (says Dr. Sharp, in a letter, and who stiles him Caliban) interrupted by many an indignant contradiction, and many a noble sentiment." He displayed some instances of his tenacious memory, talked learnedly on sonnet-writing, which subject arose from the sonnet compositions of Milton. "At twelve," says the letter, "he began to be very great, stripped poor Mrs. Macauley to the very skin, then gave her for his toast, and drank her in two bumpers." [105]

Though his predilection for the English establishments for learning was always conspicuous, yet he could find praise for the literary seminaries of the North. For when he was on his tour, with Mr. Boswell, his *fidus Achates,* the scene at Aberdeen had made such an impression upon him, that he often said, on his return to London, to Dr. Dunbar, that if he ever removed from the capital, he would incline to fix at Aberdeen.) [106] "What," said the professor, "in preference to Oxford?" "Yes, sir," replied Johnson, "for Aberdeen is not only a seat of learning, but a seat of commerce, which would be particularly agreeable." This he so often repeated, that Dunbar used to tell him, he had secured apartments for him in the King's college, which flattered him much. If he had taken a residence at this university, we possibly might have heard of the walk of Johnson at Aberdeen, as of Erasmus at Cambridge. *Localities* have charms for every body.

[Since the revise of this sheet, a publication of some of his devotional pieces is announced to the public.] [107]

He composed forty sermons. "I have no right to enquire what is become of them," said Johnson, "for I have been paid for them." The late memoir writer of Dr. Sykes relates, that his manuscript sermons are credibly reported to be sold. Good sermons, warranted originals, will always fetch a price. Little did this biographer suspect that Johnson could have found leisure or inclination for such employments. But who can tell what a friend is about, when he neither sees nor hears him?

$$\boxed{10}$$

(1785)

The Life of Samuel Johnson, LL.D.

William Cooke

When a man, celebrated for any extraordinary abilities, pays the last great debt to Nature, we become anxious to know his history — sometimes with a view to explore those gradual steps by which he rose to celebrity, and sometimes to mark those infirmities which might diminish general admiration. In either case Biography inculcates this moral purpose — *that it instructs by example*. By the good, we are taught to imitate their virtues — by the bad, to shun their deformities; but when *integrity* and *great abilities* unite in one man, he becomes not only a model for our imitation, but the object of our esteem and reverence.

To this *last* description I am about to add a conspicuous example, in the life of the late Dr. Samuel Johnson, a man whose writings entitle him to the first rank in the classes of literature — his morals, to the first classes among men.

Samuel Johnson was born in Sept. 1709, in the Parish of St. Mary, Lichfield, Staffordshire, and christened on the 7th of the said month. His father's name was Michael, and by the register of his son's birth is styled *Gentleman*, though it appears from a passage in the Lives of the British Poets, and is further confirmed by the remembrance of many now living, that he was a *Bookseller* in the town of Lichfield.

Of the father there is little known except that his credulity in the virtue of the blood of the Stuarts was so great, that he brought his son Samuel up to London at four years of age, to be stroked for the *King's evil*.[1] This story I had heard before, but did not credit it; upon enquiry, however, I found Dr. Johnson frequently acknowledged it, and added, "he was the last person touched by Queen Anne for that disorder."

He received the first rudiments of his education at the free school of his native town, which at that time flourished[2] under the direction of Mr. Hunter; and which, amongst other eminent men, produced Bishop Smalridge, Mr. Wollaston, Bishop Newton, Chief Justice Willes, &c. It is generally believed, that his early proficiency in literature induced some persons belonging to the Cathedral to send him to Oxford, and to undertake the expence of finishing his education there.

Certain it is he was admitted of Pembroke College on the 19th of October 1728, under the tuition of Dr. Adams;[3] and what is very extraordinary, though it is now near fifty-seven years since that period, the Doctor is still living in the same College, and in tolerable good health. Mr. Johnson was then nineteen years of age, and is supposed to have remained there not more than two years, having quitted the University without taking a degree.

Whether an inability to continue the expences of a College life, or a disinclination towards it, occasioned his quitting Oxford so soon, I am not informed; but the former is generally supposed to have been the case.[4] Whilst there, however, his genius was not unemployed: his College themes and declamations are still remembered; and to these he added an elegant translation of Pope's Messiah into Latin verse.

That his finances were inconsiderable at this time is further evident, as his first employment after leaving the University, was that of an Usher to the free school at Market Bosworth in Leicestershire, under the direction of the famous Anthony Blackwall; probably at a salary of not more than from twenty to thirty pounds per year. Who that can feel for the depression of genius, but will naturally lament, that a person so admirably fitted to instruct mankind should be confined to so limited a sphere! Here, however, he had leisure to devote himself to literary pursuits; and here, it is believed, he laid in those stores of knowledge which afterwards enabled him to inform, to entertain, and improve the world.

On the death of his principal, Mr. Johnson went to Birmingham, and resided in the house of one Warren, where he wrote Essays in a Newspaper, printed by his landlord; all of which are now irrecoverably lost, from that fugitive mode of publication. It was here also he translated "A Voyage to Abyssinia, by Father Jerome Lobo," and wrote those elegant lines, "On a Lady's presenting a Sprig of Myrtle to a Gentleman," generally imputed to Mr. Hammond. These verses, the Doctor very lately declared, were written at the request of a friend, who was desirous of supporting the character of a poet with his mistress.

About the beginning of the year 1735, Mr. Johnson returned to his native town of Lichfield, and undertook the education of some young gentlemen there in the *Belles Lettres*, amongst whom was the late celebrated David Garrick, then about the age of eighteen; and who, by his sprightly talents and conversation, became not only Johnson's pupil, but his companion.

This occupation, however, could not have lasted long; so, in the succeeding year, 1736, we find him advertising to board and instruct young gentlemen, in the Latin and Greek languages, at Edial, near Lichfield;[5] but, whether from the disappointment of so many schemes, or from some other cause, the following year he came up to London, determined to bring his abilities to a scene, where, as they would be sooner and more accurately discovered, they would, of course, be sooner and more liberally rewarded.

Though the circumstance of Mr. Johnson's coming up to London, may be recorded as a singular event in the literary world, it is still rendered more particular by that of his fellow-traveller, who was no less than his pupil, Garrick. Both these remarkable geniuses left Lichfield together, March, 1737, on the following letter of recommendation, from Mr. Walmesley, Register of the Ecclesiastical court of Lichfield, to Mr. Colson, a celebrated mathematician. [This letter of 2 March has been omitted.]

It appears by this letter, that Mr. Walmesley had a very particular regard for Mr. Johnson; and, that this regard was mutual, and even not abated by death, appears from Mr. Johnson's grateful remembrance of him in the life of Edmund Smith.

Speaking of his being indebted for some anecdotes of Smith's life to Mr. Walmesley, he breaks out into the following warm effusion of friendship:

Of Gilbert Walmesley, thus presented to my mind, let me indulge myself in the remembrance. I knew him very early; he was one of the first friends that literature procured me, and I hope that, at least, my gratitude made me worthy of his notice.

He was of an advanced age, and I was only not a boy; yet he never received my notions with contempt. He was a whig, with all the virulence and malevolence of his party; yet difference of opinion did not keep us apart. I honoured him, and he endured me.

He had mingled with the gay world without exemption from its vices or its follies; but had never neglected the cultivation of his mind. His belief of revelation was unshaken; his learning preserved his principles; he grew first regular, and then pious.

His studies had been so various, that I am not able to name a man of equal knowledge. His acquaintance with books was great, and what he did not immediately know, he could at least tell where to find. Such was his amplitude of learning, and such his copiousness of communication, that it may be doubted whether a day now passes, in which I have not some advantage from his friendship.

At this man's table I enjoyed many cheerful and instructive hours, with companions, such as are not often found — with one who has lengthened, and one who has gladdened life; with Dr. James, whose skill in physic will be long remembered; and with David Garrick, whom I hoped to have gratified with this character of our common friend. But what are the hopes of man! I am disappointed by that stroke of death, which has eclipsed the gaiety of nations, and impoverished the public stock of harmless pleasure.[6]

What immediate employment Mr. Johnson obtained as a translator, is unknown; it is, however, most probable, that getting acquainted with the celebrated, but unfortunate Richard Savage, he was by him introduced to Mr. Cave, the proprietor of the Gentleman's Magazine; and what seems to corroborate this, is, that Mr. Johnson has been heard to say, that the first performance that gained him any notice, was the following, published in that miscellany, in the beginning of the year 1738. [*Ad Urbanum* has been omitted.]

In May, the same year, he finished that excellent poem called "London," imitated from the third satire of Juvenal. Will it now be believed, that he offered this poem to most of the booksellers in London, for almost any thing they would give? Some shook their heads at the very word *imitation,* while others, with more civility, looked coolly in his face, and said, "It was not in their way."[7] At last, the course of rotation brought him to the shop of Mr. Robert Dodsley, brother of the present Mr. James Dodsley, in Pall-Mall. This ingenious and liberal encourager of authors instantly saw its merit; and, though the poem is not above fifteen pages, and that few imitations can boast the merit of originals, he gave him *ten guineas* for the copy: a circumstance which Mr. Johnson used often to speak of amongst his friends; adding jocularly, "Dodsley was the only bookseller in London that found out I had any genius."

The publication of this poem was fully equal to the bookseller's expectation, as I have been told by a gentleman who had an opportunity of knowing the fact, that the first edition was sold off in a week. The judicious saw a rising genius in the imitator, and Mr. Pope is said to have sought him out, who, receiving no satisfactory answer to repeated enquiries respecting him, said, "It cannot be long before my curiosity will be gratified; the writer of this poem will soon be *deterré*." — His remark was afterwards verified; for, whilst *Juvenal*, and our language shall be had in remembrance, this elegant and spirited imitation of him must be read with delight and improvement.

The price of this poem, though perhaps sufficient on the side of the purchaser, was not adequate to the labour of the author. He therefore, very prudently ceased to risque the reputation he had acquired, by any hasty productions of poetry, and turned his thoughts to *translation*. In this line, he considered he could draw upon his mind with more facility, and reduce his earnings to a greater degree of certainty: But, from the variety of discouraging circumstances, and the want of Literary friends, Mr. Johnson soon felt himself disgusted with the trade of an author, and the town together; and, in this mood, wished to return again to the country, in order to take upon himself the office of master of a charity-school in Shropshire,[8] then vacant, the salary of which was about sixty pounds per annum.

What might have accelerated this wish of retirement, at so early a period of his life, was his marriage, which happened much about this time, with Mrs. Porter, of Manchester.[9] This lady had been a widow, and though she was near twenty years older than Mr. Johnson, and had a daughter by her first husband, he behaved to her through the space of many years with great conjugal attachment, and continued his affection to her daughter, (who is now living at Lichfield) with unremitted attention to his death.[10]

But whatever formed the whole of his motives for going down to Shropshire, we find him intent on this project. The Statutes of the school, however, requiring the person so elected, to be a *Master of Arts*, which Mr. Johnson was not; the father of the present Earl Gower, who seems to have been his patron, wrote the following letter in his favour, to a friend of Dean Swift's, then in Dublin. [This letter, here dated 1738, has been omitted.]

This application, however, proved unsuccessful, which gave Mr. Johnson great uneasiness. He had set his heart upon being master of this school; as it would have relieved him from the drudgery of authorship, and given him that support which would have bounded his desires. This disappointment, however, like many others which we call by that name shews the *"vanity of human wishes,"* and on what a slender pivot the affairs of human life turn; for, had Mr. Johnson's first wish been gratified, he would have missed the opportunities of calling out his great and various abilities; and we should, in all probability, have lost those excellent works which have since enriched the purity of our language, and extended the cause of truth.

Destined therefore, to reside in London, he was forced to engage in any literary employment that could procure him the means of a decent support; and being known to Edward Cave, his original employer, at his request was induced to write the debates in parliament, which, being at the close of Sir Robert Walpole's administration, much attracted general attention. Mr. Johnson laboured some years in this business; and, as his mode of performing it must appear somewhat curious, and so very different from that practised at present by the reporters of parliamentary debates, I shall make no apology for inserting it.

The debates, at this time, were rarely given in any of the news-papers, or magazines: and it was to very particular people, and on particular occasions, that the *entrée* of the gallery was allowed. The object, therefore, in a great respect was new; and the publishing them in the Gentleman's Magazine was a matter of some consequence. Cave, however, being known to several popular members, he got one Worthington, a clergyman of a remarkable good memory, introduced into the gallery; who, in a little time, availed himself so much of his talents of retention, that he could give, not only the substance, but almost the particular words of the longest speech.

It was Mr. Johnson's province to receive these reports from Worthington, and afterwards to give them that form and impression best suited to publication. At first he found himself much perplexed, from the extent of his colleague's memory, who not only picked up the material parts of the debate, but the very *grubs and worms of digression.* He at last made it a rule to receive nothing but the *mere substance;* which he noted down shortly, and then, at his leisure, gave it all those points and graces conformable to the characters of the speakers.[11]

These speeches are to be seen in the Gentleman's Magazine, from about the year 1740, to 1744, under the disguised title of *Speeches of the Senate of Lilliput;*[12] some of which afford such fine specimens of argument and oratory, as probably induced Voltaire to say, (speaking of this period of our history) "That the eloquence of the British Senate rivalled those of ancient Greece and Rome."

It ought however to be mentioned to the credit of Mr. Johnson, that even this very innocent deception, which he was engaged in from *necessity,* afterwards dwelt unpleasingly on his mind, as no longer ago than the Tuesday before he died, he declared to a friend,[13] "That those debates were the only parts of his writings which then gave him any compunction; but at that time he had no conception he was imposing on the world, though they were frequently written from very slender materials, and often from none at all — the mere coinage of his own imagination." He likewise gave Dr. Smollett notice of this circumstance when he was writing his history of England; and some years since when a gentleman in high office was praising those speeches before him for so particular an appropriation of character, that he could name the speakers without a signature. "Very likely, Sir," said Johnson, ashamed of having deceived him; "but I wrote them in the garret where I then lived."

During the period of giving those debates, he employed himself in several biographical, and other productions, which appeared in the Gentleman's Magazine of those times; many of which are now to be seen under the title of, "Miscellaneous and Fugitive Pieces," collected and published in three volumes, by Mr. Thomas Davies. And his *Poetry* — now printing, in a small collection, by Mr. Kearsley, under the title of *The Poetical Works of Dr. Samuel Johnson.*[14]

His principal employers in these productions were Cave and Osborne: the former, one of his first friends and patrons; the latter, of "that mercantile rugged race, to which the delicacy of the Poet is sometimes exposed";[15] as the following anecdote will more fully evince.

Mr. Johnson being engaged by Osborne, to select a number of the most scarce and valuable tracts in the Earl of Oxford's Library, which he had just purchased in consequence of his Lordship's death, and which were afterwards printed in eight quarto volumes, under the title of the *Harleian Miscellany:* this work went on (agreeable to Osborne's ideas, who measured most things by the facility with which they were done) rather slowly: accordingly he frequently spoke to Mr. Johnson of this circumstance; and, being a man of a coarse mind, sometimes by his expressions, made him feel the situation of dependance. Mr. Johnson, however, seemed to take no notice of him, but went on according to that plan which he had prescribed to himself. Osborne, wishing to have the business finished, and perhaps irritated by what he thought an unnecessary delay, one day went into the room where Mr. Johnson was, and abused him in the most illiberal manner: he was an illiterate man, but by great application in his profession, had acquired some property, which had the usual effect, and made him insolent, even to his customers. This impropriety of conduct frequently brought him into scrapes and disgraceful situations.

The selection above mentioned had been at press a considerable time, and the public to whom it had been often announced, became impatient for its appearance.

Mr. Johnson heard him for some time unmoved; but, at last, losing all patience, he seized up a large folio, which he was at that time consulting, and aiming a blow at the Bookseller's head, succeeded so forcibly, as to send him sprawling to the floor: Osborne alarmed the family with his cries; but Mr. Johnson, clapping his foot on his breast, told him "he need not be in a hurry to rise; for if he did, he would have the further trouble of kicking him down stairs."

The resentments, on both sides, however, were not recorded in marble, as it appears soon after, that Mr. Johnson finished this *selection,* which he recommended to the notice of the world, by a very Critical Introduction, shewing the excellence and value of such a work, as it respected history and biography.

The death of Richard Savage, the unfortunate son of the Earl Rivers, in the year 1743, gave Mr. Johnson a fresh opportunity of shewing his biographical talents in favour of that ingenious but unhappy man. Savage was one of his earliest literary friends when he came to London,[16] and though, from this connection, it is supposed he has softened some of the irregularities of his life, it is indisputably one of the most elegant and moral performances in the English language: it, besides shewing us the novelty and vicissitudes of the life of a man of expedience, reminds us, "that nothing will supply the want of *prudence;* and that negligence and irregularity long continued, will make knowledge useless, wit ridiculous, and genius contemptible": the fact is, Mr. Johnson was not unacquainted with Savage's frailties; but, as he has, not long since, said to a friend on this subject, "he knew his heart; and that was never intentionally abandoned: for, though he generally mistook the *love* for the *practice* of virtue, he was at all times a true and sincere believer."[17]

Savage living very intimately with most of the wits of what is called our Augustan age, gave Mr. Johnson many anecdotes, with which he has since enriched his Biographical Prefaces. The following, however, I believe, has never appeared in print before.

Sir Richard Steele, Philips, and Savage, spending the night together, at a tavern, in Gerard-street, Soho, they sallied out in the morning — all very much intoxicated with liquor — when they were accosted by a tradesman, going to his work, at the top of Hedge-lane; who, after begging their pardon for the liberty of addressing them on the subject, told them — "that, at the bottom of the lane, he saw two or three suspicious-looking fellows, who appeared to be bailiffs, — so that, if any of them were apprehensive of danger, he had better take a different route." Panic-struck with this intelligence, not one of them waited to thank the man for his friendship, but flew off different ways, each conscious from the embarrassment of his own affairs, that such a circumstance was very likely to happen to himself.

The success of The Life of Savage, contributed much to Mr. Johnson's reputation; and, as his *moral* always went hand in hand with his *literary* character, his acquaintance was sought after with some avidity.

It is not my purpose, nor have I it in my power, to give the *exact dates* of all his pieces: — the difficulty of such a scrupulous attention, Mr. Johnson himself states in the Life of Dryden. "To adjust," says he, "the minute events of literary history, is tedious and troublesome; it requires, indeed, no great force of understanding, but often depends upon enquiries which there is no opportunity of making, or is to be fetched from books and pamphlets not always at hand."[18]

The piece of any consequence which Mr. Johnson next produced, was his Prologue on the opening of Drury-Lane Theatre, in the year 1747, on the commencement of his friend Garrick's management. This Prologue has been much celebrated, and with great justice, as, independent of the harmony of the versification, I cannot name a more critical history of the English Stage, from the time of Shakespeare, or a more just description of what it ought to be. Such light pieces of poetry, in general, get but a temporary reputation; but this Prologue, though admirably fitted for the occasion, will ever stand a considerable monument of his poetical and dramatic knowledge.

He seems to have written it, partly, as the test of friendship. Garrick and he, as I have before observed, started together, as the children of Fortune. They both, by this time, had been very successful — the former was very nearly at the summit of theatric excellence; and Mr. Johnson had taken equal strides in the Republic of Letters. This appears then, to have been a badge of union between them, and stands as a pleasing memorial of continued friendship between the Poet and the Actor.

Two years afterwards, Garrick had an opportunity of returning him the compliment, with equal warmth of friendship — as, in 1749, Mr. Johnson put his *Irene* into his hands, for performance. This is the Tragedy which Mr. Walmesley alluded to, in his letter to the Rev. Mr. Colson, upon his first coming up to London. He had written it at Lichfield;[19] but, as he kept it so far back as from 1737 to 1749, it is presumable he made such revisals and alterations, as a more intimate knowledge of the stage might suggest.

Garrick embraced the interest of the Tragedy, with a cordiality which became the friendship he professed for the Author. The principal characters were divided between himself and the late Mr. Barry, Mrs. Pritchard, and Mrs. Cibber; and the subordinate ones were given to Berry, Havard, Sowden, and Burton: the dresses were magnificent; the scenes splendid, and such as were well adapted to the inside of a Turkish Seraglio; and the view of the gardens belonging to it, was in all the style of Eastern magnificence.

But notwithstanding this attention, in respect to the Manager and Performers; and that the play was allowed by the best judges to possess fine sentiments and elegant language; and that the moral held up the cause of truth and virtue: yet the incidents and situations were not thought strong enough to produce that kind of effect, which, from habit, an English audience generally expect.

The strangling of *Irene* in the view of the audience was likewise disapproved of by some Critics; and though this incident, after the first representation, was removed to a greater distance, the approbation was not so general as expected. It run its *ninth* night; and then was laid upon the prompter's shelf, where it has remained to this day.

In the same year, Mr. Johnson produced a Poem, imitated from the 10th Satire of Juvenal, intitled, *The Vanity of Human Wishes,* which was published by his first patron, Mr. Robert Dodsley; and which was received by the public, with all that approbation which so classical and elegant a performance is entitled to.

The success of this Poem balancing, at least in fame, his disappointment on the stage, it was reasonable to expect Mr. Johnson would have returned to the charge as a dramatic writer; but whether from disgust, or discovering, that this species of writing was not his *forte,* he roused himself to search for fame and immortality upon more successful ground; and who will say he did not succeed in his two subsequent works — his *Dictionary* and the *Rambler?* None, but those who are equally callous to the perceptions of knowledge, and the sympathies of moral virtue.

It not unfrequently happens with great minds, that difficulties and embarrassments call them out with redoubled exertions. Had Mr. Johnson succeeded as a dramatist, he probably would have found it more for his ease and profit, to have continued to write for the stage: his friend Garrick being manager, might have forwarded his views; and his name would have, perhaps, at this day, stood in the *médiocre* list of tragedy-writers. But, foiled in this his first attempt, he was determined to rise, like Antæus, from his fall; and put in claims for higher and more substantial honours. With this view he conceived the design of one of the noblest and most useful, though at the same time the most laborious work that could possibly be undertaken by one man, viz. *A complete Grammar and Dictionary of our hitherto unsettled Language.*

He drew up a sketch of this great work, in a letter to the late Earl of Chesterfield, then one of his Majesty's principal secretaries of state; which was afterwards published under the title of "The Plan of a Dictionary of the English Language." I have now the pamphlet before me, pausing at every paragraph, so desirous am I to give an extract from such a judicious, critical, and elegant performance; but, as the nature of this work will not permit me to publish the letter in full, I dare not touch a *part*, lest I destroy the beauty and symmetry of the *whole*. It is, as far as my judgment warrants me to say, (considering the nature of the subject) one of the richest and most finished critical essays in our language.

The execution of this work cost him the labour of many years, the letter to Lord Chesterfield, when the plan was already sketched, being dated in 1747, and the whole not finished till 1755; and without doubt, previous to the first mentioned period, he must have made many preparatory collections and observations; but the manner in which it was at last executed, made ample amends for public expectation. Nor did his praises rest with his own countrymen: several of the foreign academies, and particularly the *Academia della Crusca,* paid him such honours on the occasion, as leave all encomiums in this place entirely superfluous.

When Lord Chesterfield understood this work was undertaken, he encouraged the author to proceed in it; which gave rise to the letter just mentioned: but from some of those unaccountable delays by which patronage is too generally found to cool, his lordship took no manner of notice of it till some little time previous to its publication; then he published two letters, in a periodical paper, called "The World," recommending the author, and the work, vainly enough (though under the disguise of modesty) telling the public, that for *his part* he should conform himself to the authorities of that dictionary, both in his writing and conversation.

This circumstance, attended with some previous personal slights, roused Mr. Johnson's indignation, and he no longer thought it necessary to preserve any terms of friendship with him. In conversation he freely gave his opinion of him, "That he was a Lord amongst Wits, and a Wit amongst Lords": and being complimented on his lordship's endeavours to serve him by his two essays in *The World*, he scouted[20] either their utility, or the author's good intentions; he compared them to *"two little Cock-boats,* vainly sent out to partake the triumphs of a long and dangerous voyage, without risquing the hazards of rocks and quicksand."

Mr. Johnson was not even satisfied with using the shafts of ridicule in conversation, but resented his usage of him in a letter which he wrote his lordship, *insisting on being for ever dismissed his patronage:* this letter I have not seen, but once heard a friend, to whom he read it, repeat some of it from memory; and it seemed to breathe a spirit of independence, that did great honour to the author's mind: for many years Mr. Johnson refused giving a copy of it; but some time before his death, he gave one to Mr. Langton, with an injunction never to publish it until an imperfect copy first appeared, which he judged might be the case, as he had often repeated it to several friends.

Lord Chesterfield, too late, found out the error of neglecting a man of genius, and wanted to court Mr. Johnson back to his patronage, through the mediation of Mr. [Robert] Dodsley — but in vain: Johnson was not to be shaken from his purpose; and they never spoke together afterwards.

When his lordship, however, found *the scabbard thrown away,* he was not without his resentments in turn, as appears by the following strong allusion to Mr. Johnson, in one of his letters to his son. [The "respectable Hottentot" sketch has been omitted.]

This letter shews that Lord Chesterfield was rather *angry* than *satyrical,* as the *person* of an antagonist, when he is not vain of it, should, by no means, constitute a subject for raillery: Mr. Johnson, however, gave him the *retort courteous;* for on the publication of those letters, being asked his opinion of them, he replied, "They are such as I did suppose Lord Chesterfield would write: They inculcate the morals of a W——, and the manners of a Dancing-master."

The price which the booksellers paid Mr. Johnson for his dictionary, was *fifteen hundred pounds;* a sum so inadequate to the labour, and necessary expences incurred, that the Author, *though in the habits of providing for the day that was passing over him,*[21] found the money all expended before the work was finished. In this dilemma, he called upon the booksellers for an additional *five hundred pounds;* which was objected to on their part; and, by some, called an *imposition,* as departing from the original agreement. He was then obliged to tell them, "the work must be suspended": but this had no effect; and a law-suit was talked of for some time: at last, after much grumbling, they made a virtue of necessity, and paid him the money.

I have stated the particulars of this transaction, as I have often heard it imputed to Mr. Johnson, that the demand of the additional five hundred pounds was not strictly conformable to his character; but the short answer to this is, that the work could not possibly be finished without it; the author having no other pecuniary resource to apply to; and the first sum, upon a just calculation of the labour and years employed about it, appeared to be not improvidently expended: the demand, therefore, became an act of necessity; and, indeed, that the same booksellers thought so (when interest began to open their eyes a little) is plain, as on the publication of the third edition, they voluntarily complimented him with the additional sum of *three hundred pounds*.

I cannot dismiss this article, without pointing out to the public a circumstance, which though constantly under their observation, very few have taken notice of, which is, that in Mr. Johnson's definition of the word ALIAS, in the octavo edition of his Dictionary, he takes occasion to carry his resentment against the late David Mallet,[22] in a very whimsical, and, perhaps, unprecedented manner: Mallet's original name had been *Malloch,* which he changed soon after he came to London, for *Mallet;* this duplicity, with the character he had for being a *Free-thinker* in religion, so irritated our orthodox author, that he was determined to take his revenge. The word ALIAS was the *gibbet* he chose for this purpose, which he thus exemplifies: "ALIAS, a Latin word signifying otherwise; as MALLET, alias MALLOCH — that is, otherwise *Malloch";* and here Mallet continues to *hitch*[23] to this day, and will, in all probability, long after the occasion of the example is forgotten.

During the interval of recess, necessary to the fatigue of this stupendous undertaking, Mr. Johnson, amongst other pieces of a more fugitive kind, published his *Rambler,* a series of periodical papers, which came out every Tuesday and Saturday in the year 1750, and continued for two years successively. In the course of so great a number of these papers as this long period demanded, those which the author was favoured with by others, were very inconsiderable, being assisted only in two essays by Richardson (author of Sir Charles Grandison), two by Mrs. Carter, and one by Miss Talbot;[24] and yet on the whole, this work stands in equal, if not superior rank, to the joint efforts of the *literati* who were concerned in those celebrated essays The *Tatler* and *Spectator*. What further adds to the credit of the author's genius, is, that he wrote most of these papers on the spur of the occasion — often on a journey — often in a chop-house, &c. as a temporary relief to his mind and necessities. — He has often declared this, and added, "That from such circumstances, he never had the most distant notion of their meeting with such public approbation."

The principal merit of this Work consists in disseminating philosophic and moral truths with peculiar force and energy; aided by a rich and variegated imagination, particularly in his Eastern Tales; some of which are the best models of that species of writing in our langauge. The style, though elevated and grammatically correct, has been thought by some to be bordering rather on the *turgid;* and perhaps there are a few instances which may justify this opinion. In excuse for this it should be considered, that the Author was, at the same time, deeply engaged in exploring and arranging the *orthography* and *derivatives of words;* and it was almost next to an impossibility, that the business of the one should not, in some degree, incorporate with the other. If, as he says himself in the life of Milton, "the rights of Nations and of Kings sink into questions of grammar, when *Grammarians* discuss them";[25] how difficult must it be, in the execution of two such different works, to avoid some part of this judgment!

The *Rambler* has already undergone *ten* Editions; and has, about two years since, been translated into the Russian language by order of the Empress, who was so pleased with the Work, that she has settled a very handsome pension on the translator![26] When the author of the Rambler was first told this circumstance, a suffusion of placid joy beamed upon his face, which a person in company observing, he replied — "I should be afraid to be thought a *vain* man, if I did not feel myself *proud* of such distinctions."

It will not, I hope, be thought too minute in this place to remark, (for little things are often found objects of *use,* as well as *curiosity,* to posterity) that Mr. Johnson was not paid for this work above two guineas per week, though the Booksellers have since made by it above five thousand pounds.[27]

Upon the very great repute of the Rambler, the University of Oxford complimented him with the degree of *Master of Arts,* and some years afterwards he received the degree of *Doctor of Laws* from the University of Dublin, which was finally followed up by that of Oxford conferring the like honour on him in full convocation.

The celebrity of two such productions, very justly placed Dr. Johnson at the head of the Literary profession. His name was a tower of strength to any publication, and the Bookseller was thought successful who could engage him in any line suitable to his talents. Perhaps, buoyed up a little too much with this opinion, he soon after the publication of his Dictionary, made a proposal to a number of Booksellers convened for that purpose, of writing a *Dictionary of Trade and Commerce*. This proposal went round the room without his receiving any immediate answer, at length a well known *son of the trade,* since dead, remarkable *for the abruptness of his manners,* replied, "Why Doctor, what the D——l do you know of trade and commerce?" The Doctor very modestly answered, "not much, Sir, I confess in the *practical* line — but I believe I could glean, from different authors of authority on the subject, such materials as would answer the purpose very well." [28]

The proposal, however, fell to the ground; and it is no more than probable it was happy for the Doctor's reputation it did so.

On the fifth of April, 1750, The Masque of Comus, was acted at Drury Lane Theatre, for the benefit of Milton's grand-daughter. Here an opportunity presented itself to Dr. Johnson, to do a substantial honour to the memory of our great poet, by contributing to the necessities of his descendant. He according, not only wrote the Prologue on that occasion, but announced the play by the following letter, which appeared in *The General Advertiser,* the day before its representation. [The letter has been omitted.]

It is not a little painful to observe, that notwithstanding those efforts with 20£ given by Mr. Tonson, and a large contribution, brought by Dr. Newton, the whole receipt of the House produced but, *one hundred and thirty pounds.*

In the year 1753 [1752], Dr. Johnson lost his wife, the friend and companion of many years, and one who struggled with him "against inconvenience and distraction, sickness, and sorrow," [29] with great conjugal firmness. He lamented her death with a grief which did honour to his feelings, and afterwards celebrated her memory by the following affectionate Latin epitaph, inscribed on a black marble grave stone, in Bromley Church, county of Kent.

Hic conduntur reliquiæ
ELIZABETHAE
Antiqua JARVISIORUM gente,
Peatlingæ, apud Leicestreness, ortæ;
Formosæ, cultæ, ingeniosæ, piæ;
Uxoris, primis nuptiis, HENRICI PORTER,
secundis, SAMUELIS JOHNSON,
Qui multum amatam, diuque defletam,
Hoc lapide contexit.
Obiit Londini, Mense Mart.
A. D. MDCCLIII.

The following year was distinguished by another loss, — the death of his old friend and principal employer Edward Cave, who was the first projector and publisher of the *Gentleman's Magazine;* a periodical Pamphlet, which for many years succeeded beyond every thing of the kind ever known, and still holds a principal credit amongst the accumulated monthly publications.

Gratitude to an old friend was always a predominant feature of the Doctor's character; he accordingly wrote his life (which was first published in the Gentleman's Magazine, and since collected in Davies's Fugitive Pieces) where he pays a tribute of affection to his memory. In this life he likewise states the rise of that Magazine, which, as it was the first production of the kind, deserves particular notice.

When Mr. Cave first formed this project, which was in the year 1731, he was so far from expecting the success which he afterwards found, and others had so little prospect of its consequences, that though he had for several years talked of his plan amongst printers and booksellers, none of them thought it worth the trial. That they were not restrained by their virtue from the execution of another man's design, was sufficiently apparent, for as soon as that design began to be gainful, a multitude of Magazines arose and perished; only the *London Magazine,* supported by a powerful association of booksellers, and circulated with all the art and all the cunning of trade, exempted itself from the general fate of Cave's invaders, and obtained, though not an equal, yet a considerable sale. To this undertaking he owed the affluence in which he passed the last twenty years of his life, and the fortune which he left behind him.[30]

Dr. Johnson frequently spoke of this man, with that satisfaction which people after passing the storms of life, generally find in looking back to the little incidents of their outset. He always concluded with saying, "Cave was an honest man," but then, continued he, he was a penurious paymaster, he would contract for lines by the hundred, and expect the long hundred into the bargain."

Of this industrious and intelligent printer thus presented to my mind, it likewise brings to my recollection an anecdote I heard Dr. Johnson tell of Cave's wife, which is not only curious, but should serve as an example to others, at least not to be guilty of the same neglect.

When Cave got into affluence, it was usual with him, upon the receipt of any large sum of money, to make Mrs. Cave the cashkeeper. The frequency of this, and the dependence which he had on her management of it, tempted her occasionally to practise "the little pilfering temper of a wife"; she therefore by degrees accumulated a considerable sum, which Cave knew nothing of. Her last illness was an asthma; and though she every day grew worse, she reserved this secret from her husband till her breath grew so short, that she had only time to tell him "she had concealed a part of the money which he occasionally gave her, which she laid out in India bonds." She was immediately after this seized with convulsions, and died before she had time to say where they were hid, or in whose possession they were deposited. Cave on her death made every possible enquiry after his property, but such *is the integrity of some friendships,* the bonds were never afterward found.

In 1756, we find the Doctor concerned in a periodical paper, published by T. Gardner, in the Strand, called, "The Universal Visiter," in conjunction with a number of names that promised to give permanency, and reputation to any work. But as too many doctors sometimes, only dispatch the patient the quicker, what from the indolence of some, or the opposite opinions of others, it did not continue above a year. These monthly numbers have been since collected in one volume, and to those who may be curious in distinguishing the different authors, by their different signatures, they are informed that those marked thus **, were written by Doctor Johnson; those with the letter S, by Christopher Smart; those with the letter R, by Richard Rolt; those with the letter G, by David Garrick, and those with the letter P, by Doctor Percy the present Bishop of Dromore.

In the same and subsequent year Doctor Johnson wrote *sixteen* numbers in another periodical work, published by Faden, in Fleet Street, entitled, "The Literary Magazine."[31] Those essays consist partly in a Review of Books, and partly in an answer to a pamphlet published by Jonas Hanway, called "The Eight Days Journey," in which the author takes occasion to reprobate in very aggravated terms, the unconstitutional use of *tea* drinking.

This last attack was touching the Doctor upon his favourite string; tea was to him, what gold is to the miser; honours to the ambitious, — it was the solace of his morning and evening hours; the refuge from his labours, the repast for his friends; in short it was so much the great *desideratum* of his life, that he often declared "he never felt the gripe of poverty but when he wanted money to buy tea."[32] No wonder then, that roused by this attack upon his *daily liquor,* he animadverted upon the pamphlet. Hanway answered him, and unfortunately for him having mentioned in this answer that *"he put horses to his chariot,"* and was *a Governor of the Foundling Hospital,* Johnson replied to this little swell of vanity, in the following vein of irony, which deserves to be recorded.

I now find (says he) but find too late, that instead of a writer, whose only power is his pen, I have irritated an important member of an important corporation; a man, who as he tells us in his letters, puts *horses to his chariot.*

It was allowed to the disputants of old to yield a controversy with little resistance to the Master of Forty Legions. — Those who know how weakly naked truth can defend her advocates, would forgive me, if I should pay the same respect to *a Governor of the Foundlings.*

Of the author I unfortunately said, his injunction was somewhat too magisterial: that I said, before I knew he was a *Governor* of the *Foundlings!* But he seems inclined to punish me, as the *Czar* made war upon Sweden, because he had not sufficient honors paid him when he passed through the country in disguise. Yet, was not this irreverence without extenuation. Something was said of the *merit* of *meaning well,* and the Journalist was declared to be a man, *whose failings might well be pardoned for his virtues.* This is the highest praise which human gratitude can confer on human merit; praise, that would have more than satisfied *Titus,* or *Augustus;* but which I must own to be inadequate and penurious, when offered to "this Member of an important Corporation!" &c. &c. &c.

He has however so much kindness for me, that he advises me "to consult my safety, when I talk of Corporations." I know not, what the most important Corporation can do, becoming manhood, by which my safety is endangered. My reputation is safe, for I can prove the fact; my quiet is safe, for I meant well; and for any other safety, I am not used to be very sollicitous.

I am always sorry at the sight of any being labouring in vain; and, in return for the Journalist's apprehensions for my safety, I will own compassion for his tumultuous resentment; since all his invectives fume into the air, and with so little effect on me, that I shall esteem him as one who has the *merit* of *meaning well;* that I still believe him to be *a man, whose failings* may be *justly pardoned for his virtues!*

The *Rambler* had by this time gained such universal reputation with the public, that the booksellers made a proposal to Dr. Johnson, to re-commence that species of writing which he did in the year 1758, in a series of papers published every Saturday, called "THE IDLER," since collected in two volumes duodecimo. The essays in this work are rather of a lighter kind than those of the Rambler; and as such may be compared to the last impressions of a good print, in which the likeness remains, though the strength is considerably diminished. In saying this, I do not mean generally to disparage the work; its allegories and moral essays, bear the hand of a great master, nor are some of the lighter pieces defective in fancy. I would only say, it is not the *Twin-brother of the Rambler,* and as such has not the same claim to celebrity.

During the writing of this periodical work, Dr. Johnson's mother died, and as he has dedicated a paper to her memory, the occasion of which is not generally known, I shall make no apology for giving it a place in these memoirs. I must confess to have another reason, it establishes his character as a dutiful and affectionate son, and if it wanted this additional establishment, that of a sincere and fervent Christian. [*Idler* No. 41, here reprinted in its entirety, has been omitted.]

The Doctor's affection for his parent did not even stop here. Not many days before his death, he wrote to a friend in Lichfield, [33] desiring that a large stone might be placed over the bodies of his father, mother, and brother, who were buried in St. Michael's church in that town, (inclosing the following inscription for that purpose) and hoped "it might be done while he was yet alive"; — but what are the hopes of man! death prevented him that pleasing satisfaction, though it cannot rob his memory of such a tribute of filial and fraternal attachment. [Omitted.]

In the Spring of 1759, Dr. Johnson published his "Rasselas, Prince of Abyssinia," a beautiful little novel, abounding in moral sentiments, and remarkable for a happy imitation of the Oriental writers. His design in this was, to shew the futility of our researches after happiness, in the various disguises of pleasure which this world produces; and that it is only to be found in our own minds, and a dependance on Providence. Among other topics which this literary gem treats of, is that of "Marriage," [34] which I think is better discussed here than in any other book I ever read, and as such must afford no inconsiderable instruction to all married people.

What probably might have given him the first idea of this novel, was his early translation of the *Voyages of Lobo,* whilst he resided at Birmingham, which describes the history, antiquities, government, religion, and manners of the Abyssinians; and to this translation we are, perhaps, indebted for that richness of imagery, and critical knowledge of the Eastern customs, so admirably displayed in the *Rambler* and *Idler.*

But from whatever source he drew his materials, what first suggested the idea of making use of them, should not be withheld from the public, — it was the want of *twenty pounds,* to enable him to go down to Lichfield, to pay the last duties to his mother who was dying. After having sketched the design of it, he shewed it to a bookseller, and told him his exigencies; but the other refused advancing any money till he had seen the whole of the copy. The Doctor sat down with perseverance to comply with his request; but before he had finished it his mother died. He afterwards sold it to another bookseller. [35]

Soon after the accession of his present Majesty, Lord Bute, who was then First Lord of the Treasury, being determined to pension his countryman, Mr. John Home, author of the tragedy of Douglas, he thought it prudent to associate him with an Englishman of established literary reputation. [36] Johnson was immediately thought of; but what from the natural ruggedness of his temper, and the bent of his political opinions, it was thought hazardous to make the application. His constant and intimate friend, Mr. Murphy, however, undertook it, who sought him out, and told him the subject of his message. He received it with evident marks of surprise, and after pausing a few minutes, replied, "No, Sir: They'll call me pensioner Johnson." — "Suppose they do," says Mr. Murphy, "as you will be conscious of not obtaining that title disgracefully, what's in a name?" — "Very true, Sir," says the other, "I'll consider of it: call upon me to-morrow, and I'll give you an answer." His friend pressed him not to let matters cool, and judiciously pointed out the hazard of procrastination; but he replied, "The question was momentous, and he would not be taken by surprize."

Next day he told Mr. Murphy he would accept it; and in a few days afterwards the Doctor waited upon Lord Bute to thank him. In this interview they both behaved with equal credit. Upon Johnson's introduction, after expressing his obligations to his Majesty, for this mark of royal favour, he added, "And I accept it the more readily, as I am conscious of not having obtained it by once dipping my pen in faction." — "True Doctor," said Lord Bute, "and what must give further satisfaction to a mind like yours, I hope you'll never be asked to dip your pen in faction." Here the conversation ended, and Johnson took his leave; but such was the awkward feel of this patronage to him, that from that hour he never once knocked at his Lordship's door.

"The learned leisure," which this pension enabled him to enjoy, being 300£ per year, directed the Doctor to studies more congenial to his mind than those generally suggested by booksellers. He therefore sat down to a new edition of Shakespeare, which he published by subscription in 1765, in eight volumes octavo. The general merit of this work repaid the public expectation so much, that it went through two editions in five years, and a certain literary character, Dr. [John] Campbell, since dead, said of it, "That the preface and notes were worth the whole subscription-money."

Of the merit of some of the notes I have the misfortune of differing from him; but as to the preface, I think it one of the most ingenious and critical we have in our language; it discusses with great fairness the unities of time and place, and without being blindly attached to his great author, speaks enough of his character to assign him that immortality which the united voice of the public for near two centuries have given him. He praises him, above all his cotemporaries, as the poet of nature — The Poet that holds up to his readers a faithful mirror of manners and of life; characters that are the genuine progeny of common humanity; such as the world will always supply, and observation will always find.

In the year 1770 [1773], in conjunction with Mr. Steevens, Doctor Johnson enlarged his Shakespeare to ten volumes octavo, and thus by a combination of great abilities, it is become at present our first book on the subject.

On the night previous to the publication of the first edition, he supped with some friends in the Temple, when much pleasantry passing on the subject of commentatorship, he took no notice of the hours till the clock struck five, then starting as from a reverie he exclaimed, "This may be sport to you, Gentlemen, but you don't consider there are but two hours between me and criticism."

The third edition of *Johnson and Steevens's Shakespeare* is now in the press, under the inspection of a gentleman every way fitted to the task by a critical knowledge of the drama, as well as the comparative merit of our best, and oldest English writers.[37]

Dr. Johnson's political works, consisting of "Taxation no Tyranny, — Falkland Island, — The Patriot, — and False Alarm," were published at different intervals, from about the year 1769 [1770] to 1775; and perhaps it would be more for the credit of his memory that they were never undertaken, as too many are inclined to think, and in other respects his admirers, he has sacrificed his talents to the support of Ministerial errors and corruption. I cannot entirely agree in this opinion; as, however, the positions he laid down may be *politically wrong,* all those who knew his heart must give him credit for *thinking them right;* perhaps the acrimony with which he has treated some of the leaders and measures of Opposition was his greatest fault, and this undoubtedly should preclude him the character of an *impartial* politician.

In the course of his political labours the Doctor expressed, or rather renewed a desire which "he had so long conceived, that he scarcely remembered how the wish was originally formed," to visit the Hebrides, or Western Islands of Scotland. In this journey, which was begun in the year 1773, he was accompanied by Mr. Boswell, author of the History of Corsica, and other literary pieces, "A companion," (says the Doctor in his account of this Journey) "whose acuteness would help my enquiry, and whose gaiety of conversation and civility of manners are sufficient to counteract the inconveniencies of travel in countries less hospitable than those we have passed." [38]

After his return, and about the beginning of the year 1775, he published his remarks, under the title of "A Journey to the Western Islands of Scotland."

This journey, though performed through some of the most uncultivated parts of Scotland, he has made very entertaining. He shews besides an accurate account of the country, the eye of a philosopher piercing through the manners, customs, and wants of an uncivilized people; and then compares them with the luxuries and artificial wants of more refined life. He has repaid his debts of hospitality, by several honourable and grateful accounts of the *Lairds* and leading men at whose houses he was entertained; and even in lower life, he has condescended to give some pleasing portraits of virtue and rural simplicity.

In the course of this work, he goes into an enquiry concerning the authenticity of Ossian's Poems, published some years since by Mr. James Macpherson, the result of which enquiry he gives us in the following words.[39]

I believe they never existed in any other form than that which we have seen. — The Editor, or Author never could shew the original, nor can it be shewn by any other: to revenge reasonable incredulity, by refusing evidence, is a degree of insolence with which the world is not yet acquainted, and stubborn audacity is the last refuge of guilt: it would be easy to shew it if he had it — but whence could it be had? It is too long to be remembered, and the language formerly had nothing written. He has doubtless inserted names that circulate in popular stories, and may have translated some popular ballads, if any can be found; and the names and some of the images being recollected, make an inaccurate auditor imagine, by the help of Caledonian bigotry, that he has formerly heard the whole.

Some part of this passage gave offence to the Editor of Ossian's Poems, and an epistolary altercation is said to have ensued.[40] Which of them was right, in respect to the authenticity of the Poems, would be rashness in me to decide, seeing that after much *literary dispute* on the subject, it is still unsettled: but that the Doctor differed in opinion with the Editor *rather too coarsely*, I believe, impartiality will allow. "An author no doubt may be considered as a general challenger, whose writings every body has a right to attack"; but it is of much importance to the credit of an assailant, that to a proportioned degree of judgment and information, he brings good temper and impartiality.

Though we do not find the Doctor employed in any capital work about this period, his muse was not idle in the service of his friends. He wrote the Prologue to the comedy of the Good-Natured Man, for Dr. Goldsmith; and on the Doctor's death which happened some years afterwards, paid a tribute of respect to his memory, by an elegant Latin inscription, which is since placed on his monument in Westminster Abbey.

For the widow of the late Mr. Hugh Kelly he likewise wrote an Occasional Prologue to the "Word to the Wise," performed for her benefit after her husband's decease. This comedy was originally brought out by Mr. Kelly, in the year 1770, but was damned on the second night of performance, without a fair hearing, by the violence of a party, who opposed the author as a ministerial pensioner. The writer of this account was present at both representations, and he hopes never again to see such partial treatment within the walls of a theatre; where an author, fairly putting himself on the audience as on a jury, to try the merits of his piece, is condemned on what does not come in evidence before them.

Whilst I am dwelling upon this circumstance, I cannot avoid mentioning a mode of damnation, (which then appeared to me to be quite new) practised by some professed enemies of Mr. Kelly, the second night of representation.

A body, consisting of about twenty people, spread themselves nearly in the center of the pit, with a leader at their head, to give them the cue. He accordingly watched all those little mistakes in representation, which will sometimes unavoidably happen, together with all those weak passages, or familiar words in the scene, and instantly turning them to his own advantage, set up a horse laugh, which was followed by his whole corps.

Unquestionably there was much *malice* in this procedure, but at the same time it must be confessed there was great generalship. — Hissing rather provokes indignation, than begets partizans — but *laughing* is often an irresistible impulse, which becomes contagious from example, and thus gains involuntary proselytes. That this was the case on that night was very clear, as the laughers became the majority, and the play was withdrawn.

Though Mr. Kelly failed in the representation of this comedy, he did not in the *success* of it. — He printed it by subscription, by which he got 800£ and thus obtained some proof that the sense of the public *out of doors* did not agree with that of his judges *within*.

Here so long a pause happened in Dr. Johnson's literary pursuits, that most people thought they were at an end. His age and growing infirmities encouraged this opinion, and he was at times heard to say, "he thought he had written enough." However, an accident took place, which made him alter this resolution, and gave a new accession of fame to his character as a writer.

About the year 1778, the Booksellers having agreed to publish a body of English Poetry, they applied to Doctor Johnson to write Prefaces to the works of each author. He accepted their proposals, and the agreement was struck for two hundred pounds.[41] The design at first was no more than that which we find in the French Miscellanies; containing a few dates, with a general character, and the engagement was made agreeable to this design: but the flowers of English poetry sprung up so agreeably under the cultivation of the Doctor's hand, that he voluntarily enlarged his plan, both in regard to the lives and critical remarks, "not without the honest desire (as he expresses himself in the advertisement to that work) of giving useful pleasure."[42]

When the life of Cowley, which was the first specimen, was finished, the great variety of matter and accurate criticisms, which he bestowed on that author, gave the booksellers the most certain prospect of success. The Doctor's powers had been thought to be rather on the decline, but by this and the subsequent lives, the public saw him flourish in a green old age, adding fresh vigour to his fancy, and additional experience to his judgment. His style too, which in *The Rambler* more particularly, was thought *turgid,* was admitted to be much improved, so that, when the booksellers published the whole of the lives in four volumes octavo (independent of the works of the British Poets) the sale became universally rapid, and the book is now become as great a favourite in the libraries of Europe, as any of the Doctor's most celebrated pieces.

That there is much learning and great reach of mind in this performance, I readily admit; but yet there are some few passages that I wish, for the Doctor's memory, he had left out. In the life of Waller particularly, he charges Hampden with being *"the zealot of rebellion,"*[43] forgetting that he himself becomes a *partizan* by this charge. In the life of Milton, he attributes to that great man the character of being "severe and arbitrary, that he thought *woman made only for obedience,* and *man only for rebellion."* And in another place, speaking of Milton's brother, Christopher, who was bred to the law, and made a judge by King James the Second, he remarks, "but his constitution being too weak for business, he retired *before any disreputable compliances became necessary"*:[44] by this remark, in some degree anticipating the line of conduct he *would* pursue under such circumstances.

In the life of Congreve, he commits himself to Criticism with a looseness unbecoming the general chastity of his pen:

of his plays (says he) *I cannot speak distinctly, for since I inspected them, many years have passed;* but what remains upon my memory is, that his characters are commonly fictitious and artificial, with very little of nature, and not much of life. His scenes exhibit not much of imagery or passion: his personages are a kind of intellectual gladiators; every sentence is to ward or strike; the contest of smartness is never intermitted; his wit is a meteor playing to and fro, with alternate corruscations. His comedies have therefore, in some degree, the operation of tragedies; they surprise rather than divert, and raise admiration oftener than merriment.[45]

Surely in giving so harsh and particular a criticism, on such an established author as Congreve, he ought not to have trusted to the *recollection of many years past,* particularly when the materials for more recent information were so near at hand. But these are little blemishes that perhaps are to be found in all works of any magnitude; fits of *petulance* and *indolence* will seize us at the desk, as in the more momentous affairs of life; it is by the general merit of the *writer,* as of the *man,* that his character ought to be ascertained.

The very great success of the Lives of the British Poets, induced the booksellers to make him a present of one hundred pounds more than they had agreed for, and on going to press with the third edition, they added another hundred pounds to the former.

And here it is to be observed, as a circumstance highly to the honour and integrity of Dr. Johnson's character, that when the assignment of those Lives was carried to him, he objected to the covenant, (undertaking to assign the eventual term of fourteen years, which would devolve to him if he lived to the end of the first period stated by act of parliament) saying, "it would be establishing a precedent which might be injurious to future authors": — he at the same time jocularly added, "why even then I shall be but *eighty-six.*"

I mention this fact merely to shew that he was influenced by the purest motives in this transaction, and which in the first edition of this work, from not being so minutely informed, I had, in some respect, mistated.[46]

The Doctor now determined to cease from his literary labours. He had reached his seventy-second year, and found the infirmities of old age growing fast upon him. He had likewise wisdom enough to see he had stopped at the proper time, in the full career of reputation; and that many authors passing beyond these limits, instead of reaching additional fame, had sometimes found disgrace.

He therefore composed himself for the quieter scenes of life, by making excursions to the country in summer, and enjoying the conversation of his friends in winter. Lichfield, the place of his nativity, was his general route. Here he found great pleasure in visiting those places which were the favourite haunts of his earlier days, and conversing with those friends whom the ravages of time had spared. At one period he obliged the master of the school where he had been educated, to restore to the boys an annual entertainment of *Furmenti*, [47] which had been the custom in his days, but had for some years been discontinued; and at another, he has been caught with his hat, coat, and wig off, leaping over an old rail in a field, because it was the favourite exercise of his boyish days.

His fortune enabled him to live in this manner, as the pension he enjoyed from the crown, with the addition of his former earnings, always governed by a proper œconomy, gave him the full extent of the *stium cum dignitate*.

But whilst life was thus evenly ebbing to its close, with only the interruption of some occasional sickness incident to old age, he was, during the night in the summer of 1783, attacked with a paralytic stroke, at his house in Bolt-court, Fleet-street, which deprived him of the powers of speech. He awoke with the attack; and as religion was ever uppermost in his hours of retirement, he attempted to repeat the Lord's prayer in English — but could not — he attempted it in Latin with the same effect — at last he succeeded in Greek. He immediately rung the bell, but on the approach of his servant, could not articulate a syllable. Feeling, however, that he retained the full use of his senses, he signified a desire for pen, ink, and paper, and wrote the following note to Mr. Allen, a printer, who lived next door to him; a very honest, virtuous, good man, who had been his intimate and confidential friend for many years, and at whose death (which happened suddenly last summer) the Doctor said, "he never knew a man fitter to stand in the presence of his God."

Dear Sir,

It hath pleased Almighty God this morning to deprive me of the powers of speech; and as I do not know but that it might be his further good pleasure to deprive me soon of my senses, I request you will, on the receipt of this note, come to me, and act for me, as the exigencies of my case may require.

I am sincerely your's,

S. Johnson.

To Mr. Edmund Allen.[48]

Mr. Allen immediately attended him, and sent for his usual physicians, Drs. Heberden and Brocklesby, who in the course of a few months recovered him so much, that he was able to take the air, and visit his friends as usual.

He continued every day growing better; and as he found his spirits much relieved by society, it was proposed by some friends, to establish a club in the neighbourhood, which would answer that purpose. The Doctor seemed highly pleased with the proposal, and after naming some friends, whom he wished to have about him, they met early last winter, at the Essex-head, in Essex-street, for the first time, when the Doctor being unanimously called to the chair, he surprized them with a set of rules, drawn by himself, as Ben Jonson did his *"Leges Convivales,"* which being read, and approved of by the rest of the members, were regularly entered in a book for that purpose.

These rules, to use his own words, are "founded in frequency and parsimony"; and as the public may have some curiosity in seeing so learned a man as Dr. Johnson in his hours of social relaxation, the following is an authentic copy of them, together with the names of the gentlemen who composed the club, as they stood, "on the rota of monthly attendance."

General Rules of the Essex-Head Club, commenced the 10th of December, 1783.

> "To day deep thoughts with me resolve to drench
> In mirth — which after no repenting draws."
>
>   MILTON.

I. THE Club shall consist of twenty-four members. The meetings shall be on the Monday, Wednesday, and Saturday, of every week; but on the *week before Easter-day* there shall be no meeting.

II. Every member is at liberty to introduce a friend once in a week, but not oftener.

III. Two members shall oblige themselves to attend in their turn every night from eight to ten o'clock, or procure two to attend in their room.

IV. Every member present at the Club shall spend at least *six-pence;* and every man who stays away, shall forfeit *three-pence.*

V. The master of the house shall keep an account of the absent members, and deliver to the president of the night a list of the forfeits incurred.

VI. When any member returns after absence, he shall immediately lay down his forfeits; which if he omits to do, the president shall require them of him.

VII. There shall be no general reckoning, but every member shall adjust his own expences.

VIII. The night of indispensible attendance will come to every member once a month. Whoever shall for three months together omit to attend himself, or by substitution — nor shall make any apology on the fourth month, shall be considered as having abdicated the Club.

IX. When a vacancy is to be filled, the name of the candidate, and of the member recommending him, shall stand in the Club-room three nights: on the fourth he may be chosen by ballot, six members at least being present, and two-thirds of the ballots being in his favour, or the majority, should the numbers not be divisible by three.

X. The master of the house shall give notice, six days before, to each of those members whose turn of necessary attendance is come.
The notice may be in these words: ["Sir, On ――― the ――― of ―――
will be your turn of presiding at the Essex-head; your company, is therefore, earnestly requested."]
One penny shall be left by each member for the waiter.

Nightly Rules of the Essex-head Club.

I. The president will collect *seven-pence* from each member at his entrance, marking his attendance thus V; and *three-pence* for every preceding night which is not marked against his name in the book thus V.

II. The forfeits to be paid over to the landlord. The seven-pence to be considered as part of each member's distinct reckoning.

III. Two letters of notice are to be forwarded each night, by the Penny-post, to the presidents of that day seven-night, as by list of the members.

IV. When the forfeits are paid, they should be noted in the book thus W.

List of the members of the Essex-head Club, when first instituted, as they stood on the rota of monthly attendance.

Dr. Johnson,
Dr. Horsley,
Dr. Brocklesby,
――― Jodrell, Esq;
William Cooke, Esq;
W. Ryland, Esq;
――― Paradise, Esq;
Dr. Burney,
John Hoole, Esq;

Francesco Sastres, Esq;
Mr. Edmund Allen, (dead)
Hon. Daines Barrington,
James Barry, Esq;
J. Wyatt, Esq;
Mr. John Nichols,
Edward Poore, Esq;
Rt. Hon. William Windham, M. P.
Thomas Tyers, Esq;
William Cruikshank, Esq;
W. Seward, Esq;
Richard Clarke, Esq; (now Lord Mayor of London.)
William Strahan, Esq; M. P.
Arthur Murphy, Esq;
Dr. W. Scott.

The Doctor, when his health permitted it, was a constant visitor, and seemed to reserve his spirits and conversation for those meetings, to the delight and improvement of his friends. In this career of innocent relaxation, the constant bleeding, which he was obliged to undergo for the necessary reduction of an asthma; (with which he was afflicted many years) brought on a dropsy, which again confined him to his house for some months in the spring of 1784.

In the summer of the same year he grew so much better, that supposing the air of Italy might be the best means of re-establishing his health, he hinted in conversation his desire to undertake that journey. His old and intimate friend Sir Joshua Reynolds, eager to extend a life so dear to himself, and so valuable to the public, and yet thinking the Doctor's finances not equal to the project, mentioned the circumstance to the Lord Chancellor, adding, "that if his pension could be encreased two hundred a-year more, it would be fully sufficient for the purpose." His Lordship met the proposal cordially, and took the first opportunity to speak of it to the K——g.

His M——y had been previously advertised of the Doctor's intention, and seemed to think favourably of it; but whether he did not conceive the Lord Chancellor's application to be direct, or that he understood Dr. Johnson's physicians had no opinion of this journey, when it was mentioned to him he waved the conversation.

The Chancellor, on this, wrote to Dr. Johnson, informing him, that as the return of his health might not wait the forms of the addition to his pension, he might draw immediately upon him for 500£ which lay at his banker's for that purpose.

So liberal and unexpected an offer from a quarter where he had no right to expect it, called forth the Doctor's gratitude, and he immediately wrote the Lord Chancellor the following letter:

My Lord,

After a long and not inattentive observation on mankind, the generosity of your lordship's offer raises in me no less wonder than gratitude. Bounty so liberally bestowed I should gladly receive if my condition made it necessary; for to such a mind who would not be proud to own his obligation? But it hath pleased God to restore me to such a measure of health, that if I should now appropriate so much of a fortune destined to do good, I could not escape from myself the charge of advancing a false claim. My journey to the continent, though I once thought it necessary, was never much encouraged by my physicians, and I was very desirous that your Lordship should be told of it by Sir Joshua Reynolds as an event very uncertain; for if I should grow much better I should not be willing, and if much worse, I should not be able to migrate.

Your Lordship was first solicited without my knowledge; but when I was told that you was pleased to honour me with your patronage, I did not expect to hear of a refusal; yet as I have had no long time to brood hope, and have not rioted in imaginary opulence, this cold reception has been scarce a disappointment; and from your Lordship's kindness I have received a benefit which men like you are able to bestow. I shall now live *mihi carior,* with a higher opinion of my own merit.

I am, my Lord,
Your Lordship's most obliged,
Most grateful,
And most humble servant,

S. Johnson.

To the Right Honourable
the Lord Chancellor.
Sept. 1784.[49]

The Doctor was at Lichfield when he wrote this letter, on his return from Derbyshire, in tolerable good health. However, on his arrival in town in October [November], Providence thought fit to make all pecuniary as well as medical application unnecessary. The dropsy returned in his legs, which swelled to such a thickness that his physicians had no hopes of his recovery. They however continued to visit him, and prescribe such medicines as were best calculated to compose and quiet his pains. He was likewise occasionally visited by several of his friends, and, at intervals, possessed his usual spirits and flow of conversation.

His constant friend, as well as physician, Dr. Brocklesby, calling upon him one morning, after a night of much pain and restlessness, he suddenly repeated those lines from Macbeth:

> Oh! Doctor,
> Canst thou not minister to a mind diseas'd,
> Pluck from the memory a rooted sorrow,
> Raze out the written troubles of the brain,
> And with some sweet oblivious antidote
> Cleanse the full bosom of that perilous stuff
> Which weighs upon the heart?

And when the Doctor replied in the following words of the same author: "Therein the patient / Must minister unto himself," he exclaimed, "well applied, — that's true, — that's more than poetically true." [50]

On the Thursday before his death, finding himself grow worse, he insisted on knowing from Dr. B[rocklesby], whether there were any hopes of his recovery? The Doctor at first waved the question; but he repeating it with great eagerness, the other told him, "that from the complication of disorders he laboured under, and the advanced state of life he was in, there were but little hopes"; he received his fate with firmness; thanked him, and said he would endeavour to compose himself for the approaching scene.

The next day, a friend of his, hearing this alarming sentence, and anxious to have every possible means tried for his recovery, brought Dr. Warren to him; but he would take no prescription; he said, "he felt it too late, the soul then wanted medicine and not the body." [51] Upon the Doctor's taking his leave, he told him "he must not go till he had given him his fee, and then presenting him with a copy of his *Lives of the Poets,* begged his acceptance of it, assuring him "that was all the fee he had ever given his other two physicians."

For some weeks before he died, he received the sacrament two, or three times in each week; on the mornings of those days he begged that no body might disturb him, not even his physicians, but in cases of absolute necessity. He spent a great part of the preceding nights in prayer, and in the act of communion he shewed a piety and fervency of devotion that communicated itself to all around him. An intimate friend of his coming into the room one day after this ceremony, the Doctor exclaimed (his face at the same time brightening with a ray of cheerful piety), "Oh! my friend, I owe you many obligations through life; but they will all be more than amply repaid by your taking this most important advice, BE A GOOD CHRISTIAN." [52]

The Saturday night preceding his death, he was obliged to be turned in the bed by two strong men employed for that purpose; and though he was very restless, yet when a friend asked him in the morning, whether the man he had recommended to sit up with him was wakeful and alert, the Doctor, recovering his pleasantry a little, replied, "Not at all, sir, his *vigilance* was that of a dormouse, and his activity that of a turnspit on his first entrance into a wheel." [53]

The next night he was at intervals delirious; and in one of those fits, seeing a friend at the bedside, he exclaimed, "What, will that fellow never have done talking poetry to me?" He recovered his senses before morning, but spoke little after this. His heart, however, was not unemployed, as by his fixed attention, and the motion of his lips, it was evident he was pouring out his soul in prayer. He languished in this manner till 7 o'clock on Monday evening, the 13th December, 1784, and then expired without a groan, in the 75th year of his age.

His body was opened on Wednesday the 15th December, in the presence of Drs. Heberden and Brocklesby, where the causes which produced his last disorder were discoverable, but found impracticable to have been removed by medicine. His heart was *uncommonly large,* as if analogous to the extent and *liberality of his mind:* and what was very extraordinary, one of his kidneys was entirely consumed, though he never once complained of any *nephritic,* or gravelly disorder. It is, however, to be conjectured, that he had some *presentiment* of this circumstance, as a few months before his death he had an argument with his physicians, on the possibility of a man's living after the loss of one of his kidneys.

Some time previous to his death he made a will, subscribed only by two witnesses; [54] but telling the circumstances to some friend, who knew he had a freehold of about twelve pounds a-year in Lichfield, in right of his father, another was drawn; but so tardy are some of the wisest men, even in the most necessary acts, when they awaken the fears of death — it was only a few weeks before he died, that the blanks were filled up. On the same principle of delay, the revision of many manuscripts was postponed, some of which were burned by the Doctor the week before he died, to avoid being left in an imperfect state. Amongst the rest was one book, out of two, wherein he had noted some hints for writing his life, which he committed to the flames by mistake. [55]

Though I have subjoined an authentic copy of the doctor's will to these memoirs, there are two clauses which, in justice to him, ought particularly to be explained, and commented on. — By the first, he has left an annuity of 70£ to his old faithful black servant Francis Barber, who lived with him for near forty years, [56] and who, by a faithful, and diligent discharge of his duty, has deserved this mark of his master's generosity and friendship. When he had determined on this legacy for him, he asked Dr. Brocklesby, who happened to be sitting with him, how much people in general left to their favourite servants? The other answered him, from twenty to fifty pounds a-year, but that no nobleman gave more than the last sum: "Why then," says the Doctor, "I'll be *Nobilissimus,* for I have left Frank *seventy pounds* a-year; and as it probably will make the poor fellow's mind easy, to know that he will be provided for after my death, I'll be obliged to you to tell him of it."

If we compare this generous action with that of his brother poet *Pope,* how superior Dr. Johnson rises in generous feelings and grateful remembrance of faithful services! When the bard of Twickenham died, he left but *one hundred pounds* to his favourite servant John Searle, and *one more* on the death of Mrs. Martha Blount, which was eventual; and yet he distinguishes this man, in his epistle to Dr. Arbuthnot, under the character of *good John:* "Shut, shut the door, good John, fatigued I said,/ Tie up the knocker, say, I'm sick, I'm dead." And Dr. Warburton, who had an opportunity of knowing the fact, calls him, in a note upon this passage, "his old and faithful servant." But compliments pass from the head, generous actions arise from the heart.

The other clause does his memory equal honour. When Dr. Johnson's father died, which is now above thirty years ago, he owed Mr. Innys, a bookseller, who lived in Paternoster Row, thirty pounds; after many enquiries the Doctor found out the descendant of this man, and has left him the sum of *two hundred pounds,* as a compensation for the loss of the principal, and interest for so many years.

By a computation of the Doctor's fortune, the whole is estimated at about *two thousand pounds,* which, with the pension of three hundred pounds a year, he enjoyed during his life, it seems somewhat singular that he should desire, or at least *connive* at the proposed encrease of that pension to enable him to travel. Two hundred pounds a-year was all the sum required, and as this at farthest, could not be wanted above two years, his fortune, coupled with the situation and time of life he stood at, could very well afford such a deduction, without breaking that line of independence which ought inseparably to belong to such a character.

From a sudden combination of those circumstances, therefore, it might be imagined, that the Doctor, with all his philosophy, had caught that almost inseparable vice of old age, *avarice;* but when it is considered, that a principal part of his fortune lay in the public funds, which he could not dispose of without a very material loss — and the rest was in private securities, which might require time to call in, — I trust these facts will clear him from that imputation. Indeed, what puts his immediate want of money beyond all manner of doubt, is, that his pension was under a mortgage to a particular acquaintance, and only cleared off a few days before his death.[57]

So anxious was this good man to discharge every part of his moral character with punctuality, that some time before his death he sat down to recollect what little sums he might owe in the early part of his life to particular friends, which were never given with a view to be restored. Among this number he sent a guinea to the son of an eminent printer, which he had borrowed of his father many years before, to pay his reckoning at a tavern.[58]

He likewise recollected borrowing thirty pounds of Sir Joshua Reynolds at a great distance of time; "but this sum (said the Doctor to Sir Joshua, with a manliness of mind which answered for the feelings of his friend being similar to his own) I intend to bestow on a charity which I know you'll approve of." His attention to his duty exerted itself in several little particulars, which might have escaped the generality even of good men, but which at once shewed the calmness of his mind, and the delicacy of his friendships. — Amongst these may be reckoned his sealing up several bags of letters in order to be returned to the writers of them, lest the confidence they reposed in him should suffer by any want of attention on his part.[59] In short, every action of his life reflected the character of the man, who uniformly illustrated the morals of his pen by the force of his own virtuous example.

Dr. Johnson's figure, even in his youth, could never have been calculated either "to make women false," or give him a preference in the schools of manly, or military exercises. His face was formed of large coarse features, which, from a studious turn, when composed, looked sluggish, yet awful and contemplative. He had likewise nearly lost the sight of one of his eyes, which made him *course* every object he looked at in so singular a manner, as often to create pity, sometimes laughter. The head at the front of this book is esteemed a good likeness; indeed so much so, that when the doctor saw the drawing, he exclaimed, "Well, thou art an ugly fellow, but still, I believe thou art like the original." [60]

His face, however, was capable of great expression, both in respect to *intelligence* and *mildness,* as all those can witness who have seen him in the glow of conversation, or under the influence of grateful feelings. I am the more confirmed in this opinion, by the authority of a celebrated French Physiognomist, who has, in a late publication on his art, given two different etchings of Dr. Johnson's head, to shew the correspondence between the countenance and the mind.[61]

In respect to person, he was rather of the *heroic* stature, being above the middle size; but, though strong, broad, and muscular, his parts were slovenly put together. When he walked the streets, what with the constant roll of his head, and the concomitant motion of his body, he appeared to make his way by that motion, independent of his feet. At other times, he was subject to be seized with sudden convulsions, which so agitated his whole frame, that, to those who did not know his disorder, it had the appearance of madness — Indeed, to see him in most situations, he was not favourably distinguished, either by nature, or his habits.

But the *severer* studies, though they may bring with them great learning and great knowledge, are seldom found in the company of the graces. "A man of letters, for the most part, spends in the privacies of study, that season of life in which the manners are to be softened into ease, and polished into elegance; and, when he has gained knowledge enough to be respected, has neglected the minuter arts, by which he might have pleased." [62]

Of his familiar habits, the principal and most distinguished was that of his being a severe and unremitting student. In his boyish days, he distinguished himself in this line; and when we consider, that some time after this he had been a *teacher,* for many years was employed as a *translator,* and through life an *author,* there was but little time left for other pursuits.

His domestic arrangements were always frugal, and he never aspired, even when his fame and reputation were at the highest, to exhibit, either in his dress or establishment, what the world calls a genteel appearance. A little before the death of his wife, he received into his house Mrs. Anna Williams, daughter of Dr. Zachariah Williams, who, though blind, possessed such a share of intellectual accomplishments and cheerfulness of disposition as rendered her a very amiable companion to her benefactor, who allowed her twenty pounds a-year to her death (which happened about a year ago), and otherwise behaved to her with an attention and respect every way becoming his character.[63]

The company of this very valuable woman was a great resource to him when at home, but as 'tis observed by one of Dr. Johnson's friends "that his houshold gods were neither numerous or splendid enough for the reception of his great acquaintance," [64] he constantly visited them, both in town and country, and none so much as the late Mr. and Mrs. Thrale. In the family of this gentleman he lived a considerable part of the year, and they so perfectly understood his habits, and had such a proper relish for his conversation, that he seemed more *at home* there than any where else. — He had a *suite* of apartments for himself, both at their town and country house — formed a library principally of his own selection — directed the education of the young ladies, and was, in every respect, so much "the guide, philosopher and friend" of the family, that Mr. Thrale, on his death, left him two hundred pounds, and appointed him one of his executors.

But soon after this event, by one of those trials which neither female pride, or female philosophy can withstand, this friendship was dissolved by the marriage of Mrs. Thrale. The mere report of this had such an effect on him, that for three nights he could not close his eyes. He then wrote her a long letter of five quarto pages, dissuading her from so rash and disgraceful an union.[65] To this he had no answer but a confirmation of the report, on which he exclaimed, in great bitterness of heart, *"Varium et mutabile semper fœmina."*

From the largeness of his person, the demands of nature were expected to be considerable, and Nature was true to herself. He fed without much delicacy, either in choice or quantity — but then his dinner was his last meal for the day. He formerly drank his bottle, it is said with a view to dispel that apprehension, which he dreaded through life, of approaching insanity. But afterwards suspecting danger from that habit, he almost totally abandoned it; "for," said he, in that moral and philosophic strain which generally distinguished his remarks; "What ferments the spirits, may also derange the intellects, and the means employed to counteract dejection may hasten the approach of madness. Even fixed, substantial melancholy is preferable to a state in which we can neither amend the future, nor solicit mercy for the past." In weaker liquors, however, he was more profuse, particularly in tea, which he drank at all hours, and on most occasions; and so particularly fond was he of this liquor, that he has often been known to drink twelve or fourteen cups of it between two and three o'clock in the morning, and then go to rest, without feeling the least inconvenience. To the excess of tea drinking, and the too frequent use of acids, which he freely indulged himself with upon all occasions, have been attributed that relaxed state which he was in for many years before his death. He was often told of those consequences — but in matter of personal habits, the Doctor would be his own physician.

He always sought the company of women, and was so much delighted with them, that every appearance of philosophic ruggedness was instantly exchanged for gentleness, and the pleasantries of conversation. He often acknowledged this, and at the same time would say, "There are few things we so universally give up, even in an advanced age, as the supposition, that we have still the power of ingratiating ourselves with the fair sex."

As he says of Milton, "fortune appears not to have had much of his care." [66] In his outset, and for many years afterwards indeed, he had no opportunities; but for many years past, if fortune had been his object, such extraordinary and useful talents were well entitled to it. The wits of Queen Anne's time were most of them liberally rewarded by places, some of them to a very considerable amount. The *chaste* Congreve, for instance, enjoyed above twelve hundred pounds per year, which even ministerial changes did not deprive him of; whilst Johnson, as proud a name as any of them in *literature* — a greater than most of them in *morals,* touched the meridian of his fame, and passed that of his life, without the least favour from government; and when ministers did think fit to pension him, it was perhaps more to answer the purpose of a temporary policy, than to reward the useful labours of philosophy.

In his traffic with booksellers, he shewed no great regard to money matters. By his dictionary he no more than merely supported himself, during the many years he was employed in that great undertaking. By his Ramblers, I have before observed, he did not get much above two guineas per week; and though it is reasonable to suppose he might, on a representation of the encreasing fame of those valuable papers, have got his stipend increased — he did not solicit it — "his wants being few, they were competently supplied." [67]

If it should be asked then, how he came to die worth two thousand pounds? it is not to be imputed to the profits of authorship. He had for above twenty years enjoyed a pension of three hundred pounds per year: he had, besides, some legacies; and as his wants were always very few, and those wants made less by his frequent domestication with his late friend, Mr. Thrale, and others, his savings contributed much to this sum. Old age too had been approaching for some time; and it would ill become a man of Dr. Johnson's prudence, to neglect providing for what may continue long, must be a period of inaction, and what always requires additional comforts and conveniencies.

And here it is curious to pause on the fate of different authors. Dr. Johnson, who passed a long life in the service of literature; whose writings have done so much honour to his country, and to the general cause of truth, perhaps never earned, *communibus annis,* more than two hundred pounds a year; whilst many a Journalist, and Dramatic Writer, who *never said a thing that a wise man should wish to remember,* have obtained four times that sum, by pandering to the *vices* and *follies of the day.*

In literature, perhaps, Dr. Johnson may be considered as the first man in his time — he read most of the languages which are considered either as learned, or polite — Hebrew, Greek, Latin, French, and Italian — he was in particular so perfect a master of the Greek and Latin, that he could repeat, or turn to almost any passage in any author of reputation that could be mentioned. He was not even content with the common stock of antient learning, but extended it to the authors of the middle centuries, most of whom he could not only name, but point out the scope and design of their writings.

As a Philologist, he stood *unique,* which his *Dictionary of the English Language,* and the *Lives of the British Poets,* bear honourable testimony. His criticisms, in this last production, come forward with all the depth of erudition, aided by a most powerful and discriminating genius; and though he is the first that undertook this work *generally,* he has left nothing for his successors to do.

In history he possessed an intimate knowledge of the ancient and modern parts, as well as in the annals and chronologies of most countries. In this useful study he did not merely content himself with exploring the ravages of tyrants, the desolation of kingdoms, the routs of armies, and the fall of empires, but with the different passions, tempers and designs of men — the growth and infancy of political and theological opinions, the gradual increase and declension of human knowledge.

In theology he was not less skilled, being acquainted with the writings of the primitive fathers, our soundest divines, and most of the controversial writers of past and present times. He was bred in the ecclesiastical discipline and politics, which distinguished the royalists in the last century, and he never abandoned them.

His knowledge in manufactures was extensive, and his comprehension relative to mechanical contrivances so extraordinary, that he has often, on a first view, understood both the principles and powers of the most complicated machine.

The few specimens which Dr. Johnson has given us of his poetry, are sufficient in quality, though not perhaps in *quantity,* to give him a distinguished situation amongst the sons of Parnassus: indeed they are all so highly finished in their kind, as must make every man, who has read them, wish he had written more. This question has been often put to him, and the answer he gave was, "that his *prose* cost him nothing but his present thinking — whilst his *poetry* not only demanded his thoughts in the moment of composition, but unavoidably crossed him in the hours of amusement and conversation." — "The one I can detach from my mind at will, but the other haunts me like a spirit, 'till I have laid it."

Amongst the poets of his own country, next to Shakespeare, he admired Milton; and though in some parts of the life of this great man, he has been rather severe on his political character, there are others wherein he bestows the highest praises on his learning and genius. To this I am happy to add another eulogium, which I heard from him in conversation a few months before his death: — "Milton (said he) had that which rarely fell to the lot of any man — an unbounded imagination, with a store of knowledge equal to all its calls." [68]

But great and extensive as the learning of Dr. Johnson was, (so limited is the power of human understanding) it was far from being universal. It is said he had but an imperfect knowledge of *mathematics* and *natural philosophy,* and was almost totally deficient in the polite arts. He had likewise little of the *practical* knowledge of mankind; for though few men could speak with more *acumen* on the follies and designs of the human heart, his own was too unsuspicious of the world, to resist, at all times, the infinite variety of its impositions: — he was besides tinctured with *superstition,* as particularly appeared from his credulity in the celebrated affair of the *Cock-lane Ghost,* in 1762, and his *acquiescence* at least, if not belief, in the general *doctrine of spirits.* [69]

In his conversation, he was learned, various, and instructive, oftener in the didactic than in the colloquial line, which might have arisen from the encouragement of his friends, who generally flattered him with the most profound attention — and surely it was well bestowed; for in those moments, the great variety of his reading broke in upon his mind, like mountain floods, which he poured out upon his audience in all the fullness of information — not but he observed Swift's rule, "of giving every man time to take his share in the conversation"; and when the company thought proper to engage him in the general discussion of little matters, no man threw back the ball with greater ease and pleasantry; his *bon mots* abounded upon those occasions, some specimens of which I have preserved, as no improper appendage to these memoirs. [The *bon mots* have been omitted.]

He always expressed himself with clearness and precision, and seldom made use of an unnecessary word — each had its due weight, and stood in its proper place. He was sometimes a little too tenacious of his own opinion, particularly when it was in danger of being wrested from him by any of the company. Here he used to collect himself with all his strength — and here he shewed such skill and dexterity in defence, that he either tired out his adversary, or turned the laugh against him, by the power of his wit and irony. — But whatever turn the conversation took, he always guarded against the most distant idea of *immorality* or *indecency;* and if either was started in his presence, he was the first to hunt it down by the sharpness of his reproof. He has often declared he had no fixed aversion to any one but men of those principles — and such he considered as his personal enemies.

In this place, it would be omitting a very singular quality of his, not to speak of the amazing powers of his *memory.* The great stores of learning which he laid in, in his youth, were not of that cumbrous and inactive quality, which we meet with in many who are called *great scholars;* for he could, at all times, draw bills upon this capital with the greatest security of being paid. When quotations were made against him in conversation, he either, by applying to the context, gave a different turn to the passage, or quoted from other parts of the same author, that which was more favourable to his own opinion: — If these failed him, he would instantly call up a whole phalanx of other authorities, by which he bore down his antagonist with all the superiority of *allied force.*

But it is not the readiness with which he applied to different authors, proves so much the greatness of his memory, as the *extent* to which he could carry his recollection upon occasions. I remember one day, in a conversation upon the miseries of old age, a gentleman in company observed, he always thought Juvenal's description of them to be rather too highly coloured — upon which the Doctor replied — "No, Sir — I believe not; they may not all belong to an individual, but they are collectively true of old age." Then rolling about his head, as if snuffing up his recollection, he suddenly broke out: — "Ille humero, hic lumbis . . . ." [Omitted.] [70]

But here it will be recollected, perhaps, that Dr. Johnson, in the early part of his life imitated this satire from Juvenal, under the title of, "The Vanity of Human Wishes"; and that this circumstance might impress it more strongly on his memory. Those, however, who are anywise acquainted with the business of an author, will know how little of any particular production is left upon the memory after any distance of time. Intent upon *parts,* he perhaps never reads the *whole,* and if he does, it is not with a view to recollect it, but rather to see that it is clear from *false thoughts* and *grammatical errors.* The more of *genius* too that he possesses, the less fond will he be of his own works; the pleasure of such is generally spent at the end of the performance; then feeling the strength of his own powers unabated, he looks abroad for other subjects, which, if they do not produce him more fame, will at least yield him more novelty.

But not to press any further argument upon this subject, I can produce a much more surprising instance of Dr. Johnson's memory in the following anecdote, which I give on the authority of a gentleman of known honour and veracity, a particular *friend* of the Doctor's, and one who is entitled to that name by his knowledge, his candour, and many agreeable qualities.

Some time previous to Dr. Hawkesworth's publication of his beautiful little *Ode On Life,* (since published in Pearch's Collection of poems, in four volumes), he carried it down with him to a friend's house in the country to retouch. Dr. Johnson was of this party; and as Hawkesworth and the Doctor lived upon the most intimate terms, the former read it to him for his opinion, "Why, Sir," says Johnson, "I can't well determine on a first hearing, read it again, second thoughts are best"; Dr. Hawkesworth complied, after which Dr. Johnson read it himself, approved of it very highly, and returned it.

Next morning at breakfast, the subject of the poem being renewed, Dr. Johnson, after again expressing his approbation of it, said he had but one objection to make to it, which was, that he doubted its *originality*. Hawkesworth, alarmed at this, challenged him to the proof; when the Doctor repeated *the whole of the poem,* with only the omission of a very few lines; "What do you think now, Hawkey," says the Doctor? "Only this," replied the other, "that I shall never repeat any thing I write before you again, for you have a memory that would convict any author of plagiarism in any court of literature in the world." [71]

I have now the poem before me, and I find it contains no less than *sixty-eight* lines.

Next to the extent of his memory, might be classed the very great rapidity of his mind in composition; for though in the compilation of his dictionary he has shewn the most patient labour and attention, he has on other occasions proved, that few, if any, could exceed him, *currente calamo.* Of this he has given many examples.

Whilst he was concerned in the Gentleman's Magazine he has declared it was no uncommon effort for him, to write *Three Columns* in an hour, which was faster than most persons could transcribe that quantity, and more by *one third* than the quickest parliamentary reporter can at present perform, with the matter already prepared to his hand. To approve himself in the judgment of Cave, he undertook the *Life of Savage,* and finished it in *six and thirty hours.* In one night, after spending the evening with some friends in Holborn, he composed his *Hermit of Teneriffe*. And in another wrote the *Preface to the Preceptor*.

The first seventy lines of "*The Vanity of Human Wishes*," he composed in one morning, in that small house beyond the church at Hampstead, and afterwards finished it before he threw a single couplet on paper. The same method he pursued respecting the *Prologue on the opening of Drury Lane Theatre*, changing only one word at the remonstrance of Garrick. — "And then," said the Doctor, "I did not think his criticism just, but it was necessary he should be satisfied with what he was to utter." —

Hitherto Dr. Johnson has been principally spoken of for those qualifications that distinguished him as a scholar, and a man of genius; the noblest parts of his character yet remain untouched, those of an *honest man* and *good Christian*. Pope laments that Roscommon was the only poet in Charles's days, who preserved his pen from the contagious example of the times. "Unhappy Dryden! in all Charles's days / Roscommon *only* boasts unspotted bays." But our virtuous author not only restrained his pen from pandering to the follies and vices of the times, but wholly and unremittingly wielded it in the cause of truth and virtue. He considered it as the indispensible duty of an author to endeavour to make the world better, nor would he admit the manners, or even the ignorance of the age he lived in, as any extenuation of this neglect; "for," said he, "justice is a virtue independent on time and place." [72]

His opinion of vicious authors he farther expresses with a noble indignation, which always forms that strong antipathy of good to bad.

The wickedness of a loose or profane author, in his writings, is more atrocious than that of the giddy libertine, or drunken ravisher, not only because it extends its effects wider (as a pestilence that taints the air is more destructive than poison infused in a draught), but because it is committed with cool deliberation. By the instantaneous violence of desire, a good man may sometimes be surprised before reflection can come to his rescue: when the appetites have strengthened their influence by habit, they are not easily resisted, or suppressed. But for the frigid villainy of studious lewdness, for the calm malignity of laboured impiety, what apology can be invented? What punishment can be adequate to the crime of him who retires to solitude for the refinement of debauchery, who tortures his fancy, and ransacks his memory, only that he may leave the world less virtuous than he found it? that he may intercept the hopes of the rising generation, and spread snares for the soul with more dexterity. [73]

His life reflected the purity and integrity of his writings. His friendships, as they were generally formed on the broad basis of virtue, were constant, active, and unshaken. And what rendered them still more valuable, he knew and practised that sort which was most applicable to the wants of his friends. To those in need he liberally opened his purse — To others he gave up his *time,* his *interest,* and his *advice;* and having an honest confidence that this *last* was of some weight in the world, he scarcely missed an opportunity of enforcing it; particularly to young men, whom he hoped would remember what fell from such high authority; even to children he could be playfully instructive — Thus taking every opportunity to make the age he lived in better and wiser.

Of his charities, they were unbounded; not only in relieving temporary objects, but in the regular establishment of many reduced people, that must have perished but for his support. Of the many instances that could be given of this, and which are in the recollection of most of his friends and acquaintances, I shall select but the two following:

Francis Barber, his black servant, was but ten years old when he took him under his care, and at a time when the Doctor was but ill qualified, in point of circumstances, to maintain him. The first thing he did was to have him made a *Christian.* — He afterwards sent him down to a school in Yorkshire for his education; and after some time spent there, brought him up to town and instructed him himself. He had the noblest motive for this extraordinary care in his education, intending to make him a *missionary* in order to instruct his countrymen in the principles of the Christian religion. His parts, however, after repeated and extraordinary trials, not admitting this cultivation, he took him into his service, where he experienced in the Doctor, rather the friend than the master. During his stay here, Barber married, and the Doctor, in consideration of his long and tried fidelity, not only gave him and his wife the constant privilege of living in his house, but left him a very comfortable provision for life.

The above is a fact well known; the other is an instance which I believe to be equally true, as I had it from very respectable authority.

Some years since, the Doctor coming up Fleet-street, at about two o'clock in the morning, he was alarmed with the cries of a person seemingly in great distress. He followed the voice for some time, when by the glimmer of an expiring lamp, he perceived an unhappy female, almost naked, and perishing on a truss of straw, who had just strength enough to tell him, "she was turned out by an inhuman landlord in that condition, and to beg his charitable assistance not to let her die in the street." The Doctor, melted at her story, desired her to place her confidence in God, for that under him he would be her protector. He accordingly looked about for a coach to put her into; but there was none to be had: "his charity, however, worked too strong," to be cooled by such an accident. He kneeled down by her side, raised her in his arms, wrapped his great coat about her, placed her on his back, and in this condition carried her home to his house.

Next day her disorder appearing to be *venereal,* he was advised to abandon her; but he replied, "that may be as much her misfortune as her fault; I am determined to give her the chance of a reformation"; he accordingly kept her in his house above thirteen weeks, where she was regularly attended by a physician, who restored her to her usual health.

The Doctor, during this time, learned more of her story; and finding her to be one of those unhappy women who are impelled to this miserable life more from necessity than inclination, he set on foot a subscription, and established her in a milliner's shop in the country, where she was living some years ago in very considerable repute.

That many men meeting with the same accident, would have relieved such an object, as far as *pecuniary assistance* was necessary, I readily believe — but to forego all forms, and risque the imputation of being her seducer, or at least the partner of her guilt, required such a mind — and such a heart as Johnson's; who feeling the irresistible force of his duty, performed it independent of every other consideration.

From these anecdotes, it might seem unnecessary to speak of his RELIGION, seeing that he so well performed all the great duties it inculcates. But in an age, when great learning has but too often the vanity to oppose itself against the mysteries of revelation, it must be the happiness of Dr. Johnson's friends, to promulgate to the world, that he was, in every sense of the words, "A TRUE AND SINCERE BELIEVER OF THE CHRISTIAN RELIGION." Nor did he content himself with a silent belief of those great mysteries, by which our salvation is principally effected, but by a pious and punctual discharge of all its duties and ceremonies.[74] When his health permitted it, he regularly attended divine service, and was as regular a communicant. In his illness, he either read prayers constantly himself, or enjoined some friend to do it for him; and in those moments, his fervour and devotion were exemplary.

His last advice to his friends was upon this subject, and, like a second Socrates, though *under the sentence of death,* from his infirmities, their eternal welfare was his principal theme. — To some he enjoined it with tears in his eyes, reminding them, "it was the dying request of a friend, who had no other way of paying the large obligations he owed them — but by this advice."

Others he pressed with arguments, setting before them, from the example of all religions, that sacrifices for sins were practised in all ages, and hence enforcing the belief of the Son of God sacrificing himself *to be a propitiation not only for our sins, but also for the sins of the whole world.*

To those whom he suspected to be lukewarm in their creed, he wrote down a short account of what he thought a good Christian should profess, and requested them, as they valued his memory, and their own eternal welfare, that they would read it often, and seriously ponder on the great and important truths it referred to.[75]

Such was the life of SAMUEL JOHNSON! who, whether we consider him as a *scholar,* a man of *genius,* or a *Christian,* filled each character with a degree of eminence and utility, that must render his name an ornament to this country, whilst there is a taste remaining for letters, or morality.

Dr. Johnson was buried in a public manner, in Westminster Abbey, on Monday, December 20, 1784, at the foot of Shakespeare's monument, in Poet's Corner, near the grave of his old and intimate friend, David Garrick. His pall was supported by the Right Honourable Edmund Burke, Right Honourable William Windham, Sir Joseph Banks, Sir Charles Bunbury, George Colman, and Bennet Langton, Esqrs. His executors likewise attended, as did a considerable number of his friends and acquaintances, who sincerely paid this last tribute of affection to his memory. His monument is to be placed in a niche, between that of Handel, and John Duke of Argyle.[76]

$\boxed{II}$

(1785)

Memoirs of the Life
and Writings of the Late
Dr. Samuel Johnson

William Shaw

Preface

Besides the facts already before the public, the Editor of these *Memoirs* has been favoured with the contributions of those who were long the friends of Doctor Samuel Johnson.

His servants, Mrs. Desmoulins,[1] who knew him from her infancy, and several others of his most intimate acquaintance, whose names the Editor is not allowed to mention, told him all they knew.

The late Mr. Thomas Davies, of Covent-Garden, who lived long in habits of friendship with the Doctor, not only assisted the Editor in detecting several errors, in other accounts of his life, but authenticated to him many facts, which seemed otherwise doubtful. This Gentleman had collected many anecdotes of his friend, but would not mention them, he said, to any person whatever, as he might probably have occasion to use them himself.

But the principal, and most valuable communications in this work, are from Mr. Elphinston,[2] who, with singular readiness and affability, gave the Editor every sort of information which he could desire; and the reader may easily conceive how much might be gleaned by a person of his intelligence and discernment, during a correspondence of the greatest intimacy for above the space of thirty years. The letters and anecdotes, here published, will shew how much, how sincerely, and for what a length of time, these congenial characters regarded each other.

The facts relating to the Ossian controversy are anonymous, unless the authenticity of any of them should be challenged; in that case the author will avow them, as the means of defence are fully in his power.

Memoirs of Dr. Samuel Johnson

The late Dr. Samuel Johnson, whose story I am now to relate, like every one who arrives at extreme age, survived all his earlier and most of his later acquaintance.

This man was grown grey in literature. He lived in the capacity of an author on the town for a period of near fifty years. The vicissitudes and fortunes of such a situation, protracted to such a length of time, it were impossible even for those who knew him best, to trace with accuracy or state with precision.

The anecdotes of his juvenile days have perished with the companions of his youth.[3] Few interest themselves in the history of a man without property, fame or consequence. Johnson was for many years lost in a multitude of authors, who are occupied only in collecting the occurrences of the day, polishing into form the fugitive ideas of booksellers, or in some of the numerous periodical works which engross so much of the trade, furnishing subjects of fresh speculation for the public mind. And it was not till he derived peculiar lustre from a long series of success in his literary pursuits, that he became an object of general attention and enquiry.

It is now thirty years since he lamented on publishing his Dictionary, that *most of those whom he wished to please were sunk into the grave.*[4] Nor is it when thus loaded with the frailties of age, and tottering under the accumulated decays of nature, that any man is much inclined to multiply connections or commence friendships. So great and universal however was the estimation which his virtuous principles and eminent talents at last procured, that of late it has been deemed a sort of literary discredit not to rank in the number of his acquaintance, his admirers, or his imitators.

Men distinguished by industry or genius as Johnson was, in morals, arts, sciences, or letters, serve the purposes of public utility in a double capacity. Their example stimulates those around them to exertion and perseverance in virtue or excellence. Posterity contemplates also with a mixture of reverence and emulation, the copy of an original which their ancestors were thus contented to follow and applaud.

By exhausting a long laborious life in contributing to the improvement and delight of his countrymen, Johnson finally merited and obtained their general and unfeigned approbation. His enlightened mind, which aimed only at the happiness and perfection of the species, was constantly emitting such effusions of virtuous intelligence as tended equally to clear the head and better the heart; and when his death, which had been some time expected, was announced, most of his contemporaries regarded the melancholy event with a consternation or sensibility similar to that of a family who has lost its head, or an army whose general falls.

This accounts for that extreme avidity with which every vestige of his genius, his taste, or his humour, is still received by a grateful public. And it will be long before any work, in which he had the least concern, can be indifferent to them. His transcendent abilities, and tried virtues, his oddities, which were alike original and abundant; the variety of his friends, and the length of his life, give so many shapes to his story, and such different complexions to the prompt and occasional ebullitions of his wit in different situations, that whoever had the honour of his acquaintance must be in possession of materials which, for the sake of literature and posterity, ought to be recorded.

Lichfield in Staffordshire is now very well known to be the place of Johnson's birth; a circumstance which may probably be recollected by posterity, when this ancient city, like others which have been made immortal by giving birth to great men, is forgotten.

It appears from the parish register, that Johnson was born in the month of September, 1709. His father kept a shop near the market-place, and chiefly dealt in books, stationary ware, and book-binding; articles which, especially in a country situation, where literature is but rarely an amusement, and never a business, could not be very profitable. It was from this circumstance, that Johnson was enabled to say, as he often did, that he could bind a book very well.

Old Mr. Johnson, therefore, whose story being thus blended with that of his son, becomes an object of some attention, might be reputable, but could not be rich. He was a man of reserved manners, but of acknowledged shrewdness. From habits of steadiness and punctuality he acquired great personal respectability. The oldest people in the place would often tell the Doctor, who heard them with a sensible satisfaction, that his father continued to the last such a favourite among the boys, that he was perhaps the only one in town who never received any injury from their petulance and mischief. And it was said by himself, whose regards were incapable of betraying him into the flattery even of a parent, that *he was no careless observer of the passages of the times in which he lived.*[5] His intellectual abilities unimproved and called forth by no interest or emergency, were notwithstanding perhaps but moderate, as it does not follow, that because the son made a figure, the father should be a prodigy. But that he preserved himself by his industry and attention in a state of honesty and independence, that he had prudence enough by no schemes or speculations of any kind to injure his credit with his neighbours, and that whatever disappointments and crosses occurred in his intercourse with the world, he discovered the same innate fund of satisfaction and chearfulness which marked the most prosperous circumstances of his life, are particulars well known, and it is all we do know with certainty about him.[6]

Even in the town of Lichfield, however, where so little is to be made by the practice, we find him letting out part of his house in lodgings. These at the time of Johnson's birth were occupied by a Mr. Swynfen, who had a very pretty countryhouse on an estate of his own a few miles distant from Lichfield, where he practised physic, and where for that reason he provided himself with occasional accommodation. He was a man of considerable reputation in his profession as a physician, but was still more eminent for the liberality of his mind and the goodness of his heart. This gentleman, having stood godfather for the child, interested himself not a little in whatever related to his subsequent tuition. Though perhaps not affluent he was in easy circumstances, and being of a friendly and susceptible nature, took an early liking to young Johnson, the first openings of whose genius he superintended himself with much satisfaction and confidence. These, though neither sparkling nor premature, as Johnson was always rather solid and saturnine, than volatile or forward, were yet so entirely original and spontaneous, as to afford sufficient indications that his talents were not unhappily turned for literature and science.

He imbibed the elements of erudition at the free grammar-school of Lichfield. A Mr. Hunter had then the direction of the school. To this gentleman's elegant and correct method of teaching, the Doctor has often acknowledged the highest obligations. It was a circumstance he always mentioned with pleasure, that the place of his education had produced a Wollaston, a Newton, a Willes, a Garrick, and a Hawkesworth. The two last particularly, whose names are not unknown to fame, though a few years younger, were both his school-fellows, who then contracted that regard for his character, and confidence in his talents and worth, which afterwards disposed them so readily to list among his pupils and friends. For juvenile attachments often continue to operate through life, and are generally the last to which susceptible minds become insensible.

Thus situated, Johnson entered on the initials of learning, with an eagerness equally persevering and unsatiable. His exterior was always sluggish, and he never did any thing which had the least appearance of gracefulness, taste, dexterity, or dispatch. Even in the act of devouring the sublimest passages of ancient literature, one who knew him not, would have thought him asleep with the book in his hand. But though his diligence discovered no ardour, his perseverance was so singular and exemplary, that all attempts to divert him from the task assigned, or which he assigned to himself, were uniformly without effect. The rapacity with which he commenced his primary pursuit, and grasped at every object of classical intelligence, is obvious from the stubbornness of a peculiar habit which he then contracted. To his dying day, he never thought, recollected, or studied, whether in his closet, or in the street, alone, or in company, without putting his huge unwieldy body, in the same rolling, aukward posture, in which he was in use, while conning his grammar, or construing his lesson, to sit on the form at school.

He is said, when a mere school-boy, to have read indefatigably, and probably picked up no despicable acquaintance with books, by occasionally attending his father's shop. Here he was, not unfrequently, so absorbed by his predilection for the classical lore of antiquity, as entirely to neglect the business he had in trust. Being often chid for disobliging some of the best of his father's customers and friends, in this manner, he replied with great shrewdness, *that to supersede the pleasures of reading, by the attentions of traffic, was a task he never could master.*

It was, undoubtedly, by lounging here, that he heard many of those biographical and literary anecdotes, which he has since detailed, with so much elegance and vivacity, in his *Lives of the Poets*. To such a mind as Johnson's, thus early smitten with the love of science and philosophy, every thing connected with men of genius and letters, we may well believe, would be eagerly devoured, and tenaciously retained. And it is remarkable, in what an exuberant vein of manly sensibility, those particulars, which he says, *were told him* when a boy, occasionally break from him.

We are not informed at whose expence he was sent to college. His godfather, Dr. Swynfen, was likely enough to be consulted on this occasion. And the gentlemen in the neighbourhood, prompted by his example and zeal, and sensible of the father's inability and the son's genius, probably agreed among themselves, on some mode of thus finishing an education, from which they predicted much public utility. He was entered, however, of Pembroke-college, Oxford, October 31, 1728. Here he studied several terms, and might have continued longer, nor left the university, as he certainly did, without any degree, but that he could not afford, either to continue, or to pay for those honours, to which his proficiency as a scholar must have otherwise entitled him.

His conduct, during no long residence in that illustrious seminary, is but little known, or at least has been marked by no celebrity. He is said to have treated some of the tutors with disrespect, their lectures with negligence, and the rules of the college with rudeness and contumely. But this story, besides being supported by no authority, does not suit the tenor of the Doctor's behaviour, who at the same time that he despised the rules or ceremonies of fashion, in his deportment among the idle, the whimsical, the gay, or the affectedly polite, regarded with reverence every form or regulation, which had instruction or utility for its object.

In such a situation Johnson could not be idle. It was here he contemplated the wisdom of antiquity, and stored his capacious memory with whatever is valuable on record. He was formed by nature for a sedentary and recluse life. His strongest habits were those of indolence and austerity. All his subsequent exertions originated, not in his own choice, but in stern necessity. Labour appeared to him impracticable whenever it was possible to be idle. He had not yet commenced author, nor thought of the profession. His performances then could only be such college exercises as he could not avoid. Some of these were much admired and are still remembered. He particularly translated Pope's Messiah into elegant Latin verse, which afterwards appeared in a volume of poems, published by one Husbands.

It is supposed that he remained between two and three years at college, which he left for the place of an usher to a free-school at Market Bosworth in Leicestershire.[7] This laborious capacity he sustained much longer than was expected by any who knew him. All his leisure time was employed assiduously in the pursuit of intellectual acquisition and amusement; and who can say what might have been the consequence of his continuing for life in such a situation. Some may suppose his works to have gained in quality what they might have wanted in quantity. It can hardly be conceived, he would not have produced some memorial of his genius. But it would be rash to say, that such a production must have surpassed in excellence, the most finished of those pieces which actually fell from his pen. How very few gentlemen authors have ever arrived at any superlative distinction or eminence. Writing is an art which can only be acquired by practice. Lyttelton, Chesterfield, Hume, Robertson, and Gibbon, though by means of an independent situation, were never in pay to booksellers, accustomed themselves to literary compositions from their infancy. Johnson, therefore, immersed in a school might have published less, but except he had written much, he could not, with all the advantages of leisure, retirement, and plenty, have written so well as he did, amidst the incessant bustle of a town life, exposed to the constant intrusions of the idle and officious, and precipitated by the frequent pressure of impending want.

Here, by the example and advice, probably of his friend and master, Anthony Blackwall, he formed the plan of establishing an academy of his own.

Previous however to the accomplishment of this project, we find him residing at Birmingham, in the house of one Warren, a printer. His first essays are said to have been written for a news-paper, published by his landlord, and that he wrote while here, *A Voyage to Abyssinia, by Father Jerome Lobo, a Portuguese Jesuit; with a Continuation of the History of Abyssinia down to the Beginning of the eighteenth Century; and Fifteen Dissertations on various Subjects, relating to the History, Antiquities, Government, Religion, Manners, and Natural History of Abyssinia, and other Countries mentioned by Father Jerome Lobo. By Mr. Le Grand.* He wrote at the same time and in the same place, *Verses on a Lady's presenting a Sprig of Myrtle to a Gentleman,* which have been re-printed in several miscellanies, under the name of Mr. Hammond. They were, as the Doctor declared, very late in life, written for a friend, who was desirous of having, at least from his mistress, the reputation of a poet.

I give this anecdote to the reader as it appeared in one of our monthly publications.[8] It was incorporated with an account of Johnson's life, which, so far as it went, had all the marks of authenticity. Thus connected, the fact bore an aspect so like that of truth, as must have rendered the omissions, in spite of all my suspicions to the contrary, still inexcusable.

The author of the life of Garrick, who has been intimately acquainted with Johnson for many years, from whom Johnson could not conceal a secret of his heart, or an incident in his story, mentions the beginning of the year 1735, as the time when Johnson undertook the instruction of young gentlemen in the Belles Letters at Lichfield. Garrick and Hawkesworth were of the party who became his pupils on this occasion, and who profited during the short time he acted in that station. It is not certain, nor indeed material to know in what this scheme proved defective. But in May, 1736, we find him advertising a boarding-school at Edial, near Lichfield.[9]

This is a critical period in the life of Johnson. His father could afford him no pecuniary assistance, and he had too much sensibility and manliness to continue a burthen on his friends.[10] Such an establishment could not however be accomplished without money; and the gleanings of a very few years in the situation occupied by Johnson, allowing him to be a rigid œconomist, which he never was, must have been trifling. Thus circumstanced, how then could he raise a sum adequate to the demand? The difficulty will be solved by supposing his marriage to have taken place about this time. Mrs. Porter, whom he married, had been left a widow; her husband died insolvent, but her settlement was secured. Though she had three children, she was still young and handsome. The first advances probably proceeded from her, as her attachment to Johnson was in opposition to the advice and desire of all her relations. Her brother in particular offered to settle a very handsome annuity on her for life, provided she would break her engagement.[11] But nothing would dissuade her. She brought her second husband about seven or eight hundred pounds, a great part of which was expended in fitting up a house for a boarding-school, which they had doubtless concerted between them. But this abortive scheme was likewise of short duration. He has left no documents by which to account for the failure. His manners however sufferable among the petty circle to whom his real merits excused every thing, were far from connecting popularity with his personal intercourse. Parents could not be very fond of putting their children under the care of a man whose size was gigantic, whose temper was arrogant and austere, and whose habits were all clumsy and rude. His mind was as destitute of accommodation as his exterior was of politeness or grace; and to those who estimate genius or worth only by a soft tongue, a smooth face, or ceremonious carriage, his wit would appear insolence, his honesty folly, and his learning pedantry. Such a man was more likely to create aversion, than conciliate friendship, and instead of gathering a school, to be considered by the young and ignorant as a scarecrow. He had too much good sense to overlook so material an inconvenience. It might even strike him as an insuperable obstacle to success, and have its effect in determining him to abandon the whole plan, as romantic or impracticable.

He then adopted the sudden resolution of trying his fortune with the Booksellers in town. This adventure was not perhaps so much the consequence of disappointed expectations, as of his strong propensity for literary pursuits. Mr. Garrick, though his pupil, and inferior both in years and education, was no doubt consulted on this event. The letter which introduced Johnson to a clergyman of great reputation at that time as well as Garrick, however frequently quoted by those who have gone before me on the same subject, cannot with propriety be omitted in this place. [The letter from Walmesley to Colson of 2 March 1737 (misdated by Shaw 1736) has been omitted.]

London discloses an endless variety of resources for independent merit. Here capacity and industry can never want encouragement. And when every other expedient has failed, there are still hopes of doing something in a market, where all sorts of commodities are sure to bring their price.

Johnson had not lived to the age of six-and-twenty, without occasionally exercising his talents and acquirements in composition. Walmesley mentions him both as a poet and a scholar, without saying how he knew the fact. But few have the art of writing well who are not fond of shewing it, and Johnson does not seem to possess less vanity than other men.

What reception this friendly introduction procured for him with Mr. Colson, or whether this worthy clergyman was of any real service to him, we are not told. Such manuscripts as he brought to town were now by his direction probably offered to sale. But it does not appear that his *London,* with all its merit, was treated with much respect. This literary market was then, as it generally has been, governed only by principles of knavery, envy, or caprice. Most publishers were the tools of some favorite author, in whose opinion they confided, and whom they caressed on purpose that they might at once monopolize his labours and advice. Pride has been always the foible of the profession. What justice could a stranger expect from an order of men who can never be generous, and seldom civil to one another.

The fact is, Johnson's poem was likely to be on his hand, merely because rejected by some capital Booksellers.[12] He had been strongly importuned by his godfather Dr. Swynfen, before he left Lichfield, to publish it in the country, with a dedication to Dr. Chandler, who was then Bishop of Lichfield and Coventry. But he was determined to solicit no connection with the great. The church had been the primary object of his education, but from principles of religious delicacy he had uniformly declined the honour thus intended for him by his friends. And this was one consideration which probably weighed against the advice of his godfather in the present case. But the shyness of the trade to bring forward this favourite production sufficiently punished his obstinacy; and finding he could not live on poetry, which nobody would purchase, he connected himself with the editors of newspapers, and often depended on the lucubrations of the day for the provisions of to-morrow.

It was in this fugitive and dilatory situation that he got acquainted with Cave, the printer, whose numerous literary projects afforded bread to multitudes.

This enterprising printer Johnson compliments in the following copy of beautiful Latin verses, to which an elegant English version is subjoined, which was done for me on purpose by a friend. [*Ad Urbanum* has been omitted.]

How this connection commenced, the minute transactions it produced, or how long it continued is yet ascertained by no documents before the public.

Johnson seems to have contributed his share from the beginning in the Gentleman's Magazine.[13] But in such unequal and fugitive compilations, no man is fond of writing any thing otherwise than anonymously. In the year 1738 a few petit pieces however appeared with the initials of his name, which perhaps have been excelled by nothing he has since produced. When these are excepted it will not be very easy amidst the huge mass of materials contained in a magazine, to discriminate even the pen of a Johnson. Of this particular he was himself always singularly shy. He declined pointing out any of his earlier performances, when some of his most intimate friends asked it as a favour. To others he acknowledged that he then wrote many things which merited no distinction from the trash with which they were consigned to oblivion. And whatever the Booksellers may allege, it is a fact very well known, that a perfect catalogue of his works was a task to which he has always said his own recollection was inadequate.

Great merit has been ascribed to Johnson for the speeches he fabricated for the *Senate of Lilliput.* It was by this disrespectful appellation that he marked his contempt for the British House of Commons. This series of chimerical debates commenced in the year 1740, and were continued for several sessions. He received hints from a person who attended the House regularly for that purpose. The public, who were anxious to know what their delegates were doing, gratefully accepted of Johnson's account as there was not another, and allowed that to be genuine which they had not the means of perceiving an imposture.

Men however who know what it is to report the speeches in parliament, will be struck with nothing mighty extraordinary in all this. It is well known Mr. Woodfall, and Mr. Sheridan, who is certainly next in fame as a Reporter, have sometimes exceeded within the four-and-twenty hours, Johnson's labours for a month. There is a prodigious difference between a man's compassing at his leisure in his study, surrounded with every domestic convenience, and feeling no pressure from the urgent demands of the press, and where he is incessantly molested by the bustle of those at work, and by a thousand circumstances which, though not easily described, are yet peculiarly inimical to recollection.

This is their situation to whom the public are indebted for such accounts of the parliamentary proceedings as are daily detailed in Newspapers. These gentlemen, after sitting for twelve, or sometimes eighteen hours on a stretch, crouded as closely as they can be, without victuals, perchance, or drink, hasten as fast to their respective offices as possible, where they often write six, seven, or eight hours, at the rate of a column an hour. This incredible dispatch, to which the period of diurnal publications indispensibly subjects them, absolutely precludes all revisal, either of their own copy, or any proofs from the press. The wonder is not, therefore, that there should be so many improprieties in style and arrangement, but that there are, in fact, so few.

It is habit only which can unite with such facility any degree of correctness whatever. The mechanism of the business is an art, which practice alone can give. It combines accuracy and readiness of recollection, command of language, sound health, and great rapidity in the liberal use of the pen. In the two former Johnson had undoubtedly few equals, in the two latter he seems materially deficient. Seldom, altogether, free from illness, his constitution could not have supported the drudgery of attendance. And the form of his alphabet, which inclines strongly to the left, instead of the right, is a proof that he was not much master of what may be called an expeditious hand.

His predecessor in this Herculean labour was Guthrie, who, long before he died, was reduced to the necessity of using an amanuensis. Johnson was every way superior, and it is asserted by those who ought to know, that the magazine, during his connection with it, rose considerably in the public estimation. Hawkesworth, his friend and imitator, succeeded him likewise in these cursory productions, and brought with him no inconsiderable share of his master's genius.

While thus employed in the composition of speeches, which never were spoken, his admirers imagined they perceived a striking apposition, in his stile and train of thinking, to the various speakers. This characteristic was, however, the more impossible, that Johnson never, in the whole course of his life, attended one debate in either house of parliament. This was a species of ingenuity, which no instruction could supply. And nothing exposes the mean adulation of his eulogists more, than the absurdity of thus praising him for what was, in its own nature, impracticable.

The *Life of Savage*, it is said, was undertaken and executed with peculiar expedition, in order to convince the proprietor of the Gentleman's Magazine, that Johnson was equal to this laborious employ. And he has often enough asserted, with some degree of ostentation, that he completed this long and well-written life, in little more than six-and-thirty hours.

In 1738 he began a translation of the famous Father Paul's History of the Council of Trent. It is not known on what account this work was laid aside. Though no great progress was ever made in it, a few sheets of it were certainly printed. These, it is to be hoped, will be carefully preserved by some friend to letters; and the public will be highly indebted to the editor, who shall be the first to present it with such an acceptable curiosity.

What Johnson says, in his introduction to the Life of Dryden, is so literally true in his own case, that we may as well make him speak for himself. "In settling the order of his works there is some difficulty; the time of writing and publishing is not always the same; nor can the first editions be easily found, if even from them could be obtained the necessary information." [14] The truth is, that during his engagement with Cave, he published several lives, and other detached performances, many of which were collected by his friend, Mr. Davies, and given to the world, a few years ago, under the title of Fugitive Pieces.

Among the earliest of these appeared, *London, a Poem, in Imitation of the third Satire of Juvenal.* This elegant and masterly production, in which the enormities of the metropolis, and the infinite perils to which health, reputation, and virtue, are inevitably exposed by a London life, as well without fortune as with it, could, notwithstanding, hardly find a purchaser in the whole trade. The celebrated Mr. Robert Dodsley, however, was an exception. He saw the satire was aimed with the dexterity of no common poet. Johnson asked only ten guineas, and Dodsley gave it, rather as an encouragement to go on, than from any sanguine expectation of success in the sale of an *Imitation.* Johnson is reported to have boasted among his friends, *that Dodsley was the first bookseller who found out that he had any genius.* We are told that Mr. Pope read the poem with pleasure, who, receiving no satisfactory answer to repeated enquiries after the author, said, "It cannot be long before my curiosity will be gratified, the writer of this poem will soon be *deterré.*"

Such an opinion, from Pope, was one of the highest compliments which could be made to a young author. Whether it produced any personal friendship, acquaintance, or interview, is not certain; but the rigidness which runs through his criticism, on most of Pope's works, gives some ground of suspicion, that a very early dislike had been conceived against the poet, his verses, or his commentator.

What he has written concerning the imitations of this great man, is not inapplicable to his own.

The imitations of Horace (says he) seem to have been written as relaxations of his genius. This employment became his favourite by its facility: the plan was ready to his hand, and nothing was required but to accommodate as he could, the sentiments of an old author, to recent facts, or familiar images; but what is easy is seldom excellent: such imitations cannot give pleasure to common readers; the man of learning may sometimes be surprized and delighted by an unexpected parallel; but the comparison requires knowledge of the original, which will likewise often detect strained applications. Between Roman images and English manners, there will be an irreconcileable dissimilitude, and the work will be generally uncouth and parti-coloured; neither original nor translated, neither ancient nor modern.[15]

These were his sentiments, when his judgment was matured by experience, and after a long series of studies, in which many opportunities must have occurred, of a cool and critical discussion of the subject. This may probably account for his writing so little in that way afterwards; for, notwithstanding the very high merit of *London*, as a species of imitation, in no part of his works, perhaps, does he appear more susceptible of criticism, as the few following brief strictures, communicated to me by a warm admirer of Pope, will sufficiently evince.[16] He owned, at the same time, that nothing but Johnson's nibbling, with so much indelicacy, at the beautiful versifications of a poet, whom he had always esteemed the most classical and elegant in the language, could have provoked him to read, what he acknowledged an excellent poem, with such fastidious minuteness.

> Let observation, with extensive view,
> Survey the [world] from China to Peru. [1–2]
> > *Johnson's Imitation.*[17]

Let observation survey the world, from China to Peru, and we must allow its *view to be extensive*, whether the poet tell us so or not.

> Who now resolves, from vice and London far,
> To breathe in distant fields a purer air. [5–6]
> > *Johnson's Imitation.*

If he was *far* from London, certainly the fields which he breathed in must be *distant*.

> *With slavish tenets taint our poison'd youth.* [55]
> *Johnson's Imitation.*

To taint poison'd youth, is to poison them twice.

> Spurn'd as a begger, dreaded as a spy,
> Live unregarded, unlamented die. [81–82]
> *Johnson's Imitation.*

Johnson censures Pope's epitaph on himself, which begins,

> Under this stone, or under this sill,
> Or under this turf, &c.

"When a man," says he, "is buried, the question under what he is buried, is easily decided. He forgot that though he wrote the epitaph in a state of uncertainty, yet it could not be laid over him till his grave was made. Such is the folly of wit, when it is ill employed."[18]

Johnson did not die till a considerable number of years had elapsed, though he says he was dying at the time he wrote the above line; he died too exceedingly lamented. He made a mistake on a very serious occasion, as well as the poet whom he censures.

> Fate never wounds more deep the gen'rous heart,
> Than when a blockhead's insult points the dart. [168–69]
> *Johnson's Imitation.*

Juvenal says no such thing; it is his sense, tortured to little less than nonsense. What! does a blockhead's insult give the deepest wound? Every old woman can tell us that "a fool's bolt is soon shot." No one minds it, but those who are themselves not over wise.

> *Thy satire point, and animate thy page.* [263]
> *Johnson's Imitation.*

Here Johnson is again unlucky in the concluding line of a poem. By pointing the satire, he must animate the page of course. Addison fell into this fault of tautology, as often as Johnson, but Addison was not so severe as Johnson, in criticising others.

This poem, very probably, gives an exact picture of *London,* as it appeared to his mind immediately on his leaving the country, while every rural convenience was yet recollected with regret, and those of the town had been enjoyed only to such a degree, in such company, or under such circumstances, as might rather disgust than gratify. The difficulty of securing a prospect of employment, before he could be known, the shyness of the booksellers, to interest themselves in the fortune or business of a stranger, the wants of futurity which could hope but little assistance from the present, which was unequal to its own supply, ill health, few friends, exquisite sensibility, and a temper of mind, rather melancholy than chearful, obviously account for the indignant spirit, and strong assemblage of melancholy imagery with which that performance abounds.

Under these impressions he undoubtedly meditated a return to a country situation. The bustle of the town seems to have offended his predilection for retirement, and the occupation of an author, his unconquerable love of ease. Perhaps, Mrs. Johnson might also be consulted on the like occasion, and it is likely, would rather wish to enjoy her old friends, than have the trouble, in so precarious a place as London, to cultivate new ones. It is certain he had solicitations to accept of a school in the neighbourhood of Lichfield, with which he had no other objection to comply but a want of the necessary qualifications.

The following letter ought to have been inserted before, but from the observations just made it will not be misplaced here, especially as it requires more labour than I can bestow, as well as materials, which have not yet been found, to settle the chronology of his publications and transactions, with certainty or precision. [The Gower letter, here dated 1738, has been omitted.]

It is rather odd this letter did not procure a more favourable answer, and that Johnson did not succeed to the school. We know not whether Swift, to whose friend it was addressed, knew any thing of the matter, but it is obvious Johnson has written the life of this very extraordinary genius, as if his mind had been somewhat warped, and he owed the Dean no returns of kindness or gratitude.[19] Whatever the impediment might have been, it ultimately proved insuperable. Johnson, whose sanguine imagination was easily influenced, and all whose hopes, by whatever means exerted, still glowed with incessant fervour, felt long and severely the disappointment.

It seems to be about this time that he planned and executed the poem, which he calls the *Vanity of Human Wishes,* another imitation of his favourite Juvenal.[20] This however was not brought forward till some time in the year 1759 [1749]. His situation in the Gentleman's Magazine was even then continued, and is the true reason why Cave became the publisher.[21] The train of thinking is in all respects worthy the author.

It is a poem which every where discovers the same beauties, and not a few of the same faults, which in the former offend every reader of genuine taste and correctness.

The lines with which we venture to compare a few of Johnson's, are quoted from a New Translation of the Tenth Satire of Juvenal, by Thomas Morris, Esq. late Captain of his Majesty's seventeenth Regiment of Foot, published as a specimen of a complete version of that masterly writer.[22] And when the defects of what goes by the name of Dryden, the similarity between Roman and British vices, and the singular gravity, truth and boldness of Juvenal, are duly considered, who would not wish his proposals may succeed. These quotations are chiefly selected for exhibiting to the English reader, the beauty and defects of Johnson's Imitation, as they who comprehend not the meaning of the ancient poet, are not competent to judge with propriety on his application to modern times.

This communication I likewise owe to the same gentleman, whose pertinent strictures on London have already been inserted.

> Yet still one gen'ral cry the sky assails,
> And gain and grandeur load the tainted gales;
> Few know the toiling statesman's fear or care,
> Th' insidious rival and the gaping heir. [45–48]
>
> *Johnson's Imitation.*

> The supplication in each temple heard,
> By ev'ry mortal to the gods preferr'd,
> Is, to be grac'd with pow'r, with riches blest,
> And in the forum keep the largest chest:
> Let us remember, ere we make our pray'r,
> No aconite is serv'd in earthen ware;
> That apprehend, when cups with jewels shine,
> And the broad gold inflames the Setine wine.
>
> *Translation of the Tenth Satire of Juvenal.*

Juvenal speaks out; but Johnson hints *too obliquely* at the practice of poisoning: a person unacquainted with the original, will not understand his meaning.

> *Load the tainted gales,*

is not much better than

> *Load* the *loaden* gales,
> Or, *taint* the *tainted* gales.

Johnson, speaking of Pope's epitaph says,

Op'ning virtues blooming round

is something like tautology.[23] I think *load the tainted gales* is more like it.

Or seen a new-made mayor's unwieldy state. [58]

Surely Johnson might have made something out of the Lord Mayor's shew, answering to Juvenal's description of the prætor's going to proclaim the shews of the circus. In Juvenal's time the prætor of Rome was not a greater personage than our Lord Mayor, and the figure made by the one now, is full as ridiculous as that made by the other long ago.

> For why did Wolsey, near the steeps of fate,
> On weak foundations raise th'enormous weight?
> Why but to sink beneath misfortune's blow,
> With louder ruin to the gulphs below. [125-28]
>
> *Johnson's Imitation.*

> Sejanus little thought what he desired,
> When to the highest rank his soul aspir'd;
> The vast increase of riches, pomp, and pow'r,
> Was only adding stories to his tow'r,
> The more astonishing to make it's fall,
> That buried riches, honours, lord and all.
>
> *Translation, &c.*

That the blow of misfortune might throw down Wolsey is plain enough; that it could demolish a building is not so obvious.

> *Let art and genius weep.* [173]
>
> *Johnson's Imitation.*

Johnson, speaking of Pope's epitaph, says, "in another couplet art is used for arts, that a rhyme may be had to heart."[24] Has he not fallen himself into the like mistake, without having the same excuse for it.

> Enquirer cease; petitions yet remain,
> Which heav'n may hear, nor deem religion vain. [349-50]
>
> *Johnson's Imitation.*

The sense here is strangely broken, and rendered obscure.

> Yet when the sense of sacred presence fires,
> And strong devotion to the skies aspires. [357-58]
>
> *Johnson's Imitation.*

Is not this anti-climax? Would it not be better thus?

> *Yet when devotion to the skies aspires,*
> *And the strong sense of sacred presence fires.*

These goods for man the laws of heav'n ordain.
These goods he grants, who grants the power to gain. [365–66]
Johnson's Imitation.

If Johnson thought Pope blameable for not using the singular *art* instead of the plural *arts*, for the sake of rhyme; how much more to be condemned is the critic himself, who uses the plural *goods*, instead of the singular *good*, without any reason that I can find, and in open defiance of his own decree? I appeal to his dictionary. Under the word *goods* we find, 1. Moveables in a house. 2. Wares, freight, merchandize: Under the word *good*, 4. Moral qualities.

And makes that happiness she does not find. [368]
Johnson's Imitation.

The expletive *does* in the last line of the poem, and in the most important place in that line, makes a most lame and impotent conclusion.

How wouldst thou shake at Britain's modish tribe,
Dart the quick taunt, and edge the piercing gibe? [61–62]
Johnson's Imitation.

The latter line is loaden with useless epithets, and the sense weakened by them. How much better thus!

> *How wouldst thou shake at Britain's modish tribe!*
> *How wouldst thou dart the taunt, and edge the gibe!*

Till conquest unresisted ceas'd to please,
And rights submitted left him none to seize. [107–08]
Johnson's Imitation.

The whole account of Wolsey is in the present tense. Why the author chose so ungracefully to change the tense in this couplet only, which is in the middle of the account too, I cannot guess: it has a slovenly appearance however; and how easily might it have been avoided, thus:

> *Till conquests unresisted cease to please,*
> *And rights submitted leave him none to seize.*

> *Till captive science yields her last retreat.* [144]
> *Johnson's Imitation.*

The epithet *captive* is not only useless, but nonsensical; for, if science was taken captive, what retreat could she be in possession of? We must hope that the author meant to say, that "when science yields her last retreat, she becomes a captive": This, however, is a piece of intelligence scarcely worth relating.

> *Should no disease thy torpid veins invade.* [153]
> > *Johnson's Imitation.*

That is, in plain English, should no disease invade thy diseased veins. In short it is a pleonasm, to make up the measure; but not quite so bad a one as the former.

> *He views and wonders that they please no more.* [264]
> > *Johnson's Imitation.*

A trifling change would make this line better.

> *He views and wonders they should please no more.*

> *No sounds, alas! would touch th'impervious ear.* [269]
> > *Johnson's Imitation.*

If *no* sounds *would* touch it, *it* certainly *must* be impervious.

Johnson fortunately for his reputation was soon satisfied his *forte* did not lie in making verses. His poetry, though not any where loaded with epithets, is destitute of animation. The strong sense, the biting sarcasm, the deep solemnity, which mark his genius, no where assume that union, symmetry, or collected energy, which is necessary to produce a general effect. We are now and then struck with a fine thought, a fine line, or a fine passage, but little interested by the whole. His mode of versifying, which is an imitation of Pope, may bear analization, but after reading his best pieces once, few are desirous of reading them again.

The life of Savage, which was his first biographical essay,[25] had such a reception with the public, or answered the bookseller's purpose so well, that Johnson was encouraged to cultivate this species of composition. For a series of years therefore he was constantly enriching the annals of literature, with new articles of English biography. It is impossible to be exact in stating the dates of these public actions, or giving the history of their origin and composition. The particulars they involve are the less interesting, that they seem to have grown into request only since the fame of the author has been established; that they are distinguished by no other species of excellence than fidelity and perspicuity, and they might still have continued unadmired, and even unknown, but for the superior lustre of subsequent performances.

Osborne shared the honour with Cave and [Robert] Dodsley, of being one of Johnson's first patrons. An affray with that curious bookseller, gave the trade no very advantageous idea of Johnson's temper. It was hushed at the time, in complaisance to the opulence of the one, but gradually became a subject of speculation, as the reputation of the other increased. Johnson was employed in writing an introduction to the Harleian library, which, as it gave an account of various articles, could not be done in haste. Osborne incessantly urged expedition, and had often recourse to contumelious language. Johnson who had much pride, had also much good-nature, made no other reply to this tiresome impertinence, but that he was as busy as possible. The calculations of booksellers are solely confined to the sale, and seldom involve the various avocations and deliberations which protract composition. The delicate embarrassments of genius are consequently not unfrequently treated with rudeness and vulgarity. No body of men are more uniform and eager in taking advantage of their necessities, who, like Johnson, are reduced to a dependance on their favour. Osborne was base enough to make Johnson feel his situation, by a brutal sarcasm, which he blurted in his face, on finding him reading with great coolness, while the quantum of copy promised by this time, was not yet begun. Johnson, surprised into a passion, by the bookseller's rage and ferocity, started from his seat, without uttering a word, and, with the book in his hand, instantly knocked him down.

Hitherto he had tried his genius as a translator, a satyrist, and a biographer; he was now to appear a philologist. The plan of his Dictionary, which he displays with so much elegance and dignity in an address to the late Earl of Chesterfield, was published so early as the year 1748 [1747]. This performance promised something so much like what all men of taste had long thought wanting to the purity, stability, and perfection of our language, exhibited an object of such magnitude to the public mind, and was itself so exquisite a specimen of the happiest arrangement and most polished diction, that it brought Johnson forward to general attention with peculiar advantage. The eyes of all the world were turned on what part the nobleman thus distinguished would now act in concert with the first writer, and interested by the sketch of a work the most laborious and useful of any which even then had roused the curiosity and excited the wonder of an enlightened age. From a secretary of state, still more illustrious for his elegant accomplishments than for his high birth or official situation something like substantial encouragement was expected to an undertaking which aimed at no less than a *standard Dictionary of the English tongue.* His lordship was a competent judge of the subject. He acknowledged its importance and necessity. He occupied a sphere in life, an influence among the great, and a character among the learned, which enabled him to do much. His vanity was not inferior to his power; and had the talents of Johnson stooped to the prostituted language of adulation, his toil had probably been considerably alleviated by the taste, the address, the assiduity and the countenance of Chesterfield. But nothing can be conceived more diametrically opposite and irreconcileable than the tempers, the prejudices, the habits, the pursuits, and the peculiarities of these contemporary wits. A semblance of intimacy took place, in which it is not likely that either were sincere. The oddities of the author furnished the peer with a fund of ridicule, and the fastidious elegance of the peer excited only the aversion, contempt, and pity of the author. *All the celebrated qualities of Chesterfield,* (said Johnson to an intimate friend, to whom he was then in the habit of unbosoming himself on occasion) *are like certain species of fruit which is pleasant enough to the eye, but there is no tasting it without danger.*

In this well written pamphlet it was his ambition to rival the preface to Chambers's Dictionary. How far he succeeded is not easily determined. It will not be denied, that he possesses more energy of language, and perhaps a more beautiful arrangement of the multifarious particulars to which he solicits the public attention, but he certainly wants the simplicity, and indeed is proscribed by his subject from displaying the knowledge, of Chambers.

Chesterfield joined in the general applause which followed the exhibition of a design thus replete with utility in the aim, and originality in the execution. He was proud to have attracted the regards of such a man as Johnson, and flattered himself with the hopes of fresh accession of fame, from being the patron of such a work. But the manners of the operator were so disgusting to this Mæcenas of letters, and learned men, that the only concern he took in the matter was saying a few polite things at his table, and congratulating the lovers of grammar on the improvement which that science would derive from the labours of Johnson. It is a disgrace to his memory, and to the age, that the author of an undertaking so arduous and extensive was not placed beyond the recurrence of necessity, and that while his genius was conferring permanancy on their language, the exigencies of his situation impelled him to apply to other means for daily subsistence.

The talents requisite for such an undertaking seldom meet in one man. Its magnitude was enough to stagger any resolution less vigorous, to repress any ardour less manly, to derange any intellect less collected than that of Johnson. But his capacity was competent to the object. His reading was chiefly philological, his taste was improved by an intimate acquaintance with all the classical remains of antiquity, his memory retained with exactness whatever his judgment had matured; and he possessed a penetration or discernment characteristically solid, cool, and discriminating. It was not a composition that depended on the paroxysms of genius, a vigorous imagination, fertility of invention, originality of conception, or brilliancy of style. Patient industry, laborious attention, a determination of forgetting the lassitude of fatigue by a renewal of the task; and a mind, which notwithstanding a thousand avocations and obstacles, like the water in a river, still returned to the same channel, and pursued the same course; were some of the qualifications with which Johnson formed the plan, and entered on the compilation of his Dictionary.

A work thus complicated and prodigious admits great variety in collecting the materials, and frequent relaxations from the exertions it demands. Many are the subjects which would present themselves to the author's mind, from such an association of ideas as must have accompanied the progress of his studies. And it may be rationally conjectured, that he often found relief not only in the society of his select friends, but in a great variety of literary pursuits, the more pleasing probably for the time, that they might appear to others of less importance.

His *Irene* however, which was brought upon the stage in 1749, is generally acknowledged to have been written before he came to town. Why it did not make its appearance sooner, and why it was not better received when it did, are questions which now perhaps cannot be answered.[26]

It would be a singular period in the annals of the English Theatre, in which the reception of authors were regulated by their merit. Johnson's temper was ill calculated for supplicating favours from inferiors. It was not in his heart or his nature, to hang about a manager, to associate with the critics in the green-room, to cultivate an intimacy with spouters, or to interest the patronage of loungers in the lobby of the playhouse. He either did not understand that private pliancy and public ostentation which constitute the mystery of the trade, or had the manliness to regard with contempt, every species of obliquity, even when it leads to success. The plot however, the thoughts, and the diction of his tragedy, are allowed to be beautiful and masterly. But he is sparing of that bustle and incident, which atone for the want of every excellence with a London audience. A performance which exemplified the prescriptions of an Aristotle, was not likely to please a nation tutored in this barbarous taste. It does not abound in doggerel madrigals or epigrammatic rodomontade. It degrades not scenes of dignified distress with the Pantomime of Harlequin, the gossippings or gibberish of gypsies, or the ribaldry and buffoonery of clowns. It is written only to improve the heart, to elucidate and refine the passions, to connect the interests of humanity with the dictates of reason, and to restore the union of taste and virtue.

But though the principal characters were given to those who at that time excelled in the profession, the expectation of Johnson and his friends was disappointed. The first exhibition was coldly received, and the audience it seems were more disposed to admire the author than to be affected by his scenes. A gentleman who sat in the pit, on that occasion, has told me, that on looking round him he saw nobody using their handkerchief; but the whisper was strong and prevalent, that the *poet was a prodigy of learning.*

Much, especially in tragedy, depends on the actors. Johnson's address was disgusting. He had not made any advances to conciliate their fondness, or to prompt their exertions. His manners were gruff and distant, his language was coarse and oraculous; and though Garrick was of the party, posterity who shall mourn *Irene,* will be rather apt to impute her fate to inanimate acting, than unskilful writing.

Johnson was not of a turn of mind to struggle for any thing not immediately within his reach. Under the auspices of a Garrick, whose assistance and advice he could always command, who can doubt but by a sedulous application he might have excelled in the higher species of the drama? But he who had it in his power to lead, was unwilling to continue acting only a secondary part. Other subjects less hazardous in the issue, and more easy in the execution, were incessantly occurring and engaging his cultivation, with which he ran no risk of a rival, and which, though perhaps less profitable, yet yielded his necessities a readier supply.

His disgust and contempt for the public taste suggested to him the first idea of furnishing the town with a periodical paper twice a week. In such a work he enjoyed the prospect of exposing the taste of his countrymen, and often contributing by the happy application of superior talents, to their correction and refinement. And perhaps it may be doing him no injustice to suppose, that wherever the fashionable levities of taste are censured, he glances obliquely at the usage of *Irene.*

By an incident in the history of the *Rambler,* not generally known, that celebrated work was published at Edinburgh, at the same time the publication of it went on in London.[27]

Mr. Elphinston, well known in the learned world for a variety of valuable publications, both in prose and verse, was the intimate friend of Johnson, and then on a visit to his relations in that part of the united kingdom. The first number came to him under cover, and without a name. But the author could not be concealed; and, in Mr. Elphinston's opinion, there was not, in England, another than Johnson, competent to such an undertaking. He consequently conceived the benevolent design of diffusing the work among his countrymen, as promising much instruction to them, and some profit to the author. It was immediately reprinted in Scotland in a minute and elegant manner. Mr. Elphinston not only superintended the press, and took every possible care of the edition, but likewise enriched it by a new and apposite translation of the mottos. Most of these were retained in the next edition which appeared in London, and Johnson, in a note appended to a collection of them, acknowledges the obligation in the handsomest terms.[28] Indeed this was an instance of attention and friendship, with which, as it well became him, he always expressed the most grateful satisfaction.

In the following letter we learn some particulars relating to this business. The original reception of the Rambler in Scotland is not obscurely hinted, and the author's tenderness for his labours, strongly marked by the solicitude with which he cherishes the partiality which his friend had conceived in their favour. The original, in Johnson's own handwriting, is still in Mr. Elphinston's possession. The writer's regard for true learning and worth, is happily illustrated by his kind attention to the celebrated Ruddiman.[29] The honourable testimony which he bears to the virtue of that venerable man, was a proof that his heart was always in unison with the wise and good, whoever they were, or wherever they lived.

Dear Sir,

I cannot but confess the failures of my correspondence, but hope the same regard which you express for me on every other occasion will incline you to forgive me. I am often, very often ill, and when I am well, am obliged to work and indeed have never much used myself to punctuality. You are however not to make unkind inferences, when I forbear to reply to your kindness: for be assured, I never receive a letter from you without great pleasure, and a very warm sense of your generosity and friendship, which I heartily blame myself for not cultivating with more care. In this, as in many other cases, I go wrong in opposition to conviction: for I think scarce any temporal good equally to be desired with the regard and familiarity of worthy men. I hope we shall be sometime nearer to each other, and have a more ready way of pouring out our hearts.

I am glad that you still find encouragement to proceed in your publication, and shall beg the favour of six more volumes, to add to my former six, when you can, with any convenience, send them me. Please to present a set in my name to Mr. Ruddiman; of whom I hear, that his learning is not his highest excellence.

I have transcribed the mottos and returned them, I hope not too late; of which I think many very happily performed. Mr. Cave has put the last in the Magazine, in which I think he did well. I beg of you to write soon, and to write often, and to write long letters which I hope in time to repay you, but you must be a patient creditor. I have however this of gratitude, that I think of you with regard, when I do not perhaps give the proofs which I ought of being

> Sir, your most obliged,
> and most humble servant,
> Sam Johnson

To Mr. Elphinston. [*Without any date.*] [30]

From this soothing and friendly letter Johnson seems to have been much flattered by the success of his Rambler in North-Britain. Indeed he always acknowledged, that it was by far the best edition of the work. It was, in fact, much more correct than the original one in London, though published under his own eye: for his friend spared no attention, which could by any means contribute to the author's reputation.

About this time Mr. Elphinston lost his mother, which affected him so deeply, that Johnson thought it his duty to write to him on the occasion: which, by the way, was a subject on which no writer, ancient or modern, ever excelled him. The letter breathes a spirit of the most elevated piety and of the tenderest consolation; and being handed about while the publication of the Rambler went on in Edinburgh, considerably promoted the circulation of it, especially among religious readers. We may judge of his sincerity in that letter, by perusal of the papers in the Rambler of nearly the same date. He had heard the news from Mrs. Strahan,[31] sister to Mr. Elphinston; and wrote in all probability his fifty-second and fifty-fourth numbers under that impression.

Dear Sir,

You have, as I find by every kind of evidence, lost an excellent mother; and I hope you will not think me incapable of partaking of your grief. I have a mother now eighty-two years of age, whom therefore I must soon lose, unless it please God that she rather should mourn for me. I read the letters in which you relate your mother's death to Mrs. Strahan; and think I do myself honour when I tell you that I read them with tears; but tears are neither to me nor to you of any farther use, when once the tribute of nature has been paid.

The business of life summons us away from useless grief, and calls us to the exercise of those virtues of which we are lamenting our deprivation. The greatest benefit which one friend can confer upon another, is to guard, and incite, and elevate his virtues. This your mother will still perform, if you diligently preserve the memory of her life, and of her death: a life, so far as I can learn, useful and wise; innocent; and a death resigned, peaceful, and holy. I cannot forbear to mention, that neither reason nor revelation denies you to hope, that you may encrease her happiness by obeying her precepts; and that she may, in her present state, look with pleasure, upon every act of virtue to which her instructions or example have contributed. Whether this be more than a pleasing dream, or a just opinion of separate spirits, is indeed of no great importance to us, when we consider ourselves as acting under the eye of God: yet surely there is something pleasing in the belief, that our separation from those whom we love is merely corporeal; and it may be a great incitement to virtuous friendship, if it can be made probable, that union which has received the divine approbation, shall continue to eternity.

There is one expedient, by which you may, in some degree, continue her presence. If you write down minutely what you remember of her from your earliest years, you will read it with great pleasure, and receive from it many hints of soothing recollection, when time shall remove her yet farther from you, and your grief shall be matured to veneration. To this, however painful for the present, I cannot but advise you, as to a source of comfort and satisfaction in the time to come: for all comfort and all satisfaction, is sincerely wished you by,

Dear Sir,

> Your most obliged,
> most obedient,
> and most humble servant,
> Sam. Johnson.

To Mr. Elphinston.
Sept. 25, 1750.[32]

In the history of literature, the price of copy would be a desirable piece of information; but to keep this as much in the dark as possible, is one of the mysteries of Bookselling; which, being a lottery throughout, is generally carried on under a mask. His emoluments from the *Rambler* are therefore not generally known. Some accounts have rated them at two, and others, probably not less authentic, at five guineas a week. We are only certain, that from the beginning he retained so much of the property in his own hands, till the work was half finished. He then disposed of the copy entirely, but for how much, or under what conditions we are not acquainted.[33] The moment this fact was known in Edinburgh, the translator of the mottos, who had Johnson's interest supremely at heart, and not deeming himself under any obligation to continue the same exertions for the Booksellers, desisted; though he persevered in otherwise perfecting the edition.

The truth is, even this performance, one of the most masterly and elegant in the language, was but coldly received at first. It was during the publication of the Rambler, that the literary character of *David Hume* broke forth in its strongest lustre. He was the fashionable writer of the day. He had always kept himself independant of Booksellers. This was a circumstance which considerably encreased it with some people, as they are pleased to distinguish between an author who writes for subsistence; and one, who though able to live without writing, yet sells what he writes with as much anxiety, as if he wrote for a livelihood. This, however, they call a gentleman-author, and, without much regard to the comparative merit of the two, very often, and very absurdly, give him the preference.

Such was the prejudice to which Hume owed much of his celebrity, though his merits undoubtedly entitled him to a very large share. His peculiar eccentricities and paradoxes, chiefly on moral, philosophical, and religious subjects, procured him an incredible number of votaries in both kingdoms. Nothing appeared in the literary world, about which he was not consulted; and it is well known, the critics of the times, regarded his opinion as sacred and decisive. He mentioned the Rambler, however, with respect; and only regretted there should be so much cant and so much pedantry, in a performance replete with taste, erudition and genius.

This stricture very obviously marred, though it did not absolutely prevent the success of the book. Johnson, when told of the fact, only acknowledged himself the less surprized that his papers had not been more universally read. *My countrymen,* said he, *will not always regard the voice of a Blasphemer as an oracle.* He took no farther notice of the circumstance. Perhaps he might not be altogether inattentive to its influence on the minds of men; in what follows, which is quoted from the last number of the Rambler. "I am far from supposing," says he, "that the cessation of my performance will raise any enquiry; for I have never been much the favourite of the public, nor can boast that in the progress of my undertaking, I have been animated by the rewards of the liberal, the caresses of the great, or the praises of the eminent." [34]

These, however, were not the only compositions, which occupied the attention of Johnson in consort with his Dictionary. During eight years exhausted in this prodigious work, several petty pieces made their appearance on different occasions, and at different times; which severally operated as so many advertisements of that in which he was principally employed, as tending equally to establish his reputation and conciliate the public confidence in his future labours.

This publication, which appeared in 1755, was accompanied with a preface, in which it is not easy to say, whether genius, erudition, industry, or taste is the predominating feature. But on this occasion he takes an opportunity of stating some complaints, which, as they chiefly refer to his circumstances, peculiarly mark the man, in an apology for keeping back his book so long from the public; and to defeat the censures of the captious, he has this curious passage, which gives a summary account of his own conduct. "Much of my life," says he, "has been lost under the pressure of disease. Much has been trifled away, and much has been always spent in provision for the day that was passing over me." [35] The first of his complaints is true. He had much ill health. His size was large; but he was not more aukward in his gait, than gross and cumbrous in his make. In the earlier periods of his life, he was grievously afflicted with the king's evil, but this disease was much abated, if not perfectly cured, long before his death. But from his infancy to his grave he laboured under a complication of maladies, which repeatedly baffled all the powers of physic. Had he failed however in his undertaking, this would rather have condemned the attempt, than justified the want of execution.

He acknowledged himself guilty of trifling away much of his time, and yet his habits of temperance and sobriety are well known. No man ever imputed dissipation to Johnson; but his indolence or aversion to activity, was so notorious as to become proverbial. In truth, he never would work, but in order to eat. He has often confessed composition had no charms for him, and that all the fame and reputation which he acquired by his writings, as well as the numerous and sublime virtues ascribed to them, were comprehended in the single monosyllable *bread*.

The other grievance by which he endeavours to interest the feelings of the reader, is, in my opinion, singularly whimsical: *much of my life has always been spent, in provision for the day that was passing over me*. This was literally putting his situation on a level with that of a mere labourer, whose only dependance is on the sweat of his brow. But it is well known Johnson received so much money, that at the very time of adopting this whining language he was in a capacity to have lived at the rate of three hundred pounds a year.[36]

This was at least no dispicable competence, for an individual who had no other family to maintain than Mrs. Johnson and himself.

But he adds: *"the English Dictionary was written amidst inconvenience and distraction, in sickness and in sorrow."* [37] What those inconveniences and sorrows thus solemnly asserted to have interfered with the tranquil pursuits of laborious study were, he does not inform us. It is however known, that though he never had any children, he was not wholly exempted from domestic inquietude. It has been said that Mrs. Johnson, who was much the elder of the two, had, especially in the latter part of her life, addicted herself to drinking, some say, opium. A suspicion of his conjugal infelicity on this account certainly went abroad, and procured him much commiseration among his friends: and to the disgust occasioned by this cruel misfortune, his various sarcasms on matrimony, his affected indifference to the sex, and the contempt which he frequently pours on all the expressions of the tender passions, are generally, perhaps improperly, attributed. Mrs. Johnson was otherwise a lady of great sensibility and worth; so shrewd and cultivated, that in the earlier part of their connection, he was fond of consulting her in all his literary pursuits; and so handsome, that his associates in letters and wit were often very pleasant with him on the strange disparity, which, in this respect, subsisted between husband and wife. Probably he grew peevish by study and disease, and he who piqued himself on his bluntness abroad, was not likely to be very complaisant at home. She disliked the profusion, with which he constantly gave away all the money about him; and he found with astonishment and concern, that whatever he provided or laid up for family exigence, was always gone before he expected.

Notwithstanding these petty differences, they regarded each other with true cordiality and affection. Both suffered from oddities, which it was impossible to conquer; but mutually reposed a steadfast confidence, while it was their happiness to live together. Johnson often said he never knew how dear she was to him, till he lost her. Her death affected him so deeply, that he grew almost insensible to the common concerns of life. He then stayed little within, where her image was always recalled by whatever he heard or saw. Study disgusted him, and books of all kinds were equally insipid. He carefully avoided his friends, and associated most with such company as he never saw before. And when he thought himself a burden, and felt the pressure of time becoming insupportable, the only expedient he had was to walk the streets of London. This for many a lonesome night was his constant substitute for sleep. An impression thus forcible and serious, time and vicissitude only could erase. And it was not till he found his mind somewhat composed, and his heart considerably at ease, that he began to relish the blessings of life, to enjoy his friends, and to resume his studies.

The following plain inscription to the memory of Mrs. Johnson, was then among the first productions of his pen. It is simple and concise, but contains much. Genuine sorrow, is not loquacious. There is something in the original which cannot easily be translated, but the reader may not dislike to see attempted. [Omitted.]

It was doubted whether the artifices of the booksellers by practising on the public curiosity, would not injure the performance [i.e., the *Dictionary*], and raise expectation too high to be satisfied. The enquiries after the publication were eager and universal, and yet the disappointment which attended the event was inconsiderable. It was equally ridiculous in individuals and parties, to expect their discriminating prejudices consulted in the explanation of words. But on no other ground has any solid objection been made to the English Dictionary. It is notwithstanding attacked in the twelfth number of the North Briton, with as much virulence as if it had been intended only as a register of political opinion.

When Johnson was first told of Wilkes's going to court, in consequence of his political conversion, he gave a strong proof of the pertinence of his judgment, as well as of the strength of his memory. *I hope,* said he, *Mr. Wilkes is now become a friend to the constitution, and to the family on the throne, but I know he has much to unwrite, and more to unsay, before he will be forgiven for what he has been writing and saying for many years.*[38]

In a compilation which involved so much reading, recollection and correction, rash explanations were unavoidable. The word *Furbelow* he derived originally from *Fur* and *below,* and said it was *fur* sewed on the lower part of the garment. But the fact was, a lady of distinction having once appeared at the French court in this dress, which was entirely of her own invention, was asked what she called it, and answered *c'est unfalballa.*[39] His definition of the word *oats,* was rigidly just, but the scurrilous alterations of party rendering the Scotch at that time extremely sore, they were much offended, but so may all mankind think it a disgrace to breathe because this is the mode of life in horses as well as men.

He put such a sense on *pension* or *pensioners,* as furnished petty malignity with a fund of ridicule and sarcasm against himself.

His exposition of the excise was likely to be followed by consequences still more serious and vexatious. Some people then at the head of that obnoxious board, avowed their resentment in such a manner as to threaten a prosecution.[40]

How this matter terminated is not now generally known. In a subsequent edition of the Dictionary, Johnson was desired to alter and soften the article. *No,* said he, *it has done all the mischief, and I own no complaisance to excisemen or their masters.*

Johnson's connection with Chesterfield came to an eclaircissement, the moment this great work made its appearance. *Moore,* author of the World, and the creature of this nobleman, was employed by him to sound Johnson on the subject of a Dedication. Some time before Johnson had been refused admittance to his Lordship. This, it was pretended, happened by the mistake of a porter, though it is pretty well known, few servants take such liberties without the connivance of their masters. Johnson, who saw through all the disguises of Chesterfield's pride, never forgave the indignity, and treated every apology which was afterwards suggested by the friends and admirers of this nobleman, as an insult. *Moore,* without touching on that point in the most distant manner, expressed his hopes that Johnson would dedicate his Dictionary to Chesterfield. He received a very pointed and direct negative. — "I am under obligations," said he, "to no great man, and of all others, Chesterfield ought to know better than to think me capable of contracting myself into a dwarf, that he may be thought a giant." "You are certainly obliged to his Lordship," said *Moore,* "for two very elegant papers in the World, and all the influence of his good opinion, in favour of your work." "You seem totally unacquainted with the true state of the fact," replied Johnson, "after making a hazardous and fatiguing voyage round the literary world, I had fortunately got sight of the shore, and was coming into port with a pleasant tide and a fair wind, when my Lord Chesterfield sends out two little cock-boats to tow me in. I know my Lord Chesterfield tolerably well, Mr. Moore. He may be a wit among Lords, but I fancy he is no more than a Lord among wits."

In the year following, he published the *Political State of Great-Britain, Observations on the State of Affairs,* and *Proposals for printing the Dramatic Works of William Shakespeare.*

His political performances discover all that solid reasoning and sound information without which Johnson never would write on any thing. In these, published in the year fifty-six, he discusses with his usual penetration and address our political situation in the Western world, and enters into the perplexed question, so strenuously agitated by the Courts of Versailles and London, concerning the boundaries of the colonies. Both pamphlets are replete with shrewdness, sarcasm, and profound attention to the restlessness of ambition, the effects of usurpation, the arrogant claims of princes, and the natural rights of mankind.

Johnson, so early as the year forty-five, had conceived the design of publishing a correct edition of Shakespeare's works. But Warburton, whose name was then deservedly high in the republic of letters, proposing at the same time a similar work, Johnson prudently suspended his for the present. The pamphlet, however, which he printed on the occasion, received the approbation of his rival, who, of all other men, was the least guilty of adulation. But Warburton saw Johnson's production, and regarded it as the certain presage of his future eminence. And when that great critic, in the decline of life, was treated with indignity by his contemporaries, Johnson had the manliness to retain his veneration, respect and gratitude for him to the last.

Having therefore finished the undertaking, which then attracted and commanded the most general approbation, he renewed his application to the text of Shakespeare. The scope of this work he delineates at large in a pamphlet which he then published, and which is composed with the author's usual manliness, decency, and elegance. He enumerates, as might be expected, the defects of former editors. These he promises to supply. He also specifies the general sources of their errors, which he thinks may be rectified.

From the nature of his former labours, and the consequence which he derived from genius, from industry, and from success, he presumes to think himself better qualified to do his author justice than most of those who preceded him. "With regard to obsolete or peculiar diction," says he, "the editor may perhaps claim some degree of confidence, having had more motives to consider the whole extent of our language than any other man from its first formation. He hopes that, by comparing the works of Shakespeare with those of writers who lived at the same time, immediately preceded, or immediately followed him, he shall be able to ascertain his ambiguities, disentangle his intricacies, and recover the meaning of words now lost in the darkness of antiquity."

He adds what must give the reader a very just and distinct idea of the undertaking. "When, therefore, any obscurity arises from an allusion to some other book, the passage will be quoted. When the diction is entangled it will be cleared by a paraphrase or interpretation. When the sense is broken by the suppression of part of the sentiments in pleasantry or passion, the connexion will be supplied. When any forgotten custom is hinted, care will be taken to retrieve or explain it. The meaning assigned to doubtful words will be supported by the authorities of other writers, or by parallel passages of Shakespeare himself." [41]

The only publication in which we find him engaged in the subsequent year [1758] is the *Idler*, a periodical work, which he owned to a friend, consisted chiefly of some materials he had gleaned for his Rambler, a few pieces occasionally suggested by reading, accident, or conversation, and others rescued from the fate of volumes in which they had been consigned to oblivion. He amused himself by detailing these elegant and instructive papers in the public prints. They were immediately collected and published in two volumes, but on what terms is not known. Two essays which had not appeared were added, one on the epitaphs of Mr. Pope, and one on the war-like character of our English soldiers. The first abounds in false criticism, the second is little more than the vulgar rhodomontade of a hot-house politician, who is always ready to match one of his countrymen against three of any other in the universe.[42]

There is a common prejudice in the world against second parts. But the *Idler* ought not to be considered as a continuation of the Rambler. It seems, from the introductory number to have been contrived on quite a different plan. And the character of an *Idler* is supported throughout with no inconsiderable share of propriety and spirit. Were I disposed to compare the excellence of these two valuable performances, I should not hesitate to prefer the *Idler*. The leading idea is not only more original, but it associates a greater variety of subjects, in the discussion of which the author had an opportunity of indulging his own feelings, apologizing for his own habits, and pouring out his mind in speculations the more mature, that his heart as well as his genius, was interested; and to such as knew him familiarly it is obvious that he often describes the foibles of his imaginary beings in terms applicable only to his own.

It is not improbable that his *Translation of Father Lobo's Voyage to Abyssinia* contributed to facilitate his acquaintance with the tropical language of the Orientals. His powers of imagination were vigorous and active, and notwithstanding the truth of his conceptions, he seems from the first to have been not a little dazzled by splendour of expression. The charge of an over-wrought or blown stile, which has been so frequently, and not altogether unjustly made against his writings, might arise from this taste, which all his experience and strength of mind could never finally suppress.

From the Preface of a work so little known, and yet so laborious, I cannot resist the pleasure of presenting the reader with the following short extract. It exhibits, in my opinion, Johnson's manner, and shews that whatever his improvements afterwards were, his plan of composition, his mode of thinking, and his superiority to the prejudices of the vulgar, must have been original and unvaried.

The following relation (says he) is so curious and entertaining, and the dissertation that accompany it so judicious and instructive, that the translator is confident his attempt stands in need of no apology, whatever censures may fall on the performance.

The Portuguese traveller, contrary to the general vein of his countrymen, has amused his reader with no romantic absurdity or incredible fictions; whatever he relates, whether true or not, is at least probable; and he who tells nothing exceeding the bounds of probability, has a right to demand that they should believe him, who cannot contradict him.

He appears by his modest and unaffected narration to have described things as he saw them, to have copied nature from the life, and to have consulted his senses, not his imagination; he meets with no basilisks that destroy with their eyes, his crocodiles devour their prey without tears, and his cataracts fall from the rocks without deafening the neighbouring inhabitants.

The reader will here find no regions cursed with irremediable barrenness, or blessed with spontaneous fecundity, no perpetual gloom, or unceasing sunshine; nor are the nations here described either devoid of all sense of humanity or consummate in all private or social virtues. Here are no Hottentots without religion, polity, or articulate language; no Chinese perfectly polite, and completely skilled in all sciences; he will discover, what will always be discovered by a diligent and impartial enquirer, that wherever human nature is to be found, there is a mixture of vice and virtue; a contest of passion and reason, and that the Creator doth not appear partial in his distributions, but has balanced in most countries their particular inconveniences by particular favours.[43]

It is known to many of the Doctor's friends, that his *Rasselas or Prince of Abyssinia,* was an early conception, on which his ideas were matured long before the completion of the work. He shewed the first lines of it to a Bookseller, who gave him no encouragement to proceed; but the confidence of genius was not to be baffled or repressed by the cold suggestions of interested ignorance. The stroke betrayed the hand of a master, but there wanted the taste of Protogenes to discern it. The outlines of this immortal work could not procure the author credit for twenty guineas. His mother was dying of a good old age. He wished to raise this sum that he might be able to see her on her death-bed. He sat down to finish his plan, and notwithstanding his expeditious composition, she died before he could make it convenient to visit her. The forty-first number of his Idler probably relates to the circumstance of her death. The Prince of Abyssinia was sold to another Bookseller, and had a very considerable sale.[44]

We are now come to the æra of his pension. It originated with Lord Bute, though the Doctor since the odium which attended the administration of that nobleman, drove him to the shades, affected always to give the sole merit of it to his Majesty. The manner by which he received it has been detailed especially since his death, probably by Mr. Murphy, or some one desirous of publishing the concern which he had in the transaction. It was owing however entirely to his own merit, without the solicitation of a mistress or a player in his favour.[45] He was not the man who would have owed an obligation to the creature or courtezan of any minister on earth.

Johnson had conceived a strong prejudice against Lord Bute. He dined at Mr. Elphinston's but a few days before the pension was proposed. He was there asked, why he had shewn such dislike to the minister; because, said he, he gave the king a wrong education. He had only taught him, added Johnson, to *draw a tree*.[46]

It was not above a day or two after this that the fact was mentioned in the newspapers. Mr. Elphinston hastened to congratulate his friend on this unexpected accession of good fortune. Johnson related the matter circumstantially. Nothing he said could have been given more handsomely. When proposed to his Majesty, a certain Lord, [47] whom he would not name, was abundantly sarcastic on his character, and mentioned his political principles as inimical to the House of Hanover. Lord Bute's answer was, that if these were the Doctor's principles, there was merit in his suppressing them; that if he had not made an improper use of them without any acknowledgement from court, it was not very likely he would, when that should take place, and that it was intended to reward his writings which were before the public, without any regard to such principles as he kept to himself.

Johnson was now in a state of independence; but his habit of literary composition was but little enervated, though no longer excited by necessity. The work which engrossed his attention was his long projected and promised edition of Shakespeare. This in 1765 was published by subscription, and especially since joined to the critical labours of Mr. Steevens, is become a valuable acquisition to literary criticism.

His notes in various parts of the work, his explanation of difficult passages, his development of hidden beauties, his interpretations of obscurities, and his candour and ingenuity in reconciling inconsistencies, discover no superficial acquaintance with either men or books. Many think the text not deserving the commentary, few who are judges think the commentary at least not equal to the text. This is the favourite bard of Englishmen, and he owes his immortality to their discernment, as in every other nation his absurdities had probably buried him in oblivion. It was said by one of the Popes, with the usual decency of professional impostors, that a book which required so much explanation as the Bible, ought not to have been written. This witticism applied to Shakespeare would be deemed blasphemy, and yet apart from a few splendid passages, what do we find in his plays to justify their excessive popularity, or to give the author that super-eminence which he has so long enjoyed on the English stage? Do they serve to correct the taste, improve the heart, enlighten the understanding, or facilitate any one purpose of public utility. His characters are in fact all monsters, his heroes madmen, his wits buffoons, and his women strumpets, viragos, or idiots. He confounds the relations of things by aiming at no moral object, and for pleasantry often substitutes the grossest obscenity. His creations are as preposterous as they are numerous, and whenever he would declaim his thoughts are vulgar, and his expressions quaint or turgid or obscure. He makes Achilles and other illustrious characters of antiquity hector like bullies in a brothel, and puts in the mouths of his heroines the ribaldry of Billingsgate. There is not a rule in dramatic composition which he does not habitually violate. He is called the poet of nature, and he certainly imitates her deformities with exactness, but seldom aims at that preference of art which consists in copying her excellence. The profusion of intemperate praise which accompanies his memory indicates much oftener an abject deference for the opinion of the multitude than any real sense of intrinsic merit. And many a reader fancies himself charmed with the beauties, who is only a dupe to the name of an author. Johnson was not a critic to be misled by report, while he could have access to the truth. He even says, that there is *not one of Shakespeare's plays which were it now to be exhibited as the work of a cotemporary writer, would be heard to the conclusion.*[48] And he states the excellencies and defects of his author in terms so equally pointed and strong, that he has run into paradox, where he meant only to be impartial.

From the party altercations which distinguish British politics, no Englishman of a speculative genius can be altogether free. And whatever principles are espoused, one party will always be disgusted in proportion to the merit with which these are asserted, illustrated, or defended. The abuse to which his pamphlets in favour of government exposed him, are to be attributed to this circumstance. He adopted the ministerial side of the question with all that promptitude of invention, that ardour of genius, that brilliancy of imagination, and that energy of expression which characterise his writings. And the *Patriot,* the *False Alarm, Falkland Island,* and *Taxation no Tyranny,* which were published at different times from the year 1760 [1770] to about 1775, will be read and admired, when the heats which occasioned them are forgotten.

Prior to the unfortunate failure of Fordyce, Johnson in company with his friends Hawkesworth and Goldsmith, often visited that gentleman.

An acquaintance consequently commenced between Johnson and the Rev. Dr. James Fordyce, so well known for his popular talents in the pulpit, and his Sermons to young women. These were shown to Johnson and published by his advice. He even interested himself so far in the work as to write the title and the advertisement.[49] The author consulted him with a becoming confidence, and politely attributed much of the success attending that elegant work to his good offices. In truth, Johnson conceived a very favourable opinion of this reverend gentleman. He owned himself fond, he said, of a man, who notwithstanding the illiberality which still debased the literature of his country, had *no dirty heresies sticking about him.*

In the summer of 1773, he set out on a tour to the Hebrides of Scotland. His companion was Mr. Boswell, to whose polite attention and facetious temper he attributes much of the entertainment he received. His account of this journey is written with his usual attention to men and things, the ideas he conceived of the country, and his satyrical turn of thinking. It appeared in 1775, and brought upon the author a world of enemies. He was charged with gross misrepresentation, with consulting his prejudices where he ought to have consulted his eyes, and with substituting for the localities, he affects to point out those only which his cynical opinion had disguised.

But the chief controversy which this work produced was concerning the authenticity of Ossian's Poems. This he denies in the most unqualified terms, and dares the translator to shew his originals. He regarded the whole as an impostor, and an insult on the common sense of mankind, and observed, "that to revenge incredulity by refusing evidence, is a degree of insolence to which the world is not yet acquainted, and stubborn audacity is the last refuge of guilt." [50] This challenge was conceived as indelicate, and resented, not by an immediate publication of the MSS, but the grossest menaces. The translator's letter to Johnson on this occasion was probably not preserved; it extorted however the following reply. [The letter of 20 January 1775 to James Macpherson has been omitted.]

This was dictated from memory only, when Johnson had mislaid the copy he preserved of the original, which General Melville [51] has been heard to repeat verbatim, and which is said to be much more pointed. A meeting however was so certainly expected between these two literary heroes, that for some time after Johnson never went abroad without a stout cudgel, and his antagonist it is also alleged, was furnished with a similar weapon. Whether Macpherson was ashamed of his rudeness in addressing a person of Johnson's age and respectability in foul language, or apprehensive of the consequences which might result from an assault, is uncertain, but the matter never went further.

About Christmas, 1774, the Rev. Mr. Shaw was introduced to Johnson, by the kind offices of Mr. Elphinston. Shaw being a Highland man, the Doctor interrogated him much on his knowledge of the Erse, and whether the Poems of Fingal existed in that language. The answer which Shaw made was, that he often had wished, to be clearly ascertained of the fact, whether they did or did not. This candour and frankness strongly recommended him to Johnson's notice and friendship. He was always pleased when he heard him afterwards mentioned with respect, and when Dr. Beattie,[52] in a conversation on the Ossian controversy, ventured to insinuate something derogatory to the veracity of this gentleman, Johnson's answer was, *"I never before heard so much said against Mr. Shaw, and I do not believe it."*

The present Earl of Eglinton,[53] who has an attachment to the Highlanders, and their language, requested of Mr. Shaw, a copy of the MS of his Galic Grammatical Rules, which was granted him, and Mr. Boswell having seen it in the hands of his Lordship, begged leave to lay it before Johnson, as a proof that the Erse had not been neglected. It appears that either his Lordship had forgotten to mention how he got it, or at least that Mr. Boswell did not acquaint the Doctor with that circumstance. For on a morning visit, Shaw soon after paid Johnson, he was asked by him if he knew that MS as it did not appear to be ancient. The Doctor had been perusing it, and it lay on the table before him. Shaw's name, who had written an Erse Grammar, was prefixed to the MS which he therefore told the Doctor was his composition, and in his own handwriting.

Johnson immediately instigated him to publish it, and assured him the publication would be attended with both profit and reputation. He accordingly introduced him to Mr. Strahan, who printed it, and when he presented him with a copy, he expressed satisfaction at the mention he made of Mr. Elphinston's English Grammar; and when he came, in perusing the preface, to the following sentence, relative to himself, "To the advice and encouragement of Dr. Johnson, the friend of letters and humanity, the public is indebted for these sheets," he, after some pause said, "Sir, you have treated me handsomely; *you are an honour to your country."*

Besides a natural turn for the study of language, and the advantages and credit he had now acquired among his countrymen, Shaw turned his thoughts towards making a collection of all the vocables in the Galic language that could be collected from the voice or old books and MSS.

Having communicated his idea, in 1778, to the Doctor, and pointed out the difficulties and expence necessary to make the tour of Scotland and Ireland, the limited sale of such a work, and the uncertainty of subscriptions, he replied, that the Scotch ought to raise a fund for the undertaking. Application therefore was made to the Highland Club, of which Shaw had been one of the original founders, and which was instituted for the purpose of encouraging Galic enquiries, but he found that by the underhand dealings of Macpherson and his party, and Shaw's connexion with Johnson, nothing would be contributed. His disappointment he soon communicated to the Doctor, and still expressed the most ardent zeal to record the ancient language of his native country: he said he could muster, of his own property, from two to three hundred pounds towards a journey, and other expences, if he could entertain any hopes of being refunded by the publication. By a speech he made that day on the undertaking, the Doctor fully determined him to set off with the spring, the conclusion of which was; *"Sir, if you give the world a Vocabulary of that language, while the island of Great-Britain stands in the Atlantic Ocean, your name will be mentioned."* By such a speech, and from such a man, the youthful mind of Shaw went with ardour in pursuit of the objects in question. He performed a journey of 3000 miles, persevered and finished his work at his own expence, and has not to this day been paid their subscriptions by his countrymen.

Before he set out, he laid before the Doctor his plan of collecting and arranging his materials, asked his advice, and received his directions. He told him, that though he did not implicitly believe what was said in defence of, and against the Poems of Ossian, he, however, at present, could bring no proofs to substantiate the allegations for or against them; and that as a secondary work, he would do every thing in his power, to collect specimens, if such could be got, at least be in possession of facts, if not to satisfy the public, to remove all doubts from his own mind, of their spuriousness or authenticity; and that he would afterwards talk or write as he could procure evidence. Of this the Doctor highly approved, though it has been since asserted, that it was previously settled between them what proofs he should find. But they know little of the man, who can believe such scandal; and Shaw seems altogether incapable of acting with such disguise.

The sequel hath verified the sincerity of their mutual declarations; for the enquiry of the one has confirmed the incredulity of the other. What the Doctor doubted Shaw has proved, and the virulence shown by the party for Ossian against Shaw, which has since been refuted, is but a fresh proof of the imposture.

So far was the Doctor interested in the success and fortunes of his coadjutor in this business, that he addressed him to take orders in the Church of England, but he lived not to see him provided for. Upon his going to settle in Kent, in 1780, as a curate, the Doctor wrote to Mr. Allen, the Vicar of St. Nicholas, Rochester, in his favour, the follow-ing letter.

Sir,
Mr. William Shaw, the gentleman from whom you will receive this, is a studi-ous and literary man; he is a stranger, and will be glad to be introduced into proper company; and he is my friend, and any civility you shall shew him, will be an obligation on,

Sir,
your most obedient servant,
Signed   Sam. Johnson.[54]

The enquiry into the authenticity of Ossian was published by his approbation; but he expressed his apprehensions of the treatment that succeeded. He read the whole over to Mrs. Williams, as she has been heard to say, and said that he was much pleased with the proofs adduced of the imposture of Ossian, and the manner in which he retorted the abuse and scandal which M'Nicol poured out in his book against him.[55] He gave his advice and assistance in conducting the argument, and often told Shaw, *"We shall prevail in this controversy."*

The following letter, occasioned by Clark's answer to Shaw's enquiry, which appeared in some of the periodical publications, deserves preser-vation, as it contains such a recapitulation of the subject in debate, as gave the Doctor much satisfaction.

To Doctor Samuel Johnson.
Sir,
The controversy concerning the authenticity of Ossian's Poems is at last decided in your favour. But this detection has produced a spirit of revenge as disgraceful to letters as it is shocking to humanity. Thus the vulgar often mistake for a new star, the blaze of a meteor, whose transitory splendour expires in a stench.

It is, however, to you, Sir, the rational admirers of decency and dispassionate criticism now look up, with anxiety and solicitude, for a vindication of the gentle-man, whose character, friends, and prospects have been thus generously sac-rificed in defence of truth. He is thought to have written at your instigation. It was at least in confidence of your patronage that he thus manfully avowed his convictions. He is of consequence enough to justify even your interference: nor is innocence beneath the protection of any.

To crush the potent combinations raised by this contest, against every thing dear and interesting to Mr. Shaw, requires the most vigorous exertion of no common abilities. The literati of Scotland have, for the most part, been duped by the translator of these chimerical compositions. Their interest in the republic of letters, especially in this country, is at present very powerful. Some of their moral characters are unfortunately involved in the dispute. And to substantiate a proof that the poems in question are only a mere modern fabrication, at once destroys their veracity as men, and, as they imagine, deeply affects the honour of the country.

For these reasons, every possible effort will naturally be made to re-establish the fallen credit of Ossian. The translator, by every honourable means, no doubt, has at last wriggled himself into parliament, and the Highland clergy will be assiduous to serve him, in proportion as they may now suppose it in his power to return the obligation. Your silence, Sir, while all Grub-street is in an uproar, in a matter which originated with you, will consequently be attended with a new eruption of forgeries, from the same lying spirit that has already belched up so many. These, another fresh abettor of Ossian's ghost will readily detail, in all the ribaldry of detraction, and all the malignant acrimony of disappointment. And poor Shaw may adopt for his eternal motto,

— A barbarous noise environs me,
Of owls and cuckows, asses, apes, and dogs!

If a blistered tongue be the most infallible symptom of a diseased stomach, the case of his patients surely demand the most immediate prescriptions of a master.

Malice and Scotch cunning are surely united, and exerted against this unfortunate Enquirer, in a most extraordinary degree. The man, like Job in another case, is, in one moment robbed of his all. As a scholar, a gentleman, a poet, or a preacher, he affords his old Scotch acquaintance only a little ridicule or a vulgar sarcasm. His literary talents are denied, and he is considered as a man, equally destitute of letters, decency, and decorum. Yet Clark, who pronounces thus cavalierly on his ignorance, with almost the same breath, acknowledges himself indebted to his criticism. Strange John Clark, to confess yourself corrected in your favourite Celtic study, by one whom you tell us, so often and so roundly, knows nothing about the matter.

It might well be suspected that he who composed both a grammar and a dictionary, under the patronage of the first lexicographer perhaps in Europe, would probably be deemed by the impartial part of mankind, not altogether incompetent to the task. To render the victory decisive, it was therefore necessary, as far as the blackest aspersions and most contemptible insinuations could go, to ruin his moral reputation. They foresaw his knowledge of the subject could have no weight, but in proportion to his credit with the public. This once destroyed, the argument would necessarily be their own.

In short, these Scotch literati seem to hang together in palming these nostrums on the public, like so many jugglers, equally concerned in the success of some common trick, and Mr. Shaw, for having relinquished his share in the plot, is hooted by the whole honourable fraternity as a traitor. To render his criminality for this unpardonable treachery still more enormous, his religion is classed with his literary apostacy, and both stated as irrefragable evidences that he is utterly destitute of principle. And such is the general provocation which his alacrity and adroitness in this business have given, that he would probably run the same risque on appearing once more in the Highlands of Scotland, with the man, who, after turning King's evidence, should have the temerity to re-visit the cells of Newgate.

It seems therefore incumbent on you, Sir, to state the facts at large, which first led you to a discovery of this monstrous imposition, to rescue your Gallic coadjutor from the odium incurred by espousing your cause, to enter your protest against prostituting a polemical discussion to illiberal invective and virulent detraction, and to account to the public for their conduct, who, under pretence of vindicating a very frivolous truth, have essentially injured the most important virtues. Leaving Mr. Shaw to struggle thus, in a contest commenced by you, will be considered by your joint opponents, as a damning proof of his delinquency; of their surmises, in your suffering yourself to be imposed on by his artifice; and of your yielding to the weight of their accumulated virulence against him, after defying all that sophistry could do against yourself.

ANTI-OSSIAN.[56]

In consequence of this letter, had Johnson's health permitted him, during the last six months, he intended to have drawn out and published a state of the controversy from the beginning, to balance the arguments and evidence on both sides, and to pronounce judgment on the whole. This is a piece of criticism now lost, and much to be lamented, as the question concerning the poems attributed to Ossian, from the illiberal construction put on his opinion of their authenticity, interested him as materially as any circumstance of his life.

Though the following letter came into the Editor's hands too late to be inserted in the proper place, it must not be suppressed, as it is the first Mr. Elphinston received from the Doctor, and shews how long a correspondence of the most liberal and friendly nature, has subsisted between them.

To Mr. Elphinston.
Sir,
I have for a long time intended to answer the Letter which you were pleased to send me, and know not why I have delayed it so long; but that I had nothing particular, either of inquiry or information, to send you: and the same reason might still have the same consequence; but that I find in my recluse kind of Life, that I am not likely to have much more to say, at one time than another, and that therefore I may endanger by an appearance of neglect, long continued,

the loss of such an Acquaintance as I know not where to supply. I therefore write now to assure you how sensible I am of the kindness you have always expressed to me, and how much I desire the cultivation of that Benevolence, which, perhaps, nothing but the distance between us has hindered from ripening before this time into Friendship. Of myself I have very little to say, and of any body else less: let me, however, be allowed one thing, and that in my own favour; that I am,

Dear Sir,
Your most humble servant,

April 20, 1749 Sam. Johnson.[57]

In the year 1778, as appears from the date of the following, his friend, Mr. Elphinston became a widower. Johnson, who had long known the exquisite sensibility of his nature, entered into all his sympathies with his usual tenderness. And it is impossible to read his consolatory epistle on that occasion, without sharing that amiable philanthropy which he then felt, and which formed a very distinguishing trait in his character.

To Mr. Elphinston.

Sir,

Having myself suffered what you are now suffering, I well know the weight of your distress, how much need you have of comfort, and how little comfort can be given. A loss, such as yours, lacerates the mind, and breaks the whole system of purposes and hopes. It leaves a dismal vacuity in life, which affords nothing on which the affections can fix, or to which endeavour may be directed. All this I have known, and it is now, in the vicissitude of things, your turn to know it.

But in the condition of mortal beings, one must lose another. What would be the wretchedness of life, if there was not something always in view, some Being, immutable and unfailing, to whose mercy man may have recourse. Τὸν πρῶτον κινοῦντα ἀκίνητον

Here we must rest. The greatest Being is the most benevolent. We must not grieve for the dead as men without hope, because we know that they are in his hands. We have, indeed, not leisure to grieve long, because we are hastening to follow them. Your race and mine have been interrupted by many obstacles, but we must humbly hope for an happy end.

I am, Sir,
Your most humble servant,

Signed Sam. Johnson.[58]
July 27, 1778.

The Lives of the Poets is one of his greatest, and perhaps was the best finished of his works. It was undertaken so late as the year 1778. The design, originally, was only to have given a general character of each author, and to have fixed, as nearly as possible, the period of publication.

But the subject was too fertile and pleasing to be thus briefly dismissed. The booksellers agreed to give him two hundred pounds for no more than this, but his genius expanded with the rich fields that opened to his view, and facts accumulated in proportion as he continued the search.

He was engaged in this performance by a very general concurrence in the trade, to defeat the project which had been conceived of abridging their monopoly. This was the plan of Mr. Bell, who printed the English poets at, what he called, the Apollo press.[59] His edition was cheap and dimunitive, but elegant and likely to be popular. The booksellers were in hopes, the high reputation of Johnson, would, by this undertaking, prove a protection to what they deemed their property.

The only thing to be feared was the declension of those abilities, on which they depended, as he was now arrived at a very advanced age. But he soon convinced them and the public, that notwithstanding the disease and infimities to which he was reduced, his intellects were still unimpaired. His account of the metaphysical poets, his Memoirs of Dryden, and especially his Critique on Paradise Lost, are, in my opinion, among the happiest efforts of his pen, and written with all the beauty and elegance of which our language is susceptible.

Thus, by a most fortunate choice of his subjects, has this great man in giving at once stability to our tongue, and formation to our taste, established a basis for his own fame, which shall last while a vestige of the one or the other remains.

From this period, the cessation of all his labours, the public seemed anxious about his preservation, in proportion as it every day became more and more certain that they must soon lose him. He was consequently, in the evening of his days particularly, an object of universal attention and enquiry. The progress of his declining health has accordingly been traced in every [sic] account hitherto presented of his life and literary pursuits, with a minute and tiresome exactness.

In the year 1783 he was attacked by a stroke of the palsey, which deprived him for some time of the power of speech. But by the assiduity of Dr. Heberden and Dr. Brocklesby, his usual physicians, he was soon recovered to his wonted state of ill health.

In the month of December of the same year, a club was instituted at the Essex-Head, chiefly on his account, and by several individuals who wished to monopolize his company. He composed rules for its regulation, and seemed to enjoy it while he could give his attendance; but his infirmities continued to increase, and the constant evacuations to which he was subjected by an asthmatic habit, terminated in a dropsy, which in the spring of 1784, confined him some months.

It was now his friend, Sir Joshua Reynolds, conceiving that the genial climate of Italy might help to cherish or eke out a life thus dear to him, and to mankind, signified to the Lord Chancellor how seasonable and acceptable, for that purpose, two hundred a year more would prove to the Doctor. His lordship did not hesitate a moment in mentioning the circumstance in its proper place. But Johnson never was a courtier. Other claims and other accounts were more pressing. Though the greatest princes in the world would have been glad to confer an obligation on such a man, the necessities of his situation were overlooked. The present is neither an age nor a government, in which merit like his can expect more than bare encouragement.

The Chancellor however found means to acquaint him, in the most delicate manner, that five hundred pounds at his banker's was at his service, and he should think it money well laid out, if in any degree it contributed to his convenience. Johnson's letter on this unexpected occasion, though one of his last, is not the least happy of his productions. [This letter of September 1784 has been omitted.]

No event since the decease of Mrs. Johnson so deeply affected him as the very unaccountable marriage of Mrs. Thrale. This woman he had frequently mentioned as the ornament and pattern of her sex. There was no virtue which she did not practise, no feminine accomplishment of which she was not a mistress; hardly any language or science, or art which she did not know. These various endowments he considered as so many collateral securities of her worth. They conciliated his confidence at least in what he thought she was. He consequently entertained a sincere friendship for her and her family. But her apostacy appeared to him an insult on his discernment, and on all those valuable qualities for which he had given her so much credit. The uneasiness and regret which he felt on this occasion was so very pungent, that he could not conceal it even from his servants. From that time he was seldom observed to be in his usual easy good humours. His sleep and appetite, and the satisfaction he took in his study, obviously forsook him. He even avoided that company which had formerly given him the greatest pleasure. He often was denied to his dearest friends, who declined mentioning her name to him, and till the hour of his death he could not wholly dismiss her from his thoughts.

His dying moments were replete with that piety which adorned his life. The approaches of death shocked him to a certain degree, because he did not affect to conceal what he felt. Serenity or fortitude in such an awful situation, is the gift of few minds. He died in the full conviction of an eternal world, and the important realities of futurity, were consequently regarded by him with proportionable diffidence and solicitude.

A few days before his decease he sent for Sir Joshua Reynolds, and told him that he had three favours to ask of him. Sir Joshua, confiding in the Doctor's good sense and discretion, frankly promised an implicit compliance with his request. The first was, that though he owed Sir Joshua thirty pounds, he was not to expect to be repaid. This was readily granted. The second demand was that Sir Joshua should not paint on Sundays. To this a small degree of hesitation appeared, but however no positive objection was made. He desired as his third and last request that he would regularly every day read more or less of the scriptures; Sir Joshua bogled most at this, but the Doctor assuming much earnestness, told him how much he had it at heart, and hoped Sir Joshua's pledging himself to a dying friend might insure the literal and punctual performance of a duty, which would for certain be attended with the best effects, promised to comply.

The dispositions he made in his last will have been variously construed. And some have blamed him much for treating his poor relations so harshly, by leaving his whole property almost to strangers. He consulted however his own feelings, and we know not his principles sufficiently to judge of his motives.

He was uniformly through life anxious to communicate happiness to all about him. He had innumerable pensioners. His house, especially in the latter part of his life, was an asylum for the indigent and well deserving. It was crouded for years with aged invalids of both sexes. Mrs. Williams, the blind woman, lodged with him from Mrs. Johnson's death till within a few years of his own. He has celebrated Mr. Levet in a beautiful copy of verses to his memory. He had an annual feast for a numerous collection of old ladies whom he knew, and to whom on this occasion, he always gave his company in preference to any other engagement.

About seven o'clock on Monday evening, the 13th of December, 1784, this great and worthy individual expired in the 75th year of his age without a groan. And perhaps he left few behind him either of equal goodness, ability or reputation.

In estimating the real merit of this elegant and masterly writer, it may be necessary to attend not so much to what he knew as to what he communicated. His most intimate friends could obtain but a partial acquaintance with the former, the public are in full possession of the latter. It seems of very little consequence how the fountain is supplied, while the stream preserves its fulness and its purity. The genius of Johnson from whatever source he drew his information, whether his acquaintance with philosophy or philology was solid or superficial, or whether he was a man of science or only a mere lexicographer, abounded with originality on every subject which occupied his attention. His writings are not theoretical, but he often elucidates general knowl- edge without obscuring his stile by technical phraseology. How then shall the science of an author, who attaches himself to no particular one, be decided. To infer his ignorance of specific qualities, from his acquaintance with that alone which involves them, is like upbraiding the philosopher who studies the principles of mechanics because he is not a wheelwright, or a watchmaker. Examine all his allusions in his *Ramblers,* his *Idlers,* and his *Lives,* and let his science be estimated in the same proportion as these are adopted with propriety. What is it that has thus enriched his stile, and rendered all his details so much more interesting and original than those of most other authors. Is it not the solid and profound reflections of a sagacious, discriminating, and well-informed mind? In fact, it was by passing through this intelli- gent medium, that his various and literal communications accumulated all their value and importance, and what he has said of Dryden, applies with peculiar propriety to himself. *His works abound with knowledge and sparkle with illustrations. There is scarcely any science or faculty that does not supply him with occasional images and lucky similitudes; every page discovers a mind very widely acquainted both with art and nature, and in full possession of great stores of intellectual wealth.*[60]

To a mind thus manured in learning, science, and knowledge of the world, Johnson added such amplitude of wit as answered all the pur- poses of petulance, malignity, and amusement. It is however not a little singular, that with a bluntness of address, and a coarseness of colloquial expression peculiarly characteristic, he was equally without humor and superior to every species of buffoonery.[61] All his ideas, in whatever terms he chose to exhibit them, were brilliant, original and correct. He was a painter who seldom dealt in sketches. His pictures might be sometimes preposterous or fanciful, and not unfequently monstrous for deformity, but were generally finished. He possessed in an eminent degree the talent of elevating the conversation by an exuberance of classical and interesting sentiment, but in the course of a long life, and in the enjoyment of a numerous and polished acquaintance, gave few specimens of those elegant and social pleasantries which are often to be found in the company of the learned and polite. With a large share of good-nature he could occasionally be unpardonably severe, and he never was more entertaining than when he gave a loose to the sarcastic propensity of his nature at the expence of some character absent or present. The moment he found himself the idol of fashion, his conceit of his own powers was without restraint or decency. He arrogated the distinction of Dictator in all companies, delivered his opinions with oracular promptitude and decision, and spurned with impatience and scorn the most delicate contradiction. His respect for no party, sex, or individual, when the fit of talking had once seized him, could either qualify or suppress a favourite paradox, a rude jest, or a bold apothegem. His witticisms were rather strong and pointed, than exquisitely fine and charming, and more calculated to render us dissatisfied with what we cannot help, than by a group of agreeable associations to excite our gratitude for what we may still enjoy. No man ever discovered more humanity or discovered it in a manner less capable of disguise than he did. His heart was in unison with every thing that could suffer. He had no equal in affording consolation to the sorrowful. Pity always made him serious, and he never deemed that an object of mirth which tended by any means whatever to impair the happiness of society. He had no levity of his own, and was so far from relishing it in others, that he never met with a facetious character in his life which he did not either despise or treat with incivility. In short, his genius was fettered by melancholy and caprice, he was fond of appearing sententious and dispassionate and correct, and even his most sprightly ridicule was generally tinged with reflection and solemnity.

The anecdotes which have been told of him are endless. For many he is doubtless obliged to the fabrications of his friends, as well as his enemies. Report, for a series of years, has given him the credit for most of the best things that have attracted public attention. Some of these appear only an improvement of others, the second edition of what did not please him in the first, or an echo to sayings of which no trace probably remained on his memory but the sound. Whoever would make an accurate collection of them must inviolably adhere to arrangement. A great variety were dropt originally in Booksellers' shops, where he always lounged away much of his time, with a few literary and scientific men, whose intimacy and conversation it was his ambition to cultivate; and among people of fashion and distinction, of whose attentions, adulation, and friendship he grew immoderately fond in the latter periods of his life.

Long before he broached the idea of his Dictionary, or any other work which chiefly contributed to raise and establish his literary reputation, he was much with a Bookseller of eminence, [62] who frequently consulted him about manuscripts offered for sale, or books newly published. But whenever Johnson's opinion happened to differ from his, he would stare Johnson full in the face, and remark with much gravity and arrogance, *I wish you could write as well.* This Johnson thought was literally telling a professional man that he was an impostor, or that he assumed a character to which he was not equal. He therefore heard the gross imputation once or twice with sullen contempt. One day, however, in the presence of several gentlemen, who knew them both, this bookseller very incautiously threw out the same illiberal opinion. Johnson could suppress his indignation no longer. *Sir,* said he, *you are not competent to decide a question which you do not understand. If your allegations be true, you have the brutality to insult me with what is not my fault, but my misfortune. If your allegation be not true, your impudent speech only shews how much more detestable a liar is than a brute.* The strong conclusive aspect and ferocity of manner which accompanied the utterance of these words, from a poor author to a purse-proud Bookseller, made a deep impression in Johnson's favour, and secured him, perhaps, more respect and civility in his subsequent intercourse with the trade than any other transaction of his life.

Goldsmith, who hated the prudery of Johnson's morals, and the foppery of Hawkesworth's manners, yet warmly admired the genius of both, was in use to say among his acquaintance, that Johnson would have made a *decent monk,* and Hawkesworth *a good dancing master.*

Johnson often took his revenge. He had sarcasms at will for all persons, and all places. One evening these two wits were in company with Mrs. Thrale, and a large assemblage of fine women: Goldsmith, who was the most aukward creature imaginable in such a situation, overturned the tea-things as the servant presented him with his dish. He was speechless; and the ladies, after staring at each other, burst into a fit of laughter. Johnson only continued grave, and turning to Mrs. Thrale, *Madam,* said he, *can you tell how a man who shocks so much in company, can give so many charms to his writings?*

Johnson is said never to have forgiven a lady, then present, who whispered to Mrs. Thrale in a voice loud enough to be heard through the whole room, *These gentlemen publish so much delicacy, that they reserve none for private use.*

But whatever may be thought of his genius, his science, or his wit, the benevolence, the seriousness and the religious tendency of his moral productions are eminent and incontestible. He never made any attempt in historical composition. In other walks of literature he had few superiors, and he was undoubtedly one of the most popular authors of the present age. His regards for religion were sacred and inviolable. Those virtues and qualities which administer to the decency and felicity of life, derived from his pen peculiar aid and illustration. He was the friend and advocate of whatever enlarges, heightens, refines, or perfects the happiness of humanity. To this great and prevailing object all his labours had an immediate reference, and his whole life in public and private was consecrated to the welfare and the honour of the species.

12

(1786)

An Essay on the Life, Character, and Writings of Dr. Samuel Johnson

Joseph Towers

The attention of the public was never more excited, in consequence of the death of any man of literary celebrity, than by that of the late Dr. SAMUEL JOHNSON. Innumerable anecdotes have been published of him, his most minute singularities have been recorded, and his virtues, and even his weaknesses, laboriously displayed, by those who lived with him on terms of the most perfect intimacy. It is not my design in this publication to relate the transactions of his life, or to communicate any new anecdotes of him: but as so much has been written and published concerning Dr. Johnson, there may probably be some, who may be desirous to form a rational estimate of his character and of his writings, who would judge impartially of his excellencies and his defects; and it is with a view to contribute in some degree to that end, that this Essay is now offered to the public.

It is scarcely possible for any man, who has the least taste for literary composition, to peruse the writings of Johnson, without a full conviction, that he possessed uncommon powers of mind, and uncommon energy of language. His personal character appears also to have been peculiar and extraordinary; and such as must excite the attention of those who are curious in their researches into human nature. As he attained to great eminence by his superior talents as a writer, so as a man he was also distinguished by his virtues. But as he had great excellencies, he had also great weaknesses; and the latter appear sometimes to have been nearly as conspicuous as the former.

Some of the friends of Dr. Johnson have been led, by the warmth of their attachment to him, to estimate too highly his moral and religious character. When Mrs. Piozzi tells us, that Dr. Johnson had a mind "good beyond all hope of imitation from perishable beings,"[1] we can by no means assent to the truth of the proposition; and especially when we find her relating weaknesses of him, which would be thought disgraceful even in very ordinary men. Mrs. Piozzi also speaks of him, as "one of the most zealous and pious Christians our nation ever produced";[2] and in another place says of his life, that "it was a life of seventy years spent in the uniform practice of every moral excellence, and every Christian perfection, save humility alone."[3]

Mr. Tyers observes, that "when Charles the Second was informed of the death of Cowley, he pronounced, That he had not left a better man behind him in England." This gentleman also adds, "It may be affirmed with truth, that this was the case when Dr. Johnson breathed his last."[4] I feel no inclination to controvert any assertion made by Mr. Tyers; but cases often occur, in which we cannot agree in opinion with those whom we esteem; and I am far from being convinced of the justness of this sentiment respecting Dr. Johnson. The assertion of King Charles II concerning Cowley was not true;[5] and as we refuse our assent to the royal eulogium pronounced on that poet, we may also be permitted to question the propriety of its application to Dr. Johnson, and this without the least desire to do any injustice to his memory. In Johnson, considered as a man, and as a writer, there was much that was excellent and laudable, and no inconsiderable portion of what was otherwise. In forming our ideas of his character, we must separate the one from the other, if we would make a just and rational estimate.

That the assertion of King Charles respecting Cowley was not well grounded, perhaps a little attention to the characters of that age may be sufficient to determine. That eminent poet appears to have been possessed of very amiable qualities: but at the time of his death the illustrious Robert Boyle was living, who was as much distinguished for his piety and virtue, as for his philosophical abilities. In a moral and religious view, the character of Cowley could not be placed in competition with that of Boyle. It may likewise be observed, that among other men of eminent virtue of that age, Sir Matthew Hale was also yet living.

It was very pardonable in Mr. Tyers, and the other zealous friends of Dr. Johnson, to speak somewhat too highly of his character. The warmth of attachment to the memory of a deceased friend, was a sufficient apology for their conduct. But positions must not too hastily be admitted, which are not supported by fact, and which are not consistent with a just regard to the honour of human nature. It seems also injurious to the interests of religion and virtue, to represent Dr. Johnson as a pattern of human excellence. Better models might undoubtedly be pointed out. He had great virtues, but he had also too many striking and apparent faults, to be considered as a proper object of indiscriminate imitation. Highly as he thought of himself, his attachment to the interests of virtue was too sincere to have suffered him to countenance such an opinion. When, in his last illness, he said to his surrounding friends, "Don't live such a life as I have done," [6] he had no idea of being considered as a man of exemplary piety and virtue. There have been many men, who were more uniformly pious, and more uniformly benevolent, than Dr. Johnson, and who had neither his arrogance, nor his bigotry; and such men, in a moral and religious view, were superior characters. There were such men before the death of this celebrated writer, and there can be no reasonable doubt but that such men are yet remaining.

Having made these remarks, I think it here proper to observe, that I am totally devoid of the least inclination to degrade injuriously the character of Dr. Johnson; and that I only wish to see it equitably and accurately ascertained, in such a manner as shall do justice to his real excellencies, without injury to the interests either of virtue or of truth.

In every part of Dr. Johnson's life, he appears to have had a strong sense of the importance of piety and virtue; this was constantly exhibited in his writings, and often in his actions; but his reproaches of himself for not regulating his conduct according to his principles were very frequent; and seem, on his fixed and stated days of religious recollection, to have been very pungent. When he was fifty-five, he says, that from almost the earliest time that he could remember, he had "been forming schemes of a better life." [7] He was often struggling with his own irregular propensities; and his frequent bodily complaints had a considerable tendency to prevent him from employing his time in the manner that he wished, and which his judgment and his conscience dictated.

He appears to have been under the influence of strong sentiments of piety from an early period of life: but the first prayer that he remembered to have composed, and which was published by Mr. Strahan, in the collection of his "Prayers and Meditations," was written by him in 1738, when he was twenty-nine years of age. [8] Notwithstanding his conviction of the importance of religion, he yet represents himself as having been very irregular in his attendance on public worship. When he was sixty-three years of age, he says in his Meditations, in reviewing his conduct during the preceding year, "I have, I think, been less guilty of neglecting public worship than formerly. I have commonly on Sunday gone once to church, and if I have missed have reproached myself." [9] He seems also not to have been a very diligent reader of the scriptures, till towards the latter part of his life, though he appears always to have had a firm belief in the divine origin of the sacred writings. He confesses, when he was at a very advanced age, that there was much of the Bible, at least of the Old Testament, which till then he had never read.[10] His *Meditations,* though they contain some remarkable instances of weakness and superstition, afford, however, a strong evidence of the sincerity of his piety, and of his solicitude to regulate his life in conformity to the dictates of virtue. It is not unworthy of notice, that he composed and addressed a short prayer to the Deity, on the commencement of the Rambler.[11]

It is observable, that, in his *Meditations,* in which reproaches of himself for his faults frequently occur, no mention is ever made of that arrogance of behaviour which he frequently exhibited, and which yet seems to have been a predominating feature in his character. Indeed, the humility which appears in his Meditations, and the haughtiness which he often displayed in his conduct, form a striking contrast.

The arrogance of his manners must often have been extremely offensive to those who were connected with him, or who occasionally visited him: and he can hardly be supposed to have been serious, in what he said, with apparent gravity, to Mrs. Thrale, concerning his own good breeding.[12] If he were, it is a curious instance of the ignorance of a man of great abilities respecting his own character. That he was convinced, however, of the utility and importance of good breeding, is manifest from the 98th number of the Rambler, in which he treats of the advantages of politeness to individuals and to society.[13]

The manner in which he speaks, in his Meditations, of some of his deceased friends, sufficiently evinces the warmth of his attachment to them. He seems to have had much regard for Mr. Thrale; and the language which he uses, in speaking of his death, is striking and pathetic. "I felt," says he, "almost the last flutter of his pulse, and looked for the last time upon the face that for fifteen years had never been turned upon me but with respect or benignity. Farewell. May God, that delighteth in mercy, have had mercy on thee!" [14]

His entertaining Dr. Levet, Mrs. Williams, and others, who were incapable of maintaining themselves, in his own house, is a circumstance that places his character in a very amiable point of view: and he appears on many occasions to have manifested much tenderness of disposition. Mrs. Piozzi's account of the benevolence exhibited by him in his own house, is very honourable to him. "He nursed," says she, "whole nests of people in his house, where the lame, the blind, the sick, and the sorrowful, found a sure retreat from all the evils whence his little income could secure them." [15]

Mrs. Piozzi also says, that Dr. Johnson's "attention to veracity was without equal or example." [16] This seems an extraordinary assertion. Men of strict veracity are certainly not so scarce as this ingenious lady imagines. No reasonable doubt can be entertained, but that there are many men, whose attention to veracity is fully equal to that of Dr. Johnson. But Mr. Tyers likewise says, that "He always talked as if he was talking upon oath." [17] This, however, must be understood with much limitation; for he once said to Mr. Boswell, "Nobody, at times, talks more laxly than I do." [18] And that gentleman observes, that "he could, when he chose it, be the greatest sophist that ever wielded a weapon in the schools of declamation; but he indulged this only in conversation; for he owned he sometimes talked for victory." [19] It appears also from a conversation between him and Dr. [John] Campbell, that this gentleman had conceived an idea of this being a practice with Dr. Johnson.[20]

His ideas of education seem, according to Mrs. Piozzi's account, to have been somewhat peculiar, and somewhat inconsistent. He maintained, that children were not to be taught without the infliction of pain, and yet was a strong advocate for treating them with great indulgence. "No science," said he, "can be communicated by mortal creatures without attention from the scholar; no attention can be obtained from children without the infliction of pain; and pain is never remembered without resentment." [21] The whole of this is certainly not true. It is often very difficult to fix the attention of children; but that their attention may frequently be fixed without the infliction of pain, is a truth with which no judicious instructor can be unacquainted. And it is surely not true, that pain inflicted on children, with a view to their future benefit, is always afterwards remembered by them with resentment. It is somewhat singular, that he should speak of his own tutor, at the university, as so ignorant, that he did not think his instructions worthy of any attention; [22] and yet at another time declared, that if he had had sons, he would have put them under his care, merely on account of the good temper of the man, and his attachment to his pupils.[23] Such a sentiment, from any other man, would probably have been treated by Johnson with infinite contempt.

In some of the accounts published of him, occasional remarks thrown out by him in conversation, and which seem to have been the result of that propensity to contradiction by which he was often actuated,[24] appear to be given as his real sentiments: which was probably far from being the case. It can hardly be supposed, that he thought so lightly of parental authority as Mrs. Piozzi has represented; though he might certainly, without any impropriety, think that Cyrus, when he commanded armies, and conquered nations, was of sufficient age to choose himself a wife; and also be of opinion, that the daughter of a housekeeper might be allowed to sit down in the presence of her mother, without a formal permission.[25] Johnson might very naturally contradict any ideas on this subject that he thought absurd; but when he has any occasion to speak of filial piety, in his deliberate writings, he appears to have a high sense of its importance.

Mrs. Piozzi says of him, that "every word of his merited attention, and that every sentiment did honour to human nature";[26] and also that he was "the best and wisest man, that ever came within the reach of her personal acquaintance."[27] It is, however, somewhat unfortunate, that in the account published of Dr. Johnson by this ingenious lady, though, when giving a general character of him, she speaks in the highest terms of his virtues, yet many of the anecdotes, which she has related of him, are extremely unfavourable to his memory; and such as, it might naturally be presumed, a zealous friend would have suppressed.

In his early life, he probably suffered many of the inconveniencies of indigence. It was many years before his worth was known, or his merit acknowledged. He was feelingly convinced of the truth of the observation, in his own imitation of the third satire of Juvenal, that

Slow rises worth, by poverty depress'd.[28]

It was in the year 1737, when he was about twenty-eight years of age, that he came up to the metropolis, accompanied by Garrick, in the hope of improving his circumstances by the exertion of his literary talents. His first objects were translation, either from the Latin or the French, and dramatic poetry. His friend Gilbert Walmesley particularly mentions, in a recommendatory letter of him and Garrick to Mr. Colson, that Johnson meant "to try his fate with a tragedy."[29] This was his IRENE: but he probably had not interest enough to bring it on the stage: for it did not make its appearance there till twelve years after. He engaged, however, in the business of translation; but was soon greatly dissatisfied with the employment, and his employers. It was in the month of March that he arrived in London; and it appears from a letter written in his favour by lord Gower, and dated the first of August, the same year, that he was then extremely desirous of being chosen master of a country free-school, the salary of which was sixty pounds a year, and which lord Gower said would have made him "happy for life." [30] Thus humble was the situation, which was aspired after by the man, who was afterwards to be an ornament to his country by the splendour of his talents, and the value and importance of his literary productions. But even this humble situation he could not attain. It was necessary that he should be a master of arts: and the design of lord Gower's letter was to procure for him this degree from Trinity-college, Dublin, by the interest of Dean Swift, to a friend of whom his lordship's letter was written. The application being unsuccessful, Johnson still continued in London, and engaged in such literary employment as he could procure, and particularly in writing, for the Gentleman's Magazine, an account of the parliamentary debates.

His "LONDON: a poem, in imitation of the third satire of Juvenal," was published in 1738; and was afterwards followed by "The Vanity of Human Wishes," an imitation of the tenth satire of Juvenal. These are both pieces of great merit; and, indeed, all the poetical pieces of Johnson are so excellent, that we naturally wish them to have been more numerous. It is, however, observable, that in his *London* are some very imperfect rhimes, and such as could not have stood the test of that mode of criticism, which he has himself introduced in his biographical prefaces. In his *London,* he has given a very unfavourable representation of the metropolis of the British empire: but it may be remarked, that after he became possessed of an income which would have enabled him to change his situation, London was always his favourite residence, and he seems never to have been long easy in any other place. In his *Vanity of Human Wishes,* he exhibited in some degree his political sentiments, by the manner in which he speaks of the death of Strafford, [31] and by his panegyric on archbishop Laud, whom he represents as having been brought to the block by his genius and his learning.

> See, when the vulgar 'scape, despis'd or aw'd,
> Rebellion's vengeful talons seize on LAUD.
> From meaner minds, tho' smaller fines content,
> The plunder'd palace, or sequester'd rent;
> Mark'd out by DANGEROUS PARTS, he meets the shock,
> And FATAL LEARNING leads him to the block:
> Around his tomb let Art and Genius weep,
> But hear his death, ye blockheads, hear and sleep. [32]

Archbishop Laud undoubtedly possessed both learning and abilities, and in many respects promoted the interests of literature. But it was neither his talents nor his learning to which he owed his untimely end. The arbitrary principles of government which he laboured to maintain both in the church and in the state, his zeal in support of unjust claims, his persecuting spirit, and the tyranny which he exercised in the Star-chamber, and in the court of high commission, were the real causes of his being brought to the scaffold.

Among the earlier productions of Johnson was his "Account of the Life of Mr. RICHARD SAVAGE, son of the Earl Rivers," the second edition of which was published, in 8vo. in 1748. This has been thought too favourable to Savage; but it is an excellent piece of biography, and has great merit as a composition.

His LIFE OF JOHN PHILIP BARRETIER, which was published in 1744, is a very curious pamphlet; but it has little of Johnson's manner, and there is some reason to suspect it to be only a translation. Mr. Formey, secretary to the Royal Academy of Sciences at Berlin, published a life of Barretier, in French, from materials furnished by the father of that extraordinary young man in 1741;[33] and from some passages in Johnson's publication, it seems probable, that it is only a translation of that piece. But this I cannot affirm with certainty, as I have never seen the original.

In 1747, he published in 8vo. the "Plan of a Dictionary of the English Language; addressed to the Right Honourable Philip Dormer, Earl of Chesterfield, one of his Majesty's principal secretaries of state." He had now engaged in the compilation of his Dictionary, and was flattered by the prospect of the patronage of lord Chesterfield, who had testified his approbation of the undertaking. Though many literary men were at this time not unacquainted with Johnson's merit, and, indeed, had a high sense of it; yet his name appears not then to have been much celebrated, or very generally known; and this performance, which was very elegantly written, was well calculated to excite the attention of the public, and to shew how well qualified the author was for the execution of the important work in which he had engaged.

The same year he wrote that fine prologue, which was spoken by Mr. Garrick, on the opening of Drury-Lane theatre; and in which he so happily delineated the genius of Shakespeare:

> *When learning's triumph o'er her barb'rous foes*
> *First rear'd the stage, immortal SHAKESPEARE rose;*
> *Each change of many colour'd life he drew,*
> *Exhausted worlds, and then imagin'd new:*
> *Existence saw him spurn her bounded reign,*
> *And panting Time toil'd after him in vain:*

His powerful strokes presiding Truth impress'd,
And unresisted passion storm'd the breast.[34]

It was in 1749, when he had completed his fortieth year,[35] that his tragedy of IRENE was brought upon the stage; and on this occasion he appeared, perhaps for the first time, in the character of a beau. He then wore at the theatre, as he himself informed Mr. Boswell, a waistcoat richly laced.[36] This gaiety of appearance, as it was not very natural to him, was probably not long continued. The prologue to this tragedy was written in a much more manly strain than that frequently adopted on such occasions. It contained the following lines respecting the author:

Be this at least his praise; be this his pride;
To force applause no modern arts are try'd.
Shou'd partial cat-calls all his hopes confound;
He bids no trumpet quell the fatal sound.
Shou'd welcome sleep relieve the weary wit,
He rolls no thunders o'er the drowsy pit.
No snares to captivate the judgment spreads;
Nor bribes your eyes to prejudice your heads.
Unmov'd, tho' witlings sneer, and rivals rail;
Studious to please, yet not asham'd to fail.
He scorns the meek address, the suppliant strain,
With merit needless, and without it vain.[37]

IRENE is written with an exact regard to the unities, and the language of it is elegant and nervous. But it was not received with any great degree of applause. The author of it has observed, in the preface to his edition of Shakespeare, that on our stage "inactive declamation is very coldly heard, however musical or elegant, passionate or sublime." There may, possibly, in Dr. Johnson's tragedy, be too much of this "inactive declamation." It is not in a high degree interesting, and perhaps we may say of it, nearly in his own language, that "its hopes and fears communicate little vibration to the heart."[38] Such, however, was the general merit of the piece, that it certainly deserved a better reception than it met with. But, perhaps, the reason that it had no greater success in the representation was, that it was addressed more to the head than to the heart; and abounded more in strong and just sentiments, than in pathetic incidents, or interesting situations. Though one professed design of dramatic exhibitions is to instruct, yet to procure a temporary entertainment is the chief object of those by whom they are most frequently attended. As their aim is not the acquisition of wisdom, but the amusement of an hour, a very superficial piece may sometimes obtain the preference to one of much superior excellence. If ever the stage be really made in any considerable degree the school of virtue, perhaps the exhibitions must be directed by those who are not pecuniarily interested in the conduct of it. In large audiences, or popular assemblies, it is not always merit that obtains the greatest applause. Even in the House of Commons, where men of fine taste and just discernment might naturally be expected to be found, the elegant, the classic, the accomplished Burke, will sometimes meet with less attention, than men who are only distinguished by pertness and vivacity, and who are as much inferior to him in knowledge as they are in genius. On such occasions it seems too manifest, that it may almost be said even of the majority of that house, in terms somewhat similar to those of Johnson respecting the supporters of the Bill of Rights, that they are little affected by elegance of composition, and that their ears feel no niceties of language.[39]

The RAMBLER of Dr. Johnson first began to be published, in periodical numbers, in the year 1750; and it is to this admirable performance that he owes much of his reputation. It was not, however, on its first publication, very popular, nor very generally read. He says, in his last Rambler, "I am far from supposing, that the cessation of my performances will raise any inquiry; for I have never been much a favourite with the public; nor can boast, that, in the progress of my undertaking, I have been animated by the rewards of the liberal, the caresses of the great, or the praises of the eminent."[40] But the great merit of this work was at length generally acknowleged. It has since passed through many editions, and been translated into foreign languages. In the RAMBLER, indeed, the finest sentiments of morality and of piety are rendered delightful, by the harmony and splendour of the language. In his Lives of the Poets, as well as in some of his other works, there are no inconsiderable number of exceptionable passages; but his *Ramblers* are almost uniformly entitled to applause. The morality inculcated is pure, and the piety in general rational; and the criticisms, and observations on life and manners, are acute and instructive. It is one of those works which may repeatedly be read, and which will repeatedly delight. — Hæc decies repetita placebit.

As the *Ramblers* are less calculated for general reading than the *Spectators,* they have never been equally popular; but, perhaps, they are more interesting to literary men, as containing a greater variety of acute and original observations relative to the particular views, sentiments, and pursuits of men of letters.

Among the best papers in the RAMBLER, are those on retirement, on the regulation of the thoughts, the frequent contemplation of death, the importance of the early choice of a profession, the necessity of attending to the duties of common life, the history of Eubulus, on the inconveniencies of confidence and precipitation, the disquisition on the value of fame, on the requisites to true friendship, on a man's happiness or misery being chiefly to be found at home, on the inattention of men to the shortness of human life, the story of Cupidus, the voyage of life, on the sufficiency of life to all purposes if well employed, on repentance, on the necessity of reviewing life, the visit of Serotinus to the place of his nativity, on the necessity of labour to excellence, on the fallaciousness of the hopes of youth, and on the prospects of futurity.[41] The eastern tales, and some of his allegories, have also great merit; and the last number is a very masterly composition.

His character of Prospero in the RAMBLER, we learn from Mrs. Piozzi, was intended for Garrick;[42] and it might, possibly, be under the influence of some dissatisfaction from the behaviour of that celebrated actor, that he wrote the severe character of the manners of the generality of the players, which is inserted in the life of Savage.[43] He seems to have thought, that Garrick was more applauded than he deserved;[44] and, perhaps, was of opinion, that the profession of a player was rated too high. But there is no appearance of any resentment against Garrick, in what is said concerning him in the Lives of the Poets.[45] He there speaks of him with respect and tenderness; and whatever animosities there might have occasionally been between them, they seem then to have been completely obliterated by the hand of death.

In 1755, he published his DICTIONARY OF THE ENGLISH LANGUAGE, which was eight years after the publication of his *Plan*. The earl of Chesterfield wished to have had this great work dedicated to him; but as his lordship, though secretary of state at the time when the *Plan* of the Dictionary was addressed to him, had afforded the author no beneficial patronage, Johnson, with great spirit, and great propriety, refused the compliment; and he informed the public in his preface, that his work had been executed "with little assistance of the learned, and without any patronage of the great." He seems, indeed, and not without reason, to have had a considerable dislike to the usual modes of dedication: for he says, in his last Rambler, "Having laboured to maintain the dignity of virtue, I will not now degrade it by the meanness of dedication."[46]

His Dictionary was a work of great labour, and great merit, and has not been praised more than it deserves. That it has faults cannot be denied; nor would any man, who was at all competent to judge of such a work, suppose it possible that it should be without. But by the completion of it, with all its defects, he might justly be considered as having rendered a signal service to the republic of letters. As our language had then attained to a considerable degree of perfection, it was important that a common standard should be established, which might at least have some tendency to prevent that perpetual fluctuation, to which languages are subject, and thereby to secure to the English language, and to English authors, a more permanent duration.

The preface to his Dictionary contains many just and acute observations respecting general grammar, and that of the English language in particular: and the close of his preface is highly eloquent and pathetic. During the time in which he was employed in the compilation of his Dictionary, he sometimes laboured under the accumulated distresses of ill health, and of a scanty and precarious income. "The English Dictionary," says he, "was not written in the soft obscurities of retirement, or under the shelter of academic bowers, but amidst inconvenience and distraction, in sickness and in sorrow." He adds, in the same preface, "Much of my life has been lost under the pressures of disease; much has been trifled away; and much has always been spent in provision for the day that was passing over me; but I shall not think my employment useless or ignoble if by my assistance foreign nations and distant ages gain access to the propagators of knowledge, and understand the teachers of truth; if my labours afford light to the repositories of science, and add celebrity to Bacon, to Hooker, to Milton, and to Boyle." [47]

His HISTORY OF RASSELAS, PRINCE OF ABYSSINIA, which was published in 1758 [1759], is elegantly written, and contains striking remarks upon the vanity of human pursuits, and the unsatisfactory nature of human enjoyments; together with a variety of acute observations on men and manners. But the representations given in it of human life are extremely gloomy, and more gloomy than are warranted by truth or reason. The character of Imlac is well sustained, and his enumeration of the qualifications of a poet is highly eloquent; but in some of the conversations between Rasselas and Nekayah, the princess is made too profound a philosopher. The character of the Arabian chief, by whom Pekuah was captured, is well delineated; and the disquisition concerning marriage is amusing and instructive. It is observable, that in this work the reality of apparitions is strongly maintained; and the remarks which it contains on disorders of the intellect, and the dangerous prevalence of imagination, seem to have taken their rise from those fears of some derangement of understanding, and that morbid melancholy, with which Johnson was not unfrequently afflicted.

The IDLER, which was finished in the year 1760, has, perhaps, hardly yet obtained the reputation which it deserves. It is not equal to the Rambler; but it is, upon the whole, a very pleasing collection of essays, and there are some papers in it of great excellence. Among the best papers in the Idler are those on the robbery of time, on the retirement of Drugget, on the imprisonment of debtors, on the uncertainty of friendship, admonitions on the flight of time, the journey of Will Marvel, on the necessity of self-denial, on the vanity of riches, on the decline of reputation, on the progress of arts and language, on the fate of posthumous works, the history of translations, on the sufficiency of the English language, and on the obstructions of learning.[48] Some of the characters in other papers are also well drawn; and it is a circumstance rather curious, that the character of Sober, in the 31st number, should have been intended by Johnson, as Mrs. Piozzi informs us it was,[49] as a satirical description of himself.

His edition of SHAKESPEARE was published in the year 1765; it had been long delayed;[50] and, perhaps, at last, did not fully answer the expectations of the public; but many of his notes are valuable, and the short strictures at the end of the several plays are written with his usual vigour. His preface is also a composition of great merit; though there are parts of it which have somewhat of affectation, and somewhat of inconsistency; but it contains many fine passages; and some of his remarks respecting the unities of time and place are original, acute, and rational. In characterizing the preceding commentators of our great dramatic poet, he has treated Theobald with too much severity, and appears not to have done him justice as an editor of Shakespeare; but he is partial to Warburton, and speaks of the opponents of that prelate with a degree of contempt which they certainly did not deserve. Since the publication of Dr. Johnson's edition of Shakespeare, our great dramatic poet has been farther elucidated, and his plays enriched with many valuable notes, by the successive labours of Mr. Steevens, Mr. Malone, Mr. Reed, and other gentlemen.

Of the POLITICAL WRITINGS of Dr. Johnson, it would be injurious to the interests of truth, and to the common rights of human nature, to speak in terms of much commendation, in any other view except as to their style. His FALSE ALARM was published in 1770, and chiefly relates to the proceedings respecting Mr. Wilkes in the case of the Middlesex election, and to the petitions and public meetings which were occasioned by that transaction. His FALKLAND'S ISLANDS appeared the following year, and his PATRIOT in 1774. In the latter he ridiculed the pretensions to patriotism of the leaders of the popular party, opposed the claims of the colonies to be exempted from taxation by the British parliament, and defended the Quebec act.

In these political productions many positions are laid down, in admirable language, and in highly polished periods, which are inconsistent with the principles of the English constitution, and repugnant to the common rights of mankind. As a political writer, he makes much more use of his rhetoric than of his logic, and often gives his readers high sounding declamation instead of fair argument. And, indeed, in characterizing those who differ from him in sentiment, he seems sometimes to pay so little attention to truth, equity, or candour, that, in perusing his pieces, we are inclined readily to assent to a proposition of his own, that "there is no credit due to a rhetorician's account either of good or evil." [51] However we may respect the memory of Johnson, and however unwilling we may be to speak of him with harshness, those who impartially peruse his political publications will be obliged to confess, that few party pamphlets have appeared in this country, which contain greater malignity of misrepresentation. Even Swift, who carried the rancour of party to a great height, hardly equalled the malignity of Johnson's representations of those who differed from himself on political subjects. It seems difficult to suppose, that he could seriously believe many things that he has advanced, concerning those whose political sentiments were different from his own; and, if he did not, it is still more difficult to vindicate his conduct.

The petitions presented to the King about the year 1769, and in which many of the best and worthiest men in the kingdom undoubtedly concurred, are represented by Dr. Johnson as containing "the sense only of the profligate and dissolute." [52] And he was such an enemy to public assemblies of the people, and so little inquired whether what he advanced was truth in matters of this kind, that he maintained, that "meetings held for directing representatives are seldom attended but by the idle and the dissolute." [53] No man who had ever attended many meetings of that kind could be of this opinion; and next to a man's advancing things which he knows to be false, is his asserting things which he cannot know to be true.

In 1775, he published his "TAXATION NO TYRANNY; an answer to the resolutions and address of the American congress." The style of this pamphlet must appear extraordinary to those who are acquainted with the termination of the great contest, which then subsisted between Great-Britain and the American colonies. The terms which he employs in speaking of the congress, of the people of America, and of their cause, are grossly indecent, and unworthy of a man of letters, a Christian, or a philosopher. They reflect dishonour only on himself; and we are grieved that such sentiments should be couched in such language, and should proceed from such a man.

Dr. Johnson contended, that the parliament of Great-Britain had "a legal and constitutional power of laying upon the Americans any tax or impost, whether external or internal, upon the product of land, or the manufactures of industry, in the exigencies of war, or in the time of profound peace, for the defence of America, for the purpose of raising a revenue, or for any other end beneficial to the empire"; and that they had "a right to bind them by statutes, and to bind them in all cases whatsoever."[54] Every impartial man is now convinced of the injustice and ridiculousness of these claims; and there are few who do not lament that any attempts were ever made to enforce them.

It must always be regretted, that a man of Johnson's intellectual powers should have had so strong a propensity to defend arbitrary principles of government. But on this subject, the strength of his language was not more manifest than the weakness of his arguments. In apology for him, it may be admitted, that he was a Tory from principle, and that much of what he wrote was conformable to his real sentiments. But to defend all that was written by him, his warmest friends will find impossible. In all his political writings, the passages which are, perhaps, the most worthy of regard, and the best supported by principles of reason, are those in which he has introduced such arguments, as should prevent nations from being too ready to engage in war.[55] The inhabitants of this country have always had too great a propensity of this kind; and it is on this subject only that I would recommend to them some attention to Dr. Johnson as a politician.

It was in the autumn of the year 1773, that he undertook his journey to the Hebrides, or Western islands of Scotland; of which he published an account in the year 1775. This is a very masterly performance; for, besides a very pleasing account of his journey, it also contains a variety of acute observations on human life, and many curious incidental remarks relative to the history of literature, with which Dr. Johnson was very intimately conversant. In this journey he was accompanied by Mr. Boswell; and the habitual good humour of this gentleman, his vivacity, his love of literature, and his personal attachment to Johnson, together with his natural influence in Scotland, must have rendered him a very agreeable companion to him, during the course of his tour to the Hebrides. Of this journey Mr. Boswell has himself since published an account, which is highly entertaining, and which appears to contain a very natural, exact, and faithful representation, not only of the incidents which occurred during the tour, but also of the very singular manners of his learned and celebrated friend.

In 1779, when he was seventy years of age, he published his Lives of the Poets, which seem to have been the most popular of all his productions.[56] These, considered as compositions, and as abounding with strong and acute remarks, and with many very fine, and some even sublime passages, have unquestionably great merit; but if they be regarded merely as containing narrations of the lives, delineations of the characters, and strictures on the works of the authors concerning whom he wrote, they are far from being always to be depended on; the characters are sometimes partial, and there is sometimes too much malignity of misrepresentation; to which, perhaps, may be added, no inconsiderable portion of erroneous criticism.

The first life which occurs in this collection is that of Cowley, which is very favourably written, and contains an elaborate criticism on his works. The false taste, which so frequently appears in the productions of that poet, is treated by his biographer with sufficient indulgence; and we are apt to be somewhat surprized, that so fastidious a critic, as Johnson sometimes was, should descant so copiously on such petty conceits, as Cowley frequently exhibits. He is unjustly partial to Cowley in the preference which he gives to his Latin poetry over that of Milton; but his observations on the writings of the metaphysical poets are novel and ingenious.

The second life in this collection is that of Waller, of whom Dr. Johnson says, that, in 1640, he "produced one of those noisy speeches which disaffection and discontent regularly dictate; a speech filled with hyperbolical complaints of imaginary grievances."[57] This *noisy speech,* as our author terms it, was dictated by good sense and real patriotism. The complaints in it were not hyperbolical, and the grievances that Waller enumerated were real, and not imaginary. The grievances of which he complained were the encroachments of prerogative on the rights of the people, the imprisoning their persons without law, and the power assumed by the king of taxing his subjects, and seizing their property, without the authority of parliament; and the language of the complaints made by him on this subject was not too strong for the occasion. He afterwards made a speech in favour of episcopacy: but with this his biographer was better pleased, and speaks in terms of high commendation. The character of Waller by Clarendon is given by Johnson at full length:[58] upon which it may not be improper to observe, that the noble historian's account is in several particulars manifestly erroneous; and as it is said that Waller had some animosity against

Clarendon, it seems equally apparent, that the latter wrote the character of the poet under the influence of sentiments of personal dislike.

In his life of MILTON, he has spoken in the highest terms of the abilities of that great poet, and has bestowed on his principal poetical compositions the most honourable encomiums: but he has very injuriously misrepresented his character and conduct as a man. He could not endure those high sentiments of liberty, which Milton was so ardently desirous to propagate. He viewed with aversion the man, who had dared publickly to defend the execution of King Charles the First.[59] There is something curious, in tracing the conduct of Johnson with respect to Milton, and in observing the struggle which there was in his mind concerning him, resulting from his reverence for him as a poet, and his rooted dislike against him as a political writer. It can hardly be doubted, but that his aversion to Milton's politics, was the cause of that alacrity, with which he joined with Lauder, in his infamous attack on our great epic poet, and which induced him to assist him in that transaction.[60] But Johnson was unacquainted with the imposture; and, when it was discovered, urged Lauder to an open recantation. It is well known, that the forgeries of Lauder were completely detected by Dr. Douglas, and that by that ingenious and able writer Milton was sufficiently vindicated from the charge of plagiarism. But it is, perhaps, not generally known, that Lauder died, some years since, in very indigent circumstances, at Barbadoes.

It seems to have been by way of making some compensation to the memory of Milton, for the share he had in the attack of Lauder, that Johnson wrote the prologue that was spoken by Garrick, at Drury-Lane theatre, in 1750, on the performance of the mask of Comus, for the benefit of Milton's grand-daughter; and in which the following lines appear to refer to the detection of Lauder:

> *At length our mighty Bard's victorious lays,*
> *Fill the loud voice of universal praise,*
> *And baffled spite, with hopeless anguish dumb,*
> *Yields to renown the centuries to come.*[61]

But many years after, when his Lives of the Poets appeared, his old dislike to Milton's politics was again manifested; and we see strikingly exhibited, in his account of him, his reverence for his talents, and his aversion for his principles.

Dr. Johnson says, that Milton "left the university with no kindness for its institution, alienated either by the injudicious severity of his governors, or his own captious perverseness. The cause cannot now be known, but the effect appears in his writings." [62] That Milton thought the universities needed reformation, we may, indeed, learn from his writings; and many other able men, who have received their education in these antient and celebrated seminaries, have been of the same opinion. It is unjust, therefore, to impute these sentiments to circumstances of personal disgust, or to captiousness of temper. He has shewn, by his piece addressed to Mr. Hartlib, [63] that he had conceived ideas of a more perfect plan of education; and it is not a subject of surprize, that a man, whose understanding was so highly cultivated, and who possessed a mind so comprehensive as that of Milton, should sometimes form schemes of better modes of education than those which have hitherto been adopted.

Johnson ridicules Milton, with very little reason, for hastening home from his travels, "because his countrymen were contending for their liberty, and, when he reached the scene of action, vapouring away his patriotism in a private boarding-school." [64] The fact is, that when not engaged in more important occupations, Milton employed himself in the instruction of some private pupils; but he never deserted his principles, nor was backward to exert himself in the promotion of the cause that he espoused. There is no reason to doubt, but that he would have defended it with his sword, as well as with his pen, if a proper opportunity had offered; for his personal courage was unquestioned. But no proper military office was bestowed upon him, though it seems to have been intended, and was never declined on his part. His learning and abilities, however, qualified him to serve the cause that he espoused, more advantageously by his pen than by his sword; and he engaged in it with great ardour, and great eloquence, and in such a manner as excited the attention of all Europe.

But though Dr. Johnson at first attacks Milton for inactivity in the cause that he espoused, he soon finds his activity too great. He says, that about the year 1641, Milton "began to engage in the controversies of the times, and lent his breath to blow the flames of contention." [65] The truth is, that Milton thought, that some reformation was necessary both in the church and in the state; he was desirous of promoting the interests of civil and religious liberty; and, therefore, published such pieces as he supposed calculated to promote the cause of public freedom. Of one piece which was published by Milton at this time, on the subject of "Prelatical Episcopacy," Johnson has given the title, in order to shew that our great epic poet "had now adopted the puritanical savageness of manners." [66] But by those who impartially read this title, it will be difficult to discover any thing, to which the word savage can with the least propriety be applied.

Dr. Johnson says, that Milton's "political notions were those of an acrimonious and surly Republican, for which it is not known that he gave any better reason, that that *a popular government was the most frugal; for the trappings of a monarchy would set up an ordinary commonwealth.*" [67] Every man, who is much conversant in the prose writings of Milton, must be convinced, that this assertion of Johnson is not true; and all may be convinced of it, who will peruse his "Ready and easy way to establish a Free Commonwealth, and the excellence thereof compared with the inconveniencies and dangers of re-admitting Kingship in this nation." [68]

Other writers, as well as Johnson, have spoken with severity of Milton, as being a republican. But it could be no disgrace to any man, who had lived under the tyrannical government of the Stuarts, that he should think a republic preferable. His *Defensio pro Populo Anglicano* has also brought upon him many reproaches. But in this piece he evidently wrote in conformity to his real sentiments, and his arguments have never been refuted. Charles I had violated his most solemn engagements to his people, he had trampled on their antient constitution, and most important rights, and at length, in consequence of his tyrannical administration, deservedly lost his head upon a scaffold. It was this transaction which Milton vindicated: and he may be supported by reasons which will not easily be answered, by the ablest and the warmest advocates for royalty. Those who reverence Milton as a poet will likewise find, if his conduct be accurately and impartially examined, that he is also justly entitled to our reverence as a man, and as a citizen.

Dr. Johnson has given a quotation from Milton's second Defence of the People of England, in order to prove that he flattered Cromwell; and it is certain, that in this piece great encomiums are bestowed on the protector. [69] But Milton then hoped, with many others, that Cromwell would really establish a free commonwealth; and was far from being singular in forming high ideas of the protector's merit. It should also be remembered, that, in the same performance, he exhorts Cromwell, in the strongest terms, not to desert those great principles of liberty which he had professed to espouse; and shews what an enormity it would be, if after having successfully opposed tyranny, he should himself act the part of a tyrant, and betray the cause that he had defended.

Milton was first employed as Latin secretary under the commonwealth, and though he continued to execute the office under the protectorate of Cromwell, yet he never was a confident of Oliver's, nor was employed in the promotion of his views; and seems only to have written those public dispatches, which related to the general interests of the kingdom. He never deserted his principles; and was ever ardently desirous of establishing and securing the liberties of his country. As to the story which Dr. Johnson is inclined to reject, as "an obscure story," [70] of a reply made by Milton to his wife, relative to a proposal of his continuing to execute the office of Latin secretary, after the Restoration, it is perfectly suitable to his character, and is more probable, and much better attested, than many of those which are given in these Lives of the Poets. But it implied a degree of public spirit, and of consistency, in Milton, which Johnson was unwilling to admit.

It has been much lamented by some ingenious writers, that Milton should have employed so much of the earlier part of his life in the composition of his prose pieces, on political and controversial subjects, instead of applying himself to the cultivation and exertion of his poetical talents. But Milton thought, and perhaps not irrationally, that to promote the interests of liberty, civil and religious, to exert his abilities in the advancement of truth and virtue, was a more important and a more dignified employment, than even "embellishing original tales of chivalry," or "cloathing the fabulous atchievements of the early British kings and champions in the gorgeous trappings of epic attire." [71]

Mr. Thomas Warton, to whom the public are indebted for many ingenious and elegant productions, but whose political sentiments are somewhat similar to those of Dr. Johnson, has discovered the same propensity to degrade and discredit Milton as a prose-writer.[72] He says, that "his *Defensio pro Populo Anglicano* against Salmasius, so liberally rewarded by the Presbyterian administration, the best apology that ever was offered for bringing kings to the block, and which diffused his reputation all over Europe, is remembered no more." [73] That his Defence of the People of England, as it related to a transaction which happened more than a century ago, is not now very generally read, may be readily admitted; but that it "is remembered no more," is surely a strange assertion. But Mr. Warton also observes, that "Milton's plan of education to Hartlib has more show than value. He does not recommend those studies to boys, which, as Cicero says, in a passage superficially understood, *Adolescentiam* ALUNT, *adversas res ornant, prosperis perfugium et solatium præbent, delectant domi, non impediunt foris, peregrinantur nobiscum, rusticantur.* Instead of laying a stress upon such authors as open and enlarge a young understanding, he prescribes an early

acquaintance with geometry and physics. But these will teach no generous sentiments, nor inculcate such knowledge as is of use at all times
and on all occasions." [74] It might be inferred from Mr. Warton's observations, as well as from some remarks of Dr. Johnson, that Milton had
slighted poetry, history, and moral philosophy, and recommended little
attention to any other studies but those of mathematics and natural
philosophy. But those who will take the pains to peruse his "Tractate
of Education," will find that this was far from being the case. He
recommends, indeed, an early acquaintance with physical authors;
but he also says, "The main skill and groundwork will be, to temper
them such lectures and explanations upon every opportunity, as may
lead and draw them in willing obedience, enflamed with the study of
learning, and the admiration of virtue, stirred up with high hopes of
living to be brave men, and worthy patriots, dear to God, and famous
to all ages." He also hopes, that there might be infused "into their young
breasts such an ingenuous and noble ardour, as would not fail to make
many of them renowned and matchless men. At the same time, some
other hour of the day, might be taught them the rules of arithmetic,
and soon after the elements of geometry even playing, as the old manner
was. After evening repast, till bed-time, their thoughts will be best taken
up in the easy grounds of religion, and the story of scripture." He
afterwards recommends, that they should be amply instructed "in the
knowledge of virtue, and the hatred of vice; while their young and
pliant affections are led through all the moral works of Plato, Xenophon,
Cicero, Plutarch, Laertius, and those Locrian remains." And after mentioning other objects of study, he adds, "When all these employments
are well conquered, then will the choice histories, heroic poems, and
Attic tragedies, of stateliest and most regal argument, with all the famous
political orations, offer themselves: which, if they were not only read,
but some of them got by memory, and solemnly pronounced, with right
accent and grace, as might be taught, would endue them even with
the spirit and vigour of Demosthenes or Cicero, Euripides, or Sopho-
cles." He likewise remarks, that the plan of study which he recommended, was that which he supposed to approach the nearest "to those
antient and famous schools of Pythagoras, Plato, Isocrates, Aristotle,
and such others, out of which were bred up such a number of
renowned philosophers, orators, historians, poets, and princes, all over
Greece, Italy, and Asia, besides the flourishing studies of Cyrene and
Alexandria."

But though I think it appears from these passages, and from others, that Mr. Warton has not done justice to Milton's treatise on education, yet I perfectly concur with him in approving the following admirable observations of Dr. Johnson.

The truth is, that the knowledge of external nature, and of the sciences which that knowledge requires or includes, is not the great or the frequent business of the human mind. Whether we provide for action or conversation, whether we wish to be useful or pleasing, the first requisite is the religious and moral knowledge of right and wrong; the next is an acquaintance with the history of mankind, and with those examples which may be said to embody truth, and prove by events the reasonableness of opinions. Prudence and justice are virtues, and excellencies, of all times, and of all places: we are perpetually moralists, but we are geometricians only by chance. Our intercourse with intellectual nature is necessary; our speculations upon matter are voluntary, and at leisure. Physical knowledge is of such rare emergence, that one man may know another half his life without being able to estimate his skill in hydrostatics or astronomy; but his moral and prudential character immediately appears. Those authors, therefore, are to be read at schools, that supply most axioms of prudence, most principles of moral truth, and most materials for conversation; and those purposes are best served by poets, orators, and historians.[75]

In justice to Mr. Warton, it should also be observed, that however injuriously he may have treated Milton's prose-works, he has very skilfully and ably vindicated some of his smaller poems, from several erroneous and ill-grounded criticisms that have been published against them, and particularly by Dr. Johnson; and has also illustrated these poems, in his notes, with much ingenuity and erudition.

In the account given by Dr. Johnson of the religion of Milton, he has asserted what he could not possibly know to be true, and what those, who duly attend to Milton's character, will not easily believe. He says, that "Milton, who appears to have had full conviction of the truth of Christianity, and to have regarded the holy scriptures with the profoundest veneration, to have been untainted by any heretical peculiarity of opinion, and to have lived in a confirmed belief of the immediate and occasional agency of providence, yet grew old without any visible worship. In the distribution of his hours, there was no hour of prayer, either solitary, or with his household; omitting public prayers, he omitted all."[76]

As Milton is well known to have dissented from the established church, it is not a subject of much surprize, that he should absent himself from its public services. It may also be remarked, that the Nonconformists of that period were generally Calvinists, and Milton did not probably concur with them in opinion. These circumstances might prevent him, in the latter part of his life, from connecting himself with any particular body of Christians, and from attending their religious services. But it cannot hence be rationally inferred, nor because his stated hours of prayer are not known, that he omitted private devotion. As to private prayer, indeed, Milton had learned from the New Testament, that a man's private devotions should be performed with secrecy; and, therefore, we need not wonder, that of these none of his biographers give any account. But we are not hence to conclude, that he practised no devotion. That a man, whose ordinary practice it was to have a chapter read to him out of the Hebrew Bible, at his first rising in the morning, and whose writings breathe a strain of the most fervent piety, should omit all devotions, both public and private, is incredible; and, indeed, Dr. Johnson himself at last says, somewhat inconsistently, "That he lived without prayer can hardly be affirmed; his studies and meditations were a continual prayer." [77]

In his life of Milton, he has also made some remarks on the dangers attendant on the freedom of the press, and the inconveniencies which would result from restraining it. Much more, however, is said by him against it than for it; and on that side of the question his arguments are evidently intended to preponderate. But the positions advanced by him are erroneous and ill founded. One of his arguments against the liberty of the press is, that "if every sceptic in theology may teach his follies, there can be no religion." [78] But surely it is no necessary consequence of the permission of any publications in theology, that all religion will be overturned. Every principle of real religion is founded upon arguments, and upon evidence, too powerful to be shaken by the cavils of scepticism; and those theological dogmas, which require the aid of civil authority for their support, are unworthy of defence. The other arguments of Dr. Johnson, against the freedom of the press, are equally inconclusive.

One of the most censurable passages in Johnson's Life of Milton, is the following: "As faction seldom leaves a man honest, however it might find him, Milton is suspected of having interpolated the book called *Icon Basilike,* which the council of state, to whom he was now made Latin secretary, employed him to censure, by inserting a paper taken from Sidney's Arcadia, and imputing it to the king." [79] This ridiculous charge against Milton is so totally destitute of any proper evidence, and, independently of his character as a man of honour, so improbable in itself, that it is not easy to conceive that his biographer, with all his prejudices, could even entertain a suspicion of its being true; and it was extremely unworthy of Dr. Johnson, to give the least countenance to so ungenerous and so unsupported an imputation against an illustrious man, who was distinguished not only by the sublimity of his genius, but by his integrity and virtue.

But though, in his life of Milton, a propensity to represent his actions in a very unfavourable light is manifest throughout, yet when he comes to treat of his principal poetical productions, and especially his Paradise Lost, he has displayed their excellencies in the most animated and elevated language. He says of the Paradise Lost, that it is "a poem, which, considered with respect to design, may claim the first place, and with respect to performance the second, among the productions of the human mind." [80] And in another place he observes, that "his great works were performed under discountenance, and in blindness, but difficulties vanished at his touch; he was born for whatever is arduous; and his work is not the greatest of heroic poems, only because it is not the first." [81]

After Milton, the next life which occurs in Dr. Johnson's Biographical Prefaces, is that of BUTLER. From the little that is known of the author of Hudibras, it was not to be expected that the life of him could be very interesting. But Johnson has rendered his account of him highly valuable, by the striking remarks that he has introduced on literary composition, and on the means of attaining to literary excellence.

Of DRYDEN, whom he considers not only as a great poet, but as "the Father of English criticism," [82] the account given by Johnson is very curious, and more copious than his other lives. He was inclined to be favourable to Dryden; this appears in his general narration, and in his criticisms on his writings; and his turning Papist, on the accession of a Popish king, is dextrously palliated. [83]

In his account of ADDISON, the general representation given of his merit as a writer is very just, and very happily expressed. But he seems sometimes too much inclined to speak disparagingly of him as a man, and too ready to admit stories to his prejudice, without sufficient evidence. Addison is too much degraded in the business of his marriage, and the circumstances related concerning it are probably exaggerated. [84] Some particulars, which are disadvantageous to Addison's memory, are also, perhaps, taken too implicitly from Spence's account of his conversations with Pope; who appears to have retained more malignity against Addison, "from their antient rivalry," than is admitted by Dr. Johnson. [85] It may also be here observed, that the story related of Addison, in the life of Edmund Smith, [86] is a very improbable one, and very unsuitable to Addison's character. He was not a man to treat with contempt any objection to engaging in a literary work, which arose from motives of conscience. Had the story been related by Smith himself, the testimony of a person of so dissolute a character, ought not to have been implicitly received to the prejudice of a man, whose character for integrity was so well established as that of Addison. But Dr. Johnson received it neither from Smith, nor from his friend; nor are we made acquainted even with the name of the friend of Smith, to whom the story was originally communicated.

The criticisms of Johnson on the poetical works of SWIFT are very short; and he appears to have been uninclined to speak favourably either of his character, or his writings. The abilities of the Dean of St. Patrick's have, perhaps, been over-rated; but however that be, Johnson seems, as Mr. Boswell observes,[87] to have been prejudiced against him; nor has he done justice to his talents in his life of him.

The poems of PRIOR are criticised by him with great severity; and he seems, upon the whole, to have under-rated his merit. It would, perhaps, be difficult to meet with any reader of taste, who would concur in opinion with Johnson respecting Henry and Emma.[88] It is observable, that in his life of Prior, he speaks of King William, whom in conversation he distinguished by the epithet of "scoundrel,"[89] in more respectful terms than might have been expected. "King William," says he, "supplied copious materials for either verse or prose. His whole life had been action, and no man denies him the resplendent qualities of steady resolution and personal courage. He was really in Prior's mind what he represents him in his verses: he considered him as a hero, and was accustomed to say, that he praised others in compliance with the fashion, but that in celebrating king William he followed his inclination. To Prior gratitude would dictate praise, which reason would not refuse."[90]

In his account of Dr. KING, he takes occasion to censure the *wild principles,* which, he says, were introduced by Lord Molesworth in his "Account of Denmark."[91] These wild principles were the same principles of government that were maintained and asserted by Sydney and by Locke, and by the best and ablest writers that have appeared upon the subject. Dr. Johnson is mistaken in the story which he tells, in his life of Lord Halifax,[92] of that nobleman being disconcerted, and obliged for some time to be silent, when attempting to speak in favour of the bill for granting counsel to prisoners in cases of high treason, and afterwards urging his temporary embarrassment as an argument in favour of the bill. That circumstance happened not to Lord Halifax, but to Lord Shaftesbury, the celebrated author of the Characteristics.[93]

The life of POPE contains a variety of interesting information concerning that celebrated poet; many particulars in his character are nicely and accurately discriminated; and the comparison between Pope and Dryden is very finely written. But in his life of Pope, he has given the account of the quarrel between him and Addison, with too much reliance upon the testimony of the former, whose account is far from being entitled to implicit credit. Speaking of Pope's translation of the Iliad, and of Tickell's version of the first book, Johnson says, that Pope "was *convinced*, by *adding one circumstance to another,* that the other translation (that published by Tickell) was the work of Addison himself; but if he knew it in Addison's life-time, it does not appear that he told it. He left his illustrious antagonist to be punished, by what has been considered as the most painful of all reflections, the remembrance of a *crime* perpetrated in vain." [94]

Of this charge against Addison, and of other particulars with which he is accused, relative to the quarrel between him and Pope, no proper evidence has ever been produced. Dr. Johnson seems not to have examined the matter with much care: but many of the circumstances respecting it were examined with great accuracy by the late Judge Blackstone; [95] who observes, that Addison "had been dead many years before any of the particulars were divulged, and those which are now given us come only from Mr. Pope himself." The first regular statement of these accusations against Addison was published by Ruffhead, in his life of Pope, with the materials of which he was furnished by Dr. Warburton. [96] But as Blackstone has observed, and fully proved, "it is evident from dates and facts, chiefly extant in Mr. Pope's own works, that the account given by Mr. Ruffhead cannot possibly be altogether true, and is hardly accurate in a single particular." [97] Johnson's account and Ruffhead's are both evidently derived from the same source, the account written by Spence of his conversations with Pope. [98] But an exact adherence to truth, in matters in which his own interest or fame were concerned, seems not to have been one of the virtues of Pope; for, on several occasions, his veracity appears to have been more than questionable. [99] Some of the particulars in Ruffhead's account are inconsistent with Pope's own letters; and it may also be observed, that the elegant, but severe lines of Pope against Addison, were not made public till two years after the death of the latter; though it is manifest even from those lines, as Blackstone has remarked, that Pope himself did not then believe Addison to have been the author of the translation published by Tickell. Those who would judge impartially of the whole of this controversy, should attentively peruse the paper written by Judge Blackstone upon the subject.

In the account of the life of LORD LYTTELTON is a singular passage, from which, if taken by itself, it might be presumed to be Johnson's opinion, that every man of genius must, in the earlier part of his life, be a zealous Whig. But this will hardly be supposed to have been his opinion. He says of Lord Lyttelton's "Persian Letters," that they "have something of that indistinct and headstrong ardour for liberty, which a man of genius *always* catches when he enters the world, and always suffers to cool as he passes forward." [100] He has not done justice to Lord Lyttelton's merit as a writer; and seems to have confessed to Mrs. Thrale, that he wrote his life with some personal prejudice against him. [101]

Mr. Tyers says of Dr. Johnson, that "he was fitted by nature for a critic." [102] That he had great powers of discrimination, and often displayed great critical abilities, must be acknowledged: but it is at the same time true, that his criticisms were very far from being always just. It may, perhaps, be doubted, whether his various personal and systematical prejudices did not, in a considerable degree, disqualify him, at least in many instances, for properly discharging the office of a judicious and impartial critic. His decisions seem to have been received with too implicit a reverence by his friends and admirers. Whatever the conceptions of Johnson were, he could express them with acuteness and with vigour; and his criticisms were often rendered important, not by the justness of the remarks which they contained, but by the strength of the language in which they were delivered. In his Lives of the Poets, he has not done justice to the productions of HAMMOND, GAY, or AKENSIDE; and his rude and arrogant criticisms on the sublime odes of GRAY, can be perused by a reader of true poetical taste only with disgust. Nor do Johnson's remarks on Milton's LYCIDAS do any honour to his critical abilities. Few men of real taste have been insensible of its beauties; and Dr. Joseph Warton observes, [103] that as "Addison says, that he who desires to know whether he has a true taste for History or not, should consider, whether he is pleased with Livy's manner of telling a story; so, perhaps it may be said, that he who wishes to know whether he has a true taste for Poetry or not, should consider, whether he is highly delighted or not with the perusal of Milton's Lycidas." But Dr. Johnson is of so different an opinion, that, after a variety of ill-grounded strictures on this piece, he says, "Surely no man could have fancied that he read Lycidas with pleasure, had he not known its author." [104]

He appears to have had a very unreasonable and ill-founded aversion to blank verse, and a great dislike to pastoral poetry. He had, indeed, little taste for rural scenes: [105] and when he travelled through France with Mr. Thrale, would not even look out of the windows of the carriage, to view the face of the country; [106] and seemed to think the most pleasing prospects unworthy of his attention. Such a man, therefore, could not be expected to have a very high relish for those poetical compositions, in which the beauties of nature are described; nor could it reasonably be expected, that of such compositions he would be a judicious and impartial critic.

His life of Dr. WATTS is written with great candour; and, perhaps, he might be the more inclined to do justice to that ingenious divine, though a Dissenter, not only from respect for his piety, but also from some grateful remembrance of the assistance which he had received from his works, in the compilation of his Dictionary. He has many quotations from Watts, and has incorporated into his Dictionary not a few of the definitions which occur in the *Logic* of that writer. Mr. Courtenay, in the notes to his "Poetical Review of the literary and moral character of Dr. Johnson," has given eight lines from Watts's poems, as a sufficient specimen to enable the reader to judge of his poetical merit.[107] But surely to select a few of the worst lines of an author, who wrote so much as Dr. Watts did, is not a very candid method of estimating his merit. If Mr. Courtenay, instead of the lines which he has selected, had given Dr. Watts's ode to lady Sunderland, its elegance and beauty would have been acknowledged by every reader of taste.

The life of Dr. YOUNG, which is inserted among Dr. Johnson's biographical prefaces, but of which he was avowedly not the author, is not favourably written.[108] There is in it much zeal for the honour of Dr. Young's son, who appears, indeed, to have been injuriously treated; but too little regard for the honour of the father. Young had great weaknesses; but he had also considerable virtues, and great literary merit. In the life, however, which is given of him in this collection, his foibles are much more laboriously displayed than his excellencies; and if the son of Dr. Young be as dutiful as he is represented, which I am willing to believe, he cannot be much pleased at the account which is given of his father in the Lives of the Poets. Young is, indeed, justly censured for the many instances of adulation which occur in his writings; and his anxiety for preferment was unworthy of his character. But, in other respects, he is treated with too much severity; and his great work, the *Night Thoughts,* surely deserved to be spoken of in better terms than those of "the mournful, angry, gloomy *Night Thoughts.*"[109] In justice to the writer of the life of Young, it should, however, be observed, that in other places he stiles the Night Thoughts "extraordinary poems," and "ornaments to our language"; and that in some parts of this life the style and manner of Johnson are very happily imitated.

The principal fault of Johnson, as a biographical writer, seems to have been, too great a propensity to introduce injurious reflections against men of respectable character, and to state facts unfavourable to their memory, on slight and insufficient grounds. Biographical writers in general are charged with the contrary fault, too great a partiality in favour of the persons whose lives they undertake to relate. Impartiality should certainly be aimed at; and the truth should be given, when it can be obtained. But truth, at least the whole truth, is often not attainable; and, in doubtful cases, candour and equity seem to dictate, that it is best to err on the favourable side. No benefit can be derived to the interests either of virtue, or of learning, by injurious representations of men eminent for genius and literature.

Notwithstanding the errors, and instances of partiality and misrepresentation, which occasionally occur in the Lives of the Poets, they contain so many accurate and just observations on human nature, such original and curious remarks on various literary subjects, and abound with so many beauties of style, that they cannot be perused by any reader of taste without a great degree of pleasure. Besides their general merit as compositions, they also contain many particular passages of distinguished excellence. The character of Gilbert Walmesley, in the life of Edmund Smith, is finely drawn; the account, in the life of Addison, of the rise and progress of the Tatler, Spectator, and Guardian, and of the effects produced by those admirable essays on the manners of the nation, is just and curious; and there are many excellent observations on the modes of study, and on literary composition.[110]

Besides the works already enumerated, Dr. Johnson was also the author of many small pieces, some of which were re-printed in Davies's collection of "Miscellaneous and Fugitive Pieces." Among these are his preface to the Preceptor, and the lives of Roger Ascham, Peter Burman, and Sir Thomas Browne. The Vision of Theodore, the Hermit of Teneriffe, which was first published in the Preceptor, and which is also preserved in this collection, is a beautiful and instructive allegory. Indeed, all these pieces have considerable merit; and his Latin compositions, which have appeared in different publications, are elegant and classical.

His "Review of Dr. Blackwell's Memoirs of the Court of Augustus," which is printed in Davies's collection,[111] is written with great asperity. Blackwell's style, was, indeed, in some respects, liable to just exceptions;

but it seems sufficiently evident, that the high sentiments of liberty, which are displayed in Blackwell's book, was a principal cause of the extreme severity with which Johnson treated him. The "Dissertation on the Epitaphs of Pope," contains many just observations; but few compositions of this kind will stand the test of so rigorous a mode of criticism.

It has been lately observed, by Mr. Courtenay,[112] that "the papers in the Adventurer, signed with the letter T, are commonly attributed to one of Dr. Johnson's earliest and most intimate friends, Dr. Bathurst; but there is good reason to believe that they were written by Dr. Johnson, and given by him to his friend."[113] And, indeed, some of the papers in the Adventurer, marked T, contain such strong internal evidence of their being the productions of Johnson, particularly numbers 45, 58, 69, 74, 84, 85, 95, 99, 102, 108, 111, 115, 119, 128, 131, 137, and 138, that I have not the least doubt but that they were really written by him; and they have always appeared to me to be some of the best essays in this valuable collection.[114]

Dr. Johnson has been represented as a man of little reading. Had this been true, the observation of Churchill would have been just, that "he could not have been the author of the works which are attributed to him." Mr. Tyers, to whom he was well known, says, that "he knew all that books could tell him."[115] This is a strong expression; but it is manifest from his writings, that his reading must have been extensive. The same gentleman also says, that "with French authors he was familiar";[116] and Mrs. Piozzi remarks, that "he was a great reader of French literature."[117] We learn likewise from that lady, that in the latter part of his life, when he probably read less than in his earlier years, reading in bed "was his constant custom."[118] He seems sometimes to have spoken in low terms of his own acquisitions, from his high ideas of the powers of the human mind, and of the great intellectual attainments that might be made by industry and perseverance.

The particulars that are related, with respect to the celerity with which he composed his pieces, seem hardly credible. They appear, however, to be well attested;[119] and, if they are only nearly true, they imply an energy of mind, and a rapidity of composition, that are very extraordinary and uncommon.

Instances of considerable inconsistency were sometimes discoverable in Dr. Johnson's conversation, and in his writings. In London, he was an advocate for treating children with great indulgence;[120] and in Scotland, he contended for treating them with severity.[121] He maintained in conversation one day, that no child was better than another, but

by difference of instruction; and two days after, that "we inherit dispositions from our parents."[122] In his life of Pope, speaking of his private
edition of Bolingbroke's Patriot King, he observes in one place, that
"Warburton supposes, with great appearance of reason, that the
irregularity of his conduct proceeded wholly from his zeal for Bolingbroke,[123] who might perhaps have destroyed the pamphlet, which
Pope thought it his duty to preserve, even without its author's
approbation":[124] and in another place he says, that Pope's private
impression of Bolingbroke's work "must have proceeded from his general
habit of secrecy and cunning; he caught an opportunity of a sly trick,
and pleased himself with the thought of outwitting Bolingbroke."[125]
In his life of Milton, he treats with great ridicule the idea, that some
seasons of the year are more favourable to composition than others;[126]
and yet it is observable, that he says in his *Meditations*, "Between Easter
and Whitsuntide, having *always considered that time as propitious to study*,
I attempted to learn the Low Dutch language."[127]

It is a circumstance somewhat singular, that George Psalmanazar,
many years of whose life were passed in a course of deceit and imposture, should have been spoken of by Dr. Johnson as "the best man he
had ever known."[128] But that this was his real sentiment, appears not
only from the testimony of Mrs. Piozzi, but also from his *Meditations*.[129]
Psalmanazar was, indeed, evidently a real penitent; and many of the
latter years of his life appear to have been passed in a very conscientious
adherence to the rules of piety and virtue.

It is related by Mr. Boswell, that Dr. Johnson once said, that "he
believed hardly any man died without affectation."[130] When he made
this declaration, he seems to have been influenced by his own habitual
dread of death, which was certainly beyond what men ordinarily experience. There can be no reasonable doubt, but that men of great and
noble minds have often died, even on public scaffolds, and especially
in causes of the justice of which they were fully persuaded, with firmness, and even with chearfulness, without affectation. It is dishonourable
to human nature, and injurious to some of the most illustrious characters
that ever existed, to suppose otherwise.

In recording Dr. Johnson's sentiments concerning Mr. Hume, of
whom he had formed a very ill opinion, Mr. Boswell has made some
just animadversions on the character given of that celebrated writer
by Dr. Adam Smith.[131] It is surely extraordinary that Mr. Hume should
be represented "as approaching as nearly to the idea of a perfectly
wise and virtuous man as perhaps the nature of human frailty will permit." In support of this high encomium, no proper evidence has ever

been produced by Dr. Smith, nor by any other of Mr. Hume's friends and admirers. He might be a man of polite manners, a chearful and agreeable companion, be equitable in his dealings with others, and occasionally charitable to the poor; he might view the approach of death with composure and tranquility; he might be possessed of all the virtues that his friends attribute to him; and yet be very far inferior to many characters which have appeared among the professors of Christianity. Nor is there the least reasonable doubt but that this was really the case. Many men have been found among Christians, as much superior to Mr. Hume in virtue, as in rectitude of sentiment. Of Mr. Hume's fortitude in adversity, of great generosity displayed by him, or of any uncommon benevolence, no instances are recorded: but these virtues have been eminently and illustriously conspicuous in many Christian characters. If the character of David Hume be compared with that of Bernard Gilpin, a country clergyman, or with that of Thomas Firmin, a tradesman of London, but both acting under the influence of the great truths of Christianity, the striking inferiority of this celebrated sceptic will be apparent to every impartial man. These men were not merely of gentle and inoffensive manners, and of a mild and placid deportment; but they were distinguished by active and exemplary virtue, their minds were ardently engaged in the promotion of the happiness of their fellow creatures, and in their labours for this purpose they were indefatigable. But these men were formed by the sublime views of Christianity; and such men were never produced by scepticism or infidelity.

Having made this digression, I shall again return to Dr. Johnson, who is the principal subject of the present Essay.

He could not endure even a tolerable degree of moderation in a writer, when political characters or topics were the subject of discussion. He spoke of Mr. Granger in abusive terms to Mr. Boswell, as being a Whig; [132] though the fact was, that if Mr. Granger had any political prejudices, they were rather on the Tory side. But Mr. Granger was a very amiable man, and possessed much candour and ingenuousness of disposition. He was, therefore, inclined to do justice to those who differed from him, either in politics or religion; and this moderation led him to speak well of respectable characters of different sects and parties. It was this impartiality which gave offence to Dr. Johnson.

The style of Johnson appeared suited to his peculiar character, and mode of thinking. It seems too learned for common readers; and, on the first publication of his Ramblers, many complaints were made of the frequent recurrence of hard words in those essays. It was with a view to this accusation against him, that he wrote that essay in the Idler, which contains a defence of the use of hard words, and in which he remarks, that "every author does not write for every reader."[133] He was not ambitious of illiterate readers, and was willing to resign them to those writers whose productions were better adapted to their capacities. "Difference of thoughts," says he, "will produce difference of language. He that thinks with more extent than another will want words of larger meaning. He that thinks with more subtilty will seek for terms of more nice discrimination." It is certain, that passages sometimes occur in his writings, which are not very intelligible to ordinary readers. Thus, in the preface to his Dictionary, he puts the following question: "When the radical idea branches out into parallel ramifications, how can a consecutive series be formed of senses in their nature collateral?"[134]

He was occasionally fond of antithesis and of alliteration; and his periods are sometimes too artificial, and his phrases too remote from the ordinary idiom of our language. But notwithstanding the peculiarity of his style, he has seldom made use of words not to be found in preceding writers. "When common words," says he, "were less pleasing to the ear, or less distinct in their signification, I have familiarized the terms of philosophy by applying them to known objects and popular ideas; but have rarely admitted any word not authorized by former writers."[135] He considered himself as having contributed to the improvement of the English language. He says in his last Rambler, "I have laboured to refine our language to grammatical purity, and to clear it from colloquial barbarisms, licentious idioms, and irregular combinations. Something, perhaps, I have added to the elegance of its construction, and something to the harmony of its cadence."[136] Whatever may be the faults of his style, it has certainly great strength and great dignity, and his periods are often highly polished; and, perhaps, it would be difficult to point out any of his contemporaries, by whom the English language was written with equal energy.

When the great intellectual powers that Dr. Johnson possessed are considered, and the rapidity with which he finished his compositions, when he could prevail on himself to sit down to write, little doubt can be entertained, but that he might have produced much more than he did: and it was probably this consciousness that occasioned his frequent self-reproaches. The works, however, that he did produce, were very considerable, and such as will undoubtedly secure to him a great and lasting reputation.

With a slight sketch of some of the principal features of his character, I shall conclude this Essay.

He possessed extraordinary powers of understanding, which were much cultivated by study, and still more by meditation and reflection. His memory was remarkably retentive, his imagination uncommonly vigorous, and his judgment keen and penetrating. He had a strong sense of the importance of religion; his piety was sincere, and sometimes ardent; and his zeal for the interests of virtue was often manifested in his conversation and in his writings. The same energy, which was displayed in his literary productions, was exhibited also in his conversation, which was various, striking, and instructive; and, perhaps, no man ever equalled him for nervous and pointed repartees.

The great originality which sometimes appeared in his conceptions, and the perspicuity and force with which he delivered them, greatly enhanced the value of his conversation; and the remarks that he delivered received additional weight from the strength of his voice, and the solemnity of his manner. He was conscious of his own superiority; and when in company with literary men, or with those with whom there was any possibility of rivalship or competition, this consciousness was too apparent. With inferiors, and those who readily admitted all his claims, he was often mild and gentle: but to others, such was often the arrogance of his manners, that the endurance of it required no ordinary degree of patience. He was very dextrous at argumentation; and, when his reasonings were not solid, they were at least artful and plausible. His retorts were so powerful, that his friends and acquaintance were generally cautious of entering the lists against him; and the ready acquiescence, of those with whom he associated, in his opinions and assertions, probably rendered him more dogmatic than he might otherwise have been. With those, however, whom he loved, and with whom he was familiar, he was sometimes chearful and sprightly, and sometimes indulged himself in sallies of wit and pleasantry. He spent much of his time, especially in his latter years, in conversation; and seems to have had such an aversion to being left without company, as was somewhat extraordinary in a man possessed of such intellectual powers, and whose understanding had been so highly cultivated.

He sometimes discovered much impetuosity and irritability of temper, and was too ready to take offence at others; but when concessions were made, he was easily appeased. For those from whom he had received kindness in the earlier part of his life, he seemed ever to retain a particular regard, and manifested much gratitude towards those by whom he had at any time been benefited. He was soon offended with pertness, or ignorance: but he sometimes seemed to be conscious of having answered the questions of others with too much roughness; and was then desirous to discover more gentleness of temper, and to communicate information with more suavity of manners.[137] When not under the influence of personal pique, of pride, or of religious or political prejudices, he seems to have had great ardour of benevolence; and, on some occasions, he gave very signal proofs of generosity and humanity.

He was naturally melancholy, and his views of human life appear to have been habitually gloomy. This appears in his *Rasselas,* and in many passages of his writings. It was also a striking part of the character of Dr. Johnson, that with powers of mind that did honour to human nature, he had weaknesses and prejudices that seemed suited only to the lowest of the species. His piety was strongly tinctured with superstition; and we are astonished to find the author of the Rambler expressing serious concern, because he had put milk into his tea on a Good Friday.[138] His custom of praying for the dead, though unsupported by reason or by scripture, was a less irrational superstition. Indeed, one of the great features of Johnson's character, was a degree of bigotry, both in politics and in religion, which is now seldom to be met with in persons of a cultivated understanding. Few other men could have been found, in the present age, whose political bigotry would have led them to style the celebrated John Hampden "the zealot of rebellion";[139] and the religious bigotry of the man, who, when at Edinburgh, would not go to hear Dr. Robertson preach, because he would not be present at a Presbyterian assembly, is not easily to be paralleled in this age, and in this country.[140] His habitual incredulity with respect to facts, of which there was no reasonable ground for doubt, as stated by Mrs. Piozzi,[141] and which was remarked by Hogarth,[142] was also a singular trait in his character; and especially when contrasted with his superstitious credulity on other occasions. To the close of life, he was not only occupied in forming schemes of religious reformation, but even to a very late period of it, he seems to have been solicitous to apply himself to study with renewed diligence and vigour. It is remarkable, that, in his sixty-fourth year, he attempted to learn the Low Dutch language;[143] and, in his sixty-seventh year, he made a resolution to apply himself "vigorously to study, particularly of the Greek and Italian tongues."[144]

The faults and the foibles of JOHNSON, whatever they were, are now descended with him to the grave; but his virtues should be the object of our imitation. His works, with all their defects, are a most valuable and important accession to the literature of England. His political writings will probably be little read, on any other account than for the dignity and energy of his style; but his Dictionary, his moral essays, and his productions in polite literature, will convey useful instruction, and elegant entertainment, as long as the language in which they are written shall be understood; and give him a just claim to a distinguished rank among the best and ablest writers that England has produced.

$$\boxed{13}$$

(1786)

The Life of Samuel Johnson, LL.D.

Anonymous

There is, perhaps, no instance of an individual that has sustained so much injury to his posthumous reputation from the ill-directed zeal of injudicious friendship, as Doctor SAMUEL JOHNSON. A life marked only by the common sterility of inactive literature, has been expanded into a source of voluminous anecdote — been tortured into becoming the vehicle of almost general history — and what is still worse, of no small portion of individual calumny. Under the Presentation of his Biography, the weak have shot their bolts of folly, and the malicious exhausted their resources of insidious traduction. Circumstances have been related which could not do him honour, and have given others pain. With a new and base species of intellectual anatomy, they have laid open his heart after his death, and have produced to the observation of mankind parts of its constituent materials not always creditable to the dead, but what is perhaps of still more consequence, in the highest degree, afflicting to the living. There are men, and those of the highest distinction and most approved ability, who have, doubtless, reposed often on the memory of past connection with Doctor JOHNSON — who have solaced present vexation with such a remembrance — who have cheared the hour of care and depression with the recollection of an intimacy of which they knew the value and never doubted the sincerity — of which they felt the loss but experienced also that gratification which resulted from the conviction that the affection, was once equal, and the esteem, reciprocal. These new historians, however, are too severely moral to permit men to derive their felicity from visionary sources — they have put a very abrupt period to several of these endearing illusions — they make Doctor JOHNSON speak from the grave to disavow esteems, which were once thought rooted, and by consequence to disclaim attachments that were once fondly believed to be immutable. — The writer of these few pages declines to comment upon such proceedings with the dilated vehemence which the subject would so well sustain; he depends upon honest sympathy, to which he trusts with so implicit a confidence, that he will not believe there can exist a cultivated mind that does not feel a ready and animated abhorrence of a conduct that tends at once to give instability, to every humane opinion, and to diffuse uncertainty and suspicion through every human attachment.

The authors of this recent invention of biography do not at all appear to have considered that if the style of criticism which they have adopted in the instance of Doctor JOHNSON were to prevail to any great degree, it would operate to the exclusion of men eminent for talents or literature from all the enjoyments of society. Labour demands relaxation, and genius pants for its native luxury in the embrace of indolence: but for these gratifications they must look in vain, when it is known that from the moment they have given any indication of intellectual superiority, they cease to have the capacity of friendship about them; and that instead of the companions of careless privacy, or the participators of thoughtless merriment, they must expect to be surrounded only by a set of people who are the spies upon their minutest actions, and the historians of their most indigested opinions. Under such circumstances a man's very virtues are at war with him, and turn traitors to his repose; his *pénates* are no household gods to him, since they try in vain to obtain him a security from inauspicious intrusion, or to afford him any protection against the enmity of injudicious friendship. A person will stand for ever on tip-toe, and of course be for ever uneasy, who knows that wherever he is placed, whether on high change, or with his back to his own fire-side, he is equally under the eye of scrutiny, and exposed to the operation of a critical measurement.

This practice, however, is not less injurious to the moral and literary character of an author, than it is destructive of his comfort. The hastiness of occasional impatience, — the effusions of constitutional irritability, — the suggestions of temporary suspicion as to the motives or intentions of those with whom a person lives which fly before the least discussion or consideration, and which he blames himself for having given birth to, — the paradoxes of mere colloquial display — the whims of indulged speculation, and all the other almost involuntary perspirations of the mind which escape from it in the gentle exercises of relaxation, and which, like the similar effect of corporeal motion, a man wishes to wipe away almost the moment it appears, are to be fixed and localized by the operation of this modern invention, are to be incorporated into his system, and made a part of himself, with this additional disadvantage to him, that in the proportion as this new accession to his frame is less perfect, it is more vulnerable, and as it is more exposed it is equally fatal.

The above are the reasons co-operating indeed with the almost indispensible necessity for circumscription in a plan like this, that have added at least an objection of principle to the obligation resulting from the locality of this life, to induce me to reject the detail of little petty anecdote that characterize the histories alluded to. There is a degree of information as to a man's more latent habits, the turn and tenor of his feelings and sentiments in situations of secession from observation, that is not only entirely as interesting as any other possible part of his description, but essentially and perhaps above every other circumstance necessary to the comprehensive and philosophical understanding of his character. It is an act, however, of somewhat superfluous benevolence, because much is wanted therefore to give *all,* and to distress by unwholesome repletion merely because the pain of inanition requires to be removed. It is with the view of the human character as with all other prospects, too many circumstances confound; they destroy what critics call integrity or wholeness; they make particular features too large to admit the collective countenance into the eye at once. — A man's power of witticism is as well demonstrated by ten specimens as by a hundred; his pregnancy or facility in making them will be as satisfactorily received on the credit of a general assertion, as by any accumulation of sayings that friendship can retain. No man can have pretensions to the distinction of a colloquial wit without saying many things that are either huddled into premature oblivion by the illiberal suppression of envy, or lost to society by the fallibility of friendly recollection. At last, therefore, it will probably happen, that general assertion is the ground we must resort to in a great measure, as the basis of our opinion. It is enough to have instances sufficient to demonstrate the existence of the quality; and whether it is in wit, benevolence, power of combination, or any other operation of the mind or intellect, multiplied examples must after this point be unnecessary if not useless; and as they cannot increase the conviction may perhaps only terminate at last, in confounding the recollection.

As the transcription of an author's works, therefore, does not make a necessary part of his personal history, it may perhaps be practicable to convey a correct idea of Doctor JOHNSON's general character, without pursuing him through the uniform tract of his daily occurrences, without following him through a tedious relation of domestic incidents of little variety and less importance, and above all, without making him guilty of the posthumous treachery, of violating established friendships, and spreading wanton injuries among the illustrious individuals, from whose confidence and familiarity he once appeared to derive pride and happiness. The avoidance of such a practice is a species of negative merit I make a bold claim to, but is, perhaps, the only pretension to biographical ability that I could urge with any propriety, or maintain with any proof.

It will surprize some of our readers, but is nevertheless a fact which a very few months will incontestibly establish, that the still, quiet, eventless life of Dr. Johnson will have given rise to a larger number of volumes in size, as well as in quantity, than was found sufficient by a most correct, acute, and elegant writer[1] to embrace the whole history of the British people, with the philosophical development of the causes of their progress, in manners, laws, commerce, literature, and politics, from the period of Julius Cæsar's landing on the Island to the æra of the Revolution in 1688. — Either the minuteness of communication in the one case must be extended to a length of superfluous and almost ridiculous expansion, or else our knowledge of our own history must be dark and imperfect to a degree of unpardonable contraction. — The reader will decide to which quarter he feels a stronger bias, in the application of the more unfavourable alternative.

SAMUEL JOHNSON was born in Sept. 1709, in the parish of St. Mary, Lichfield, Staffordshire, and christened on the 7th of the said month. His father's name was Michael, and by the register of his son's birth is styled *Gentleman*. With that noble contempt, however, of distinction, merely collateral and accidental, which is so apt to adhere about minds that feel any foundation for a just confidence in themselves, Doctor Johnson declines availing himself of the *gentility* of his father, and describes him in a passage in the lives of the poets, under the denomination that is now well known to be his real designation, "as an old bookseller."[2]

The following account of some of the earlier circumstances in the life of Mr. Johnson, are related by a writer [Mrs. Piozzi] as easy and elegant in the style of her communications, as injudicious in the principle of them, who possesses a sufficient portion of female virtue to entitle her to a lenient consideration of a few female frailties, and who is so singularly paradoxical in the frame and constitution of her mind, that her veracity may be implicitly trusted to for facts, when it is by no means certain that her ardent and high-flown professions of friendship can be always confided in for sincerity.[3] [Omitted.]

Mr. JOHNSON received the first rudiments of regular school education from a Mr. Hunter, at that time a popular teacher of Lichfield, and a man not without talents, so far at least as classical attainments extended, abundantly adequate to his situation. But he was in other respects a man so unconciliating and overbearing, that the esteem for his erudition was lost in the abhorrence of his inurbanity; and as Johnson used very emphatically to describe the durable impressions of his tyranny, "No man that had ever been educated at that school was known to send his son there."[4] There was a success about his instruction, however, sufficiently rare in the history of a country pedagogue, as he had the good fortune to prepare for their public figure in life, men the most eminent in the times they lived in: namely, Bishop Smalridge; the acute and able metaphysician, Mr. Wollaston; the learned and pious Bishop of Bristol, Dr. Newton; that able lawyer, Lord Chief Justice Willes; and the last great ornament of his learned labours, our Author himself.

At the age of eighteen Mr. Johnson quitted school and was admitted on the 8th [31st] of October 1728, of Pembroke College, Oxford, under the tuition of Mr. Jorden, a man more distinguished, as Johnson constantly described him, for the parental zeal and the unaffected good nature shewn in the exercise of his office, than for any transcendency of natural endowment, or proficiency in literature.[5] Doctor Adams and Doctor Taylor were his cotemporaries and associates, and are now living to lament the loss of so early and valuable a friend.

Doctor JOHNSON did not stay to take a degree at the University, but left it after a residence of two years. There are no well attested instances of any extraordinary indication of his uncommon talents during this period, although he always remembered his *alma mater* with a fervour of attachment not likely in a proud mind to generate in indifference, or to remain during a life of difficulties, but under the warmest impressions of gratitude. He indeed was himself fond of relating a circumstance of a half-remembered declamation which he pronounced while a student of Pembroke, and which in consequence of imperfect recollection, being obliged to eke out with mere improvisation, he succeeded so well in as to excite the admiration of the whole society.

It would not be fair, however, to omit the mention of one testimony of early poetical genius, begun two years before he went to College, but not finished till many years after the usual period of academical education, not till he was sixty-eight. It is a translation of ANACREON's DOVE.[6] — If we contemplate this little effusion as an effort of juvenile talents, it is a promise of early excellence in poetry, certainly not surpassed in the real essentials of the art by his subsequent advances in it. If, as the tardier produce of his climacteric, it is a proof, amongst many others, that the opinion which prevails, that the poetic spirit sympathises with the corporeal decay, and declines into the vale of impotence in amicable association with the body, is a notion better calculated to encourage an indolent resignation of the intellectual powers, than firmly attested by fact, and more a calumny of speculation, than an approved decision of experience.

The following is a copy of it, and I have no hesitation in declaring, for so my judgment, such as it is, gives me an irresistible bias to pronounce, there is a certain unembarrassed freedom of poetical movement, a gaiety, a vividness, and an ease, that whatever may be the other excellencies of his more important and later offerings to the Muse, I have in vain endeavoured to see equalled. [Omitted.]

There is reason to believe Doctor Johnson left the University entirely from his incapacity to support the expence of it. That his finances were inconsiderable at this time is further evident, as his first employment after leaving the University, was that of an usher to the free school at Market Bosworth in Leicestershire, under the direction of Mr. Anthony Blackwall; probably at a yearly stipend of not more than from twenty to thirty pounds.

On the death of his principal, Mr. Johnson went to Birmingham, and resided in the house of one Warren, where he wrote essays in a newspaper, printed by his landlord; all of which are now lost. It was here also he translated "A Voyage to Abyssinia, by Father Jerome Lobo," and wrote those elegant lines, "On a Lady's presenting a Sprig of Myrtle to a Gentleman." He relates the circumstance that attended the formation of this little elegant poetic *prijoux* as follows:[7] — A young fellow had a sprig of myrtle given him by a girl he courted, and asked Mr. Johnson to write some verses, that he might present her in return. He promised, but forgot, and when he called for his lines at the time appointed, "Sit still a moment," said the Doctor, "dear Mun, and I'll fetch them thee," so slipped aside for five minutes, and wrote the following extempore. [Omitted.]

About the beginning of the year 1735, Mr. Johnson returned to his native town of Lichfield, and undertook the education of some young gentlemen there in the *Belles Lettres*, amongst whom was the late celebrated David Garrick, then about the age of eighteen. This employment, however, could not have lasted long, for in the year 1736, we find the following advertisement in the Gentleman's Magazine: — "At Edial, near Lichfield in Staffordshire, young gentlemen are boarded and taught the Latin and Greek Languages, by SAMUEL JOHNSON."

Who would not regret the humiliation of genius, and mourn over the miserable expedients thrust upon its adoption by the hand of poverty, were it not for the recollection that it requires an influence strong and potent as its own inaction to rouse it into exertion, and that was it not for the pinch of some severe and biting calamity, the ill demon of indolence, which nature sends into the world, as the almost inseparable associate of a gifted intellect, would still oftener than it does, prevail over its powers, and triumph in its resignation to oblivion. No man had less of constitutional tendency to industry than Johnson, and with all his powers, had he been placed in circumstances of original affluence, that man would have been now included in the number of the unhonoured dead, who occupies the very first place in the literary ranks of Europe, and who, in the energetic eulogy of a panegyrist,[8] at least his own equal in genius, "has made our language live."

He did not remain long in the situation of schoolmaster, probably because he did not meet with much success in it, for the year following we find him determined to bring his talents to a scene more propitious to the display of genius, and more pregnant with expedients for livelihood. He determined to visit the metropolis. He was accompanied in his journey by his pupil, now become his friend, David Garrick, and under the guidance of the same auspices, and stimulated by the same motives, these two distinguished individuals entered London together. The following letter from Gilbert Walmesley appears to have been the principal dependence of Mr. Johnson for his introduction into his new scene of life. [This letter of 2 March 1737 has been omitted.]

It would be injustice to the memory of this friend of Mr. Johnson's early youth, to withhold a subsequent tribute of gratitude, addressed to him in the course of the Lives of the Poets. It would be injustice also to Mr. Johnson, as it demonstrates the warmth and duration of his attachments, and proves that there was a talent for a sort of magnificent pathos about him, that if oftener exercised, might have turned out equally honourable to himself and advantageous to the drama.

Speaking of his being indebted for some anecdotes of Smith's life to Mr. Walmesley, he adds . . . . [Omitted.] [9]

When Mr. JOHNSON arrived in town, he took lodgings in a miserable street behind Exeter-change, up two pair of stairs, where he met in full sympathy of talents, pride, and poverty, that mixed, eccentric and unfortunate character, Mr. Richard Savage. It will readily be believed, that the peculiarity of their mutual fortune could not but produce a very early and ardent friendship. Such a meeting indeed must have operated as a most powerful mitigation of the severities of the other parts of their fate. A man is gratified to perceive he is not the exclusive butt of fortune, and the opportunity given for the reciprocal display of talent before a companion able to comprehend its extent, and from sympathy ready to admit its value, must perhaps be of all other consolations to misery, the most efficacious and heart-felt. It brings vanity into the field to contend against the bitterness of disappointment, and the flattery of an admired friend, to oppose to the neglect of a despised world. They have been frequently known to walk in the squares of London till five o'clock in the morning, for want of money to carry them to a coffee-house. They had the good fortune also to agree in politics, so that when the circumstances of their own individual misfortunes failed to supply them with conversation, they conspired to lament the disasters of their country, and to execrate the blunders of the then administration, for Johnson had not then commenced his reverence for courts, nor had conceived his opinion, that infallibility was attached even to the representatives or instruments of royalty.

He appears to have regarded Savage with more than common affection. He accompanied him to Greenwich, to attend his departure to his place of retirement in Wales, and wept violently at taking leave. He afterwards distinguished him, and alluded to this circumstance in his poem of London, where, under the appellation of Thales, he speaks thus of Savage.

> Though grief and fondness in my breast rebel,
> When injur'd Thales bids the town farewell;
> Yet still my calmer thoughts his choice commend,
> I praise the hermit, but regret the friend;
> Who now resolves, from Vice and London far,
> To breathe in distant fields a purer air,
> And fix'd on Cambria's solitary shore,
> Give to St. David one true Briton more.[10]

He was introduced by Savage to Mr. Cave, the proprietor of the Gentleman's Magazine; and Mr. Johnson has been heard to say, that the first performance that gained him any notice, was the following little poem, published in that miscellany, in the beginning of the year 1738. [*Ad Urbanum* has been omitted.]

In May, the same year, he finished his poem of "London," imitated from the third satire of Juvenal. He offered this poem to most of the booksellers in London, for almost any thing they would give. At last, the course of application brought him to the shop of Mr. Robert Dodsley, brother of the present Mr. James Dodsley, in Pall-Mall. He gave him *ten guineas* for the copy: a circumstance which Mr. Johnson used often to speak of amongst his friends; adding jocularly, "Dodsley was the only bookseller in London that found out I had any genius."

The publication of this poem was a source of much accession of character to him, and amidst the general observation which it excited, had the good fortune to raise the curiosity of Mr. Pope, who having for some days in vain endeavoured to discover the author, relinquished his pursuit at last, with these words: "It cannot be long before my curiosity will be gratified — the writer of this poem will soon be *deterré.*"

For the present, however, the poem of "London" operated much more to the gratification of Mr. Johnson's vanity, than to the satisfaction of any of his other appetites; and conspired, perhaps, with other more powerful causes, to induce him to wish for a more substantial and advantageous connection than a mere union with the Muse. About this time he married Mrs. Porter, of Manchester [*sic*], a widow lady, and twenty years older than himself. She brought him, however, a portion of eight hundred pounds, with which sum, united to the mastership of a charity-school in Shropshire, worth about sixty pounds a year, which was then vacant, and the appointment to the succession of which, Johnson thought he had interest enough to obtain, he had speculated to sit down in quiet and retirement. This was an illusion, however, not fated to be realized, and which the experience of a few subsequent weeks totally dissipated. His father, much about this time failed in business, and Johnson, with that enthusiasm of filial piety which always distinguished him, readily parted with the greatest part of his new wealth, to relieve the exigencies of an aged parent, and to put his affairs into some situation of tolerable ease again.

In his other scheme respecting the school he was not more fortunate. The statutes of the school required the person who should be elected to the vacant mastership, to be *Master of Arts,* which Mr. Johnson was not. He had obtained the patronage of Earl Gower, the father of the present Marquis of Stafford, who wrote the following letter in his behalf to a friend of Dean Swift at that time in London. [This letter, here dated 1738, has been omitted.]

This interference, however, proved unsuccessful, and Johnson, much to his mortification, was again thrown amongst all the shoals, storms and difficulties of a life of professional literature. He returned to London, and being in want of employment, he applied to Mr. Edward Cave, with whom he had had various engagements previous to his expedition into the country, and who retained him now to write the debates in parliament, for the Gentleman's Magazine. Johnson did not attend personally to take the debates, not having interest enough to obtain admission which at that period was extremely difficult to procure, almost every day being pregnant with discussions that menaced the dissolution of an administration that had stood for fourteen years. This defect was supplied by the agency of Mr. Worthington, a clergyman, a man of excellent memory, who furnished Johnson with the detail of the day's occurrences; and he afterwards gave the last finish to the manufacture, by moulding the several speeches into the form of argument, and investing them in all the graces of verbal decoration.

The fact is, these debates are executed in a uniform tone of mischievous elegance that destroys the discrimination of character, and subverts the reality of History. He continued in this employment for four years, namely from 1740 to 1744. The debates were entitled (as it was at that time held such a breach of privilege as never failed to call for the interference of the houses, to publish any account of parliamentary proceedings, under that ostensible character) *The Speeches of the Senate of Lilliput.* Doctor Johnson himself felt a consciousness of some impropriety attached to this mode of executing his employment, as he has been known repeatedly to declare, and that but a few days previous to his death, "that those debates were the only parts of his writings which then gave him any compunction; but at that time he had no conception he was imposing on the world, though they were frequently written from very slender materials, and often from none at all — the mere coinage of his own imagination." He likewise gave Dr. Smollett notice of this circumstance when he was writing his history of England; and some years since when a gentleman in high office was praising those speeches before him for so particular an appropriation of character, that he could name the speakers without a signature. "Very likely, Sir," said Johnson, ashamed of having deceived him; "but I wrote them in the garret where I then lived." How a man could describe the peculiar manners of individuals he had never seen, or the characteristic traits of eloquence he had never heard, is not altogether so intelligible.

During the period of giving those debates, he employed himself in several biographical, and other productions, which appeared in the Gentleman's Magazine of those times; many of which are now to be seen under the title of, "Miscellaneous and Fugitive Pieces," collected and published in three volumes, by Mr. Thomas Davies. And his *Poetry—*

now printing, in a small collection, by Mr. Kearsley, under the title of *"The Poetical Works of Dr. Samuel Johnson."* [11]

His principal employers in these productions were Cave and Osborne: the former, one of his first friends and patrons; the latter, a rich man and a brute, as the following anecdote will prove.

Mr. JOHNSON being engaged by Osborne, to select a number of the most scarce and valuable tracts in the Earl of Oxford's Library, which he had purchased in consequence of his Lordship's death, and which were afterwards printed in eight quarto volumes, under the title of the *Harleian Miscellany:* this work went on (agreeable to Osborne's ideas, who measured most things by the facility with which they were done) rather slowly: accordingly he frequently spoke to Mr. Johnson of this circumstance; and, being a man of a coarse mind, sometimes by his expressions made him feel the situation of dependence. Mr. Johnson, however, seemed to take no notice of him, but went on according to that plan which he had prescribed to himself. Osborne, wishing to have the business finished, and perhaps irritated by what he thought an unnecessary delay, one day went into the room where Mr. Johnson was, and abused him in the most illiberal manner: he was an illiterate man, but by great application in his profession, had acquired some property, which had the usual effect, and made him insolent, even to his customers. This impropriety of conduct frequently brought him into scrapes and disgraceful situations.

The selection abovementioned had been at press a considerable time, and the public to whom it had been often announced, became impatient for its appearance.

Mr. JOHNSON heard him for some time unmoved; but, at last, losing all patience, he seized up a large folio, which he was at that time consulting, and aiming a blow at the Bookseller's head, succeeded so forcibly, as to send him sprawling to the floor: Osborne alarmed the family with his cries; but Mr. Johnson, clapping his foot on his breast, told him "he need not be in a hurry to rise; for if he did, he would have the further trouble of kicking him down stairs."

The resentments, on both sides, however, were not recorded in marble, as it appears soon after, that Mr. Johnson finished this *Selection.*

The death of his early associate in difficulties, Mr. Richard Savage, in the year 1743, gave Johnson a fresh opportunity of introducing himself to the observation of the town. — He published the life of his friend a few months after his decease, and gave a specimen of philosophical biography, such as had never before been equalled, and hardly indeed attempted in this country — and yet it may be doubted whether this life, pregnant as it is with all the excellence of superior composition, has done more service or injury to the posthumous reputation of the unfortunate man who is the subject of it. His profligacies are more fully established in point of fact than they almost could have been by any other interposition, because they come attested to us now on the high authority of a man who could not be deceived, because he had ocular and personal preservation of the circumstances he describes, and who, as he was in this instance removed from all practicability of imposition himself, is equally superior to the suspicions of any such sinister practice upon others. — His conduct appears worse in point of principle, because it is now demonstrated to be such as the warmest affection could not palliate, nor the most powerful eloquence defend or obscure. Whatever else therefore may be said of this celebrated production, it will be hardly denied, that it is at least equivocal, when considered as a specimen of efficacious friendship.

Mr. JOHNSON's next production was his prologue on the opening of Drury-Lane theatre in the year 1747, being the year of the commencement of Mr. Garrick's managerical authority.

Two years afterwards he presented to Mr. Garrick his tragedy of *Irene*, the performance alluded to in Mr. Walmesley's letter to Mr. Colson, eight [twelve] years previous to this first preparation for its public appearance in 1749. — Nothing was wanting to the support of this tragedy that the internal activity of the manager within the theatre, or the partiality of external expectation without, could supply. — It dragged on a difficult existence till the ninth night of its representation; and beyond that period, the manager himself, who sustained the principal part in the performance, did not think it expedient to extend it.

The same year Mr. Johnson published his poem imitated from the 10th satire of Juvenal, entitled, *The Vanity of Human Wishes*. About the same time he published the plan of his Dictionary of the English Language, in a letter to the late Earl of Chesterfield. This letter is dated in the year 1747, and the work itself was not published till 1755, so that the preparation for this great undertaking cost him eight years labour. Every one has heard of the original friendship, and the subsequent quarrel of Doctor Johnson and the Earl of Chesterfield; and the effects of their mutual resentment have been repeatedly related among the other specimens of their respective powers of wit. — Lord Chesterfield takes an opportunity to indulge his enmity, in the following allusion in one of his letters to his son. [The "respectable Hottentot" sketch has been omitted.]

Johnson took his revenge when the book appeared, by describing it as a production "that inculcated the morals of a prostitute with the manners of a dancing master." Passion, however, is not often favourable to the display of wit — Lord Chesterfield destroyed almost the whole effects of his satire by a weak exaggeration — by making the similitude too remote, he made the application more doubtful, and the severity of course less personal. Doctor Johnson seems to have derived his retort from any thing but the book which it purports to describe. — That a set of instructions, calculated exclusively for the direction of one sex, should be founded on feelings alone applicable to the other, and that a book, a greater part of which consists in recommending reserve in sensual gratification, excepting in instances, where the pride of difficult conquest, added to the other pleasures of the enjoyment, should be grounded on the principles of a profession the very nature and business of which is constant, habitual, unreserved, and indiscriminate indulgence, are hard things easily said, but require more difficulty when they are either to be proved or explained.

The price which the booksellers paid Mr. Johnson for his Dictionary was fifteen hundred pounds, a sum evidently not a reasonable compensation for the learned labours of eight years. He felt himself poor, and applied to his employers for a further sum of five hundred pounds. They refused, and menaced application to a Court of Justice. He treated their threat with contempt, and disclaimed all intention of proceeding with the Dictionary. They at last acquiesced in the demand, and the book proceeded. This occurrence has been much discussed, and different opinions have been entertained respecting it, but the fact seems to have been, that neither party were violently to blame about it. — The booksellers founded their refusal upon the letter of an original compact, and Doctor Johnson rested his claim upon the spirit of its obvious equity.

In the year 1750, Mr. Johnson began his Rambler, which came out every Tuesday and Saturday in that year, and continued to do so for two years successively. He had fewer co-adjutors in the composition of this work than was ever known in a periodical publication, having received no more assistance in the whole course of its long and gradual formation, than five [four] essays; namely, two [one] from Richardson, two from Miss Carter, and one from Miss Talbot. The book has undergone ten editions, and has been recently translated into the Russian language, by order of the Empress. When Johnson was told of this circumstance, he replied, "I should be afraid of being thought a *vain* man if I did not feel myself *proud* of such distinction." This year the University of Oxford thought proper to acknowledge his literary merits by a voluntary admission of him to the degree of *Master of Arts,* an honour which they finally confirmed a few years after, by creating him Doctor of Laws in full convocation.

On the 5th of April, 1750, the masque of Comus was performed at Drury-Lane theatre, for the benefit of Mrs. Elizabeth Foster, Milton's grand-daughter. Johnson wrote a prologue, and Garrick performed one of his best parts, but the usual repulsion of charity thinned the house, and the whole produce, including various private contributions, amounted to no more than one hundred and thirty pounds.

In 1753 [1752] Mrs. Johnson died. The Doctor felt the loss severely, and wrote the following plain but affectionate epitaph to her memory, on her tomb in Bromley Church, Kent. [Omitted.]

In 1756 we find the Doctor concerned in a periodical paper, published by T. Gardner, in the Strand, called, "The Universal Visiter," in conjunction with several other gentlemen of literary distinction of that day. The work did not continue a year. The contributors were Dr. Johnson, whose lucubrations are marked with two asterisks; Christopher Smart, Richard Rolt, David Garrick, and Doctor Percy, each of whose papers are distinguished by having the initial letter of their surname prefixed to them.

In the year 1758 he wrote the Idler, in a series of papers published every Saturday. They were read with less avidity than the Rambler, and the town distinguished rightly in the different reception they gave them. This year [1759] he lost his mother, whose death he laments in the 41st Number of the Idler.

In the spring of 1759 he published his Rasselas, Prince of Abyssinia; the occasion of this publication should not be withheld from the public — it was the want of *twenty pounds,* to enable him to go down to Lichfield, to pay the last duties to his mother who was dying. After having sketched the design of it, he shewed it a bookseller, and told him his exigencies; but the other refused advancing him any money till he had seen the whole of the copy. The Doctor sat down to comply with his request; but before he had finished it his mother died. He afterwards sold it to another bookseller. This year [1762] he was honoured with an annual pension of 300£. The circumstances attending this distinction are related in a printed account of Doctor Johnson's life as follows. [Omitted.] [12]

The story respecting Mr. John Home has never been sufficiently attested to entitle it to much belief. Anecdotes of this kind should never be given to the public but when the evidence on which they rest is decisive and incontestible. Such communications are wrong, because in the first place they tend to impose punishment without a certainty of guilt; and in the second operate to shut the gates of bounty upon genius, as no man will be very forward in benevolence to literature who finds that he thereby exposes himself to the chance of having his motives publickly perverted, and runs the risque of incurring obloquy when he expected praise.

In 1765, he brought out his Shakespeare in eight volumes.

In the year 1770 [1773], in conjunction with Mr. Steevens, Doctor Johnson enlarged his Shakespeare to ten volumes octavo.

Dr. Johnson's political works, consisting of "Taxation no Tyranny — Falkland Island — The Patriot — and False Alarm," were published at different intervals, from about the year 1769 [1770], to 1775.

In the year 1773, he undertook an excursion which he had long meditated, a journey to the Hebrides. Mr. Boswell has given a description of some of the circumstances that led to this tour, so much in that style of simplicity, oddity, sense, and something like an occasional tendency to the contrary, that characterize his peculiar manner of writing, that I have selected it for the entertainment of my readers. [Omitted.] [13]

Whatever animadversions the book from whence the above extracts are taken may be liable to, from the tendency it has in every part to excite uneasinesses among families, by the unnecessary communications which it contains of the sentiments, which one set of individuals entertain of another, there is no denying it would have been abundantly pregnant at least with entertainment, had it not been for one little secret that Mr. Boswell, with by no means the usual dexterity of artifice, satyrically imputed to his countrymen, suffers to escape him almost in the very commencement of it. That Mr. Johnson was every morning favoured with a sight of Mr. Boswell's manuscript history of their proceedings of the preceding day — who after this can for a moment expect an impartial communication of Mr. Boswell's real sentiments. No man meant more sincerely than Mr. Boswell, but no man could execute an intention of sincerity with such a restraint upon him. We can have no other impression of the Journal, therefore, after such a discovery, than that of its being a constrained selection of morning compliments, a mere preparation of diurnal flattery, gratifying to the vanity of Doctor Johnson, but not descriptive of his real manners, nor at all decisive upon his general character.

In 1770, the Doctor again wielded his pen in the cause of benevolence, and wrote an occasional prologue to the Word to the Wise, acted for the widow of the author, the late Mr. Hugh Kelly. The four last lines in this prologue are equal to any thing in any part of Doctor Johnson's poetry.

> Yet then shall calm reflection bless the night,
> When liberal pity dignifi'd delight,
> When pleasure fir'd her torch at virtue's flame,
> And mirth was bounty with an humble name.[14]

In the year 1778 [1777], he undertook to supply the booksellers with the Lives of the British Poets, and in 1780 [1779–81] the design was fully executed, and the books published at first in ten volumes, small octavo; they were accompanied by a revised edition of the works of all the several writers, whose lives were given in four volumes of large octavo. This was the last great effort of Dr. Johnson's pen — and with the account of his literary history must pretty nearly terminate the relation of every thing that can be important or interesting in a life like his. The following I have reason to believe is a correct statement of the few remaining incidents which the vigilance of friendship has collected, and which the fondness for his memory have given an interest to, hardly derived from their own magnitude or importance.

During the night of the summer of 1783, he was attacked with a paralytic stroke, at his house in Bolt-court, Fleet-street, which deprived him of the powers of speech. He awoke with the attack; and as sentiments of religion were ever the prevalent suggestions of mind in every situation not only of danger, but even of retirement, he attempted to repeat the Lord's prayer in English — but could not — he attempted it in Latin with the same effect — at last he succeeded in Greek. He immediately rung the bell, but on the approach of his servant, could not articulate a syllable. Feeling, however, that he retained the full use of his senses, he signified a desire for pen, ink, and paper, and wrote the following note to Mr. Allen, a printer, who lived next door to him; a very honest, worthy man, who had been his intimate and confidential friend for many years, and at whose death (which happened suddenly last summer) the Doctor said, "he never knew a man fitter to stand in the presence of his God." [Omitted.]

Mr. Allen immediately attended him, and sent for his usual physicians, Drs. Heberden and Brocklesby, who in the course of a few months recovered him so much, that he was able to take the air, and visit his friends as usual.

He continued every day growing better; and as he found his spirits much relieved by society, it was proposed by some friends, to establish a club in the neighbourhood. The Doctor seemed highly pleased with the proposal, and after naming some friends, whom he wished to have about him, they met early last winter, at the Essex-head, in Essex-street, for the first time, when the Doctor being unanimously called to the chair, he surprized them with a set of rules, drawn by himself, which being read, and approved of by the rest of the members, were regularly entered in a book provided for that purpose.

These rules, to use his own words, are "founded in frequency and parsimony"; and as the public may have some curiosity in seeing such a production from Dr. Johnson in his hour of social relaxation, the following is an authentic copy of them, together with the names of the gentlemen who composed the club, as they stood, "on the rota of monthly attendance." [Omitted.]

In the summer of the same year he grew so much better, that supposing the air of Italy might be the best means of re-establishing his health, he hinted in conversation his desire to undertake that journey. His old and intimate friend, Sir Joshua Reynolds, anxious for the preservation of such a life, and yet thinking the Doctor's finances not equal to the project, mentioned the circumstance to the Lord Chancellor, adding, "that if his pension could be encreased two hundred a-year more, it would be fully sufficient for the purpose." His Lordship heard the proposal cordially, and took the first opportunity to mention it to the K——g.

His M——y had been previously advertised of the Chancellor's intention, but when it was mentioned to him waived the conversation.

The Chancellor, on this implication of refusal, wrote to Dr. Johnson, informing him, that as the return of his health might not wait the forms of the addition to his pension, he might draw immediately upon him for 500£ which lay at his banker's for that purpose.

So liberal and unexpected an offer from a quarter where he had no right to expect it, called forth the Doctor's gratitude, and he immediately wrote the Lord Chancellor the following letter. [This letter of September 1784 has been omitted.]

The Doctor was at Lichfield when he wrote this letter, on his return from Derbyshire, in tolerable good health. However, on his arrival in town in October [November], his disorder returned with so much violence as to make all expectation of change of abode quite chimerical. The dropsy returned in his legs, which swelled to such a magnitude, that his physicians relinquished all hopes of his recovery. They however continued to visit him, and prescribe such medicines as were best calculated to compose and quiet his pains. He was likewise occasionally visited by several of his friends, and, at intervals, possessed his usual spirits and flow of conversation.

His constant friend, as well as physician, Dr. Brocklesby, calling upon him one morning, after a night of much pain and restlessness, he suddenly repeated those lines from Macbeth:

> Oh! Doctor,
> Canst thou not minister to a mind diseas'd,
> Pluck from the memory a rooted sorrow,
> Raze out the written troubles of the brain,
> And with some sweet oblivious antidote
> Cleanse the full bosom of that perilous stuff
> Which weighs upon the heart?

And when the Doctor replied in the following words of the same author:

> Therein the patient
> Must minister unto himself.

— He exclaimed, "well applied, — that's true, — that's more than poetically true."

On the Thursday before his death, finding himself grow worse, he insisted on knowing from Dr. B[rocklesby], whether there were any hopes of his recovery? The Doctor at first declined an answer; but he repeating it with great eagerness, the other told him, "that from the complication of disorders he laboured under, and the advanced state of life he was in, there were but little hopes"; he received his fate with firmness; thanked him, and said he would endeavour to compose himself for the approaching scene.

The next day, a friend of his, apprized of this alarming sentence, and anxious to have every possible expedient exerted for his recovery, brought Dr. Warren to him; but he would take no prescription; he said, "he felt it too late, the soul then wanted medicine and not the body." Upon the Doctor's taking his leave, he told him "he must not go till he had given him his fee," and then presenting him with a copy of his *Lives of the Poets*, begged his acceptance of it, assuring him "that was all the fee he had ever given his other two physicians."

For some weeks before he died, he received the sacrament two, or three times in each week; on the mornings of those days he begged that nobody might disturb him, not even his physicians, but in cases of absolute necessity. He spent a great part of the preceding nights in prayer, and in the act of communion he shewed a piety and fervency of devotion that communicated itself to all around him. An intimate friend of his coming into the room one day after this ceremony, the Doctor exclaimed (his face at the same time brightening with a ray of cheerful piety), "oh! my friend, I owe you many obligations through life; but they will all be more than amply repaid by your taking this most important advice, BE A GOOD CHRISTIAN."

The Saturday night preceding his death, he was obliged to be turned in the bed by two strong men employed for that purpose; and though he was very restless, yet when a friend asked him in the morning, whether the man he had recommended to sit up with him was wakeful and alert, the Doctor, recovering his pleasantry a little, replied, "not at all, sir, his *vigilance* was that of a dormouse, and his activity that of a turnspit on his first entrance into a wheel."

The next night he was at intervals delirious; and in one of those fits, seeing a friend at the bedside, he exclaimed, "What, will that fellow never have done talking poetry to me?" He recovered his senses before morning, but spoke little after this. His heart, however, was not unemployed, as by his fixed attention, and the motion of his lips, it was evident he was pouring out his soul in prayer. He languished in this manner till seven o'clock on Monday evening, the 13th of Dec. 1784, and then expired without a groan, in the 75th year of his age.

His body was opened on Wednesday the 15th of December, in the presence of Drs. Heberden and Brocklesby, where the causes which produced his last disorder were discoverable, but found impracticable to have been removed by medicine. His heart was *uncommonly large,* and what was very extraordinary, one of his kidneys was entirely consumed, though he never once complained of a *nephritic* complaint at any period of his life. It is, however, to be conjectured, that he had some *presentiment* of this circumstance, as a few months before his death he held an argument with his physicians, on the possibility of a man's living after the loss of one of his kidneys.

Some time previous to his death he made a will subscribed only by two witnesses; but telling the circumstances to a friend, who knew he had a freehold, of about twelve pounds a-year in Lichfield, in right of his father, another was drawn; but it was only a few weeks before he died, that the blanks were filled up. On the same principle of delay, the revision of many manuscripts was postponed, some of which were burnt by the Doctor the week before he died, to avoid being left in a state of imperfection. Amongst the rest was one book, out of two, wherein he had recorded some hints for the history of his life, which he committed to the flames by mistake.

[An authentic copy of his will is here subjoined.] [Omitted.]

So anxious was he to discharge every tie of moral obligation with punctuality, that some time before his death he set down to recollect what little sums he might owe in the early part of his life to particular friends, which were never given with a view to be restored. Among this number he sent a guinea to the son of an eminent printer which he had borrowed of his father many years before, to pay his reckoning at a tavern.

He likewise recollected borrowing thirty pounds of Sir Joshua Reynolds at a great distance of time; "but this sum (said the Doctor to Sir Joshua, with a manliness of mind which answered for the feelings of his friend being similar to his own) I intend to bestow on a charity which I know you'll approve of." His attention exerted itself in several little particulars, which would have escaped the vigilance of almost any other person under such circumstances, but which at once indicated the calmness of his mind, and the delicacy of his friendships. — Amongst these may be mentioned his sealing up several bags of letters to be returned to the writers of them, lest the confidence they reposed in him should suffer by any subsequent conduct when he could no longer protect them. — An example of good faith in the termination of his earthly friendships, in which some of his acquaintances had not refinement enough to sympathize, nor, what is worse, grace to imitate.

Of Dr. JOHNSON's literary estimation, high and almost unparalleled as it is, we must trace the sources, full as much in the variety and diversity of his talents, as in the transcendency by which he can be proved to have been distinguished in any particular endowment. No man can be named who has filled the collective departments of literature, as scholar, critic, essayist, poet, and philologist, with more skill and versatility than himself; but that he so excelled in each of these particular and distinct provinces of art, as to bid defiance, perhaps, even to very modern competition, it will hardly be entirely safe to maintain. Variety however is the first strong character of genius, and as the possession of a certain degree of excellence in *all* the senses is the proof of perfection in the body, a man ought no more to regret that he is outdone in one department of science by a person incompetent to all the rest, than he should consider himself excelled in organization by one who can see farther without the faculty of hearing, or with a more exquisite sensibility of taste is without the advantage of feeling.

As a scholar, there is no vestige in any of Dr. Johnson's works, nor tradition transmitted by his familiar associates, of an uncommon profundity in any particular science. He had appropriated no part of his time to the attainment of mathematics — in natural philosophy he affected no more than the casual gleanings, which to a mind like his, always prepared for the reception of science, and unprecedentedly tenacious in the preservation of it, the common intercourse with learned society could not fail to produce. — Of the abstractions of metaphysical philosophy he does not appear to have been fond, and indeed no subject of literature seems with much violence to have attached his affection, such only excepted as tended to develop the mysterious operations of the mind of man, or the more awful indications of the intention of the Deity. A vast comprehension, therefore, of general information, hardly so exact, perhaps, as to amount to system, nor in the capricious distinctions of literature entitled to the name of science, was the character of his erudition. — The maxim that was very early taught him by a relation,[15] "to learn a little of every thing," seems to have pervaded the whole system of his future life; so that a mind perhaps more generally illumined than Doctor Johnson's at the time of his death, has not been often found amongst the ornaments of society. — He knew enough of almost every branch of learning to understand its principles, and the detail by the prosecution of which, lesser men contrive to make their heavy way to honours in literature that have been fastidiously denied to him, would have only been a clog and an incumbrance to the activity of such a genius. — He appears to have made his way through the various and involved paths of learning with the same intention and success that actuated Ulysses in his tour from Troy to Ithaca, to record the powers and extent, and to detect the peculiarities of the νοον ανδρων, the best theme and most beneficial subject of human observation. — It has been said, and with so much confidence, as to have it publickly mentioned by his friends as the weak part of his literary character, that he was no great proficient in Greek. It is difficult to controvert assertions so countenanced, and yet the whole tenor of his composition, the familiarity of his allusion to Grecian history and anecdote, and the promptitude of his quotations from Grecian writers conspire to make the report at least extremely improbable. — Nothing can be more easily distinguishable by an eye of the least discrimination, than the voluntary ebullitions of memory issuing from a cultivated mind, on an occasion that suggests them, and the little prepared *morccaus* of classical ornament, the little patches of meretricious decoration, frequently used perhaps to conceal a blemish, rather than to set off a beauty, which have recently stolen into prevalent adoption, and which it would be literary blasphemy to impute to Dr. Johnson. The charge, therefore, of want of knowledge on this subject can mean only an insinuation of comparative inferiority, and can tend only to prove not an ignorance of the tongue, but the voluntary neglect perhaps of some of its verbal technicalities.

As a critic we contemplate that part of Doctor Johnson's character; in which perhaps he is to be viewed with the most unimpaired reverence. To an accurate and extensive information in all the peculiarities of the mere bearings and tendencies of words, he united a comprehensive and philosophical knowledge of the general structure of the mind, and the particular operation of particular passions, such as is but rarely met with. In the prosecution of the more professional and technical parts of the art, such as depend upon an acquaintance with local usage and transitory prejudices, he had the discretion never to indulge himself in the fastidious habit, of rejecting the unambitious assistance of plain common sense. And to give him more praise than mere literary excellence could alone entitle him to, he introduced a spirit of urbanity into the science, a disposition of politeness to the persons of his competitors, and of candour to the consideration of their labours, estimable at once from its value to the art itself, and pleasing from its novelty, in all modern practice. From the arrogant reliance of one of his cotemporaries in the first dictates of an imperious mind, he had seen literature excite disgust, and ingenuity degenerate into chimera. From the absorption of another in the humbler drudgeries of the profession, he had reason to apprehend that a new species of criticism was to be instituted, that was to exist independently of all exercise of the judgment, and that the art itself was to sink into a mere compilation of authorities, and an unenlightened succession of ostentatious quotation. By adding moderation and reflection to the ability of the one, and mind and philosophy to the attainments of the other, he accomplished all the *desiderata* of an annotator, and laid down at least such a system of the principles of elegant criticism, as can never be sufficiently praised nor too anxiously imitated.

This however is more true of his notes upon Shakespeare than in his animadversions upon the poets, in his account of their Lives. In the latter work he has trusted too much to general impressions, and has given too free an indulgence to the operation of all his prejudices.

As a poet, Dr. Johnson is not justly to be ranked even as a member of the higher class. His language, though select and powerful, does not bend to the delicacy nor acknowledge the authority of those lighter graces which the muses dictate and delight in. Fancy and creation in the degree of them that are necessary for eminent proficiency in poetry, do not appear to have been in the number of his gifts from nature. Knowledge made him timorous, and his weight of understanding impeded his capacity of soaring. Sense, observation, cultivated and magnificent diction, a managed movement in the flow of his verse, strong satire and witty antithesis, will not be denied to him; but these alone will not make poetry. — There is a subtle spirit of which "nothing but itself can be the parallel," and which perhaps it is almost as difficult to define as to create, that must be present for the formation of real poetry. This Dr. Johnson appears to have wanted, and when I describe his poetical productions, as being with a very few exceptions, nothing more than eloquence in rhyme, as correct versifications of splendid sense, I shall not have much dread of having incurred the disesteem of those who have either themselves delighted to travel in the fairy-land of the muses, or have taken pleasure in the histories of their arts, manners, or produce.

As an essayist, Doctor Johnson yields to Addison. — The wisdom of the former steps into our system invested in all the stiff formality of her primitive magnificence — that of the latter comes chearfully into our familiar habits, and appears amongst us like Apollo in his exile from heaven, a conscious divinity in a garb of plainness. Johnson is fond of pomp, ceremony, and procession; he is the *Doge of Venice,* proceeding in accumulated finery to celebrate his nuptials with the Adriatick, while Addison with more power and less state comes amongst us like *Peter the Great,* and thinks nothing that belongs to life or manners too minute for observation, too trifling for use, or too insignificant for description. His humour also is more easy, more exuberant, and more natural. Not that Johnson is quite destitute of the quality, but what he has is of the grand and epic cast. It would have enabled him to have given a tolerably correct idea of the language, and character of the Knight of *La Mancha* himself, but would have deserted him totally in attempting to convey the most remote similitude of his incomparable *Squire.*

Johnson's stories and apologues have also less of the glow of real life than Addison's. They have the rigidity of theoretical fabrication; the incidents are not badly made, but it is evident they *are* made. With all these drawbacks to his disadvantage, however, it is not to be denied that we not infrequently discover in the lucubrations of Johnson, instances of strong original observation, of commanding powerful combination, and of noble and sublime morality, such as we in vain hope to find in the neater pages of Addison.

Of Dr. Johnson's Dictionary of the English Tongue, of which it would more immediately become me to speak, I find myself relieved from all necessity of a dilated mention, by the universality at once of its reception and its fashion. The book that is to be found in every library, and is the acknowledged umpire of every difficulty in the subject of which it treats, possesses better evidence of merit than any arts of partial declamation can possibly bestow upon it.

14

(1786)

The Life of Dr. Samuel Johnson

James Harrison (?)

The history of a man who, by the mere strength of his abilities, forced himself into the first seat of literary eminence, and continued to preserve during life the merited situation, with little envy and less opposition, cannot fail to interest the many who must always admire and the few who may ever hope to emulate such very extraordinary talents.

Dr. Samuel Johnson, born at Lichfield, the 7th of September 1709, was the eldest son of Mr. Michael Johnson, a respectable bookseller in that city, by his wife, Mrs. Sarah Johnson, sister of Dr. Joseph Ford, an eminent physician, and who was father of the famous Cornelius Ford, supposed to have been characterized by Hogarth, as a drunken parson, in his celebrated print of the Modern Midnight Conversation.

The father of Dr. Johnson is said to have been a remarkably pious and worthy man; but positive, and afflicted with melancholy: whether the last of these infirmities, which the son certainly possessed in a very great degree, was hereditary or accidental, has never been ascertained. There is, however, considerable reason to think, that Mr. Michael Johnson might be deeply affected by a circumstance which had occurred to him in early life.[1] A young woman of Leeke, in Staffordshire, where he had served his apprenticeship, conceived so violent an affection for Michael, that she followed him to Lichfield, on his settling in that city, and took lodgings opposite his house. That there had been any previous intimacy, though highly probable, by no means appears; but it is certain he had not, at this time, the smallest inclination to return her love, till he was assured that the life of the poor girl was in danger: then, indeed, he waited on her, with a tender of his hand in marriage. But it was too late! The wound so long neglected had become incurable: she declined the offer; fell a victim to her sensibility; and was interred in the cathedral of Lichfield, where Mr. Johnson caused a stone to be placed over her grave with this simple inscription —

Here lies the Body of
Mrs. ELIZABETH BLANEY, a Stranger.
She departed this Life
2d of September 1694.

From the peculiar style of the inscription — "Mrs. ELIZABETH BLANEY, *a Stranger*" — it is natural to suppose that the young woman was of obscure origin. The appellative "*Mrs.*" is doubtless a vulgar error: she could not be a married woman, and was hardly a widow. No widow has ever been known to die for love.

It is not altogether improbable, that she might have lived servant in the family where Mr. Michael Johnson was an apprentice; since there is nothing more common than juvenile attachments, in such situations, which the indiscreet youth afterwards discovers to have been formed without a sufficient attention to worldly prudence, and then sometimes dissolves with an equal disregard to moral obligations.

This, however, in the present case, is merely conjecture, and must not tend to criminate a man whose general character was irreproachable.

Whatever might be the particulars of this obscure though well-authenticated story, or however the melancholy event might affect the mind of Mr. Michael Johnson, it is likely that the impression long continued to retard his union with any other woman; as it was full fifteen years from this period to the birth of his first child, Dr. Samuel Johnson.

Either from real or affected delicacy in his mother, the new-born infant was suckled at the breast of a stranger;[2] and it seems to have been the fate of poor Johnson, from his birth, that he should *fall into bad hands*. With the milk of his nurse, he imbibed the seeds of that disease which is called the King's Evil, and which deprived him of the sight of his left eye, and continued to incommode him through life; though he was taken to London by his mother, at the age of two years, where he received the royal touch from Queen Anne, and had the customary amulet of gold hung round his neck, which the superstitious sentiments of his parents, who were notoriously attached to the Stuarts, had considered as an infallible remedy.

About the time when Dr. Johnson was born, a physician of the name of Swynfen, who chiefly resided on his own estate in Staffordshire, at some distance from Lichfield, occasionally occupied apartments at Mr. Michael Johnson's. This gentleman, who perhaps succeeded to the practice of Mrs. Johnson's father, became godfather to the infant, and is reported to have taken an active part in cultivating his early genius.

There are few parents who have not remarked some prodigious display of sagacity in their little ones; whether the children ever afterwards realized the expectations raised by such flattering prognosticks, or not. It would, therefore, be extremely wonderful, if the childhood of such a man as Johnson afforded no anecdote presageful of extraordinary genius.

Only one story of this kind, however, is extant, which deserves to be particularly recorded; and that has been so often repeated, and every time in a form so very different, that the authenticity of the whole account might fairly be doubted, if the fact had not been indisputably established.

When he was "about *three* years old," says Sir John Hawkins; Mrs. Piozzi says, *"five";* his mother had a brood of eleven young ducks, which she permitted him to call his own: and, as he was one day playing heedlessly among them, he had the misfortune to tread on one of the little creatures, and crush it to death. Alarmed at the accident, and full of emotion, he immediately snatched up the duck; and, running to his mother, bade her take a pen, and write. "Write, child!" said she, too much astonished at the request to be concerned at the accident; "what must I write?" — "Why, write," answered the child, "so."

He then gave his first indication of poetical genius, by prompting an Epitaph, which is thus recorded by Sir John Hawkins —

> Here lies good Master Duck,
>   That Samuel Johnson trod on;
> If 't had liv'd 'twould have been good luck,
>   For then there'd been an odd one.

Mrs. Piozzi publishes the Epitaph in these words —

> Here lies poor Duck,
>   That Samuel Johnson trod on;
> If it had liv'd it had been good luck,
>   For it would have been an odd one.[3]

Some readers may perhaps think that the manifest aukwardness still unfortunately subsisting in this little poetical effusion, has been moulded by Sir John and Mrs. Piozzi, to their respective ideas of what ought to have been, rather than what actually was, dictated by the child. To those who love truth and simplicity, and who do not expect metrical perfection in an infant, the lines in their original state will be far more acceptable, than with any adventitious ornaments, however successfully laboured. The genius of Johnson is to be looked for, on this occasion, and not the ingenuity of his biographers. This wonderful Epitaph, then — and wonderful it was for a child of five years old, miraculous for one of three — in its simple original state, appears to have run thus —

> Here lies poor Duck,
>   That Samuel Johnson trod on!
> If it had liv'd, 'twould have been good luck,
>   Because it was an odd one.

And in this, it is hazarding little to assert, that the intelligent reader will discover more of nature, and of genuine poetry too, than in either of the elaborate copies by which it has been preceded. Though the verse halts, it is neither turgid nor harsh: qualities always to be found in the best productions of those who have the knack of *making,* without the gift of *creating,* Poetry.

Having thus laboured to restore, not amend, this first poetical effort of Dr. Johnson, with all the zeal of a faithful annotator, it must not be dismissed without a comment.[4]

Cowley, Milton, Pope, and most other eminent poets, have given very early displays of that genius which afterwards rendered them so famous: but there is no single distich on record, pretended to have been written by them so early as these verses were composed by Dr. Johnson; even admitting, as probably must be admitted, that they were not produced till he had compleated his *fifth* year. But though the peculiarity of the accident might call forth this power soonest from him, there is little doubt that an equal portion of genius existed as early in them. Certain it is, that they wrote many excellent productions in their minority, which are constantly printed in their works; while this Epitaph is almost the only known juvenile essay of Dr. Johnson, who might doubtless have written, and perhaps actually did write, at the same time of life, many little poems equally well worth preserving.[5]

Criticism would be degraded by any remarks on a child's verses. His mother or nurse, like most other mothers and nurses, had without doubt taught him many absurdities; and, among the rest, the ridiculous old saying, *that odd things are lucky.* This idea the infant very naturally applied to the odd Duck; though it proved, in reality, the most unfortunate of the whole brood.

Young Johnson, however, was certainly a prodigy of early under-standing; and that pride which is natural to the parents of uncommonly brilliant children, frequently inducing his father and mother to teaze him for some display of his abilities in the presence of strangers, he often ran away, on such occasions, and concealed himself by climbing up a tree, to escape those exhibitions which his own good sense disap-proved.

From extreme ill health, he was not sent to school till the age of eight years; so that, from his mother, and her old maid Catharine, he received the rudiments of his education: and he is said to have perfectly well remembered sitting in the lap of the latter, while she explained to him the story of St. George and the Dragon. Tales of giants and of castles were, indeed, his chief delight; and such tales will perhaps always convey the highest degree of entertainment to a young and capa-cious mind filled with the enthusiasm of genius.

At the free-school of Lichfield, where Mr. Hunter was then master, his progress was such as might be expected from a pupil so very promis-ing, under a tutor of acknowledged great abilities. The character of an aspiring boy is soon manifest to a discerning eye; and those peculiar traits in that of Johnson, which were to distinguish the future dictator in the republick of letters, were not long before they began to develop themselves.

Besides his superiority in learning over every other boy of the same class, he was found to possess an uncommonly bold and enterprizing spirit, which made even the senior youths regard him as their chief and leader on all occasions. This universal deference was perhaps not a little aided by his extraordinary strength and size, which were consid-ered as almost gigantick; and experience convinced his associates, that though he often engaged them in mischief, he seldom failed to extricate them by his address and ability.

Indeed, so huge and unwieldy was the person of young Johnson, that when he visited at the house of Mr. Butt, of Lichfield, father of the Reverend Mr. Butt, now one of the King's chaplains,[6] as he often did, during his school vacations, the children in the family, with whom he good-humouredly played, though sometimes, it is by no means improbable, rather roughly, used commonly to call him the great boy: which their father once overhearing — "You call him," said he, "the great boy; but, take my word for it, he will one day prove a great man."

A school is the world in miniature; and a boy in power, like a man in power, has his flatterers and his minions. To gain Johnson's assistance in their tasks, or secure his aid in tyrannizing over other boys, a confederacy of three politick youths accustomed themselves, for a long time, to call him every morning, by turns; on one of whose backs, supported by the other two, he rode triumphantly to school. This was a double treat to Johnson; it indulged his indolence, and gratified his ambition. His aversion to business was so great, that he always procrastinated his exercises to the last hour, and even then seldom failed purposely to leave a few faults, that he might obtain longer time for finishing. He readily enough dictated verses or themes to reward the servilities of his favourites, but would never take the trouble to write a single line. Eager in the search of knowledge, he was inquisitive to gain information from every probable source: books and conversation, therefore, had for him stronger attractions, than the usual boyish sports, in which he seldom participated.

This eagerness to obtain knowledge was equalled by his faculty of retaining it; for, what he once read, or heard, he never forgot: and it is confidently asserted, that on hearing ten or twelve lines of poetry only once read, he could instantly repeat them verbatim, except sometimes altering an epithet, not unfrequently for the better.

It was one of his chief luxuries, to ramble about the fields during the holidays, with his favourite of the hour; yet, in these perambulations, it has been observed, he was accustomed to talk much more to himself than his companion.

To a boy of no talents, or a man of superficial understanding, this might appear a blameable waste of time; but the eye of discernment will not fail to perceive that these were no idle hours. He was then imperceptibily exerting himself, with more than any corporeal industry, in the most profitable intellectual employ; and enriching that vast hive of human wisdom, his capacious mind, not only, like that chief favourite of Labour, the bee, from every herb, plant, and flower he beheld, but from thousands of other natural objects which caught his excursive eye, and afforded food for his young imagination, which it is not in the nature of bees particularly to notice, and from which men of narrow ideas, *though abundantly busy with their hands,* are but little better calculated to extract any substantial advantage.

Garrick and Hawkesworth were both schoolfellows with Johnson; but, as the former was near seven years younger than Johnson, and the latter about ten, it is not likely that there was at that time any particular intimacy between them.

Hunter, though an excellent classical scholar, was a very strict and severe master; and, having probably disgusted young Johnson by the infliction of some arbitrary punishment, he was sent, about the age of sixteen, to an academy at Stourbridge, in Worcestershire, kept by a person of the name of Wentworth, to compleat his school education.

At this place, however, he had remained but a short time, when his father took him home, and seems to have now entertained a design of bringing him up to his own business. This was probably owing to some pecuniary difficulties; since it is abundantly manifest that young Johnson had been hitherto intended for one of the learned professions.

It is astonishing that neither his godfather, Dr. Swynfen, nor his cousin, Cornelius Ford, at this juncture interferred, and assisted to compleat the work they are reported to have aided in its commencement, by contriving that he should proceed in his studies. To raise expectations in a young and ingenuous mind, and then to cut them off by neglect, is one of the cruelest species of deception. The disappointment of all his hopes, which the aspiring youth at this period felt, and continued to feel near two years, during which time he not only attended the shop, but is said to have assisted in binding books and other mechanical occupations, was sufficient to sour his disposition, and render it both morose and melancholy, without the successive elevations and depressions he was afterwards destined to experience.

Young Johnson had just compleated his nineteenth year, when Mr. Andrew Corbet, a gentleman of Lichfield, intending to send his son to Pembroke College, Oxford, made a proposal that Johnson, who had been the youth's schoolfellow, should attend him thither as an assistant in his studies. This proposal being readily accepted, the young men were both entered, on the 31st of October 1728; Corbet as a gentleman-commoner, and Johnson as a commoner.

The college tutor, whose name was Jorden, was the very reverse of their old master, Hunter: he was neither a strict disciplinarian nor a great scholar. He had, therefore, very little respect from his pupils; though his attachment to them was so great, that he never suffered any young man under his care to be punished for slight improprieties.

There seems to be no good foundation for asserting that Johnson's talents were as eminently conspicuous at the university, as they had been at school. In Oxford and Cambridge, whatever may be pretended by common-place declaimers, there are always a very considerable number of young men who possess great abilities; and it often requires a nice eye to distinguish the brightest star in a brilliant constellation.

The stories generally circulated respecting Johnson's behaviour at the university are no more applicable to him than to every other young man of the smallest spirit in the same situation. Though he was generally assiduous in his private studies, he sometimes joined his fellow-students in trifling levities; and, not unfrequently, like most others, absented himself from lectures and early prayers. For this last offence, his tutor Jorden, who had sufficient penetration to discover his pupil's skill in Latin versification, imposed on him the task of translating Pope's Messiah; which was so well executed that, on its being transmitted to Mr. Pope, he very handsomely returned the copy, accompanied by this flattering encomium — "The writer of this poem will leave it a question for posterity, whether his or mine be the original."

But no proof of ability could greatly avail Johnson, while his genius was depressed by poverty. Mr. Corbet only paid for his commons, and his father was unable to afford him any material assistance; so that, merely through want of pecuniary supplies, he was obliged to go home at the end of thirteen months, and with much difficulty raised friends to send him back, and support him two years longer at the university.

About the time of Johnson's return to college, Mr. Jorden had quitted Oxford, on being presented to a living, and was succeeded by the present Dr. Adams, a gentleman of very superior ability.

This change, so propitious to Johnson's studies, determined him to pursue them with redoubled ardour; and he was, accordingly, constant in his attendance both at publick and private lectures, diligent in performing his exercises, and eager to embrace all opportunities of improvement.

But his ardour was still checked, and his mind clouded with melancholy, by painful reflections on the untoward circumstances of his father, who about this period became insolvent,[7] and the impossibility of continuing long enough at college to obtain a degree, or secure any decent situation in either of the learned professions, however eminently qualified.

His wretchedness, while at the university, was at one time so great, that he wanted many of the necessaries and all the conveniences of life. His whole wardrobe was on his back; and his toes were not concealed by the single pair of shoes he possessed. By order of some gentlemen of the college, a new pair of shoes were placed at his chamber-door; but Johnson, with all the resentment of an insulted man, indignantly threw them away. For this he has been censured by those who boast their superior knowledge in the art of improving adverse circumstances; and who, probably, in the same situation, would have accepted even an old pair. But Johnson possessed a delicacy to which such men are strangers, and which was very little consulted on the occasion. Shoes would have been the last things in the world which a liberal man, of true sagacity and refinement, could have thought of sending to a scholar who needed them.

Though the spirit of Johnson was too great to sink under this depression, it is certain that his pecuniary wants obliged him to quit the university sooner than had been intended.

In December 1731, soon after he left Oxford, his father died; whose business had been continued by the friendly assistance of Mr. Innys,[8] then a bookseller in St. Paul's Church-yard, who advanced 200£ on the occasion, and was now carried on by Mrs. Johnson and her son Nathaniel.

In the March following, destitute of friendly assistance, and with only 20£ for his patrimony, a mind naturally aspiring, which had been taught, and which deserved to soar, was obliged to accommodate itself to the humiliating situation of an usher at a free grammar-school. The patron of this seminary, which was situated at Market Bosworth, in Leicestershire, was Sir Wolstan Dixie, Bart. a descendant of the original founder;[9] and such was the haughty Baronet's supercilious treatment of poor Johnson, who boarded in his house, that he quitted the place within five months, wisely preferring the wide world to such misnamed protection.

It does not appear that Johnson was in any regular employ from this period to about the middle of the year 1733, when he is known to have resided with a Mr. Jarvis of Birmingham, and to have been engaged in translating from the French, Father Lobo's Voyage to Abyssinia, with the additions of Monsieur Le Grand, in a single octavo volume, for some printer of that place.

Having compleated this translation, in a style of no remarkable elegance, but accompanied with a preface in which the genius of Johnson is manifest, and being at a loss for farther employ, in the February following he returned to Lichfield; and, a few months afterwards, finding himself destitute of other resources, issued proposals, from his brother's shop,[10] for publishing by subscription an edition of Politian's Poems, in a five shillings octavo volume. This design, however, met with no encouragement, and was consequently obliged to be abandoned.

His next effort to profit by the genius he possessed, was that of addressing a Letter, dated November 25, in the same year 1734, to Mr. Cave, the printer and publisher of the Gentleman's Magazine, and tendering his services to assist in the compilation of that work.

Sir John Hawkins, who has given a copy of this letter,[11] which required an answer, *"directed to S. Smith, at the Castle, in Birmingham,"* observes that it was answered by Cave, who accepted his services: but Sir John should not have suppressed the answer; especially as he makes that very circumstance the ground of censuring some anonymous account of Johnson's life, in which it is erroneously asserted that Savage first introduced him to the acquaintance of Cave.[12]

There is nothing more common, than for young authors to labour under the delusion, that considerable profit is to be derived from assisting in a periodical miscellany of this kind; whereas the truth is, that such works are generally in the hands of a single Editor, and even he receives monthly but a very small sum indeed, unless capable of supplying all the articles which are not occasionally transmitted by gratuitous correspondents.

Cave, as an intelligent man, was no doubt willing to accept the services of so promising a contributor; but, from the nature of the thing, though he had a liberal mind, he could not possibly afford Johnson any adequate compensation for the proposed supplies, while he had a regular Editor to pay, who assisted him in the general execution of the work.

The fact seems to be, that though this application might be productive of some contribution to the Gentleman's Magazine, it produced no pecuniary gratification to Johnson, and was therefore very unlikely to keep him from seeking other means of support.

From the requisition to have Cave's answer transmitted to Birmingham, it is probable that, on the failure of his subscription, he had returned to that town, and obtained some occasional literary employ from the person [Thomas Warren] who had published his translation of the Voyage to Abyssinia, and who is said to have been the printer of a newspaper. There is no other reasonable way of accounting for the manner in which he obtained a livelihood till the beginning of the year 1735; when, indeed, his distress must have been great, as he tendered his services to Mr. Budworth, master of the Grammar-school, at Brerewood, in Staffordshire, who was under the necessity of declining them, lest those convulsive gesticulations to which his features were subject through life, should render him an object of ridicule to the inconsiderate boys.

In this humilitating situation, rejected even as the usher of a free-school, and without any other prospect of support, there was yet one way presented itself for the improvement of his circumstances.

Mrs. Porter, relict of Mr. Henry Porter, a mercer of Birmingham, had long cast a favourable eye on Johnson. Her maiden name was Jarvis, and she was probably a sister of the person at whose house he resided.

It is true she must have been nearly double the age of Johnson, then under twenty-seven, as she had at that time a son and daughter both grown up;[13] but she is said to have retained some personal beauty, and it is certain that she possessed a few hundred pounds. This last, it may be presumed, was to him the chief attraction, though he has never been considered as greedy of gain: and, Johnson no more resembling Milton, whose wives were all virgins, and who thought it indelicate to marry a widow, in his matrimonial than in his political notions, the union immediately took place.

Thus emancipated from distress, by entering into connubial bondage, and being now in some degree qualified to make choice of a profession, he opened an academy at Edial, near Lichfield, for the instruction of Young Gentlemen in the Latin and Greek Languages.

Mr. Gilbert Walmesley, register of the ecclesiastical court of the Bishop of Lichfield, and always the firm friend of Johnson, having the care of David Garrick at this period, whose education had been interrupted by a voyage to Lisbon, and who was then about eighteen years of age, placed him as the pupil of Johnson, with whom he had a few years before been a school-fellow.

Whether the dramatick genius of Garrick was awakened by Johnson's propensity to write a tragedy, or whether that propensity in Johnson was called forth by the disposition of Garrick to pursue theatrical in preference to more severe studies, is not easy to be determined: but it is certain that Johnson's Irene was written about this period.

It is equally certain that Johnson, after expending most of his property in vainly endeavouring to raise a school, and finding himself unable to procure more than about eight boys, became disgusted with his situation, and determined to seek his fortune in London.

This extraordinary tutor and pupil set out for the metropolis together, on the 2d of March 1737: Garrick, to receive philosophical and mathematical instruction under Mr. Colson; and Johnson, with a recommendation from Mr. Walmesley to that gentleman, that he might obtain some employment as a translator from the Latin or French, or procure an introduction for his tragedy on a London stage.

There is no proof, however, that Mr. Colson ever troubled himself about Johnson; who addressed, from Greenwich, a letter to Cave the printer, dated July 12, 1737, proposing a new translation of Father Paul's History of the Council of Trent.[14] This proposal of Johnson's being encouraged by Cave, an interview took place at St. John's Gate; where Garrick accompanied him, and is said to have given a fine specimen of his dramatick ability.

From this time, Johnson became the constant visitor of Cave; and, as many of the writers of that day occasionally resorted to St. John's Gate, he gradually introduced to his new guest several authors by profession; and, among the rest, that unfortunate and imprudent genius, Savage, with whom Johnson contracted a most strict intimacy.

Either from accident, or for the sake of being as much as possible together, they both had apartments in Exeter Street, behind Exeter Exchange, in the Strand; and the distress of these two celebrated characters was at this time so great, that they often wanted money to purchase the necessaries of life, and rambled a great part of the night through the streets of London and Westminster, solacing themselves with mutual condolence. Their political sentiments were the same; they were both conscious of the talents they possessed; and they felt themselves equally neglected. What was their course of life it would be idle to enquire, when they had barely the means to live. Perhaps, when either obtained a temporary supply, they participated in an evening's hilarity, and again relapsed into every thing but absolute want. This, if true, was not prudent; but it was natural to men fond of conviviality; and even Johnson has been heard to assert, that "a tavern-chair is the throne of human felicity."

His reasoning on this subject is curious, and furnishes the best possible apology for a practice which the rigid moralist will condemn. "As soon as I enter the door of a tavern," said Johnson, in vindication of this propensity, "I experience an oblivion of care, and a freedom from solicitude: when I am seated, I find the master courteous, and the servants obsequious to my call; anxious to know, and ready to supply my wants. Wine, there, exhilarates my spirits, and prompts me to free conversation, and an interchange of discourse, with those whom I most love: I dogmatize, and am contradicted; and in this conflict of opinion and sentiments I find delight." [15]

These, it may be remarked, are the sentiments of a man who seems to possess little domestick happiness. To seek comfort in a tavern, or an alehouse, is the deleterious remedy of the vulgar for matrimonial infelicity; and, like most poisonous medicines, though capable of much good, if not cautiously used, is likely to be productive of far greater evils than those which it is intended either to mitigate or cure.

Mrs. Johnson had been sent for, on her husband's having made good his footing in London; [16] and they are known to have lived on such terms as were naturally to be expected from the disparity of the match.

Johnson was barely settled in the metropolis, when he composed his satirical poem on London, in imitation of the third satire of Juvenal.

This, with that favourite mysteriousness of authors, which renders their veracity always suspected, and so frequently operates to their prejudice, he inclosed in a letter to Cave, to whom he offered it as the production of a person in distress.[17]

Cave had too much experience in the artifices of literary adventurers, not to know perfectly well who was the author; and, his heart being as good as his head, he returned a guinea or two for present use, and agreed to print the poem for the sole benefit of the writer.

It has been said, that [Robert] Dodsley, the bookseller, gave Johnson fifty pounds for the copy-right of London; but it is far more probable that he only published it, by the recommendation of Cave, and accounted to Johnson for the profit, which could hardly amount to half that sum.[18]

Lord Lyttelton and Mr. Pope spoke highly of this poem; and the latter, in particular, was very importunate with the publisher to know who was the author. But Dodsley possessed too much honour to betray the trust which had been reposed in him; and Pope consoled himself with remarking, that a man of such abilities could not long remain concealed.

It was about this period that Johnson lost his companion Savage, who quitted the metropolis with an idea of taking up his future residence at Swansea, in Wales, where he was to be supported by a subscription among his friends. This retreat is adverted to by Johnson, in his poem of London, where he mentions Savage, under the appellation of Thales.

> Tho' grief and fondness in my breast rebel,
> When injur'd THALES bids the town farewel;
> Yet still my calmer thoughts his choice commend,
> I praise the hermit, but regret the friend,
> Who now resolves, from Vice and London far,
> To breathe in distant fields a purer air,
> And, fix'd on Cambria's solitary shore,
> Give to St. David one true Briton more![19]

Neither the pecuniary advantage derived from the sale of this manly poem, nor the just reputation it produced, joined with the inclination of Cave to render Johnson any reasonable service, had yet reconciled him to the profession of an author. It was published in May 1738; and, in the month of July following [1739], the mastership of Appleby School being vacant, with a salary of sixty pounds a year, he was encouraged to go into the country and become a candidate. But the statutes of the school required that the person chosen should be a Master of Arts; and though Lord Gower was prevailed on so far to interest himself in getting over this difficulty, as to direct an application, through Dean Swift, to the university of Dublin, for a master's degree, the intercession failed, and Johnson lost his election.

Under this disappointment he returned to London; and seems now to have resolved on making authorship his profession, with a determination to exert all the powers of his vigorous mind in overcoming the many difficulties to which he perceived it was liable.

In the month of October, proposals were issued for the plan he had suggested to Cave, of translating from the Italian Father Paul's History of the Council of Trent, with Notes and the Author's Life from the French of Le Courayer. There is, however, considerable reason to think, that Johnson had at this time very little knowledge of Italian;[20] and probably meant to adopt the customary but disgraceful practice of English translators, relying wholly on the French version, though pretending to consult the original. While this translation was preparing, Cave regularly advanced small sums to Johnson, with whom he was to partake in the profit, on a truly liberal plan.

But while the work was yet in embryo, its progress was checked by one of those singular circumstances which, though they often happen in real life, are considered as quite out of nature when related in an acknowledged romance.

A gentleman of precisely the same name,[21] a Mr. Samuel Johnson, who then had the care of Dr. Tenison's Library, was at this very time engaged in the identical design, under the patronage of Dr. Zachary Pearce, most of the bishops, and many of the dignified clergy. The two editions, therefore, thwarted each other, and both were in consequence declined; though twelve sheets of Johnson's had been already printed off, comprehending the Life of Father Paul, which he afterwards abridged, and inserted in the Gentleman's Magazine.

Cave, though more a printer than a publisher, was determined that such talents as Johnson's should not remain wholly unencouraged; he, therefore, not only recommended him to the booksellers for whom he occasionally printed, but contrived to give him some trifling employ, till better business should offer from other quarters. Accordingly, in November 1738, Cave published An Examination of Pope's Essay on Man, translated by Johnson from the French of M. Crousaz, professor of philosophy and mathematicks, at Lausanne, in Switzerland; which gave rise to Warburton's celebrated Vindication of that poem.[22]

This pamphlet added nothing to Johnson's literary reputation: and, resolved, as it should seem, to produce something which must inevitably bring him into notice, his next work was an inflammatory piece of irony, called "Marmor Norfolciense; or, an Essay on an ancient Prophetical Inscription, in Monkish Rhyme, lately discovered near Lynn, in Norfolk, by Probus Britannicus"; in which he made such reflections on the Hanoverian succession, and disseminated other Jacobitish principles with so much virulence, that warrants were issued, and messengers employed by government to apprehend the author, who was fortunate enough to elude the pursuit, by retiring with his wife to an obscure lodging in Lambeth Marsh, where he remained till, the pamphlet being suppressed, the business was considered by the ministry as unworthy of farther attention.[23]

His Marmor Norfolciense made its appearance in 1739; and, in the same year, a licence having been refused for the performance of Mr. Brooke's tragedy of Gustavus Vasa, Johnson was employed by Corbett, the bookseller, to write a justification of the author, in an ironical quarto pamphlet, under the title of "A Compleat Vindication of the Licensers of the Stage from the malicious and scandalous Aspersions of Mr. Brooke, Author of Gustavus Vasa."

In 1740, Johnson succeeded Guthrie, as assistant Editor with Cave for his Gentleman's Magazine.[24] This, though not a very profitable, was at least a regular establishment; and he continued in this situation till the end of the year 1743, when he relinquished it in favour of Dr. Hawkesworth.

Much has been said about the parliamentary debates reported during this period by Johnson, who never attended to hear them, but dished up the loose memorandums received from a person present. This has been considered as miraculous by the blind idolaters of a name; who, with the usual absence of reason, have never once seemed to reflect, that the same thing was done, if not with so much elegance, with the same degree of precision, by his immediate predecessor Guthrie. The truth is, that neither of them were very attentive to facts; and that these boasted speeches, penned by Johnson, in a style of great but uniform elegance, want the superior recommendation of historical verity, and formed almost the only productions which, at the close of his life, he repented that he had ever written.

Cave felt the advantage of such a coadjutor as Johnson, who was continually enriching the work with valuable biographical and critical articles, in the increased demand for his magazine, the sale of which rose from ten to fifteen thousand, and he was not guilty of ingratitude.

Among these biographical articles, was the Life of Savage; who died the 31st of July 1743, in Bristol gaol, where he had been suffered to remain upwards of six months for a debt of only eight pounds. The extraordinary incidents which the life of this unfortunate man afforded, and the address with which they were detailed by Johnson, added much to his literary fame, though the whole is reported to have been written in a space of time barely sufficient for the transcription by an expert penman, which these recorders of wonders, with a curious disregard of consistency, deny that he ever was.

Johnson's life of his friend Savage is, perhaps, a little tinctured with that fault which so greatly abounds in the several biographical memoirs of himself, penned by his own particular friends; who, however, have gone as far beyond him in that excess of candour, which lays bare every foible of a friend with less reserve than a generous enemy would think it necessary to adopt, as they have fallen short of his exquisite manner in all the valuable qualities of composition.

Characters who, while they pretend friendship for another, from a dissembled conviction meanly abandon his interests and his fame, to obtain from the blind multitude the reputation of extraordinary candour and impartiality, form a very large tribe in the class of modern deceivers of the superficial, in this age of excessive refinement. By the intelligent they are discovered and despised.

The painter who is a master of his art, may give a flattering, a fair, or a frightful likeness: from a friend the former may be expected, from an impartial stranger the second; but the last, whatever may be pretended, can only proceed from an enemy. The principles of biography, and of portrait-painting, are precisely the same.

But if Johnson, in his Life of Savage, inclined rather to the manner of an enemy, than that of a friend, it must be allowed that he acted not from personal pique, but on principle, and that he was as little sparing of palliatives as he judged would be advantageous to the interests of morality. In Johnson's life, his *inimical friends* can offer no such excuse for their conduct: his moral character, they acknowledge, was every thing that could be expected from a man, and that man a Christian. Surely, they have promulged his imbecilities with a most unchristian zeal!

The Life of Savage compleatly established Johnson's character as an able writer; and the celebrated Henry Fielding [*sic*], with all the liberality of congenial talents, recognized his great ability, by publishing a fine encomium on this biographical essay, in a periodical paper of that day, called the Champion.

About the time when Johnson produced his Life of Savage, he was engaged by Osborne, the bookseller, who had just given 13,000£ for the then lately deceased Earl of Oxford's library of printed books, to assist the completion of a very curious catalogue of what was called the Harleian Library, in four octavo volumes, with remarks on each article.

Though the first and second volumes of this famous catalogue are supposed to have been planned and compiled by Mr. Maittaire and Mr. Oldys, the two last are considered as the work of Johnson, who certainly wrote the preface, and was afterwards retained to select all the most scarce and valuable small tracts this vast library contained, which were accordingly published in eight quarto volumes, in the year 1749 [1744–46], under the title of the Harleian Miscellany, preceded by an original Treatise on the importance of fugitive essays.

While Johnson was employed in this undertaking, which was perhaps less disagreeable to him than has been imagined, since it gave him the opportunity of looking into many valuable books which he might else never have seen, a memorable incident occurred, which has been variously related.

Osborne, who possessed all the characteristicks of an illiterate but mercenary bookseller, and whom Johnson, in his Life of Pope, has described as "entirely destitute of shame, and without sense of any disgrace but that of poverty,"[25] had taken into his head, the common mechanical cant against men of genius, that Johnson was idle. Such beings, having no ideas themselves, are unwilling to allow those who have any time for thinking, and can only judge of industry by the quantity produced; which, in the present case, Osborne's avaricious disposition considered as by no means proportioned to his own conception of what the pittance he grudgingly afforded for the work entitled him to expect. Full of these notions, and alive only to self-interest, having narrowly watched an opportunity, when the work was under a temporary delay, to detect Johnson in the act of perusing a book more than seemed to him necessary for the present purpose, he attacked the quiescent author with a torrent of the most illiberal invective. It was in vain that Johnson offered a reasonable justification of his conduct, by urging the temptation he was perpetually under, from the peculiar nature of the business: the bookseller saw no reason in what opposed his interest; and, with all the insolence of a beggar risen to opulence, had the hardiness to give Johnson the lye. To such language, and from a creature so truly inferior, there is only one reply, and it was instantly made; for the words were scarcely uttered, when Johnson, seizing a huge folio volume, hurled it at Osborne's head, and literally knocked him down: he was about to rise; but Johnson's passion had not yet subsided, and he plainly told him not to be in a hurry, as he should in that case be under the necessity of again levelling him with his native dirt. The meanness that could thus insult had all the accustomed cowardice of such a disposition; and Osborne was now as abject in his submission and apologies, as he had been haughty in the commission of the offense. Johnson was not implacable, and such an accommodation took place as induced him to compleat the work.

In the year 1745, Johnson projected a new edition of Shakespeare; and actually published "Miscellaneous Observations on the Tragedy of Macbeth, with Remarks on Sir Thomas Hanmer's Edition of Shakespeare," and proposals for an edition by himself. This production was not so universally received as to encourage his hastily proceeding in the proposed work; though its merit was acknowledged by Dr. Warburton to be very far above all the Essays, Remarks, and Observations, on Shakespeare, which he had ever examined.

This was the period when Johnson began to rise most rapidly in reputation. His great talents were generally known, and as generally acknowledged; the circle of his acquaintance had become considerably extended; and some of his early friends had already acquired considerable fame. Mr. Garrick, in particular, had for some time been in possession of the most extravagant popular applause, and was now joint-manager with Mr. Sheridan, in the Smock Alley Theatre, Dublin, where the admiration of his unrivalled abilities was to the full as great as in England.

The idea of a new edition of Shakespeare might be suggested by Mr. Garrick, or it might suggest itself to Johnson from the circumstance of that great performer's celebrity in Shakespeare's characters.

An offer of more certain advantage fully determined Johnson to abandon for the present his designs on Shakespeare. This was a proposal from certain booksellers, to compile that celebrated Dictionary of the English Language, which the present biographical Sketch has the honour to accompany in the first edition comprized in a single volume. The agreement for this undertaking was signed on the 18th of June 1746; and Sir John Hawkins, who says he writes with the original contract in his hand, states the sum stipulated to be paid for the work, which was to be two volumes in folio, at fifteen hundred guineas.[26]

Sir John, who has no mean skill in the art of acquiring the reputation of a man of letters, with more servility than most of those writers for bread as well as fame, whom he affects to despise throughout his vast budget of Anecdotes, entitled Johnson's Life, would descend to practise, strains hard for a compliment to the liberality of those who, confederating together for the monopoly of wit and learning, to enslave genius, plunder the publick, and enrich themselves, in direct opposition to the laws of their country, impudently arrogate to themselves the farcical appellation of the *body of booksellers,* though not a fiftieth part of the persons who sell books even in London, nor one single country book-seller, is comprized in the curious idea of this self-created body of con-gregated dulness.

The influence of these men, as proprietors of Reviews, Magazines, and Newspapers, has been long experienced; and Sir John, in the course of his extensive reading, having learned that Cerberus, the triple-headed porter of hell, was to be appeased by a sop, sagaciously resolved to try the effect of throwing one to *a monstrous body without any head at all.*

But sapience is not confined to the magisterial chair: periodical prints are become more numerous, some few are in liberal hands, and cunning that passed current a few years ago is now soon detected. New arts, it is true, are not wanting: but the generality of readers have more sense than many reputed authors; and those who are as willing as ever to deceive, dare not always trifle with the understanding of the publick. The consequence is, that Sir John's egregious Life of his learned friend, Johnson, instead of being complimented with the expected return of unmerited praise, has been universally abused in every literary review, with more indiscriminate censure than, perhaps, after all, it really deserves.

In adventitiously speaking of Sir John, it is difficult to avoid running into his long digressions. The liberality of his imagined friends, *the booksellers,* will be judged by every reader of the subsequent facts.

To acquire this vast sum of 1575£ it is allowed, that Johnson, who had hitherto occupied apartments in different parts of the metropolis, was under the necessity of taking a house in Gough Square, Fleet Street, that he might be near Mr. Strahan's printing-office; and not only to fit up a large room with desks and other conveniences for the purpose, but actually to employ, as Sir John asserts, "five or six amanuenses con-stantly under his eye," out of his own pocket.[27] When it is added, that the Dictionary was not published till May [15 April] 1755, a period of almost nine years, it will hardly be thought that his employers had any great right to expect they should be praised for uncommon generos-ity.

To establish the liberality of these gentlemen booksellers, in opposi-tion to the almost unanimous sentiments of the House of Peers, on the famous decision respecting literary property,[28] who with great truth and justice characterized them, in the memorable debates on that occasion, "as scandalous monopolizers, fattening at the expence of other men's ingenuity, and growing opulent by oppression," Sir John Hawkins has involved himself in the labyrinth of contradiction.

These are his words —

Johnson, who was no very accurate accountant, thought a great part would be coming to him on the conclusion of the work; but upon producing, at a tavern-meeting for the purpose of settling, receipts for sums advanced to him, which were indeed the chief means of his subsistence, it was found, not only that he had eaten his cake, but that the balance of the account was greatly against him. His debtors were now become his creditors: but they, in a perfect consistency with that liberal spirit which, in sundry instances, the *great booksellers* are known to have exercised towards authors, remitted the difference, and consoled him for the disappointment by making his entertainment at the tavern a *treat*.[29]

That is, with hardly to be expected generosity, they paid his share of the reckoning. A vast proof of booksellers' *liberality!* Sir John, in his great zeal for the reputation of booksellers, might have added, of their *piety*, too! It was a literal compliance with a scriptural injunction, and is perhaps the strongest proof that can possibly be adduced, of their attention to any precept in the sacred writings. *"Give strong drink unto him that is ready to perish, and wine to those that be of heavy hearts. Let him drink, and forget his poverty, and remember his misery no more."* Prov. xxxi. 6, 7.

The praise of a tavern treat being thus allowed, it remains to examine what Sir John Hawkins has advanced, which militates against the assertion that Johnson was overpaid. This, then, is comprized in a well-known anecdote related by Sir John, as it has often been by others, that Andrew Millar, who was treasurer for his colleagues, the booksellers, *on paying for the last sheet of the dictionary*, wrote the following laconick note to Johnson.

"Andrew Millar sends his compliments to Mr. Samuel Johnson, with the money for the last sheet of copy of the Dictionary, *and thanks God he has done with him.*"

This very *liberal* and *religious* note was immediately answered by Johnson with great good-humour.

"Samuel Johnson returns his compliments to Mr. Andrew Millar, and is very glad to find, as he does by his note, *that Andrew Millar has the grace to thank God for any thing.*"[30]

Now, if Johnson was paid for each sheet, as the work proceeded, and did not receive the money for the last sheet till it was actually finished, how could there be any after-settlement or over payment?

This is the labyrinth into which Sir John has entered; and, as we are all apt to be bewildered, when we have a favourite object in view, it is the duty of every individual to assist his stray-brother.

The clue to these incongruous accounts seems to be contained in an anecdote which Sir John has not thought it convenient to relate, as it rather tends to overthrow his position, respecting the vast liberality of Johnson's employers. The story is this — In the course of his arduous task, Johnson finding himself, with all his exertions, most miserably poor, applied to the booksellers for an augmentation of the agreed price; this was not only refused, but he was menaced with a suit in equity, to compel him to proceed under the original contract: but, at length, finding he despised their threats, and convinced that nothing less than a complete acquiescence could induce him to go on, they prudently put the best face on the business, and acceded to his proposition. It was probably at a meeting to settle this new arrangement, and not at the conclusion of the work, that Johnson had received a trifle more than he would have been entitled to from the first agreement, which was then allowed him, with the addition of a tavern supper; after which he was to proceed at so much a sheet, as the best possible way of avoiding any future misunderstanding.[31]

If this transaction reflects but little disgrace on the booksellers, it certainly does not entitle them to any great praise for their generosity.

A truce, then, to the liberality of associated booksellers! of which, it is hoped, there may hereafter be better proofs than any at present before the world. As in individuals, some of them deserve esteem; but, as a body, they are as truly despicable as a gang of smugglers, or any other confederacy of marauders, linked together for the purpose of levying contributions on the publick in despite of legal authority.

Leaving Sir John Hawkins to reconcile his great veneration for the laws of his country, with his attachment to those who confederate for the purpose of defeating them, it will be proper to go back to the period when Johnson commenced the work which has given rise to these circuitous remarks.

The great lexicographer, as he has been usually called, had not proceeded far in his Dictionary, when it was intimated that the Earl of Chesterfield, then one of his majesty's principal secretaries of state, had expressed his approbation of the design in such handsome terms as implied an inclination to patronize the undertaking, if not to assist it, as a man of genius, with his advice. This hint induced Johnson to draw up a plan of his intended work, which was transmitted to the Earl, and published under his sanction, in the year 1747.

Nothing could be more unnatural than such an association; the Earl
was the quintessence of what is called good-breeding, and Johnson has
seldom been praised for politeness. At the formal interviews which this
transaction occasioned, Johnson felt himself very ill at ease; and they
were soon mutually disgusted with each other. Having called, by
appointment, one morning, Johnson was informed that the Earl had
a gentleman with him, and was shown into an anti-chamber, to wait
his departure. After remaining upwards of an hour, he by some means
received information that the gentleman with whom the Earl was
engaged, was no other than the celebrated Colley Cibber. On obtaining
this intelligence, he immediately rushed out of the house, with a determination never to enter it again;[32] and, hastening home, wrote a very
angry letter, expressing his sense of the indignity which he conceived
had been offered him, and renouncing for ever his lordship's patronage.
Though the Earl made no reply to this letter, he instructed Sir Thomas
Robinson and Sir Joshua Reynolds to apologize to Johnson; and, when
the work was compleated, went so far as to write an essay in its favour,
for that well-known periodical paper, called the World.[33] Johnson, however, was not to be appeased; though this transaction seems to have
first brought him acquainted with Sir Joshua.[34]

He had, he said, in his printed Address to the Earl of Chesterfield,
laboured to gild a rotten post; the Earl's accomplishments, he found,
were only those of a dancing-master; and, though he might be considered as a wit among lords, he was no more than a lord among wits.
The character which the Earl gave of Johnson, whom he called a respectable Hottentot, in the celebrated Letters to his Son, has already been
sufficiently promulged.

In the year 1747 [1748], that ingenious and truly liberal bookseller,
Mr. Robert Dodsley, having projected his plan of the Preceptor, engaged
Johnson's advice and assistance in the undertaking. The preface, which
in itself forms a miniature introduction to science, was accordingly written by Johnson; and his Vision of Theodore, the Hermit of Teneriffe,
produced for this work, is one of the finest moral allegories, if not
the very finest, that ever proceeded from the pen of man. This is
a bold assertion, but it is not a hasty one: and those who peruse the
Vision of the Hermit of Teneriffe with attention; consider its excellent
adaptation to the work; and reflect on the valuable precepts it inculcates;
if they are at all zealous for the virtue of the rising generation, and
the consequent felicity of their fellow-creatures, will not deem any
encomium too great for its deserts.

About this time, Mr. Garrick became joint-patentee with Mr. Lacy, in the Theatre-Royal, Drury Lane; and, on opening for the season, in the autumn of 1747, an occasional prologue was written by Johnson, and spoke by Garrick, highly to the credit of both parties.

It may appear rather wonderful, that Johnson, having long since written a tragedy, had not, on his friend Garrick's theatrical success, procured its introduction to the stage. But the theatres were then, as theatres always will be while they continue a monopoly, accessible only to those who possess a certain degree of pliability not often found to exist in persons of real genius.

On Garrick's becoming manager, the hopes of Johnson revived; as the intimacy they had always preserved seemed to him a sufficient security against the usual duplicity, caprice, and insolence, so much dreaded by men of great talents who are at all conversant in the intrigues of a theatre-royal. A good play, he knew, might be so got up as to procure its certain condemnation, and a bad one obtain for a time the semblance of general applause, by artifices as easily detected as it would be difficult to avoid their effects. In the pride of conscious ability, he would probably have preferred starving to these risques; but, with the advantage of a manager's friendship, and that manager Garrick, he must have been unpardonably inattentive to his own interest, had he declined the offer to bring forward his tragedy.

Having undergone a strict revisal, to receive the improvements of his more mature judgment, and aided by the practical hints of Garrick, it was brought out with the whole strength of the house, in the winter of 1749. But neither the excellence of a Dramatis Personae which will hardly ever be equalled — Garrick, Barry, Mrs. Cibber, and Mrs. Pritchard — with all the aids of splendid dresses, and the most magnificent scenery, could protract the existence of the piece beyond the ninth night.

With many of the excellences, Irene has almost all the faults of Addison's Cato. Like that, though vastly inferior, it is at best a mere scholar's play, and fit only for academical exhibition. A mixed audience, accustomed to the impassioned scenes, and glowing language of Nature, as they flow spontaneously from Shakespeare, will never be delighted by the languid business, and frigid sentiments, of critical precision, conveyed with all the elegance that can possibly result from study. Johnson has sacrificed every thing to moral; which is, it must be confessed, the most valuable quality in the idea of a perfect drama: but moral, alone, will always fail of effect; and, if a strict attention to the unities, and the striking beauties which pervade much of the language, are excepted, Johnson has not discovered, throughout this juvenile effort, as it ought always to be called, the smallest proof that he possessed any dramatick ability. The truth of history is not only unnecessarily, but injuriously violated; the plot is miserably conducted; the characters are inconsistent, and without energy; and the incidents are disgustingly insipid and unnatural.

If Johnson really thought his Irene so good a tragedy, that he should never write a better, he acted wisely in not attempting another. But the specimens it contains of just and noble sentiments, cloathed in elegant and manly diction, afford much cause for regret that he did not, when his judgment was compleatly ripened, make at least a second effort.

Though the Dictionary now occupied the bulk of Johnson's time, he still found leisure for occasional exercises of his genius.

Soon after the failure of his tragedy, he published a second imitation of Juvenal, from the tenth satire, which he entitled The Vanity of Human Wishes;[35] and, about this time, to enjoy his favourite relaxation from the severity of study, he established a weekly select club, of which Hawkesworth was a member, at the King's Head Beef-steak House, in Ivy Lane, within a few doors of Paternoster Row.

One of the associates at this club,[36] being concerned in the publication of Lauder's infamous and well-known attack on the literary reputation of Milton, submitted the proof-sheets of that work, as they came from the press, to the inspection of his brother members, who appear to have felt a malicious delight in what was judged a compleat detection of his plagiaries. How any men of sense, in the smallest degree acquainted with the genius of Milton's works, could encourage an idea, that it was possible for his divine poem of Paradise Lost to have been hashed up from scraps of obscure authors, is truly astonishing; and it is greatly to be regretted that such a man as Johnson suffered himself to be so blinded by his political prejudices against the divine bard, as to be one of the greatest dupes to this flagitious deceit. The truth of history requires that it should be added, he was not only deceived himself, but so far assisted to deceive others, as actually to write the very specious preface to that scandalous work, the forgeries and impositions of which were so clearly detected and exposed, a short time after the book appeared, by the Reverend Dr. Douglas, now Bishop of Carlisle. Let it, however, be also added, that he was no sooner convinced of his error, than he not only expressed his concern at having been thus instrumental in the propagation of a falsehood, but exerted himself so effectually to undo what he had unadvisedly done, that he actually wrote, and procured Lauder to publish his own, the famous recantation of his infamy.

At the beginning of the year 1750, either to relieve his mind from the irksome task of incessant labour at his Dictionary, or with a view to improve the scanty allowance which his slow progress in the work would permit him to draw from that source, happily for the interests of morality, he was induced to begin that exquisite periodical paper, called the Rambler; which is so well known, and so universally admired, in every civilized part of the globe. To speak of this work collectively, can do it no sort of justice; and, to enter into a minute discussion of its various excellences, would require a volume. Its defects lie in a narrow compass: the language, though equally nervous and elegant, is sometimes encumbered by words which possess too much Latinity for a mere English reader; and, in the partiality for these expressions, which are fatal to every attempt at humour, the discriminations of character are often wholly neglected or destroyed.

The first number of the Rambler was published on Tuesday, the 20th of March 1750; and an additional essay was produced every succeeding Tuesday and Saturday, till March 14, 1752, when the work was compleated in two hundred and eight papers, only four of which are known to have been written by other hands: Number 30, by Mrs. Catherine Talbot; Number 97, by Mr. Samuel Richardson; and Numbers 44 and 100, by Mrs. Elizabeth Carter.

At the commencement of this fine moral work, Johnson composed a short prayer; from which it is apparent, that his grand objects in the undertaking, were the glory of God, and the best interests of society.

Almighty God, the giver of all good things, without whose help all labor is ineffectual, and without whose grace all wisdom is folly; grant, I beseech thee, that in this undertaking thy Holy Spirit may not be withheld from me, but that I may promote thy glory, and the salvation of myself and others. Grant this, O Lord! for the sake of thy Son, Jesus Christ. Amen.[37]

The conclusion of Johnson's Rambler possesses a spirit of piety, which proves his religious ardour to have been unabated, when he finished the work which he had so laudably begun.

The essays professedly serious, if I have been able to execute my own intentions, will be found exactly conformable to the precepts of Christianity, without any accommodation to the licentiousness and levity of the present age. I therefore look back on this part of my work with a pleasure which no praise of man shall diminish or augment. I shall never envy the honours which wit and learning obtain in any other cause, if I can be numbered among the writers who have given ardour to virtue, and confidence to truth. "Celestial powers! that piety regard; / From you my labors wait their last reward."[38]

Perhaps, however, the distich, from a Greek verse, with which the Rambler closes, may be liable to critical objection, as introducing a polytheistical mode of expression — *"Celestial powers!"* — in a solemn Christian address.

The papers of the Rambler, as they came out, were immediately reprinted in Scotland, under the direction of Mr. Elphinston, who was intimate with Johnson, and furnished those translations of the mottos which have accompanied every subsequent edition.

About the time of beginning the Rambler, it having been accidentaly discovered that Mrs. Elizabeth Foster, a woman of very advanced age, the grand-daughter and only known surviving descendent of Milton, was then living, in great obscurity, if not in absolute distress, Johnson felt himself called on to make some amends to the last posterity of a man whose fame he had so unjustly injured, and solicited his friend Garrick to perform the Masque of Comus for her benefit. Garrick, who was never backward in this kind of benevolence, not only chearfully complied with his request, but agreed to speak a prologue, if Johnson would write one on the occasion. It was accordingly written in a few hours; and, on the 5th of April 1750, delivered by Mr. Garrick, at Drury Lane theatre. But though considerable interest was exerted, and the liberal manager even made it a free benefit, it is said only to have produced the poor woman about a hundred and thirty pounds. This transaction, therefore, is far more to the honour of Garrick, and of Johnson, than to the publick of that day. Among all the vices of more modern refinement, a benefit for the posterity of Milton would now be hardly so ill attended. The prologue, which is not remarkable for possessing any great degree of poetical merit, mentions the recent attack on Milton's fame, and congratulates the publick on the defeat of his calumniators.

About this time, in the spring of 1751, Mrs. Lennox having finished Harriet Stuart, the first novel of that ingenious and then very young lady, Johnson, who had ever been partial to her great abilities, from the earliest dawn of her infant genius, which had appeared two or three years before in a small collection of beautiful little poems, proposed to the Ivy Lane club, and some other friends, a meeting at the Devil Tavern, and a whole night's festivity, for the purpose of celebrating what, in the whimsicality of the hour, he had thought proper to call, the birth of Mrs. Lennox's first literary child. This strange fancy being complied with, the meeting took place; and Mrs. Lennox attending, with her husband and a female acquaintance, a sprig of laurel was presented to the fair author, as a proper compliment to her genius.

Sir John Hawkins, who was present, asserts, "that a magnificent hot apple-pye was stuck with bay-leaves on the occasion": and adds, "that Johnson had prepared a crown of laurel for the purpose; with which, after invoking the Muses, by some ceremonies of his own invention, he actually encircled her brows." [39]

The learned knight, however, must certainly have either had recourse to his own ample fund of *invention,* or mistaken what might be jocosely proposed at the club for what actually took place at this celebrity; since Mrs. Lennox has lately been heard to declare, that she can by no means remember what is so very ingeniously represented as a coronation, though she perfectly well recollects the circumstance of receiving a sprig of laurel stuck in her glass of jelly.

The business, whatever it was, exhibits Johnson in no unamiable view. It indicates great goodness of heart, and manifests the friendliest disposition towards kindred genius. He considered Mrs. Lennox as possessing talents of the first order; and the event has proved, that he was not mistaken in his judgment. How few, among the many female authors of past or present times, deservedly risen to fame, have written so much, so variously, and so well! To her Henrietta, General Burgoyne's popular comedy of the Heiress is indebted for its very best scenes; and the author who has dramaticised with so much ability would not have been disgraced by a candid acknowledgement of his source. Mrs. Lennox, it is reported, has just finished another novel, equally rich in invention; which may probably afford plot, character, and incidents, for future dramatists, who will do well to be more grateful.

It has been said, that Johnson would never write without being paid for his labor, and particular instances are adduced in support of this assertion: but it is well known that he, with some other learned friends, assisted Mrs. Lennox in her very arduous task of translating Father Brumoy's Greek Theatre; and her acknowledgment, in the preface, of these friendly aids, with a reference to what those aids were, formed the whole return which was either expected or made on the occasion. He also favored her with a few essays for the Lady's Museum, and wrote a paper of the Trifler in that respectable miscellany. [40]

Though the sale of the Rambler had been very confined, while it was publishing in numbers, the work was no sooner concluded, and collected into volumes, than its success began to bear some proportion to its merits. This was probably the inducement of Dr. Hawkesworth to begin, towards the end of the same year, his almost equally celebrated, and at first more popular paper, the Adventurer, which was continued till the spring of 1754. Johnson supplied those essays, in this work, which are signed with the letter T; and it has been asserted, but without sufficient authority, that he received a stipulated sum for each paper.[41]

At the beginning of 1753 [1752], Johnson experienced a most severe shock in the loss of his wife, who died on the 28th of March, and was buried by Dr. Hawkesworth, in his own parish church, at Bromley, in Kent, under a piece of plain black marble; on which Johnson, many years afterwards, and only a few months before his own decease, placed the following inscription. [Omitted.]

It is observable that Johnson has neither mentioned the day of his wife's nativity, nor her age at the time she died. Whether the omission was by design or accident, different readers may entertain different opinions.

The constitutional melancholy of Johnson increased on the decease of his wife; and the anniversary of her death he most religiously observed, during the many years he survived her loss, by making it a day of abstinence, of prayers, and of tears. This has been ascribed, by Sir John Hawkins, with his customary display of wit, consistency, and candour, partly to the hypocrisy of Johnson, and partly to apprehensions "that his deceased wife was *gone to the devil.*"

Lest this should seem exaggerated, let Sir John speak for himself. "I have often been inclined to think, that if this fondness of Johnson for his wife was not *dissembled,* it was a lesson that he had learned by rote, and that, when he practised it, he knew not where to stop till he became ridiculous."

"That affection," proceeds Sir John, "which could excite in the mind of Milton the pleasing images described in his sonnet on his deceased wife, 'Methought I saw my late espoused *saint,*' wrought no such effect on that of Johnson: the *apparition* of his departed wife was altogether of the terrifick kind, and *hardly afforded him a hope* that she was in *a state of happiness.*"[42]

If this does not mean, that she was in a *state of misery,* or *actually gone to the devil,* what does it mean? And so much for the wit, the candour, and the consistency, of Sir John Hawkins.

But the subject is a serious one! Johnson was no hypocrite; and the loss of a virtuous and affectionate wife will generally be best estimated by the husband who is destined to bear it. Whatever may have been the imperfections of the deceased; it is probable that, on such occasions, the survivor, who has sense and feeling, suffers less from the recollection of them, than the consciousness of what were his own. He must be, indeed, a paragon of a husband, who has never been betrayed by warmth of temper into some too violent assumption of authority: who has at no time been cruel when kindness was necessary; who has never been harsh instead of tender, never blamed where he should have pitied, or resented what he should have forgiven. These are the sources of regret to an ingenuous mind, when the power of reparation is for ever lost; and while every amiable quality of the deceased is felt to have been too slightly regarded, there is but little leisure, and still less inclination, to reflect on failings of no uncommon magnitude.

That something like this was the state of Johnson's mind, is extremely obvious, from his having prayed, in express terms, on the first anniversary of his loss, *"to be forgiven all the sins he had committed, and all the duties he had neglected, in his union with the wife whom God had taken from him; for the neglect of joint devotion, patient exhortation, and mild instruction."* [43] This was the contrition of a man conscious of his own infirmity; and, in whatever light it may appear to the ignorant or the evil, there can be but little doubt that it was accepted by Him who is the Fountain of all wisdom and goodness.

Mrs. Johnson, there is great reason to believe, was a very intelligent woman, and had a good heart: but, as Johnson has himself been heard to say, "She was one of those wives who have a particular reverence for cleanliness, and desire the praise of neatness in their dress and furniture, till they become troublesome to their best friends, slaves to their own besoms, and only sigh for the hour of sweeping their husbands out of the house as dirt and useless lumber." [44]

The most careless observer of human nature can hardly fail to perceive that this peculiarity was alone sufficient to produce occasional bickerings with a man of Johnson's hasty disposition.

Her rebuke to Johnson, who was perpetually finding fault with his dinner, when he one day rose as usual to say grace, deserves to be recorded. "Nay! hold, Mr. Johnson; and do not make a farce of thanking God for a dinner which in a few minutes you will pronounce not eatable!" [45]

In January 1754, the death of Mr. Cave deprived Johnson of a most sincere friend, whose memory he has honoured with a biographical sketch in the Gentleman's Magazine, which owed its origin to that worthy and ingenious printer.

At the latter end of the same year, Johnson compleated his Dictionary; and, in the last paragraph of his Preface, which few readers of sensibility can attentively peruse without tears, pathetically laments, that "he has protracted his work till most of those whom he wished to please had sunk into the grave!" [46]

In May [April] 1755, this great work was published; the university of Oxford having, on the 10th [20th] of February preceding its appearance, constituted him Master of Arts, in full convocation.

Nor was this the only academical compliment he received on the occasion; for, Lord Corke being then at Florence, and presenting the British Lexicon, in the Author's name, to the Academy della Crusca, the members of that learned body transmitted to Johnson, in return, a beautiful copy of their celebrated *Vocabulario:* and the French Academy signified their approbation of the work, about the same time, by sending him their famous *Dictionnaire,* which he received from the hands of his friend Mr. Langton.

Mr. Garrick, too, complimented the author with a few lines of that familiar poetry, in the manufacture of which he so eminently excelled. [*On Johnson's Dictionary* has been omitted.]

The forty Frenchmen, whom Garrick thus pays his friend Johnson the compliment of having beaten, it may be necessary to observe, were that number of members of the French academy, who had been employed in settling their language.

The witlings of the time did not fail to attack the petty blunders in this great work; which, it must be acknowledged, like most other stupendous literary performances, has been sometimes extolled much beyond its real desert. It has been represented, as that perfect work which no human talents can ever produce; and the prodigious labour of accomplishing such a task has been magnified by those who have but little considered the subject, and who have possibly understood it less. Yet it is a work of labour; and, every thing considered, of wonderful perfection too: but, if the vast merit of the original definitions in general is excepted, there are, perhaps, many dull fabricators of books, who could have produced a more useful, regular, and less inaccurate, English lexicon. To be more useful, the mere labour of collecting more words would be sufficient; to be more regular and uniform in the illustrations of words, nothing more would be necessary than a diligent and patient attention to the object; and the superior correctness would require little else than particular care in transcribing the several quotations. These qualities are attainable by a mere mechanical writer, of competent diligence and good sense, without the smallest degree of what is properly denominated genius; and of which Johnson had abundantly too much for the drudgery of such an employ. Perfection might, indeed, be expected, if we could ever hope to see great genius, and indefatigable corporeal industry, united in the same person: but the exertions of genius are to the mind, what labour is to the body, with an aggravation of fatigue which those who have never so laboured can but ill conceive;

and, as the necessary relaxations require to be proportioned, the union of such opposite powers will rarely or never happen.

No man could be more sensible of the imperfections of his work than Johnson himself; who has repeatedly cautioned the reader, both in his Preface to the first, and the Advertisement to future editions, against the vain expectation of finding such a work free from inaccuracy.

Much he has certainly accomplished; but much is still wanting, before we can boast that we have a national dictionary which reflects the highest degree of honour on our character as a polished and literary people. However individuals may be flattered by their own vanity, or the partiality of friends, it is what we shall hardly ever see accomplished by the sagacity of a single person; and the man will have much reason to be proud, be he whom he may, who shall ever contribute as largely, from his own intellectual sources, towards the completion of so desirable a performance, as Johnson has certainly done.

Should a small portion of the exuberant patronage which the ARTS have for some years been accustomed to receive, be at any future period happily directed to the encouragement and promotion of SCIENCE, the purity of the English language might soon gain the summit of mundane perfection, and a compleat English Lexicon be expected to issue from a *Royal Academy of Science.*

When Johnson had finished his Dictionary, which was too copious, as well as too extensive, to be calculated for general use, the booksellers prevailed on him to make an abridgment in two octavo volumes, the sale of which has been astonishingly extensive.

These works being ended, and his advantage concluding where that of his employers began, he was under the necessity of retrenching his expences. Accordingly, he quitted his house in Gough Square, where he had, since the death of Mrs. Johnson, very humanely entertained her acquaintance, Miss Anna Williams, and took chambers in Gray's Inn. Mrs. Williams, for so she was always called, was the daughter of Mr. Zachariah Williams, a surgeon by profession, and a very ingenious man; but who had devoted too much time and attention to longitudinal experiments; which turning out unsuccessful, produced, as is generally the case with unfortunate projectors, the sad reverse of real poverty instead of expected riches. A cataract on both her eyes, had deprived this very sensible young woman of her sight; and Johnson, to procure her the best surgical assistance, had taken her under his immediate protection. On his going into chambers, he placed her in a respectable family; and prevailed on Mr. Garrick to give her a benefit, which produced her two hundred pounds. This sum, with the addition of another hundred which she afterwards gained by the publication of a small volume of miscellanies in prose and verse of her own composition, afforded her a little income, which Johnson took care to augment into a decent competency.

In the year 1756, Johnson wrote a few essays in a work, called the Universal Visiter, or Monthly Memorialist, printed for Gardner in the Strand; to which Mr. Garrick, Mr. Christopher Smart, Mr. Richard Rolt, and Dr. Percy, the present Bishop of Dromore, also contributed. But, such is the uncertainty of success in all literary adventures, that even these associated abilities were incapable of prolonging the existence of the work beyond a few months. The essays of Johnson are distinguished by two asterisks, those of the other writers by the initials of their respective names.

In the same year he was also induced to assist Mr. Faden, the printer of the Public Ledger, in the compilation of a new miscellany, called the Literary Magazine. In this work, which was carried on only two years, Johnson's Memoirs of the late King of Prussia first appeared; which have recently been reprinted, with Notes and a Continuation, by the Author of this Biographical Sketch, and published in an octavo volume.[47] Johnson wrote the Preface to the Literary Magazine; and in this it is asserted that different departments of the work were assigned to different writers. The Review of Books appears to have fallen principally to his own share; and that peculiarity of style which is not easily mistaken, seems discernible ,in several other articles. It was in this magazine that poor Jonas Hanway, *"whose chief failing,"* Sir John Hawkins, with great fellow-feeling, observes, *"was a propensity to writing and publishing books, which, for the triteness and inanity of the sentiments contained in them, no one can read!"* [48] unfortunately encountered the severity of Johnson's criticism, on printing his curious Eight Days Journey from Portsmouth to Kingston upon Thames, in two large octavo volumes.

About the beginning of the year 1757 [1756], Johnson revived his design of producing a new edition of Shakespeare; and accordingly published, in April, his plan and proposals for a Subscription, at two guineas for the eight volumes in octavo; his booksellers agreeing that he should receive all the advantage of a subscription to the first edition, on condition that he relinquished to them the future copyright.

Though Johnson certainly meant, when he issued proposals, to get through his edition of Shakespeare with the greatest possible expedition, he seems to have been diverted from his intention by the want of what he might properly enough deem sufficient encouragement. Subscriptions might, perhaps, come in slowly; and the damp which an author feels, when the warm and sanguine expectations he naturally forms at the commencement of an important undertaking begin to evaporate, and leave only the dread of neglect and disappointment, produces a mental relaxation which is with great difficulty repaired, even by that best restorative, the chearing influence of brighter days.

In April 1758, the Idler began to appear, which was first printed in a weekly newspaper, called the Universal Chronicle, published by Mr. Newbery, in St. Paul's Church Yard.[49] It was continued till the 5th of April 1760, when it closed with the hundred and third number. Twelve of these essays are acknowledged to have been furnished by correspondents; and three of them, on the subject of painting, are known to be the productions of Sir Joshua Reynolds.

This is a more familiar production than the Rambler. There the author appears cloathed in all the heavy pomp and splendor of a rich birth-day suit; the Idler presents him in a light and pleasing undress; but the peculiarity of his gait is in both equally discernible.

It has been said that Johnson, about the end of the year 1758, when his mother was on her death-bed, communicated his plan of Rasselas, Prince of Abyssinia, to one of his booksellers, whom he requested to advance twenty guineas, that he might be enabled to visit her at Lichfield, in her last moments: but the money was refused till the manuscript should be compleated, which he accordingly sat down to finish, in a state of mind which might well induce him to describe the world as containing little else than misery and wretchedness. In the mean time, he procured the loan of eight guineas from his neighbour, Mr. Allen, the printer, which he sent into the country for her present relief; and had just finished a task the most irksome that can be conceived, with the hope of once more seeing a tender and affectionate mother, when he received information that she was actually dead.

It was under the immediate impression of this loss, that he penned those excellent reflections on the death of a friend, which appear as a letter from a correspondent in the forty-first number of the Idler.

The copy of Rasselas being compleated, was sold to another bookseller, in February 1759, by the recommendation of Mr. Baretti; and the man who had been shabby enough to refuse the trifling assistance required, felt the mortification of seeing a rival in trade derive that advantage from the extensive sale of the work which he had himself lost by his meanness and ingratitude.[50]

At the latter end of 1759, Johnson attacked the design of Mr. Mylne, the architect for Black Friar's Bridge;[51] contending, with great strength of argument, and with more knowledge of the subject than might have been expected, against the preference which was given to elliptical instead of semicircular arches. Indeed, it is highly probable that he received some professional hints from a rival architect who had no inclination to appear in the controversy.

At the beginning of 1760, Johnson removed from Gray's Inn to Inner Temple Lane.[52] How he was at this exact period employed, after the conclusion of the Idler, unless in preparations for his Shakespeare, it would be difficult to trace. Yet must he not always be supposed inactive, when his biographer is unable to state that he was engaged in any particular production. It is well known that, at almost every period of his life, he occasionally wrote sermons for several of the clergy; that he aided the literary exertions of many who knew the value of his assistance in what was to pass as their own; and that he was ever a very large contributor to reviews, and other periodical miscellanies. So numerous, indeed, were his miscellaneous productions, that he has frequently been heard to declare it was by no means in his own power to collect them all.

The accession of his present majesty, towards the end of this year, opened a new and unexpected scene to Johnson. While he was brooding over his constitutional melancholy; and, probably, considering himself, as he had reason to do, notwithstanding the celebrity of his works, very inadequately rewarded by the mere remuneration of booksellers, who profited at least ten times as much as himself by his genius and labour; he received information from Lord Bute, through the medium of Mr. Murphy, that the King was disposed to grant a pension of three hundred pounds a year, as some recompence to the merits of a man whose writings had so materially conduced to promote the interest of morality, and enlarge the publick stock of useful knowledge.

The surprize and confusion of Johnson, at this unexpected proposal, made him wisely decline an immediate answer to the question whether it would be acceptable. The next day, however, having fully considered the matter, he prudently determined not to refuse what had been so handsomely offered.

What passed in Johnson's mind during this interval, the Great Searcher of hearts alone knows with any certainty: but there can be little doubt that he weighed, with an integrity which was never known to have forsaken him, his own merits and defects. His early prejudices against the Hanoverian succession had probably been long worn away by the maturity of reason, and an enlarged view of things. His writings, for more than twenty years back, though frequently on political subjects, had not been in the smallest degree tinctured with disaffection: he now saw a prince on the throne whose character was irreproachable; and whose love of liberty, and veneration for justice, were so great, that he had, as the first act of his reign, voluntarily rendered the judges independent even of himself. Under such a sovereign, he reflected, no prostitution of his talents was at all likely to be required; and he knew that, if the monarch ceased to be virtuous, and any such degradation should be expected, the remedy against an evil which no consideration on earth could ever have tempted him to endure, was always at hand. The event has abundantly proved, that he judged wisely: for, whatever diversity of sentiments may at different times have unfortunately prevailed, as to the mal-administration of particular statesmen in the present reign, there seems happily but one opinion as to the uniform character of the sovereign; who is justly considered as not having a single subject throughout his dominions, who is, at once, a better christian — a better friend — a better husband — a better father — in short, a better man — than himself. This, though it does not usually constitute the eulogy of Kings, is no mean praise; and it is a praise which, perhaps, few Kings, besides our own, can justly claim. The hand that pens this would not fear to censure the greatest monarch on earth where censure was conceived to be due; but, surely, a man like Johnson, whose abilities rendered him capable of irradiating the minds of a great people, and who had, at once, actually diffused both wisdom and morality, from the labours of a long series of years, might be so far from blushing to receive his reward from their royal representative, though stigmatized by the name of a pension, that he had reason to think such a distinction one of the greatest honours that could possibly be conferred upon him.

The idle stuff, invented by impudence, and which ignorance has so industriously promulged, that Johnson altered his definition of the word *pension,* in the subsequent editions of his Dictionary, after becoming a pensioner, is without the smallest foundation in fact. The definition stands exactly the same in all the editions; and those who could suppose him capable of altering a single word on such an occasion, knew little of the man. He had a mind infinitely too strong to be at all affected, either by the hissings of Envy, or the brayings of Folly!

The attention of Johnson was employed on higher objects than considering what the frivolous or malicious might amuse themselves with saying about his pension: he began to consider how he might employ it with the most satisfaction to himself, and render it useful to such others as he had hitherto been less able than willing to assist.

Besides Mrs. Williams, he had Francis Barber, the negro, to provide for, whom Dr. Bathurst[53] had some years before brought from Jamaica, and who was now sent to school at Bishop Stortford, where he remained five years at Johnson's expence; and Mr. Levet, a sort of itinerant professor of medicine, but in whose skill he placed much confidence, had been several years an humble dependant on his bounty. The number of others he was in the habit of relieving, besides occasional acts of charity, is known to have been prodigious, when his trifling ability is considered; and affords the most irrefragable proof that, however rough his disposition might sometimes be, he had a heart exquisitely tender, and a truly philanthropick mind.

In 1762, the credulity of Johnson in the affair of the Cock Lane Ghost, subjected him to much popular raillery, and even the more durable satire of Churchill. Foote, too, ever watchful for publick topicks, meditated the design of caricaturing him on the stage, with all that mimickry and humour of which he was so capable; but Johnson being apprized of his intention, gave the modern Aristophanes to understand that, if he should have the audacity to perform what he proposed, he would not only attend the exhibition himself, but assuredly furnish a very suitable prologue, by actually leaping on the stage, and cudgelling his representative in the face of the whole audience. Great wits do not always possess great courage; and Foote wisely preferred the certainty of sleeping in a whole skin, to the uncertain profit which he might derive from such a performance to console him for the ignominy of a publick chastisement.

Long before this period, Johnson was visited by all the principal literati, who were very properly solicitous to become acquainted with a man of his extraordinary talents; and, in the winter of 1763, the association in Ivy Lane having been some years dissolved, without any diminution in his love of sociality, a new institution was arranged, which has obtained the appellation of the Literary Club; though, being composed of only nine members, it was certainly on too contracted a scale to merit that distinction.

During all this time Johnson seemed to be making very slow advances with his Shakespeare; and the neglect was, probably with much truth, charged on his pension. But though it may seem that he was not indefatigable, it would be unfair to say he was quite idle, without fuller evidence that he had no necessary avocations, and greater reason to think lightly of his task than good sense will warrant. The collations of different editions; the consideration of difficult passages; the search for illustrations of obsolete phrases and provincial expressions; and the deliberate examination of what preceding commentators have advanced, before a difference of opinion is hazarded; are all necessary acts in an undertaking of this kind, and the time which they consume, in a work of such extent as the whole of Shakespeare's plays, must be very considerable. Indeed, there is great reason to believe that Johnson never appropriated half the time to this business which such an undertaking required. It was published in 1765; and, with a consciousness of what was wanting, and a mind scorning deceit, when he ventures to say, in his preface, that "he has collated such copies as he could procure"; he very candidly adds, that *"he wished for more."* [54]

The Preface, and accounts of the respective plays, were doubtless the most compleat parts of the work; and the former, in particular, which is a most incomparable performance, unites the finest critical disquisition on the writings of Shakespeare, with one of the best dissertations on dramatick composition in general, ever yet produced.

In the subsequent editions of Shakespeare, Mr. Steevens became his coadjutor; a gentleman well calculated to supply the defects of Johnson, and whose assistance might have been sensibly felt in a new edition of the Dictionary.

In July 1765, he was complimented by the university of Dublin, with the degree of Doctor of Laws: a title which, however, he never very cordially accepted or assumed; probably, from the remembrance that they had not given him that of Master of Arts, at a time when the honour was solicited, and when it would have been more conducive to his advantage.

It was in this memorable year that he became first acquainted with Mr. Thrale, the brewer; and that he had the still higher honour of a conversation with his Majesty, at Buckingham House. [55]

His meeting with the King was in the Queen's library; but it is not known whether it was accidental or by appointment. Johnson, however, derived great satisfaction from the event, and always mentioned his majesty's politeness and attention in terms which implied the most profound respect, veneration, and gratitude.

In the course of their conversation, the King asked him, if he intended to give the world any more of his compositions; to which Johnson replied, that he believed he should not, for that he thought he had written enough. "I should have thought so too, " returned his Majesty, with exquisite neatness and address, "if you had not written so well."

The acquaintance of Johnson with Mr. Thrale originated in Mrs. Thrale's ardent desire to rank with literary characters. The desire is not illaudable; and her success has been beyond what she might have expected.

A scheme was concerted between Mrs. Thrale and her literary friend

Mr. Murphy, to draw Johnson to Mr. Thrale's house, in the Borough, under pretence of meeting Woodhouse, the poetical shoemaker, who had distinguished himself by writing some ingenious verses, and who was accordingly invited to dine there.[56] The stratagem succeeded. He met Woodhouse, it is true; whom, probably, neither of the parties ever saw or at all regarded again: but an acquaintance, from that day, commenced between Johnson and Mr. Thrale; and this soon ripened into a friendship, which was only terminated by the death of the latter, after a duration of about sixteen years.

The manner in which Mr. Murphy had himself become intimate with Johnson, some years before, was extremely curious. While the Rambler was publishing, Mr. Murphy being engaged in writing a periodical paper, called the Gray's Inn Journal, happened to meet with a story in a French *Journal Litteraire,* which he thought would make a valuable article in his own work; this he accordingly gave an English dress, and inserted as an original. It was, however, immediately recognized by the publick as an oriental tale from the Rambler, which had been recently translated into French; and Mr. Murphy waiting on Johnson, to apologize, the acquaintance commenced.[57]

In 1766 [1765], Johnson quitted the Temple; and, taking a house in Johnson's Court, Fleet Street, Mrs. Williams, Mr. Levet, and Francis, the black, became part of his domestick establishment. The continual bickerings among these and his other houshold dependents, for a considerable number of years, would have tempted one who made less allowance for the frailties of human nature, to soon rid himself of such troublesome guests. But he bore their infirmities, as he knew they were obliged to do his, with a wonderful degree of patience.

Indeed, most of his leisure time was now spent at Mr. and Mrs. Thrale's; and he frequently resided with them, at their Streatham house, several months together, making only occasional excursions home.

For about seven years, from the commencement of his acquaintance with Mr. Thrale, he wrote little else than his two political pamphlets, the False Alarm, and Falkland Island; the former, in 1770, and the latter in 1771.

His time was chiefly taken up, when his health would permit, in visiting with Mr. and Mrs. Thrale, or entertaining their visitors. In this last situation, at least, there was somewhat humiliating, and he seems at times to have felt it.

The friendship of Mr. Thrale, who was a plain, blunt, good-hearted man, there is every reason to believe, was cordial, sincere, and wholly disinterested; that of his wife, there is abundant foundation to suspect, was of a very different nature.

Johnson was not the man to feed insatiable vanity; and, though he is said to have commended her Three Warnings, he did not advise the publication of the many other trifles to which she was continually soliciting his attention. *He was too anxious for the reputation of his friend's wife!* This is the clue to that otherwise unaccountable resentment which has pursued him beyond the grave.

Towards the end of the year 1773, having finished, in conjunction with Mr. Steevens, a new edition of Shakespeare; his good-nature was prevailed on to take that wild-goose excursion to Scotland with Mr. Boswell, called his Journey to the Hebrides, the celebrated Journal of which he published on his return. The severe animadversions, in this work, on Mr. Macpherson's pretended poems of Ossian, occasioned that gentleman to send Johnson a letter, threatening him with corporal punishment.

Johnson's spirited answer cannot be too generally known, as it includes the best possible prescription for the cure of irascibility. [Omitted.]

Having dismissed this letter, Johnson procured a stout oak plant about six feet high, with a large knob at the end, which was for some time his constant companion. But the precaution was needless; for he heard no more of the matter.

In 1774, he published the Patriot; and in 1775, his Taxation no Tyranny.

On the 30th of March, in this last year, the university of Oxford conferred on him the honorary degree of Doctor of Laws, accompanied by an elegant Latin eulogy on his vast literary acquirements.

In the summer of this year, he accompanied Mr. and Mrs. Thrale, in an excursion to France; but nothing of any particular moment appears to have occurred during their journey.

Soon after his return, he removed from Johnson's Court, to a larger house in Bolt Court; and was now, in point of circumstances, a happy man: but his constitutional melancholy still constantly attended him whenever he was much alone, and he had been afflicted with indisposition for the greater part of several preceding years. He had consequently written but little, and felt no great inclination to write more. But a confederacy of booksellers, who knew the value of his works, and who were alarmed by Mr. Bell's proposals to furnish a new edition of the English Poets in miniature, had sufficient address to procure his power-

ful assistance for a rival publication. He accordingly proceeded to write
the Lives of the English Poets; which were published, with their works,
in the year 1778 [1779–81].

This was his last great performance; and it may be considered as
the expiring flame of a genius which has seldom been equalled in any
age or country. The metaphor may be persisted in: for the language
and sentiments blaze out occasionally with a brilliancy and vigour, equal
at least, if not superior, to any thing he ever produced; and if, as the
intellectual lamp was near extinction, these bright emanations sometimes
sunk for a moment into a temporary gloom, it was only to recruit the
nearly exhausted spirit, that the last coruscations might glow with a
more powerful refulgence.

While Johnson was engaged in his lives of the poets, Mrs. Kelly, widow
of Mr. Hugh Kelly, having procured her husband's comedy of a Word
to the Wise, to be performed for the benefit of herself and five children,
at Covent Garden Theatre, he furnished a very beautiful little prologue
on the occasion, which was spoken in the year 1777.

In this year, too, he warmly interested himself in the affairs of Dr.
Dodd, whose face he had then never seen:[58] and not only penned the
speech which that unhappy man delivered at the bar of the Old Bailey,
to the court and jury; but, after his conviction, wrote the famous petition
to the King and Queen for a pardon, and several other papers.

From about the time of compleating the lives of the poets, Johnson
seems to have been suffering a gradual decay. The chief topicks of
his future conversations and epistles were, therefore, those which generally engross all serious convalescents, medicine and religion.

In 1781, Mr. Thrale died, leaving his friend Johnson one of his
executors; and Mrs. Thrale feeling more inclination to become the wife
of another man, than continue Johnson's nurse, soon contrived the
means to free herself from so incommodious a visitant.

In January 1782, Mr. Levet died suddenly at Johnson's house; who
relieved his own mind, and immortalized his old humble friend and
companion, by writing a few most elegant stanzas to his memory.

To relieve himself, in some degree, from the increasing pressure of
melancholy and disease, he now made occasional excursions to Dr.
Adams's, at Oxford; to Mrs. Porter, his daughter-in-law, at Lichfield;
and to the country residences of other friends.

His maladies, however, gained ground; and, in June 1783, he had
a sudden stroke of the palsy, which wholly deprived him of speech.
In a few days, with the assistance of Dr. Heberden and Dr. Brocklesby,
his articulation was restored; and, in less than a fortnight, he was able

to amuse himself with watering the little garden behind his house, an exercise in which he always greatly delighted. It was giving health, and food, and comfort, to languid and oppressed nature!

Though he now seemed no longer paralytick, the symptoms of an incipient dropsy were apparent; and the uneasiness he felt from this discovery, was not a little aggravated by the illness of Mrs. Williams, who died on the 6th of September, leaving her little all to a charitable institution, in the parish of St. Sepulchre, for the maintenance and education of poor deserted females.

At this time, the disease of Johnson was making a rapid progress; and, as he expected every hour would prove his last, he was incessantly employed in meditation and prayer. While he was thus piously engaged, the dropsy, to the surprize of every one, passed off, by a gradual evacuation of water, to the amount of twenty pints.

The ease and comfort which he derived from his favourable change, gave him renovated spirits; and, in the December following, to compensate in some measure for the loss of his domestick companions, he instituted a new club, at the Essex Head, Essex Street, in the Strand, where he regularly attended three times a week.

In the Spring of 1784, he sat to Mr. Opie for his portrait, which had been begun in the preceding year. He had, indeed, a great respect for this young artist, and was highly pleased with his performance. With the clumsy, vulgar portrait, by his friend, Sir Joshua Reynolds, he is known to have been exceedingly disgusted. "I will not," said he, one day, at Mr. Thrale's, in the room where the offensive picture was placed, "go down to posterity as *blinking Sam*, let Sir Joshua do his worst." [59]

While Johnson was preparing for his summer excursion this year, being alarmed by the report that a marriage was expected at Bath, between the widow of his friend Thrale, and Signor Piozzi, an Italian singer, he is said to have written a letter to that lady, *which she has prudently suppressed in her late curious collection,* on the degradation of herself, and the desertion of her children, which such an event must necessarily produce.

The union, however, took place: and Johnson found, as Sir John Hawkins elegantly expresses himself, that "he had been labouring to hedge in the *cuckow*."

"In a letter which he afterwards wrote to me," continues Sir John, "he thus delivered his sentiments."

"*Poor* THRALE! *I thought that either her virtue or her vice,* [meaning, as I understood by the former, the love of her children, and, by the latter, her pride] *would have restrained her from such a marriage. She is now become a subject for her enemies to exult over, and for her friends, if she has any left, to forget or pity."* [60]

The story of Lord Thurlow's application to his Majesty for an augmentation of Johnson's pension to five hundred pounds a year, that he might be enabled to visit Italy for the benefit of his health; the disinclination of the King to have his munificence prescribed; and the generous substitute which the greatest man in this country proposed on the occasion; has been too vaguely published, to justify any reflection on the royal patron of Johnson, whose inconsiderate friends seem most to blame in that business. [61]

Having spent all the summer in the country, and finding himself relapsing very fast into the dropsy, he quitted his native city, for the last time, about the middle of November, and returned to London.

On arriving in town, his legs were found to be so enormously swelled, that Dr. Brocklesby and Dr. Heberden, who immediately attended him, entertained but little hope of his recovery.

Indeed, Johnson now considered himself as a dying man: he received the sacrament almost every day; and was continually employed in prayer, or reading the Scriptures and other religious writings. His friends flocked around him, and he exhorted those whom he most loved to live and die good Christians. From Sir Joshua Reynolds, in particular, he is said to have extorted a promise that he should no more paint on Sundays, and that he should once every day of his future life read some portion of the Sacred Writings.

Much has been urged against the disposition which he made of his property in favour of Francis Barber, to the prejudice of such relations and other poor dependants as he had been accustomed to support or relieve during his life-time. It is more than probable that he was teazed into a hasty execution of his will; and that, as is often the case under such circumstances, he unfortunately overlooked those for whom, in a state of greater ease, and on more mature deliberation, he would have thought it his duty to make some provision. The mere accident of Frank's name being joined with his master's, in the annuity of seventy pounds a year for two lives, might be the trifling cause from whence sprung the to him material event of obtaining that annual sum.

Johnson's dread of death, and concern for his eternal interest, was indeed so great, that any neglect of temporal concerns can be little wondered at by those who knew the state of his mind at this late period of his existence.

He had, however, sufficient recollection to make a bequest of two hundred pounds to the representatives of Mr. Innys, the bookseller, who had fifty years before generously advanced that sum to prevent the total ruin of his father.

Nor was he quite unmindful of what his fame might suffer from the posthumous publication of fragments and imperfect papers; and when he was informed that Sir John Hawkins had taken the liberty to pocket two manuscript books of this description, he was enraged almost to madness, and could hardly be pacified. However Sir John may palliate his own conduct in this transaction, he has said much too little to convince any man of common understanding that he was not actuated by improper motives. His apprehension that the books would be stolen, might be a good reason for narrowly watching the suspected person, or even giving them to one of Johnson's domesticks, that they might be kept carefully locked up; but it could be no reason at all, with a man who had the smallest pretensions to delicacy, for putting the papers of a dying friend in his own pocket.

It seems evident that Johnson did not permit Sir John to retain the books, since one of them was that strange medley of prayers and meditations which Mr. Strahan has so indiscreetly published.

This circumstance is doubly to be lamented: it unquestionably served to disarrange the mind of Johnson in his last hours; and probably occasioned that hasty and indiscriminate havock with his writings, in which he, by mistake, unfortunately consigned to the flames a diary of all the principal occurrences of his life.[62]

As the dropsy increased, his legs had been scarified, at his own particular request, with the hope of procuring a favourable discharge. These scarifications he was very desirous should be enlarged more than his medical friends judged adviseable. He insisted that they were cowards, and that he would himself abide the consequence. The consequence, accordingly, he did abide; for, a few mornings afterwards, being in extreme agony, he ordered Frank to give him a case of lancets from his cabinet; and, taking one of them out, in spite of the remonstrances of those about him, made a considerable incision in one of his legs. The effusion of blood was soon stopped, and the lancet placed out of his reach. However, fancying himself relieved by the operation; and, perceiving a pair of scissars lay near him, he snatched them up, and hastily plunged them deep into both his calves. Mr. Cruikshank, the surgeon, was then sent for; and the wounds were dressed: but the loss of blood had been considerable; the effusion brought on a dozing; and, in that dozing, seemingly without pain, at about a quarter past seven in the evening of the next day, being the 13th of December 1784, he expired without a single groan.

Thus died, in his seventy-fifth year, Dr. Samuel Johnson! a man who excelled in the art of accumulating human wisdom, and in the talent of widely diffusing it to others: who, though not *"a faultless monster,"* was a pious christian, and a worthy man; and whose memory will find esteem and veneration from the wise and good, in those grateful bosoms which his works shall contribute to enlarge, wherever the beams of science irradiate the earth, till time is swallowed up in eternity.

Cue Titles

Anecdotes — Hester Lynch Piozzi, *Anecdotes of the late Samuel Johnson, LL.D.*, ed. S. C. Roberts (Cambridge, 1925).

Churchill — *Poetical Works of Charles Churchill*, ed. Douglas Grant (Oxford, 1956).

Clifford — James L. Clifford, *Young Sam Johnson* (New York, 1955).

Courtney — W. P. Courtney and D. Nichol Smith, *A Bibliography of Samuel Johnson* (Oxford, 1915).

Davis — Bertram H. Davis, *Before Boswell: A Study of Sir John Hawkins' LIFE OF SAMUEL JOHNSON* (New Haven, 1960).

Gleanings — Aleyn Lyell Reade, *Johnsonian Gleanings*, 10 parts (Privately printed, 1909–46).

Greene — Donald J. Greene, "The Development of the Johnson Canon," *Restoration and Eighteenth-Century Literature*, ed. Carroll Camden (Chicago, 1963), pp. 407–22.

Hawkins — Sir John Hawkins, *The Life of Samuel Johnson, LL.D.*, ed. Bertram H. Davis (New York, 1961).

Letters — *The Letters of Samuel Johnson*, ed. R. W. Chapman, 3 vols. (Oxford, 1952).

Life — *Boswell's Life of Samuel Johnson*, ed. G. B. Hill, revised and enlarged by L. F. Powell, 6 vols. (Oxford, 1934–50); vols. 5 and 6, 2nd ed., 1964.

Lives — *Lives of the English Poets*, ed. G. B. Hill, 3 vols. (Oxford, 1905).

Kelley and Brack — Robert E. Kelley and O M Brack, Jr., *Samuel Johnson's Early Biographers* (Iowa City, 1971).

Miscellanies — *Johnsonian Miscellanies*, ed. G. B. Hill, 2 vols. (Oxford, 1897).

Sledd and Kolb — James H. Sledd and Gwin J. Kolb, *Dr. Johnson's Dictionary* (Chicago, 1955).

Waingrow — *The Correspondence and other Papers of James Boswell Relating to the Making of the LIFE OF JOHNSON*, ed. Marshall Waingrow (New York, 1969).

Works — *The Works of Samuel Johnson, LL.D.* . . . 9 vols. (Oxford, 1825). Supplementary Vols. X and XI contain Debates in Parliament.

Yale *Works* — *The Yale Edition of the Works of Samuel Johnson* (New Haven, 1958–).

Notes

I

W[illiam] R[ider]. *An Historical and Critical Account of the Lives and Writings of the Living Authors of Great-Britain. Wherein their respective Merits are discussed with Candour and Impartiality.* London, 1762, pp. 7–10. The primary evidence of William Rider's authorship of this pamphlet is that it is signed "W. R." (p. 34) and that in an entry under "Mr. RIDER" (pp. [29]–[30]), the "utmost Candour and Impartiality" he claims to maintain is foregone in favour of unblushing praise of his *Dictionary* and *History of England*. Hawkins's comment (in his long footnote about the early contributors to the *Gentleman's Magazine*) that Rider, "bred in the same prolific seminary, was a writer in the magazine, of verses signed Philargyrus" (p. 282), is supporting evidence for his having known Johnson and therefore of his having written this relatively generously-proportioned sketch about him. If Rider knew Johnson when they were both writing for the *Gentleman's Magazine*, he either did not know exactly what pieces he had contributed or thought them too slight to be included in the sketch. The pamphlet must have been published early in 1762 since it was reviewed in the May number of the *Critical Review* (13:441–42), and since Rider was unaware of the pension Johnson was granted in July of the same year. His observation of the value of Johnson's escape from rural obscurity, his praise of the oriental compositions, and his comparison of the prose to poetry were to be echoed by most of the early biographers. (See Kelley and Brack, pp. 125–28.)

The present text is reproduced from a copy in the Yale University Library. This copy of *An Historical and Critical Account of the Lives and Writings of the Living Authors of Great-Britain* will be reprinted with an introduction by O M Brack, Jr. in the Augustan Reprint Society's 1973–74 series.

1   This remark is slightly exaggerated; a second edition of *Irene* appeared in 1754. See Courtney, p. 24.

2   The following lines from *Irene* correspond roughly to III. i. 32–34, 38–41; 44a, 46b–47; V. xii. 35–36; Yale *Works*, 6:152, 213.

2

[David Erskine Baker]. *The Companion to the Play-House: or, An Historical Account of all the Dramatic Writers (and their Works) that have appeared in Great Britain and Ireland, from the Commencement of our Theatrical Exhibitions down to the Present Year 1764.* London, 1764, II, S6ᵛ–T1ᵛ; "Irene," I, K6ᵛ. This sketch was later revised and expanded for inclusion in Isaac Reed's edition of this work: *Biographia Dramatica, or, A Companion to the Playhouse* (London, 1782). See below, pp. 19–22. This account, in both its versions, influenced every biographical sketch of Johnson through the "Memoirs" in the *Universal Magazine*. This text is reproduced from a copy in the Yale University Library.

1   Johnson did not take his degrees.

2   Catherine Talbot wrote No. 30, Samuel Richardson No. 97, and Elizabeth Carter Nos. 44 and 100. Hester Mulso (Mrs. Chapone) contributed to No. 10, David Garrick wrote the second letter in No. 15, and Joseph Simpson, Johnson's former classmate, composed the second letter in No. 107. See Yale *Works*, 3:xxi n. 1.

3   A list of the "Eastern Tales" is given in Yale *Works*, 3:xxvi n. 6.

4   Charles Goring, *Irene, or the Fair Greek* (1708).

3

[James Tytler?]. *Gentleman and Lady's Weekly Magazine* [Edinburgh], January 28, 1774, pp. 1–3. According to a *Biographical Sketch of the Life of James Tytler for a considerable time A Liberal Contributor to the Encyclopaedia Britannica* (Edinburgh, 1805) attributed to Robert Meek, Tytler published this magazine during its brief existence from 28 January 1774 to 29 March 1775 (pp. 26–27). Although it is likely that Tytler did most of the writing for the magazine, it cannot be known with certainty that he wrote this particular "Account." The sketch is taken in large part from *The Companion to the Play-House*. This text is reproduced from a copy in the Edinburgh Public Library.

1   They made the trip on horseback. See Clifford, p. 171.

2   This is an earlier attribution than that listed by Greene, p. 413.

3   All of the Drury-Lane "Prologue" was quoted except lines 42–45. See Yale *Works*, 6:89.

4   This passage is garbled. Johnson's lives of Admiral Robert Blake and Sir

Francis Drake appeared in the *Gentleman's Magazine* [10 (June 1740), 301–07, (August, 389–96; (September), 443–47; (October), 509–15; (December), 600–03; 11 (January 1741), 38–44] and then were appended to the 1767, 1769, and 1777 editions of the *Life of Savage.* See Courtney, pp. 11, 16.

4

[Isaac Reed?]. *Westminster Magazine* 2 (September 1774): 443–46. This sketch is largely an embellishment of the account in the *Companion to the Play-House* (see pp. 5–7 above) with a partial repetition of the "Short Character of Dr. Johnson" which appeared in the *London Magazine* 43 (March 1773): 109–10. To this was added a brief record of Johnson's tour of Scotland from the *London Magazine* 44 (January 1774):26–27, the "respectable Hottentot" sketch, and a few anecdotes. John Nichols, in his "Biographical Memoir of the Late Isaac Reed, Esq." [*Gentleman's Magazine* 77 (January 1807):80], states that Reed was "a valuable contributor to the Westminster Magazine from 1773–4 to about the year 1780. The biographical articles are from his pen." There is a possibility that the "Account" in the *European Magazine* was also by Reed. See Kelley and Brack, pp. 146 n. 9, 157 n. 2, and pp. 301–02 below. Reed may have revised the account in the *Companion to the Play-House* for *Biographia Dramatica,* since he was editor of the work. This text is reproduced from a copy in the Yale University Library.

1   In March, 1737.

2   "Except what I had from the bookseller, I did not get a farthing by them." See *Life,* 2:147; also 1:373.

3   ". . . for righteous monarchs
        Justly to judge, with their own eyes should see;
        To rule o'er freemen, should themselves be free"

are the last lines of Act I of Henry Brooke's *The Earl of Essex* (1761). According to Arthur Murphy, Thomas Sheridan, who acted in the Drury-Lane production, was the person who inspired Johnson's parody. See *The Life of David Garrick, Esq.* (London, 1801), 1:365. When the tragedy was reprinted in Brooke's collected works in 1778, this passage was rewritten.

4   Murphy says that this remark was addressed to Garrick (*Miscellanies,* 1:405).

5   The version given by Boswell seems to be more pointed: "This man (said he) I thought had been a Lord among wits; but I find, he is only a wit among Lords" (*Life,* 1:266 and n. 1). Both of these anecdotes were popular and exist in a variety of versions. See below.

6   The first edition of Chesterfield's *Letters* appeared in 1774. See *The Letters of Philip Dormer Stanhope, 4th Earl of Chesterfield,* ed. Bonamy Dobrée, 6 vols.

(London, 1932), 4:1684–85. At this time his portrait of the "respectable Hottentot" was mistakenly thought to represent Johnson. See *Life*, 1:266–67.

7　See pp. 6–7 above.

5

This text is reproduced from a copy of *Biographia Dramatica, or, A Companion to the Playhouse* (London, 1782),1:256–58, in the Yale University Library. This is a revised edition of *The Companion to the Play-House,* edited by Isaac Reed. See the note to 2 above, p. 294. Since the account of *Irene* in this edition does not differ substantively from that in *The Companion to the Play-House,* it has not been reprinted. See p. 7 above.

1　Davies's *Memoirs of the Life of David Garrick* (London, 1780) was published, according to the *St. James's Chronicle,* about 6 May. In the fourth edition (1784) the date is changed to 1736. The project did not get under way until late autumn or early winter 1735. See Clifford, p. 160.

2　The Appleby Grammar School application was made in 1739. See Clifford, p. 220.

3　Oxford conferred the M.A. degree in 1755, Trinity College, Dublin the LL.D. degree in 1765. He received the LL.D. degree from Oxford in 1775.

6

[William Cooke?]. This account appeared in the fifth edition, part II, of the *Beauties of Johnson* (London, 1782), pp. vii–xv. Approximately two-thirds of it was taken, with only minor changes, from the *Biographia Dramatica* (see pp. 19–22 above). The sketch was filled out with information taken from Thomas Davies's *Memoirs of the Life of David Garrick* and the now well-known letter from the Earl of Gower to a friend of Swift's in an abortive attempt to get Johnson a master's degree. The letter was probably taken from Herbert Croft's *Love and Madness* (London, 1780), pp. 71–72. These *Memoirs* may have been compiled by William Cooke, author of the *Life of Samuel Johnson, LL.D.* Both works were published by G. Kearsley and Cooke incorporated about two-thirds of the *Memoirs* into his *Life.* It does not necessarily follow, however, that Cooke was the author of the *Memoirs* because he borrowed heavily from it since it was a common practice among the early biographers to draw freely on the materials available to them. See Kelley and Brack, p. 157 n. 3. It is not known when he met Johnson but he was a member of the Essex Head Club founded in December 1783. There is certainly no evidence that the compiler of these *Memoirs* was personally acquainted with Johnson, although Cooke in his later *Life* (1785) makes little effective use of his acquaintance. (In Kelley and Brack, p. 92, Cooke is incorrectly identified as professor of Greek at Cambridge. This was another William Cooke.) This text is reproduced from a copy in the Yale University Library.

1 *Lives*, 1:373; 2:37.

2 Gilbert Walmesley, whom Boswell called "Johnson's first friend." See *Life*, 2:466. John Colson was made Lucasian Professor of Mathematics at Cambridge in 1739.

3 This letter was first made public in the *Cambridge Chronicle* for Saturday, 19 October 1765, and was printed in the *Gentleman's Magazine* for October 1765 (35:451). See *Gleanings*, 6:56, 150–53. The letter also appeared in Davies, *Memoirs of the Life of David Garrick*, 1:11–12.

4 John Leveson-Gower, 1st Earl. The date of the letter should be 1739, not 1737. For a discussion of the letter's subsequent printing history, see Davis, pp. 103–05. Davis was unaware of its previous appearance in *Love and Madness*. Croft states that the letter was shown him by a clergyman who assured him that it was authentic (p. 70). There are some two dozen variants, all of them minor, between this version of the letter and that in *Love and Madness*.

5 *Lives*, 1:290.

6 Life of Dryden [A]. *Lives*, 1:454. The quotation is from Johnson; the metaphor is the author's.

7

[L.]. This account first appeared in the *Universal Magazine* 75 (August 1784): 89–97. It was reprinted in the *London Chronicle*, December 14–16, 1784 (pp. 577–78); December 16–18 (pp. 585–86); *Lloyd's Evening Post*, December 13–15, 1784 (p. 569); December 15–17 (p. 575); December 17–20 (p. 581); December 20–22 (p. 591); *The Craftsman; or Say's Weekly Journal*, December 18, 25, 1784; *Scots Magazine* 46 (December 1784):609–12; (Appendix), 683–87; *Town and Country Magazine* 16 (December 1784):619–23; (Supplement), 707–10; *Boston Magazine* 2 (May 1785):172–76; (June 1785):209–12; (July 1785):249–51. When the "Memoirs" was reprinted the section discussing biography was dropped and it began with the paragraph: "Dr. Samuel Johnson . . . was born at Lichfield" (p. 33 below). Usually the reprints added an account of Johnson's death and a brief character sketch. Typical is that in *Lloyd's Evening Post* for 20–22 December which was itself reprinted a number of times:

On the 15th [*sic*] of December 1784, about seven in the evening, Dr. Johnson died, at his house in Bolt-court, Fleet-street, aged 77 [*sic*]. The loss of so valuable a member of public and private society will long be felt, while experience tells us, he has not left a worthier character to lament his death.

Whether we consider Dr. Johnson as a man or as a writer, his character will in the one case be found to rise to real goodness, and in the other to true greatness. Charitable to the poor, even to a degree of munificence, he enjoyed the lasting satisfaction of doing good, of relieving merit, and cheering the heart of the poor and needy. To a head stored with human learning, he added a heart on which habits of pious meditation had left deep impressions.

His enemies must allow, that his faults were not proportioned to his abilities; and when the shades of his character are deepened ever so much, they do not deprive the whole of its beauties.

Those who knew him best in private life will agree with the writer of this article, that he had a dignified mind, capable of sublime conceptions both in conduct and in expression. To the meannesses which deform many literary characters he was wholly a stranger. His peculiarities might perhaps be disagreeable and hurtful to his health and happiness, but they were a portion of that weakness without some of which no human character ever existed. His company was much courted by the learned and by the great, because no man ever left his company without reaping some lasting benefit. His death was preceded by a lingering and painful illness, which he bore like a Christian and a philosopher. By his death, the world has lost one of its true friends, and he has obtained the reward of a pious life — the laurels that never will fade — the happiness that knows no end.

Such was Dr. Johnson! Such was the character he maintained amidst the vicissitudes of elevation and depression. May his example be as long powerful as his precepts will be read and admired!

Although the "Memoirs" draws heavily on the *Biographia Dramatica* and contributes little new information about Johnson's life as such, it is important because it identifies a number of his works for the first time. The text is reproduced from a copy in the Yale University Library.

1　*Rambler* No. 164; Yale *Works,* 5:107.

2　Rambler, Vol. II. page 40 [A]. No. 60; Yale *Works,* 3:322–23.

3　Life of Addison [A]. *Lives,* 2:116.

4　Worth is often unknown, or known imperfectly, till after death; *till that period, when it is too late to learn particular circumstances with accuracy.* Knox's Essays, Vol. II. p. 51 [A]. Vicesimus Knox, *Essays, Moral and Literary,* 2 vols. (London, 1778); the quotation is from Chap. 94, "Cursory Thoughts on Biography."

5　*Lives,* 1:331.

6　"Coadjutor" is misleading, for Johnson revised Sir Herbert Croft's "Life of Young"; he did not collaborate with him, as "L's" word seems to imply. See *Life,* 4:58–59, 482.

7　*Lives,* 3:362, 391.

8   Ibid., p. 379.

9   Life of Addison, *Lives*, 2:124.

10   Life of Sprat [A]. *Lives*, 2:37.

11   The reference is to John Hawkesworth. There is no evidence to substantiate "L's" claim; Johnson probably first met Hawkesworth while both men wrote for the *Gentleman's Magazine*. See *Thraliana*, ed. K. C. Balderston, 2nd ed., 2 vols. (Oxford, 1951) 1:173 and n. 2; and *Anecdotes*, pp. 23–24; *Gleanings*, 5:45. It is unlikely, given the context, that "pupil" refers to Hawkesworth's imitation of Johnson's style. But see John Courtenay, *A Poetical Review of the Literary and Moral Character of the Late Samuel Johnson*, 3rd ed. (London, 1786), p. 24, where "pupil" applies to imitation. Reprinted with an introduction by Robert E. Kelley, Los Angeles: Augustan Reprint Society, 1969 (Publication No. 133).

12   Gentleman's Magazine for June 1736, page 428 [A]. The correct citation for the June number is page 360; the advertisement in the July number appeared on page 428. There was only one school. The author has been misled by the wrong date in Davies; the school at Edial was established in late autumn or early winter of 1735.

13   See the Universal Magazine for March 1782, page 138 [A]. See *Lives*, 2:20–21. This paragraph is a close paraphrase of two of Davies's sentences, 1:12.

14   Appollon apprit aux bergers quels sont les charmes de la vie champetre, &c. Telemaque, livre II [A]. Francois de Salignac de la Mothe Fénelon, *Les Aventures de Télémaque*, ed. Albert Cahen, 2 vols. (Paris, 1920), 1:78.

15   This is the first attribution of this title to Johnson. Since Greene overlooked the "Memoirs," some of his citations of first attributions are incorrect (Greene, p. 415).

16   *London*, ll. 85–90; Yale *Works*, 6:52–53.

17   The story of Edward Cave's deception in this matter is not supported by any available evidence. Johnson received only ten guineas from Robert Dodsley. For the history of the publication, see *Life*, 1:120–27; Yale *Works*, 6:45–46.

18   Nos. 150, 166; Yale *Works*, 5:35, 116.

19   Although somewhat oblique, this ascription of the *Parliamentary Debates* to Johnson antedates those in the *European Magazine* and Tyers cited by Greene, p. 415.

20   The Life of Edward Cave, written in 1754, by Dr. Johnson, has been recently admitted into the new edition of the Biographia Britannica, Vol. III [A]. See 2nd ed. (London, 1784), 3:313–15. It also appeared in *A New and General Biographical Dictionary* (London, 1784), 3:216–21. Johnson's biography was first published in the *Gentleman's Magazine* 24 (February 1754):55–58, shortly after Cave's death.

21   Ll. 345–68; Yale *Works*, 6:107–09.

22   *Irene* was performed nine times between 6 February and 20 February. See *Life*, 1:198 n. 1, 2.

23   See p. 20 above.

24   Sherlock's Letters on several subjects, Vol. I. p. 29 [A]. Martin Sherlock, *Letters on Several Subjects*, 2 vols. (London, 1781).

25   Knox's Essays, Vol. I. p. 136 [A]. *Essays, Moral and Literary;* the quotation is from Chap. 28, "On the Periodical Essayists."

26   No. 10, 15, 30, 44, 97, 100, 107 [A]. See Yale *Works*, 3:xxi n. 1.

27   These are Nos. 34, 39, 41, 45, 50, 53, 58, 62, 67, 69, 74, 81, 84, 85, 92, 95, 99, 102, 107, 108, 111, 115, 119, 120, 126, 128, 131, 137, 138 [A]. Greene, p. 416, credits Hawkins with first identifying Johnson's contributions to the *Adventurer;* thus his conclusion (p. 415) that Johnson's contributions, "a sizable part" of this periodical, were unknown in his lifetime, is erroneous.

28   Philological Enquiries, p. 25 [A]. James Harris, *Philological Inquiries*, 2 vols. (London, 1780–81).

29   *Preface; Works*, 5:51.

30   No. 100, 101 [A]. These papers were dated 28November and 5 December 1754. Edward Moore, the editor, was a fabulist and dramatist. Johnson's presumed failure to be admitted to Chesterfield antedates the publication of these essays. Johnson told Boswell that no particular incident produced a quarrel between them. Because of Chesterfield's continued neglect Johnson "resolved to have no connection with him." See *Life*, 1:257. For discussions of the Johnson-Chesterfield relationship see Sledd and Kolb, pp. 85–104; and Paul J. Korshin, "The Johnson-Chesterfield Relationship: A New Hypothesis," *PMLA* 85 (1970):247–59. William Hayley gives it extended treatment in his fictional *Two Dialogues: Containing a Comparative View of the Lives, Characters, and Writings of Philip, the Late Earl of Chesterfield, and Dr. Samuel Johnson* (London, 1787). Reprinted with an introduction by Robert E. Kelley, Gainesville, Fla.: Scholars' Facsimiles and Reprints, 1970.

31   See *Lives*, 1:216, 409.

32   Page 188. See a very copious account of this Romance, with the Dissertation on the Art of Flying, and the History of Imlac, the Philosopher, in our Magazine for May 1759 [A]. *Rasselas,* Chap. 31.

33   *Churchill*, Bk. 2, ll. 653–808, pp. 97–101.

34   This edition was published in 1773; George Steevens was the nephew of Admiral Charles Steevens.

35   For an extract from 'The Patriot,' see our Magazine for October 1774; and for another from 'Taxation no Tyranny,' our Magazine for March 1775 [A].

36   See Helen Louise Guffie's unpublished dissertation, "Samuel Johnson

and the Hostile Press" (Columbia University, 1961), and Donald J. Greene, *The Politics of Samuel Johnson* (New Haven, 1960), pp. 189–92.

37   Thomas Pennant's description of his tour of the mainland of Scotland in 1769 was published in 1771 as *A Tour in Scotland, 1769.* His second tour through western Scotland and the Hebrides was made the summer before that of Johnson and Boswell but the account, *A Tour in Scotland and Voyage to the Hebrides, 1772,* was not published until 1774.

38   The first four volumes were published in 1779, the last six in 1781. The octavo edition first appeared in 1781. See Courtney, pp. 132, 141–42.

39   See the Life of Edmund Waller, *Lives,* 1:249. John Hampden was Waller's cousin.

40   Henry Sacheverell violently advocated the high-church and Tory cause in numerous sermons and pamphlets. Robert Filmer's most famous work, the *Patriarcha* (1680), presented a patriarchal theory of the divine right of kings.

41   Thomas Davies's unauthorized *Miscellaneous and Fugitive Pieces* published in 1773 and 1774 (and the analysis of the authorship of its contents by the reviewer in the *Gentleman's Magazine*) was the most important contribution to the establishment of a "canon" before Johnson's death. Greene, pp. 413, 414; Courtney, pp. 116–17.

42   Johnson married Elizabeth Porter on 9 July 1735; she died on 17 March 1752.

43   Anna Williams died on 6 September 1783.

44   *The Life of the Emperor Julian; trans. from the French and improved, with coins, notes, and genealogical tables* (London, 1746). For the Wilkinson sisters, see *Miscellanies,* 2:171–72, 174–75.

45   Her *Miscellanies* was published in 1766. "L" is the first to mention Johnson's contributions to this volume, but the identification of specific titles was left to Boswell. See *Life,* 2:25–26. Greene, p. 415, gives Tyers credit for attributing the "Preface" to Johnson, but was unaware of "L's" more general ascription.

8

European Magazine 6 (December 1784):411–13; 7 (January 1785):9–12; (February 1785):81–84; (March 1785):190–92; (April 1785):249–50. The claims for authorship of this "Account" are almost equally divided between Isaac Reed and George Steevens. According to John Nichols in his "Biographical Memoir of the late Isaac Reed, Esq." [*Gentleman's Magazine,* 77 (January 1807):80] Reed was "very early one of the proprietors of the *European Magazine,* and was a constant contributor to it for many years, particularly in the biographical and critical departments." This would certainly leave open the possibility that the "Account" was his. It is also known that Reed had an "extensive and accurate knowledge of English literary History" (*Life*, 4:37) which Johnson had drawn upon for his *Lives of the Poets*. Since most of Johnson's works were published anonymously, the author of this "Account" must have known Johnson and have had enough interest in literary history to feel compelled to collect this information. Boswell certainly felt that Reed would have information about Johnson's publications at his fingertips when he asked him to send "a chronological note of what you understand to be written by Johnson between 1757 and 1765 inclusive. My servant will call tomorrow before 12 for your answer" [*Letters of James Boswell*, ed. C. B. Tinker (Oxford, 1924), 2:396]. (See Kelley and Brack, pp. 146 n. 9, 157 n. 2.) Davis argues for Steevens's authorship: "its scholarly precision, its intimate knowledge of Johnson, particularly of the *Shakespeare*, its vivid and easy style, and its praise of Boswell in the manner of the January letters to the *St. James's Chronicle*, make it difficult to avoid the conclusion that its author was the eminent George Steevens" (p. 47). Dr. Richard Brocklesby in a letter to Boswell, 13 December 1784, reports hearing that Steevens had taken away the Catalogue of Johnson's works. This Catalogue served, no doubt, as the basis of the "Account." Waingrow suggests that it was probably written by Steevens, though he may have had some help from Reed. See Waingrow, pp. 26 and n. 6, 146 n. 1. As biography, this essay is virtually negligible; as an account of Johnson's works, it is of great value. Greene's estimate of the importance of the "Account" (p. 417) in making first attributions to Johnson's canon is slightly exaggerated, however, because it overlooks "L's" "Memoirs" in the *Universal Magazine*. This text is reproduced from a copy in the University of Iowa Library.

1   Life of Dryden, 12mo. edit. 92 [A]. *Lives*, 1:373.

2   A few years before Dr. Johnson's death, he wrote an Epitaph for his parents, and a brother who lived to man's estate [A]. Johnson mentions the epitaphs in a letter of 2 December 1784; see *Letters*, 3:251–52, and *Life*, 4:393 n. 2.

3   Bishop Newton's Life, p. 8 [A]. *The Works of Thomas Newton: with Some Account of His Life*, 3 vols. (London, 1782). Newton was Bishop of Bristol and Dean of St. Paul's.

4   Nash's History of Worcestershire [A]. Treadway Russell Nash, *Collections for the History and Antiquities of Worcestershire*, 2 vols. (London, 1781–99), 1:529 n. [d] 1. Nash gives the correct date, 31 October 1728. William Adams was a junior fellow during Johnson's matriculation, and became tutor at about the time Johnson left Oxford. See Waingrow, p. 10 n. 1. Johnson's tutor was William Jorden. Johnson was at Oxford about fourteen months, from October 1728 to December 1729.

5   Thomas Warren published the *Birmingham Journal*. These essays, still undiscovered, were first attributed to Johnson here. See Greene, p. 415. The "Account" misdates his residence with Warren, which lasted about six months

in 1732–33. Johnson ceased writing for Warren by 21 May 1733. See Clifford, pp. 143–44, 340 n. 41; Courtney, p. 2.

6 It is probable the recollection of this early performance induced him, many years afterwards, to write "The Prince of Abyssinia" [A].

7 See particularly "The Union, 1766," p. 157 [A].

8 The "friend" was Morgan Graves, brother of Richard, the novelist. Edmund Hector, Johnson's close friend, not Graves, requested the verses. For a discussion of the controversy surrounding this poem, see Waingrow, pp. 439 and n. 2, 575–76 and n. 3, 5, 6. None of the recent commentators on this issue mentions this "Account."

9 Life of David Garrick, p. 7 [A].

10 See Gent. Mag. 1736, p. 428. "ADVERTISEMENT. At Edial, near Lichfield, in Staffordshire, young Gentlemen are boarded, and taught the Latin and Greek languages, by SAMUEL JOHNSON" [A].

11 See Dr. Johnson's account of this gentleman, in his "Life of Edmund Smith." Mr. Walmesley translated Dr. Byron's [*sic*] famous Song. See Gent. Mag. 1745, p. 102. He died August 3, 1751, aged 69 [A]. Gilbert Walmesley was born in 1680 and, hence, was not 69 when he died. He was not the translator of "My time, O ye muses," by John Byrom; the translator was Geoffrey Walmsley (*Life*, 6:488, Errata). Boswell followed this erroneous attribution. See *Life,* 1:81 n. 2.

12 Thus one of his antagonists addresses him: "Yet, surely if it be upon such terms that you are become a pensioner, it were far better to return back to that poor but honest state, when you and the miserable SAVAGE, on default of the pittance that should have secured your quarters at the Club, were contented — *in the open air* — to growl at the *Moon,* and Whigs, and Walpole, and the House of Brunswick." *Letter to Samuel Johnson, LL.D.* Printed for Almon, 8vo. 1770, p. 33 [A]. The "antagonist" was probably John Wilkes. See Courtney, p. 114.

13 That Johnson was introduced to Cave by Savage is unlikely; the reverse is more plausible. For discussions of this question, see Hawkins, p. 28; *Life,* 1:125 n. 4, 533; *Lives,* 2:434 n. 2; *Gentleman's Magazine* 201 (September 1856): 275; *Gleanings,* 6:77–84; Clifford, p. 207.

14 Gent. Mag. 1738, p. 156 [A]. The entire poem was reprinted here.

15 The full title is *Ad Ricardum Savage, Arm. Humani Generis Amatorem;* Yale *Works,* 6:43–44.

16 These newspapers were probably reprinting the "Memoirs" from the *Universal Magazine.* See p. 35 and n. 17 above.

17 Appleby Grammar School was in Leicestershire.

18 This Letter has been reprinted with the date 1737. It was evidently writ-

ten after the publication of LONDON, consequently at least some months later [A]. The correct date is 1739. See pp. 24–25 and n. 4 above.

19   See Gentleman's Magazine, December 1784, p. 891 [A].

20   P. 581 [A].

21   The writer of this article has now before him a Life of Father Paul; with some account of his Writings, printed in 8vo. This was probably intended as part of the rival edition. It has no title-page, nor does it appear, after a strict enquiry, *that it was* ever to have been published [A]. It was long thought that another Samuel Johnson had undertaken this project; however, the "rival" was the Rev. John Johnson. See Edward Ruhe, "The Two Samuel Johnsons," *N & Q* 199 (1954):432–35; Clifford, pp. 200–01. Zachary Pearce, who later aided Johnson on the *Dictionary*, was Bishop of Bangor, later of Rochester.

22   This is an incorrect attribution. The author of "The Apotheosis of Milton" was William Guthrie. See *Life*, 1:140. Also, the following attribution is confused: Elizabeth Carter translated Crousaz's *Examination*. Johnson wrote the *Commentary*.

23   This appears to be an unfounded assertion. Clifford, p. 213, argues that this tract was not among Johnson's favorite pieces, but there is no evidence that he desired to suppress it.

24   After having written this piece, it will appear extraordinary, that Dr. Johnson should have been so far misled, as to suppose the Prophecy in Swift's Works a genuine one, and gravely to declare, that though not completed in all its parts, it should not be read without amazement. See Swift's Life, p. 24, 12mo [A]. *Lives*, 3:14 and n. 2. This is clearly an imaginative interpretation of Johnson's remark: "He [Swift] wrote . . . an explanation of an *Ancient Prophecy*, part written after the facts, and the rest never completed, but well planned to excite amazement."

25   See *Life*, 1:142, and Courtney, pp. 9–10.

26   This Pamphlet is ascribed to Dr. Johnson, on the authority of an old Bookseller, who remembered the publication of it [A].

27   "First essays" is ambiguous. Johnson contributed a paragraph satirizing George Lyttelton to an "Extract of Mr. Gulliver's Memoirs Relating to the Characters of the Principal Members of the Senate of Lilliput" in the *Gentleman's Magazine*, 10 (March 1740):99–103, and (May 1740):227–30. See Donald J. Greene, "Some Notes on Johnson and the *Gentleman's Magazine*," *PMLA* 74 (1959):75–84. According to F. V. Bernard, Johnson probably composed the debates on the Navy Estimates in the December 1740 number, the Registration of Seamen in the January 1741 number, and all of the debates from July 1741 through the 1744 Supplement. See "Johnson and the Authorship of Four Debates," *PMLA* 82 (1967): 408–19. For extended discussion of Johnson's authorship, see *Life*, 1:501–12; Hawkins, pp. 59–60; and Benjamin Beard Hoover, *Samuel Johnson's Parliamentary Reporting* (Berkeley and Los Angeles, 1953), pp. 23–30, 207–18. Hawkesworth, it is now generally agreed, succeeded Johnson in this project.

28   They appeared in four issues of the *Gentleman's Magazine* for 1746: May, September, October, November.

29   In some Miscellanies, an Epitaph on Claudy Philips, a Musician, has been ascribed to Dr. Johnson; but as it appeared in this year's Magazine, p. 464, with the signature G, accompanied by other Pieces, known to be written by Mr. Garrick, marked in the same manner, it probably should be given to that Gentleman [A]. Johnson did write the "Epitaph." See Yale *Works*, 6:68; Courtney, p. 11.

30   This is the first attribution of the translation of Fontenelle's *Éloge* on Morin to Johnson (Greene, p. 415). Boswell assigned this piece to Johnson on the basis of internal evidence. See *Life*, 1:17, 150.

31   John Swan's translation of Sydenham's works first appeared in 1742. Johnson's *Life* was included in later editions (1763, 1788) without acknowledgement. See Courtney, pp. 12–13.

32   The anecdote of Johnson's "extraordinary correction" of Thomas Osborne by striking him with a folio was repeated, with various embellishments, by a number of the early biographers. Boswell gives the definitive version, *Life*, 1:154.

33   The first volume of the *Catalogue* is dated 1743. See Courtney, p. 13.

34   The "Preface" to the *Harleian Miscellany* appeared in 1744. See Courtney, p. 15. William Oldys was the noted antiquarian.

35   *Lives*, 2:413–14.

36   No letters between Johnson and Savage are extant.

37   Fielding resigned from *The Champion* on 29 June 1741, and was succeeded as editor by James Ralph the following year. See Wilbur L. Cross, *The History of Henry Fielding*, 3 vols. (New Haven, 1918), 1:259–60. In a note to Boswell, Isaac Reed identifies Ralph as the author of "this Eulogium." See Waingrow, p. 497 and n. 10.

38   The Oxford Edition of Shakespeare edited by Thomas Hanmer appeared in 1743–44. For Johnson's comments, see Yale *Works*, 7:43–45, 96–98.

39   (1747), p. xiii. See *Life*, 1:175–76.

40   See a Letter from Dr. Francis Hutchinson to Orator Henley, published in *Oratory Transactions*, No. 1. p. 10. 8vo. 1728 [A]. Francis Hutcheson, the Scots moralist; his name was sometimes wrongly given as Hutchinson. John Henley was an eccentric preacher. Addison's latest biographer, Peter Smithers, does not corroborate the story of Tonson's offer. See *The Life of Joseph Addison*, 2nd ed. (Oxford, 1968), p. 435, where he mentions Addison's consideration of such a project.

41   Addison's Life, p. 65. 12mo. edition [A]. *Lives*, 2:113. This section is a close paraphrase of Johnson. John Locker, miscellaneous writer.

42   Johnson did not write this biographical sketch.

43   *Works,* 5:20. This passage from the *Plan* does not infer that Pope and Johnson were acquainted.

44   It may be necessary here to mention, that an Epilogue was spoken on the same occasion by Mrs. [Peg] Woffington, evidently the production of Mr. Garrick, though erroneously, in a late Miscellany, ascribed to Dr. Johnson [A]. The Epilogue was written by Sir William Yonge. See Waingrow, p. 591 and n. 1.

45   See *Poems;* Yale *Works,* 6:80–87.

46   William Lauder published his attack in 1750. See *Life,* 1:228–31; Court-ney, pp. 36–37.

47   "Milton vindicated from the Charge of Plagiarism, brought against him by Mr. Lauder, and Lauder himself convicted of several Forgeries, and gross Impositions on the Public, in a Letter to the Earl of Bath. By John Douglas, M.A." 8vo. 1751. P. 77 [A]. This pamphlet by Douglas, Bishop of Salisbury, appeared in November, 1750. See Courtney, p. 37. The Earl of Bath was William Pulteney.

48   This Letter not answering Lauder's expectation, he took upon himself his own defence on another ground, and abused both his Detector and Defen-der. See "King Charles vindicated from the Charge of Plagiarism, brought against him by Milton, and Milton himself convicted of Forgery, and a gross Imposition on the Public." 8vo. 1754. P. 4. This effort of spleen and malice was also abortive, and the Author soon afterwards retired to Barbadoes, where he died (1771), as he had lived, an object of general contempt [A].

49   This is a condensed version of Johnson's account in the Life of Milton. See *Lives,* 1:160.

50   The letter is dated 12 May 1750. See *Letters,* 1:33. The blind "owner" of the manuscript was Anna Williams.

51   Thomas Birch did not include this work in his edition of *The Works of Sir Walter Raleigh,* 2 vols. (London, 1751). The work was, however, "Printed for the EDITOR," in 1751, and sold by John Newbery. This attribution still requires investigation. See Greene, p. 415.

52   The installments appeared in *The Student,* 2:260–69, 290–94, 331–34.

53   Husbands's *A Miscellany of Poems By several Hands* is dated 1731. See Courtney, p. 1.

54   See her Epitaph in our Magazine for December, p. 414. His feelings on this occasion may be read in *The Idler,* published some years afterwards [A]. Elizabeth Johnson died 17 March 1752. On his epitaph Johnson errone-ously gives 1753. *Idler* No. 41 (27 January 1759) expresses his feelings on the death of his mother.

55   The following character, in Letter 112, cannot be applied to any other

person: [the "respectable Hottentot" passage has been omitted]. In these terms did this flimsy, superficial Peer speak of Dr. Johnson, in the year 1751 [A].

56   *Works,* 5:51.

57   The number of the French Academy employed in settling their language [A]. Garrick's "On Johnson's Dictionary" first appeared in the *Public Advertiser,* 22 April 1755, and in the *Gentleman's Magazine* 25 (April 1755):190, beneath an advertisement for the *Dictionary.*

58   *Preface; Works,* 5:50.

59   This Gentleman printed a paper [*North Briton*], in which he ridiculed the following passage in the Grammar of the English Tongue prefixed to the Dictionary. *"H* seldom, perhaps never, begins any but the first syllable." It contained a few score instances, in opposition to this remark. It began, "The Author of this observation must be a man of quick *appre-hension,* and of a most *comprehensive* genius" [A]. See *Life,* 1:300.

60   See Advertisement at the end of the Review of Dr. Johnson's Shakespeare [A]. The Advertisement in *A Review of Dr. Johnson's new edition of Shakespeare* (London, 1765) promises further attacks not on the *Dictionary,* but on his *Shakespeare.* The author later mentions Kenrick's attack in the proper place, see p. 56 below. William Kenrick was a notorious reviewer and libeller of literary figures.

61   *Lexiphanes* (London, 1767) was the work of Archibald Campbell. See *Life,* 2:44.

62   Zachary Williams was, it is said, a surgeon and physician in South Wales, who, allured by the reward offered by Parliament, laid aside the business of his profession to apply himself to the study of the longitude. Having formed his system, he came up to London, where he laid his proposals before a number of ingenious gentlemen, who agreed that, during the time required to the completion of his experiments, he should be supported by a joint subscription, to be repaid out of the rewards to which they concluded him entitled. Among his subscribers was Mr. Rowley, the constructor of the Orrery; and amongst his favourers, Lord Piesley. About 1729, his subscribers explained to the Lords of the Admiralty his pretensions, and the Lord Torrington declared his claim just to the reward assigned in the last clause of the act to those who should make discoveries conducive to the perfection of the art of sailing. This he pressed with so much warmth, that the Commissioners agreed to lay his Tables before Sir Isaac Newton, who excused himself from examining them on account of his age. [Newton died in 1727.] That great man, however, on hearing that Mr. Williams held the variation at London to be still encreasing, which he and other philosophers thought to be stationary, declared that he believed the system was visionary. On Sir Isaac Newton's declining the office assigned him, it was given to Mr. Molyneux [died 1728], who being suspected of clandestinely availing himself of the author's discoveries, altercation and a rupture ensued between them. About the same time he was admitted a Pensioner into the Charter-House, and continued his philosophical pursuits. He exhibited to the Royal Society

proof of the reasonableness of his theory, by a sphere of iron, on which a small compass moved in various directions, exhibiting no imperfect system of magnetical attraction. "After this (he adds, in Dr. Johnson's words) I withdrew from public notice, and applied myself wholly to the continuation of my experiments, the confirmation of my system, and the completion of my Tables, with no other companion than Mr. Gray, who shared all my studies and amusements, and used to repay my communications of magnetism with his discoveries in electricity. Thus I proceeded with incessant diligence; and perhaps in the zeal of enquiry did not sufficently reflect on the silent encroachments of Time, or remember that no man is in more danger of doing little than he who flatters himself with abilities to do all. When I was forced out of my retirement, I came, loaded with the infirmities of age, to struggle with the difficulties of a narrow fortune, cut off by the blindness of my daughter from the only assistance which I ever had, deprived by Time of my patrons and friends, a kind of stranger in a new world, where curiosity is now diverted to other objects, and where, having no means of ingratiating my labours, I stand the single votary of an obsolete science, the scoff of puny pupils of puny philosophers." The retirement from which he had been driven was the Charter-House, from whence he was expelled May 23, 1748, in a manner which would lead one to conclude he must have been guilty of some gross misbehaviour. At that period he was 75 years old, and consequently, when the above pamphlet was published, had reached the age of 82. He probably died soon after. In the year 1749 was printed a pamphlet, called "A true Narrative of certain Circumstances relating to Zachariah Williams, an aged and very infirm poor Brother Pensioner in Sutton's Royal Hospital the Charter-House; declaring some few of the many ill Treatments and great Sufferings he endured, and the great Wrongs done to him in order to his Expulsion out of the said House, and for a Pretext to deprive him of his just and appointed Rights therein" [A]. This information is largely taken from Johnson's *Account.* See *Works,* 5:298–99, 300–01.

63   Yale *Works,* 7:56.

64   *Letters,* 1:91.

65   For a discussion of Johnson's indebtedness to others see Arthur Sherbo, *Samuel Johnson, Editor of Shakespeare* (Urbana, 1956), particularly pp. 28–45; 102–13.

66   According to Boswell, items one, two, and six were not written by Johnson. See *Life,* 1:19; Courtney, pp. 74–75.

67   The *European Magazine* reads "chum." The earliest publications of this letter had this reading. See *The Letters of Tobias Smollett,* ed. Lewis M. Knapp (Oxford, 1970), p. 75 and n. 2; Waingrow, p. 537.

68   Thomas Francklin, Regius Professor of Greek at Cambridge, deprecated one of Arthur Murphy's tragedies in *A Dissertation on Antient Tragedy* (London, 1760), p. 24. For the "account of the former," see *European Magazine* 5 (March 1784):177–78.

69   Johnson's pension was not increased, although efforts in this direction

were made late in his life. See *Life,* 4:327–28, 348–50, 367–68; Hawkins, pp. 262–63.

70   See, for example, the *North Briton,* Nos. 11 (14 August 1762) and 12 (21 August 1762); *Churchill,* Bk. 3, ll. 817–20, p. 127. Johnson had defined *pension* as "An allowance made to any one without an equivalent. In England it is generally understood to mean pay given to a state hireling for treason to his country."

71   More properly, this is a character sketch of William Collins, not a life. See Courtney, pp. 101–02.

72   Johnson was, according to Percy, responsible for the "finest strokes" of the Dedication. See Percy's letter to Robert Anderson of 18 June 1800 in Anderson's *Life of Johnson,* 3rd ed. (London, 1815), p. 309 n.

73   It seems unlikely that the *Preface* was written this quickly, although precise information is lacking. See Sherbo, *Samuel Johnson, Editor of Shakespeare,* p. 13.

74   George Adams, *A Treatise describing and explaining the Construction and Use of New Celestial and Terrestrial Globes.*

75   In this year was published a Satire, by Cuthbert Shaw (an author of whom we should be glad to receive some account), entitled THE RACE, in which Dr. Johnson was spoken of in the following terms:

> Here Johnson comes — unblest with outward grace,
> His rigid morals stamp'd upon his face.
> While strong conceptions struggle in his brain;
> (For even Wit is brought to-bed with Pain)
> To view him, porters with their loads would rest,
> And babes cling frighted to the nurse's breast.
> With looks convuls'd, he roars in pompous strain,
> And, like an angry lion, shakes his mane.
> The Nine, with terror struck, who ne'er had seen
> Aught human with so horrible a mien,
> Debating whether they should stay or run —
> Virtue steps forth, and claims him for her son.
> With gentle speech she warns him now to yield,
> Nor strain his glories in the doubtful field;
> But wrapt in conscious worth, content sit down,
> Since Fame, resolv'd his various pleas to crown,
> Tho' forc'd his present claim to disavow,
> Had long resolv'd a chaplet for his brow.
> He bows, obeys; for Time shall first expire,
> E'er Johnson stay, when Virtue bids retire [A].

2nd ed. (London, 1766), pp. 16–17. Shaw wrote a number of poems, of which this is probably the best known.

76   The correct date for the edition of Ascham is 1761. Johnson was the

actual editor but credit was given to James Bennet. See *Life,* 1:550–52; Courtney, p. 100.

77   The concluding lines to *The Traveller* are generally ascribed to Dr. Johnson [A]. For Goldsmith's poem (1764) Johnson wrote lines 420, 429–34, 437–38. *Collected Works of Oliver Goldsmith,* ed. Arthur Friedman, 5 vols. (Oxford, 1966), 4:268–69.

78   Yale *Works,* 9:118.

79   *Letters,* 2:3.

80   For Johnson's publications in 1776, see Courtney, pp. 127–28.

81   The play was a revival of *A Word to the Wise* by Hugh Kelly. Thomas Hull acted at Covent Garden for forty-eight years and managed the theater from 1775 to 1782.

82   George III. See *Life,* 1:42 n. 2; 4:410.

83   John Hoole edited and wrote a prefatory life to *Critical Essays on Some of the Poems, of Several English Poets* (London, 1785) by John Scott, the Quaker poet. Hoole had introduced Scott to Johnson.

9

T[homas] T[yers]. *Gentleman's Magazine* 54 (December 1784):899–911; (Supplement), 982; "Additions," 55 (February 1785):85–87. Issued with revisions as a pamphlet (London, 1785). Reprinted in the *London Magazine Enlarged and Improved* 4 (May 1785):331–48 [Taken from December *GM*]; *New Annual Register . . . For the Year 1784,* 1 (London, 1785):23–47 [Taken from pamphlet]. The *Gentleman's Magazine* version was reprinted in *Miscellanies,* 2:335–81. This text is reproduced from the copy of the pamphlet with marginal annotations by Tyers in the Columbia University Library. Tyers's corrections have been incorporated into the text. This copy was reprinted with an introduction by Gerald D. Meyer, Los Angeles: Augustan Reprint Society, 1952 (Publication No. 34).

1   William Cumberland Cruikshank, the anatomist, who attended Johnson during his final illness. The executors were Sir John Hawkins, Sir Joshua Reynolds, and Sir William Scott, the international and maritime lawyer.

2   See, for example, *Lives,* 2:123; 3:199–200.

3   *Works,* 5:51; John Horne Tooke, *A Letter to Mr. Dunning, on the English Particle* (London, 1778), p. 56 n.

4   There is no reliable support for this last assertion. See Clifford, pp. 37 and 330 n. 16.

5   This is the first attribution of this poem to Johnson (Greene, p. 415). In the first version of the "Sketch," Tyers had given the age as three. For a discussion of the other versions of the poem, see *Gleanings*, 3:72–74; Waingrow, pp. 64 n. 2, 79–80; and pp. 249–50 and n. 4 below.

6   This is probably a reference to Andrew Corbet of Shropshire, who matriculated at Pembroke College, and who never fulfilled his promise of financial aid to Johnson. See *Life*, 1:58; Waingrow, p. 102 n. 29.

7   Clifford, p. 121, cites Tyers's account as one of the "dramatic exaggerations" of Johnson's behavior at Oxford.

8   It is unlikely that Johnson was ever usher under Blackwall, who died 8 April 1730. See *Gleanings*, 5:75–77.

9   John Green, later master at Lichfield Grammar School and Bishop of Lincoln; Isaac Hawkins Browne, the poet, whose conversational abilities Johnson admired. See *Anecdotes*, p. 113. Clifford remarks that Johnson knew Browne long before the time Tyers assigns (p. 59). See also *Gleanings*, 3:123; 5:49.

10   Smollett disregarded Johnson's warning. See *A Complete History of England*, 4 vols. (London, 1757–58), 3:73.

11   *Works*, 10:355–56. Horace Walpole was Robert Walpole's brother.

12   See Arthur Murphy's more detailed account, *Miscellanies*, 1:378–79. The "gentleman in a high employment" may have been Alexander Wedderburne, 1st Baron Loughborough. See also *Miscellanies*, 2:342 n. 5.

13   This lapse of chronology makes it clear that Tyers exaggerates Johnson's motivation for writing Savage's life, as well as the speed with which it was composed.

14   James Harris's *Philological Inquiries*.

15   The "shameless Aristophanes" was Samuel Foote. See *Life*, 2:299.

16   *Marmor Norfolciense* was reprinted in 1775.

17   Actually five bookselling firms were partners in the publication of the *Dictionary:* Robert Dodsley, Charles Hitch and L. Hawes, Andrew Millar, John and Paul Knapton, and Thomas and Thomas Longman.

18   There are several conflicting versions of this episode in the early biographies. For a discussion of them, see Sledd and Kolb, p. 108 and n. 10.

19   Ephraim Chambers, whose *Cyclopaedia, or an Universal Dictionary of Arts and Sciences* first appeared in 1728.

20   Joseph Spence, anecdotist and friend of Pope.

21   John Gilbert Cooper published his *Life of Socrates* in 1749.

22   Boswell, on the basis of information supplied by Bennet Langton, says that Chesterfield gave Johnson ten pounds. See *Life*, 1:261 n. 3.

23   Langton later gave a transcript of the letter to Boswell. See *Life*, 1:260–61.

24   William Adams, Master of Pembroke College, Oxford. See Waingrow, p. 21.

25   The exact amount was £1,575; *Life*, 1:183, 304.

26   John Boyle, 5th Earl of Corke and Orrery. Tyers added the following manuscript note: "of this literary Peer Johnson used to say, 'I loved him, more than I esteemed him': the reverse of what many of his acquaintance pronounced of himself."

27   The octavo abridgement appeared in eight editions from 1756 to 1786; see Sledd and Kolb, p. 114. There is no evidence that he received additional remuneration for the abridgement; see *Life*, 1:304 and n. 1.

28   Possibly *The Beauties of Johnson;* see *Life*, 1:214.

29   Samuel Richardson contributed only one essay, No. 97.

30   See Yale *Works*, 2:xxi n. 3.

31   See *The Letters of William Shenstone*, ed. Marjorie Williams (Oxford, 1939), p. 549; quoted in *Life*, 2:452–53. Shenstone attended Pembroke College, but did not enroll until two years after Johnson's departure.

32   *Lives*, 3:222. *Lexiphanes* was by Archibald Campbell.

33   Yale *Works*, 9:119.

34   "An ambassador" is said to be "a man of virtue sent abroad to tell lies for the advantage of his country." Quotation from *Idler* No. 30; Yale *Works*, 2:94.

35   See Johnson's "Prologue to *A Word to the Wise*," l. 4; Yale *Works*, 6:290.

36   With Henry Thrale, Johnson's "will" was not always "law." See *Anecdotes*, pp. 90–91, 185.

37   For details of the exchange of letters between Johnson and Mrs. Thrale, see James L. Clifford, *Hester Lynch Piozzi (Mrs. Thrale)* [Oxford, 1952], pp. 227–29, and *Letters*, 3:172–78. The "adumbration" appeared in *Gentleman's Magazine* 54 (December 1784):893.

38   G. B. Hill, *Miscellanies*, 2:354 n. 4, suggests that George III is referred to here.

39   Johnson was not a Non-juror. See *Life*, 2:231, and Maurice J. Quinlan, *Samuel Johnson: A Layman's Religion* (Madison, 1964), p. 172.

40   *Churchill*, Bk. 3, ll. 819–20, p. 127.

41   John Douglas, who exposed Lauder.

42   Edmund Burke.

43 John Campbell, miscellaneous writer. Johnson attended his Sunday evening gatherings in Queen Square. See *Life*, 1:417–18.

44 "The Winter's Walk," 1.20; Yale *Works*, 6:84.

45 Tyers has enclosed this paragraph in square brackets in ink.

46 Because he lacked the M.A. degree.

47 Thomas Warton, historian of English poetry.

48 The offer of a living in Lincolnshire was made by Bennet Langton, father of Johnson's close friend. See *Life*, 1:320.

49 William Dodd, preacher, author, and forger; *The Holy Bible, with a commentary and practical improvements*, 3 vols. (London, 1765–70).

50 See *Letters*, 2:409–10. John Hoole was the translator. Warren Hastings, Governor-General of India, 1772–85.

51 Joseph Warton, the critic, brother of Thomas.

52 A few of Johnson's letters had appeared in periodicals. Mrs. Piozzi published her two-volume edition of Johnson's correspondence in 1788.

53 William Jones, the Orientalist and member of The Club.

54 Martin Sherlock, *Letters of an English Traveller translated from the French* [by John Duncombe] (London, 1780); originally published in French and Italian in 1779. An additional volume, *New Letters from an English Traveller*, appeared in 1781.

55 Giuseppe Baretti came to England in 1751; Johnson had learned Italian before this time. See *Life*, 1:115, 302 and n. 1.

56 The Rev. Edward Lye published a *Dictionarium Saxonico-et Gothico-Latinum* (London, 1772), in which Johnson was actively interested. See *Letters*, 1:176.

57 We have been unable to identify Johnson's "guide" in Hebrew. See Yale *Works*, 1:154–55.

58 Edward Barnard, Provost of Eton.

59 Christopher Smart introduced Tyers to Johnson about 1755; see Arthur Sherbo, *Christopher Smart: Scholar of the University* (East Lansing, 1967), p. 101.

60 Hanway published a *Journal of Eight Days Journey from Portsmouth to Kingston upon Thames . . . To Which is Added an Essay on Tea* (London, 1756). Johnson published a review in the *Literary Magazine*, No. 7 (1756):335–42, and, in reply to Hanway, made additional comments in No. 13 (1757):161–67. See *Works*, 6:20–37. Although somewhat oblique, this ascription of Johnson's reply to Hanway antedates that in Hawkins cited by Greene, p. 416.

61 Murphy says that Johnson transcribed this remark in the margin of a passage in *Remarks on Johnson's Life of Milton*, part of *The Memoirs of Thomas*

Hollis (London, 1780) by the Rev. Francis Blackburne. See *Miscellanies,* 1:398 and n. 3.

62   Robert Vansittart, Regius Professor of Civil Law at Oxford, was Johnson's friend, but there seems to be no evidence that he went to India or that Johnson offered to accompany him. Tyers is perhaps confusing Robert with Henry Vansittart, Governor of Bengal, with whom, apparently, Johnson was not acquainted. For Johnson's desire to visit India with Joseph Fowke, see *Life,* 3:20, 471.

63   Johnson wrote to his printer, William Strahan, that the title would be "The choice of Life or The History of ——— Prince of Abissinia." See *Letters,* 1:117. The story of Seged appears in *Rambler* Nos. 204–05; Yale *Works,* 5: 296–305.

64   The text has "lump" but "lamp" seems a more likely reading.

65   Charles Pratt, Lord Camden, well-known for his antipathy towards Scotsmen. See *Life,* 2:514.

66   See *Miscellanies,* 2:388.

67   William Gerard Hamilton. For his generosity, see *Letters,* 3:100, 102, 119.

68   James Dunbar, professor of philosophy, King's College, Aberdeen and author of *Essays on the History of Mankind in Rude and Cultivated Ages* (London, 1780).

69   Daniel Burgess, non-conformist divine, whose parish was sacked by Sacheverell's mob in 1710. Tyers implies that despite Sacheverell's fanatic devotion to High Church principles Johnson would have nevertheless regarded him as the lesser of two evils.

70   Johnson wrote the two-page introduction to *Proceedings of the Committee Appointed to Manage the Contributions Begun at London . . . for Cloathing French Prisoners of War* (London, 1760). See Courtney, p. 99.

71   *London,* 1. 177; Yale *Works,* 6:56.

72   See the *Life of Ascham; Works,* 6:512.

73   See *Life,* 3:191; 4:37; *Lives,* 1:226 n. 8; 3:396.

74   Johnson thought *Henry and Emma* a "dull and tedious dialogue." See *Lives,* 2:202–03.

75   See *Lives,* 3:440, 434–35.

76   Robert Potter, author of *An Inquiry into Some Passages in Dr. Johnson's Lives of the Poets: Particularly His Observations on Lyric Poetry, and the Odes of Gray* (London, 1783). Potter also published *The Art of Criticism as Exemplified in Dr. Johnson's Lives of the Poets* (London, 1789). See H. G. Wright, "Robert Potter as a Critic of Dr. Johnson," *RES* 12 (1936):305–21. Johnson did not regard Potter's translation of Aeschylus (1774) very highly. See *Life,* 3:256.

77   John Young, professor of Greek at Glasgow, author of *A Criticism on*

The Elegy Written in a Country Church Yard. Being a Continuation of Dr. J——'s Criticism on the Poems of Gray (London, 1783). See Courtney, p. 138.

78   For a brief account of some of the attacks on the *Lives,* see Courtney, pp. 135–40. See also *Lives,* 3:457–58; *Life,* 4:64; *Thraliana,* 1:495; 2:622–23; *Miscellanies,* 2:417.

79   The *Elements of Criticism,* by Henry Home, Lord Kames, was published in 1762.

80   Thomas Warton's *Observations on the Faerie Queene of Spenser* had appeared in 1754.

81   Arthur Murphy's *A Poetical Epistle to Samuel Johnson* appeared in 1760, and is an imitation of Boileau's *Epître à Molière.* The last line, as quoted by Tyers, is a paraphrase of the last two lines of the poem: "And, since I ne'er can learn thy classic lore,/Instruct me *Johnson,* how to write no more." Goldsmith dedicated *She Stoops to Conquer* to Johnson (*Collected Works of Oliver Goldsmith,* 5:101).

82   Thomas Francklin's translation of Lucian's *Demonax* appeared in 1780. Only a portion of the translation was dedicated to Johnson. See *Life,* 4:479–80.

83   Wilkes, in the *North Briton,* No. 12, ridiculed Johnson for his definition of a pensioner. Johnson attacked Wilkes in *The False Alarm.* See *Works,* 6:155–78.

84   Andrew Millar.

85   This was a popular anecdote, although repeated in slightly different forms. See, for example, *Life,* 2:363 and *Anecdotes,* pp. 168–69.

86   Tyers is confused about this anecdote. According to Mrs. Piozzi, Johnson's sally, in reply to a question by Dr. Hugh Blair (the Scots divine and critic and a supporter of the authenticity of *Ossian*), was directed against James Macpherson. See *Anecdotes,* p. 168, and *Life,* 1:396. *Douglas,* a tragedy by John Home, was originally performed at Edinburgh in December 1756, and, with success, at Covent Garden the following March. For Johnson's dislike of the play, see *Life,* 2:320; 5:360–62.

87   Joseph Nollekens made a bust of Johnson in 1777. See *Life,* 4:554.

88   This bust by James Hoskins is now in the Royal Literary Fund (London). See Ronald Mac Keith, "The Death Mask of Samuel Johnson," *New Rambler* (June 1968), pp. 41–47.

89   Possibly James Burnett, Lord Monboddo. Johnson's dialect would have been that of Staffordshire.

90   We have been unable to identify this quotation from Humphry Hody.

91   Tyers may have in mind Johnson's remark about "a giant and a dwarf" in the *Preface to Shakespeare.* See Yale *Works,* 7:64.

92   This poem is lost; see Yale *Works,* 6:395.

93   *Works,* 5:51.

94   The executor was Sir John Hawkins. See Hawkins, p. 273.

95   Johnson bequeathed his house to his executors with instructions to sell it. It was sold to the Corporation of Lichfield. See *Life*, 4:440. An "exhibition" is a form of monetary assistance to university students.

96   Robert Freind, noted writer of inscriptions. Hester Maria Salusbury was Mrs. Piozzi's mother.

97   Paul Henry Maty conducted the *New Review* from 1782–86. For his praise of Johnson's epitaph on Henry Thrale, see 5 (1784):269–71.

98   Johnson left more than £2,000.

99   *Lives*, 1:149.

100   The actual cost was £45.6.1. An itemized list of expenses is given by J. Carter Rowland, "The Controversy Over Johnson's Burial," *New Rambler* (January 1970), p. 6.

101   This document was burned by Johnson shortly before his death. See *Life*, 4:405–06.

102   Johnson's account of William Tytler's *An Historical and Critical Enquiry into the Evidence produced by the Earls of Moray and Morton, against Mary Queen of Scots* (Edinburgh, 1760) appeared in the *Gentleman's Magazine* 30 (October 1760): 453–56. This is the first attribution of this work to Johnson. See Greene, p. 416.

103   Johnson contributed the "Advertisement" to Anna Williams's book, a "Dedication" to Charlotte Lennox's translation of *Sully's Memoirs*, and a "Dedication" to Adams's book. See Allen T. Hazen, *Johnson's Prefaces and Dedications* (New Haven, 1937), p. 112.

104   Johnson visited Oxford in July, 1759. Westmoreland's speech was given on 7 July. It is likely, in the absence of concrete evidence, that *Idler* No. 65 (14 July) and, perhaps, *Idler* No. 66 (21 July) were written at Oxford.

105   John Sharp, Archdeacon of Northumberland. His account of Johnson's visit appeared in a letter in the *Gentleman's Magazine* 55 (March 1785):173. See *Life*, 1:487, 517–18.

106   For Johnson's remarks on Aberdeen, see Yale *Works*, 9:13–18.

107   George Strahan edited Johnson's *Prayers and Meditations;* the preface is dated Islington, 6 August 1785. See Yale *Works*, 1:xvi–xviii; Courtney, pp. 158–59.

I O

[William Cooke]. *The Life of Samuel Johnson, LL.D. with Occasional Remarks on His Writings, an Authentic Copy of His Will, and a Catalogue of His Works. To Which*

are Added, Some Papers Written by Dr. Johnson, in Behalf of a Late Unfortunate Charac-
ter [Rev. William Dodd], *Never Before Published.* London, 1785. The first edition
was published on Monday, 27 December 1784 two weeks after Johnson's death;
the second edition is dated 22 February 1785. That the book was put together
in great haste is quite evident. The first edition draws heavily on previously
published information, such as that in the *Biographia Dramatica* and the
"Memoir" in the *Universal Magazine.* When Cooke prepared the second edition
he corrected some errors and made a few revisions, but mostly the biography
is filled out by the insertion of blocks of material. *Ad Urbanum,* the "respectable
Hottentot" sketch, the epitaphs for Johnson's parents and the rules of the Essex-
Head Club, for example, are simply inserted in the proper place in the narrative.
He also took advantage of the Johnsoniana which appeared after the first edition, particularly that of Tyers and George Steevens (?) [*European Magazine*
7 (January 1785):51–55], to flesh out his characterization. For a more detailed
discussion, see Kelley and Brack, pp. 11–13 and n. 21–24; and pp. 91–108
and n. 16–28. This text is reproduced from a copy of the second edition in
the Yale University Library. Only the *Life* itself has been included.

1   Johnson was not quite three years of age when his mother, not his father,
took him to London to be touched by Queen Anne on 30 March 1712.

2   Bishop Newton's Life, p. 8 [A].

3   Nash's History of Worcestershire [A]. Johnson was admitted to Pembroke
College on the 31st of October and William Adams was not his tutor. Apart
from these errors, Cooke implies that Adams was much older than Johnson;
in fact, Adams was only about three years older.

4   As a proof of this latter opinion, he has been often seen with his naked
feet appearing through the upper-leathers of his shoes; yet once when a new
pair was left at his door, he threw them away with indignation, disdaining to
accept of any thing so indelicately obtruded on his necessity [A].

5   See Gentleman's Magazine, 1736, p. 428 — Advertisement. "At Edial,
near Lichfield in Staffordshire, young gentlemen are boarded and taught the
Latin and Greek languages, by SAMUEL JOHNSON [A].

6   *Lives,* 2:20–21.

7   It seems unlikely that the poem was submitted to a number of booksellers.
See Clifford, pp. 188–94.

8   The Appleby Grammar School was in Leicestershire.

9   Of Birmingham.

10   In addition to Lucy, there were two sons.

11   This anecdote is unsubstantiated. See Clifford, p. 351 n. 12.

12   The correct title is *Debates in . . . .*

13   The friend was probably John Nichols. See *Life,* 4:407–08.

14   Published 15 February 1785. For a brief summary of the publishing history of Kearsley's collection, see *The Poems of Samuel Johnson,* ed. D. Nichol Smith and E. L. McAdam (Oxford, 1941), pp. xiv–xv, xix.

15   Johnson's Life of Dryden [A]. This is a loose paraphrase of *Lives,* 1:407.

16   Dr. Johnson acknowledged, that he and Savage, more than once, rambled all night about the streets, because their joint purses could not raise a sum sufficient to pay for the most humble lodging [A]. See *Life,* 1:164.

17   The first quotation is from *Lives,* 2:434. The phrase, "he mistook the love for the practice of virtue," appears in *Lives,* 2:380.

18   *Lives,* 1:368.

19   Johnson did not write all of the play at Lichfield. See *Life,* 1:100, 106, 107; Yale *Works,* 6:109.

20   Johnson defined this term: "To ridicule; to sneer. This is a sense unauthorized, and vulgar."

21   Vide Preface to his Dictionary [A]. *Works,* 5:49.

22   Mallet was a Scots poet and essayist.

23   "To catch, to move by jerks," *Dictionary.*

24   Richardson contributed only one essay and Cooke neglects Hester Chapone's contribution.

25   *Lives,* 1:113.

26   No eighteenth-century Russian translation is known. See *Life,* 4:529.

27   Johnson received two guineas for each number, thus four guineas a week. See Courtney, p. 26.

28   Johnson contributed the Preface to *A New Dictionary of Trade and Commerce* (London, 1756) by Richard Rolt.

29   Vide the Preface to his Dictionary [A]. *Works,* 5:51.

30   *Gentleman's Magazine* 24 (February 1754):57; *Works,* 6:432.

31   William Faden was the printer of the *Rambler.*

32   The quotation which follows is loosely taken from Johnson; *Works,* 6: 33–34, 37.

33   Richard Green, antiquary and apothecary; *Letters,* 3:251–52.

34   Chapters 26, 28–29.

35   Cooke is the first to mention the unlikelihood of Johnson's having offered *Rasselas* to two booksellers before it was published by the Dodsleys, William Johnston and William Strahan, the printer.

36   Home received a pension of £300 in 1760; therefore, Cooke's assertion seems doubtful. Murphy does not mention Bute's alleged effort to connect Home and Johnson; see *Miscellanies*, 1:417–18.

37   Isaac Reed; the edition was published in 1785.

38   Yale *Works*, 9:[3].

39   Ibid., p. 118.

40   See *Life*, 2:511–13.

41   The booksellers approached Johnson in 1777. The initial agreement was for 300 guineas. See Courtney, p. 130.

42   From the Advertisement to the third edition; see *Lives*, 1:xxvi.

43   *Lives*, 1:249.

44   Ibid., pp. 157, 85.

45   Ibid., 2:228.

46   Cooke had written in the first edition: ". . . on going to press with the third edition, willing to make him a further compliment, they offered him *two hundred pounds* more for his reversion of the copyhold: but the Doctor meeting the offer with the same generosity, after pausing some time, replied — 'Why, let me see — fourteen years hence, why I shall be but *eighty-six* then — no — I'll even keep the reversion as a nest egg for old age'" (pp. 76–77).

47   Furmenti or Frumenty is a dish made of hulled wheat boiled in milk, and seasoned with cinnamon, sugar, etc. Furmenti was customarily eaten on Mid-Lent Sunday and on Christmas Eve. See *Gentleman's Magazine* 13 (July 1783):578.

48   This is the first publication of this letter of 17 June 1783. See *Letters*, 3:32.

49   *Letters*, 3:220–21.

50   V. iii. 40–46. This anecdote was variously reported. See Waingrow, pp. 27, 32–33.

51   Richard Warren, member of The Club and physician to George III, Boswell, and Reynolds. The friend, or perhaps more properly, friends, cannot now be identified. See *Life*, 4:399; Waingrow, p. 27. This effort to secure the services of Dr. Warren parallels closely John Hoole and Francesco Sastres's attempt on Saturday and Sunday, 27 and 28 November, regarding Dr. Heberden. See *Miscellanies*, 2:149–50 and *Journal Narrative Relative to Doctor Johnson's Last Illness Three Weeks Before His Death Kept by John Hoole*, ed. with a preface by O M Brack, Jr. (Iowa City, 1972).

52   Possibly Dr. Richard Brocklesby. See *Life*, 4:414 and n. 3.

53   Hawkins affirms that Johnson made this quip on Friday, 10 December (p. 274).

54   The will of 8 December was witnessed by George Strahan and John Desmoulins, the Codicil of 9 December by John Copley, William Gibson, and Henry Cole. See Hawkins, pp. 265, 268–69, 273; *Miscellanies,* 2:149; *Hoole's Death of Johnson; Life,* 4:402 n. 2.

55   It is not known that Johnson burned his diary by mistake. Boswell claims that Hawkins's pocketing of the diary threw Johnson into such "agitation" that he burned it (*Life,* 4:406 n. 1). See Hawkins, pp. 271–72 and n. 9.

56   Barber joined Johnson in 1752.

57   This seems doubtful; Cooke is the only biographer to mention it.

58   The son of William Faden, editor of the *Literary Magazine.* Murphy identifies him as a "geographer near Charing Cross," *Miscellanies,* 1:447.

59   It is known that he burned a large quantity of letters. See, for example, *Life,* 4:405.

60   By Thomas Trotter. See *Life,* 4:421 n. 2, 461–62.

61   Johann Caspar Lavater was Swiss. Cooke must have seen the French translation, *Essai sur la Physiognomie,* which began publication in 1781. (See John Graham, "Lavater's *Physiognomy:* A Checklist, " *Papers of the Bibliographical Society of America* 55 [1961]:297–308.) The two heads appear on p. 200 of Part I. See *Life,* 4:463–64.

62   *Rambler,* vol. I. p. 85 [A]. *Rambler* No. 14; Yale *Works,* 3:79.

63   There is no other evidence of Johnson's giving such an allowance to Anna Williams. He assisted Garrick in giving her a benefit. See *Letters,* 1:83–84, 85–86. He also offered her occasional financial aid. See *Letters,* 1:375, 377, 382.

64   Thomas Tyers. See p. 72 above.

65   Cooke refers to Johnson's letter of 2 July 1784 (*Letters,* 3:174). Since the body of the letter is comprised of only ninety-seven words, it could hardly have filled five quarto pages.

66   *Lives,* 1:152.

67   Ibid., p. 153.

68   For a similar appraisal, see *Lives,* 1:183.

69   Cooke exaggerates Johnson's credulity, ignoring the fact that he helped to expose the imposture of the Cock-Lane ghost.

70   Cooke quotes nineteen lines from Juvenal (ll. 227–45, Loeb Classical Library) and then gives Dryden's translation (ll. 368–87, *The Poems of John Dryden,* ed. James Kinsley, 4 vols. [Oxford, 1958], 2:729–30).

71   Hawkesworth's poem was first published in the *Gentleman's Magazine* 17 (July 1747):337. We have not been able to identify Johnson's "particular friend."

72   *Preface to Shakespeare;* Yale *Works,* 7:71.

73 *Rambler* No. 77; Yale *Works,* 4:43–44.

74 As readers of Johnson's prayers and meditations realize, this is not always the case.

75 Johnson asked John Hoole, Francesco Sastres, and Dr. Brocklesby to write down his admonitions, but there is no evidence to suggest that Johnson composed in writing the sort of document that Cooke describes. See Waingrow, p. 134 and n. 6.

76 Johnson's monument is in St. Paul's Cathedral.

I I

[William Shaw]. *Memoirs of the Life and Writings of the Late Dr. Samuel Johnson; Containing Many valuable Original Letters, and several Interesting Anecdotes both of his Literary and Social Connections. The Whole Authenticated by Living Evidence.* London, 1785. William Shaw, Gaelic scholar and dissenting minister, was introduced to Johnson by James Elphinston in 1774. Shaw's account of his relationship with Johnson during the next ten years is given below. Although Shaw drew on previously published lives for the broad outline, and a few details, of Johnson's career, there is a good deal of new biographical material. As he makes clear in his "Preface," he obtained valuable information from Mrs. Desmoulins, Thomas Davies, and Elphinston. He also indicates that he has consulted other of Johnson's "most intimate" acquaintances and goes to great pains to establish the authenticity of his information and to prove himself qualified to be Johnson's biographer. Whatever the shortcomings of his biography might be, Shaw, unlike the other early biographers, did make an effort to discover the facts. He gives us important information about Johnson's wife, the publication of the Edinburgh edition of the *Rambler,* and the Ossian controversy. The account of the Ossian debate is particularly revealing since Shaw was one of the principals. This text is reproduced from a copy in the library of Herman W. Liebert.

1 Mrs. Desmoulins was the daughter of Johnson's godfather, Samuel Swynfen. She was among the group of Johnson's dependents and was in attendance when he died. Boswell also found her communications useful.

2 James Elphinston, educationalist and translator, brought out the Edinburgh edition of the *Rambler* and "enriched it with translations of the mottos." See *Life,* 1:210 and n. 3.

3 This is an exaggeration. Shaw did not take advantage of the available materials concerning Johnson's early life.

4 *Works,* 5:51.

5 *Lives,* 2:37.

6   Michael Johnson was probably not so cheerful as Shaw represents him. See *Gleanings*, 3:100.

7   Johnson was probably at Market Bosworth from March to July 1732. See *Gleanings*, 5:80.

8   *European Magazine* 6 (December 1784):412. See p. 44 above.

9   Shaw has the events of this period rather confused. The school at Edial probably did not get under way until autumn or early winter of 1735 and there is little reason to believe that Hawkesworth was ever one of his pupils (*Gleanings*, 6:45). Johnson inserted the advertisements for the school in the *Gentleman's Magazine* for June and July 1736. His marriage had taken place 9 July 1735.

10   Johnson's father had died in 1731.

11   The reference is probably to Joseph Porter, a wealthy London merchant and Tetty's brother-in-law. See *Gleanings*, 6:32.

12   The account of the publication and reception of *London*, like those in the *Universal Magazine* and Cooke, is unreliable. See Clifford, pp. 188–94.

13   Johnson wrote Cave on 25 November 1734 to offer his services in the poetry section of the magazine; see *Letters*, 1:3–4. His first known contribution is *Ad Urbanum*, published in March 1738, seven years after the founding of the periodical. See Clifford, p. 187; Courtney, pp. 5–6.

14   *Lives*, 1:335.

15   Ibid., 3:247.

16   We have been unable to identify this "warm admirer of Pope."

17   The first two lines quoted are from *The Vanity of Human Wishes;* the remainder are from *London*. See Yale *Works*, 6:91, 47–61. The second line of *The Vanity of Human Wishes* should read: "Survey mankind, from China to Peru."

18   *Lives*, 3:271.

19   This incident probably did not lead to Johnson's prejudice against Swift. See *Gleanings*, 6:113–14.

20   Tenth Satire [A]. Shaw has collapsed the events of these years, for it is unlikely that Johnson spent this much time planning the poem.

21   Shaw has again confused the chronology. Johnson was editor from 1738 to 1745 (with some interruption), and performed editorial duties occasionally thereafter. See Edward A. Bloom, *Samuel Johnson in Grub Street* (Providence, R. I., 1957), p. 8.

22   Subscriptions are taken in by Mr. [John] Murray, in Fleet-Street [A]. Thomas Morris, brother of the song writer, Charles Morris.

23 *Lives,* 3:271.

24 Ibid.

25 This was his first extended biography. Shorter biographies had appeared earlier in the *Gentleman's Magazine.*

26 Between 1737 and the production in 1749, Johnson tried unsuccessfully to have his play read by the theatre managers. When Garrick, who had aided Johnson's earlier efforts, assumed the managership of the Drury Lane Theatre in 1747, the production of *Irene* was assured. See Yale *Works,* 6:109.

27 The first number of the *Rambler* appeared 20 March 1750; the first number of Elphinston's edition appeared 1 June 1750. See Courtney, p. 32.

28 See Yale *Works,* 3:xxxi n. 1; 6:241–42. For Johnson's expression of gratitude to Elphinston, see 3:3.

29 Thomas Ruddiman, librarian and grammarian.

30 *Letters,* 1:39–40. Chapman dates the letter 1751 or 1752.

31 Margaret Penelope Strahan, wife of William, the London printer.

32 *Letters,* 1:34–35.

33 Johnson was paid two guineas a number or four guineas a week. He retained the copyright until after the expiration of the series, but later sold it. See Bloom, *Samuel Johnson in Grub Street,* p. 145.

34 Yale *Works,* 5:316.

35 *Works,* 5:49.

36 Shaw's imposition of an economic interpretation on the "provision" is foreign to Johnson's meaning and is factually inaccurate.

37 *Works,* 5:51.

38 For an account of Wilkes's "conversion" see George Rudé, *Wilkes and Liberty* (Oxford, 1962), pp. 191–93.

39 "Falbala" was probably borrowed from French-Provençal "farbélla" (fringe, lace); also, the Auvergnat "ferbelà" (to wear clothes in rags, tatters). See Oscar Bloch, *Dictionnaire Étymologique de la Lange Françoise* (Paris, 1968).

40 Johnson defined excise as "a hateful tax levied upon commodities, and adjudged not by the common judges of property, but wretches hired by those to whom excise is paid." He did not revise it. See *Life,* 1:295 n. 9.

41 Yale *Works,* 7:56–57.

42 Johnson received two-thirds of the profits on a printing of 1500 copies. See Yale *Works,* 2:xxiii. "A Dissertation on the Epitaphs written by Pope" origi-

nally appeared in the *Universal Visiter* (1756), pp. 207–19; "Bravery of the English Common Soldiers" first appeared in the *British Magazine* (January 1760), pp. 37–39. Both were added to the third edition (the second collected edition) of the *Idler* (London, 1767). See Courtney, pp. 75, 84.

43   *Works*, 5:255–56.

44   This is a highly imaginative account of the publication of *Rasselas*. Johnson submitted it to William Strahan, who, with the Dodsleys and William Johnston, published it.

45   Memoirs of G[eorge] Anne Bellamy [A]. (London, 1785.) This is largely a condensation of *An Apology for the Life of George Anne Bellamy* published in the same year. There is no specific reference to Johnson's pension in either of these works. Murphy, one of the first, if not the first (see *Life*, 1:374–75), to suggest the idea of Johnson's receiving a pension, published a short account of his role in the affair in the *Monthly Review* 76 (May 1787):374–75, but his full account was not published until 1792. See *Miscellanies*, 1:417–19.

46   Probably a humorous allusion to John Joshua Kirby's having been appointed drawing master to the Prince of Wales through the Earl of Bute.

47   We have been unable to identify this Lord.

48   Yale *Works*, 7:91.

49   This "failure" was the result of a quarrel with his assistant and a subsequent split in his congregation; Fordyce retired from his church in London in 1782. *Sermons to Young Women* was published in 1766. Fordyce published a sermon, "On the Death of Dr. Samuel Johnson," in *Addresses to the Deity* (London, 1785), pp. 209–32.

50   Yale *Works*, 9:118.

51   Probably Robert Melville, antiquarian.

52   James Beattie, Scots poet and rhetorician.

53   Archibald Montgomerie, eleventh Earl of Eglinton.

54   *Letters*, 2:408.

55   Donald M'Nicol had attacked Johnson in his *Remarks on Dr. Johnson's Journey to the Hebrides* (London, 1779). See *Life*, 2:308 n. 1. John Clark solicited M'Nicol's assistance in the *Answer to Mr. William Shaw's Reply* (Edinburgh, 1783); see *Life*, 4:526. See also Robert F. Metzdorf, "M'Nicol, Macpherson, and Johnson" in *Eighteenth-Century Studies in Honor of Donald F. Hyde*, ed. W. H. Bond (New York, 1970), pp. 45–61.

56   See the *London Magazine* 51 (December 1782):574–75.

57   *Letters*, 1:30–31.

58   Ibid., 2:253.

59 The series was called "Bell's British Poets" and extended to 109 volumes, published 1772–82.

60 *Lives,* 1:417.

61 As readers of Fanny Burney's *Diary* know, Johnson had a great fund of humor and was not above clowning and buffoonery.

62 Perhaps Thomas Osborne.

12

[Joseph Towers]. *An Essay on the Life, Character, and Writings of Dr. Samuel Johnson.* London, 1786. Joseph Towers, dissenting minister and miscellaneous writer, edited the *British Biography* (1766–72), was joint-editor of *Biographia Britannica* (1778–93), and was author of a biography of Frederick III of Prussia (1788). Towers had animadverted on Johnson's political pamphlets as unworthy of the author of the *Rambler* in his *A Letter to Dr. Samuel Johnson, occasioned by his late political Publications* (1775). Boswell reprinted excerpts from the *Letter* and concluded: "I am willing to do justice to the merit of Dr. Towers, of whom I will say, that although I abhor his Whiggish democratical notions and propensities . . . I esteem him as an ingenious, knowing, and very convivial man" (*Life,* 2:316). The heavy indebtedness of this biography, particularly to Boswell, Piozzi, and Tyers, is amply shown in the author's 106 footnotes. Towers's contributions are largely confined to a discussion of Johnson's political and critical views. This text is reproduced from a copy in the library of Herman W. Liebert.

1 Anecdotes of the late Dr. Samuel Johnson, p. 294 [A]. P. 188.

2 Ibid. p. 18 [A]. P. 15.

3 Ibid. p. 220 [A]. P. 142.

4 Biographical Sketch of Dr. Johnson, in the New Annual Register for 1784, p. 23 [A]. See p. 61 above.

5 This remark may be apocryphal, but it was widely accepted as true in the eighteenth century. Charles II's praise was first recorded by Thomas Sprat, repeated by Richard Hurd and Johnson; see *Lives,* 1:17–18. The authenticity of the remark is accepted by a recent critic, Robert B. Hinman, in *Abraham Cowley's World of Order* (Cambridge, Mass., 1960), p. 24.

6 Tyers's Biographical Sketch, ut supra, p. 24 [A]. See p. 62 above.

7 Prayers and Meditations, composed by Dr. Johnson, and published by Mr. Strahan, p. 52 [A]. See Yale *Works,* 1:81.

8   Prayers and Meditations, p. 3 [A]. Johnson's first surviving prayer was composed on 7 September 1736; Yale *Works,* 1:36–38.

9   Ibid. p. 106 [A]. Yale *Works,* 1:147.

10   Ibid. p. 106, 112 [A]. Yale *Works,* 1:147, 151.

11   Ibid. p. 9 [A]. Yale *Works,* 1:43.

12   Anecdotes, p. 36 [A]. P. 26. " 'He [Edward Barnard, Provost of Eton] was the only man too (says Mr. Johnson quite seriously) that did justice to my good breeding; and you may observe that I am well-bred to a degree of needless scrupulosity. No man, (continued he, not observing the amazement of his hearers) no man is so cautious not to interrupt another; no man thinks it so necessary to appear attentive when others are speaking; no man so steadily refuses preference to himself, or so willingly bestows it on another, as I do; no body holds so strongly as I do the necessity of ceremony, and the ill effects which follow the breach of it: yet people think me rude; but Barnard did me justice.' " But see also Mrs. Piozzi's statement that "no one was indeed so attentive not to offend in all such sort of things as Dr. Johnson; nor so careful to maintain the ceremonies of life . . ." (p. 165).

13   Yale *Works,* 4:159–64.

14   Meditations, p. 184, 185 [A]. Yale *Works,* 1:304.

15   Anecdotes, p. 85 [A]. P. 57.

16   Ibid. p. 221 [A]. P. 143.

17   Biographical Sketch of Dr. Johnson, p. 38 [A]. see p. 79 above.

18   Tour to the Hebrides, p. 441 [A]. *Life,* 5:352.

19   Ibid. p. 7 [A]. *Life,* 5:17.

20   Ibid., p. 406 [A]. *Life,* 5:324.

21   Anecdotes, p. 22 [A]. P. 17.

22   Ibid. p. 30 [A]. P. 22.

23   Ibid. p. 38 [A]. P. 27. Johnson later described his conduct to Jorden on this occasion as "stark insensibility." See *Life,* 1:59–60. Despite what he considered Jorden's defects in learning, he sincerely admired his tutor. See *Life,* 1:272.

24   Vid. Mrs. Piozzi's Anecdotes, p. 223 [A]. P. 144.

25   Ibid. p. 26, 27 [A]. Pp. 20–21.

26   Ibid. p. 269 [A]. P. 172.

27   Ibid. p. 295 [A]. P. 188.

28   *London,* l. 177; Yale *Works,* 6:56.

29   Davies's Life of Garrick, vol. I. p. 11 [A].

30   Johnson came to London in March 1737; Gower's letter was written in 1739.

31   Ll. 131–34; Yale *Works,* 6:97.

32   Ll. 167–74; Yale *Works,* 6:99–100.

33   Vid. Formey's account of his own life, prefixed to the translation of his *Philosophical Miscellanies,* printed at London in 1759, p. 7 [A]. Towers is partially correct. Johnson wrote his first two installments [*Gentleman's Magazine,* 10 (December 1740):612; 11 (February 1741): 87–88, 93] from correspondence furnished him by the Reverend Mr. Nicholas Carter, father of Elizabeth Carter, his fellow contributor to the *Gentleman's Magazine* (see Montague Pennington, *Memoirs of Mrs. Elizabeth Carter* [London, 1808], 1:70–94). The third installment [12 (May 1742):242–45] was taken from Jean Henri Samuel Formey's *La Vie de Mr. Jean Phillippe Baratier* (1741). Johnson again drew on Formey's information when he revised and reissued his articles as a pamphlet in 1744.

34   Ll. 1–8; Yale *Works,* 6:87–88.

35   He was born on the 18th of September, 1709 [A].

36   Tour to the Hebrides, p. 458 [A]. *Life,* 5:364.

37   Ll. 21–32; Yale *Works,* 6:111–12.

38   For both of these quotations see Yale *Works,* 7:84.

39   *Thoughts on the Late Transactions Respecting Falkland's Islands.* See *Works,* 6:205–06.

40   Yale *Works,* 5:316.

41   Numbers 7, 8, 17, 19, 24, 26, 43, 49, 64, 68, 71, 73, 102, 108, 110, 155, 165, 169, 196, 203 [A]. The title of *Rambler* No. 26, "The mischief of extravagance, and misery of dependence," is omitted.

42   Anecdotes, p. 49 [A]. P. 34. *Rambler* No. 200; Yale *Works,* 5:276–81.

43   *Lives,* 2:334. See also *Life,* 1:167, for Boswell's assertion that this passage from the *Life of Savage* expresses Johnson's aversion to actors.

44   Vid. Boswell, p. 31, 299 [A]. *Life,* 5:38, 273.

45   Johnson praises Garrick in his *Life of Smith; Lives,* 2:21.

46   *Works,* 5:51; Yale *Works,* 5:317.

47   *Works,* 5:51, 49–50.

48   Numbers 14, 16, 22, 23, 43, 49, 52, 59, 62, 63, 64, 65, 68, 69, 91, 94 [A].

49   Anecdotes, p. 41 [A]. P. 34.

50   The proposals for his edition of Shakespeare was printed in the year 1756, and the work itself was not published till 1765 [A].

51   Life of Roger Ascham, prefixed to his Works, p. 11 [A]. *Works,* 6:514.

52   False Alarm, p. 48 [A]. *Works,* 6:175. For a discussion of the petitions and petitioners of 1769, see Rudé, *Wilkes and Liberty,* pp. 105–48.

53   Political Tracts, p. 157 [A]. The quotation is from *The Patriot; Works,* 6:219.

54   Taxation no Tyranny, p. 30. edit. 1775 [A]. *Works,* 6:237.

55   Vid. Political Tracts, p. 106, 107, 108, 109, 158 [A]. The references are to *Thoughts on the Late Transactions Respecting Falkland's Islands; Works,* 6:199–200; and to *The Patriot; Works,* 6:220.

56   Only the first four volumes appeared in 1779. The remaining six followed in 1781.

57   Life of Waller, p. 15. edit. 1779 [A]. *Lives,* 1:255.

58   *Lives,* 1:278–79. Like Towers, Johnson felt that Clarendon's account of Waller was open to question, pp. 279–80.

59   For Johnson's sarcastic reference to Milton's *The Tenure of Kings and Magistrates* (London, 1649), see *Lives,* 1:110.

60   Whether or not Johnson was motivated by "his aversion to Milton's politics," he seems to have been aware that the pamphlet was an attack on Milton's reputation — Boswell's arguments to the contrary notwithstanding. See Hawkins, p. 119 and *Life,* 1:231.

61   Ll. 15–18; Yale *Works,* 6:240–41.

62   Life of Milton, p. 10 [A]. *Lives,* 1:89–90.

63   The reference is to Milton's *Of Education* (London, 1644), addressed to his friend, Samuel Hartlib.

64   Life, p. 25, 26 [A]. *Lives,* 1:98.

65   Ibid., p. 32, 33 [A]. *Lives,* 1:101.

66   Ibid. p. 34 [A]. *Lives,* 1:102. Johnson gives the title as follows: *Of Prelatical Episcopacy, and whether it may be deduced from the Apostolical Times, by virtue of those testimonies which are alledged to that purpose in some late treatises, one whereof goes under the name of James, Lord Bishop of Armagh.* Towers has made a crucial deletion. Johnson said: "I have transcribed this title to shew, by his contemptuous mention of Usher, that he had now adopted the puritanical savageness of manners."

67   Ibid. p. 142 [A]. *Lives,* 1:156.

68   In this piece, Milton says, "A free Commonwealth was not only held by wisest men in all ages, the noblest, the manliest, the equallest, the justest government, the most agreeable to due liberty, and proportioned equality, both human, civil, and Christian, most cherishing to virtue and true religion, but also (I may say it with greatest probability) plainly commended, or rather

enjoined, by our Saviour himself to all Christians, not without a remarkable disallowance, and the brand of Gentilism upon Kingship." — "That people must needs be mad, or strangely infatuated, that build the chief hope of their common happiness or safety on a single person; who, if he happen to be good, can do no more than another man; if to be bad, hath in his hands to do more evil without check, than millions of other men. The happiness of a nation must needs be firmest and certainest in a full and free council of their own electing, where no single person, but reason only sways." — "Of all governments a commonwealth aims most to make the people flourishing, virtuous, noble, and high spirited." *Milton's Prose Works*, Vol. II. p. 786, 787, 795: edit. 1698.

In his *Defensio pro Populo Anglicano*, he also says, *Deus nisi invitus, populum suum sub regio imperio esse noluit; natura quid suadeat et recta ratio, non ex pluribus, sed ex prudentissimis nationibus optimè perspicitur. Græci, Romani, Itali, Carthaginienses, multique alii suopte ingenio vel optimatium vel populi imperium regio prætulerunt; atque hæ quidem nationes cæterarum omnium instar sunt. Hinc Sulpitius Severus,* Regium nomen cunctis ferè liberis gentibus semper invisum, *fuisse tradit.* DEFENSIO, p. 101 edit. London, 4to. 1651.

From sundry other passages in Milton's prose-works, there seems, however, reason to believe, that he would not have been dissatisfied under the government of a king, if the liberties of the people had been properly secured, and the power of the prince restrained and limited, according to the true principles of the English constitution [A].

69   *Lives*, 1:118.

70   P. 91 [A]. *Lives*, 1:131–32.

71   Vid. [Thomas] Warton's Preface to his edition of Milton's Poems, p. 12 [xii] [A]. *Poems upon Several Occasions, English, Italian, and Latin, with Translations by John Milton* (London, 1785).

72   Vid. the notes to the new edition of Milton's Poems, p. 587, 588 [A].

73   Ibid. p. 589 [A].

74   Ibid. p. 117 [A].

75   Life of Milton, p. 28, 29, 30 [A]. *Lives*, 1:99–100.

76   Ibid. p. 140, 141 [A]. *Lives*, 1:155–56.

77   Ibid. p. 142 [A]. *Lives*, 1:156.

78   Life of Milton, p. 45, 46 [A]. *Lives*, 1:108.

79   P. 51 [A]. *Lives*, 1:110–11. William R. Parker, *The Life of John Milton* (Oxford, 1967), 2:964–66, presents evidence that Milton did not interpolate the prayer from Sidney.

80   Ibid. p. 169 [A]. *Lives*, 1:170.

81   Ibid. p. 223 [A]. *Lives*, 1:194.

82   *Lives*, 1:410.

83 Johnson "dextrously palliated" Dryden's conversion in *Lives*, 1:404.

84 *Lives*, 2:110–11.

85 Life of Addison, p. 64 [A]. *Lives*, 2:112.

86 P. 44 [A]. *Lives*, 2:14. Addison's most recent biographer accepts the truth of this story. See Smithers, *The Life of Joseph Addison*, p. 124.

87 Boswell's Tour to the Hebrides, p. 38 [A]. *Life*, 5:44.

88 *Lives*, 2:202–03. See p. 314 n. 74 above.

89 Ibid. p. 312 [A]. *Life*, 5:255.

90 Life of Prior, p. 10 [A]. *Lives*, 2:185.

91 Life of King, p. 3 [A]. *Lives*, 2:27. Robert Molesworth published an *Account of Denmark* in 1692.

92 P. 5 [A]. *Lives*, 2:43.

93 Vid. Torbuck's Parliamentary Debates, vol. III. p. 46 Biographia Britan. General Dict. &c [A]. See *Lives*, 2:43 n. 2.

94 Life of Pope, p. 106, 107 [A]. Johnson discusses this famous quarrel in *Lives*, 3:128–34; the quotation appears on pp. 132–33.

95 In the new Edition of the Biographia Britannica, art. ADDISON, note [U] [A]. The new edition appeared in 1778.

96 See Owen Ruffhead, *The Life of Alexander Pope* (London, 1769), pp. 184–93.

97 Ibid. [A]. The reference is to the *Biographia Britannica* article in n. 95.

98 Joseph Spence, *Observations, Anecdotes, and Characters of Books and Men,* ed. James M. Osborn, 2 vols. (Oxford, 1966), 1:68–72, 335; 2:623–24.

99 Vid. Johnson's Life of Pope, p. 121, 137, 142. Life of Savage, p. 48, 49. edit. 1781. Life of Broome, p. 5, 6 [A]. See *Lives*, 3:141–42, 150, 153; 2:362–63; 3:77–79.

100 Life of Lyttelton, p. 2 [A]. *Lives*, 3:446.

101 Anecdotes, p. 161 [A]. P. 105.

102 Biographical Sketch, p. 41 [A]. See p. 82 above.

103 In Thomas Warton's Edition of Milton's Poems, p. 34 [A]. Thomas, in his note on the last line of "Lycidas," is quoting his brother Joseph.

104 Life of Milton, p. 157 [A]. *Lives*, 1:165.

105 Vid. Boswell, p. 119 [A]. *Life*, 5:112.

106 Anecdotes, p. 99, 100 [A]. P. 66.

107   P. 2 n. 2 of the third edition, reprinted with an introduction by Robert E. Kelley, Augustan Reprint Society (Publication No. 133).

108   This life was written by Herbert Croft.

109   *Life of Young*, p. 39 [A]. *Lives*, 3:371. The two quotations appear in *Lives*, 3:384, 373.

110   *Lives*, 2:20–21, 91–98.

111   Davies's collection is the *Miscellaneous and Fugitive Pieces*. For Johnson's review of Thomas Blackwell's *Memoirs of the Court of Augustus*, 3 vols. (Edinburgh, 1753–63), see *Works*, 6:9–16.

112   Literary and Moral Character of Dr. Johnson, p. 20 [A].

113   Mr. Courtenay, however, adds [p. 20 n. 42], that "at that time Dr. Johnson was himself engaged in writing the *Rambler*, and could ill afford to make a present of his labours." But in this particular this ingenious writer is mistaken. The *Adventurer* was not published till some time after a period was put to the publication of the *Rambler* in numbers [A]. For Richard Bathurst's role in the *Adventurer*, see Yale *Works*, 2:333–35.

114   Towers omits twelve essays written by Johnson.

115   Biographical Sketch, p. 25 [A]. See p. 63 above. Tyers is also the source for Churchill's remark, pp. 66–67 above.

116   Ibid. [A]. See p. 78 above.

117   Anecdotes, p. 283 [A]. P. 181.

118   Ibid. p. 237 [A]. P. 152.

119   Vid. Piozzi's Anecdotes, p. 41, 48, 201. Boswell's Tour, p. 65. Tyers's Biographical Sketch, p. 27 [A]. *Anecdotes*, pp. 34, 37, 108; *Life*, 5:67; p. 66 above.

120   Piozzi, p. 21, 22 [A]. Pp. 18–19.

121   Boswell, p. 103 [A]. *Life*, 5:99.

122   Ibid. p. 258 [A]. *Life*, 5:215.

123   This appears to have been the real motive of Pope's conduct in this transaction [A].

124   Life of Pope, p. 219 [A]. *Lives*, 3:194–95.

125   Ibid. p. 230 [A]. *Lives*, 3:201.

126   P. 102, 103, 105 [A]. *Lives*, 1:136–38.

127   P. 123 [A]. Yale *Works*, 1:158.

128   Anecdotes, p. 173 [A]. P. 113.

129   P. 96 [A]. Yale *Works*, 1:134.

130   Tour to the Hebrides, p. 500 [A]. *Life,* 5:397.

131   Tour, p. 21, 22, 23 [A]. *Life,* 5:30–31.

132   Tour to the Hebrides, p. 312 [A]. *Life,* 5:255. James Granger, the print collector and biographer.

133   Both quotations are from *Idler* No. 70; Yale *Works,* 2:217, 218.

134   *Works,* 5:36.

135   *Rambler* No. 208; Yale *Works,* 5:319.

136   Ibid., 5:318–19.

137   Vid. Piozzi's Anecdotes, p. 96, 97 [A]. Pp. 64–65.

138   Meditations, p. 140 [A]. Yale *Works,* 1:258.

139   Life of Waller, p. 1 [A]. *Lives,* 1:249.

140   *Life,* 5:121. William Robertson, the historian.

141   Anecdotes, p. 140 [A]. P. 92.

142   Ibid. p. 137 [A]. P. 90.

143   Meditations, p. 123 [A]. Yale *Works,* 1:160.

144   Ibid. p. 145 [A]. Yale *Works,* 1:261.

13

This anonymous biography appeared in 16 unnumbered pages at the beginning of volume I of Johnson's *A Dictionary of the English Language,* printed by J. Jarvis and sold by J. Fielding (London, 1786). See Kelley and Brack, pp. 108–13 and n. 29. This account is largely derivative and borrows heavily from Cooke, Mrs. Piozzi, and Boswell. About a fourth of this essay is made up of word-for-word transpositions from the *Tour* and the *Anecdotes;* these have been deleted. Also deleted are some blocks of information taken directly from Cooke and large quotations from Johnson used as filler. This text is reproduced from a copy in the Yale University Library.

1   David Hume [A].

2   *Lives,* 1:373.

3   *Anecdotes,* pp. 6–15. The quotation begins with the first complete paragraph on page 6 and ends with "poor Bathurst is dead!!!" on page 15.

4   *Anecdotes*, pp. 16–17.

5   Johnson was nineteen when he entered Oxford, 31 October 1728; he remained about fourteen months.

6   *Anecdotes*, pp. 32–33. Mrs. Piozzi made another entry (25 March) in *Thraliana* saying that Johnson had *intended* translating the lines at sixteen but never did until he was sixty-eight. See *Thraliana*, 1:232–33 and Yale *Works*, 6:296–98.

7   This version is taken from the *Anecdotes*, pp. 24–25. In the "true history" of the poem as related by Edmund Hector Johnson took thirty minutes to make the verses. See Waingrow, p. 575. For a discussion of the complex history of this anecdote, see Waingrow, p. 439 n. 2. "Mund" was Johnson's nickname for Hector.

8   R. B. Sheridan, Esq; M. P. [A].

9   *Lives*, 2:20–21.

10   There has been much controversy as to whether Johnson had met Savage at the time; Clifford's suggestion that, while Savage may not have been the model for Thales, there may be much of him in the portrait, is probably closer to the truth (pp. 207–08). Ll. 1–8; Yale *Works*, 6:47–48.

11   This volume of poetry was in print by this time. The author takes this information from Cooke, retaining the phrase "now printing." See p. 97 above.

12   This is taken from Cooke; see pp. 109–10 above. The three-paragraph quotation begins "Soon after the accession" and ends "the whole subscription money."

13   *Life*, 5:13–16, 18–19. The quotation begins with the opening paragraph and ends: "With such propitious convoys did he proceed to my native city" (p. 16). The quotation begins again with the sentence on page 18: "He was now in his sixty-fourth year . . ."; it continues to the end of the paragraph on the top of page 19.

14   Ll. 21–24; Yale *Works*, 6:290–91.

15   Probably Cornelius Ford, Johnson's cousin. They first met in 1725. See *Anecdotes*, p. 12; Clifford, pp. 284–85.

14

[James Harrison (?)]. This biography appears in 18 unnumbered pages at the beginning of Johnson's *A Dictionary of the English Language* published by Harrison and Company (London, 1786). (See Kelley and Brack, p. 154 n. 29). On p. iii appeared the following "Advertisement to Mr. Harrison's Life of the Author":

> The world has already been so glutted with Anecdotes and Memoirs of Dr. Johnson, that every new account, for some years, will probably be considered rather as an evil than a good.
>
> Of evils, the least are to be chosen. This, after much deliberation, has determined the Editor to present his Readers with a more concise Life of the Doctor than he had originally intended.
>
> But though Mr. Harrison is equally desirous to avoid the errors of those who have wearied by long heterogeneous digressions, and disgusted by minute recitals of insignificant facts, he is not without the hope that he shall omit no circumstance of importance in the Doctor's character; and he has the peculiar felicity to know, that whatever may be the imperfections discoverable in this little biographical sketch, it can never appear to have been delineated by the hand of that worst species of enemy, a *pretended friend.*

The last sentence in this advertisement is particularly ironic in view of the author's having taken most of his information from Hawkins. The sketch cannot be dismissed, however, as a mere condensation of Hawkins. When the author had information not found in his source, he inserted it in the proper place in the narrative; notable examples are his new version of the "Epitaph on a Duck" and his information on Johnson's writings for Charlotte Lennox. One wonders whether Harrison took the trouble to write this life himself; it would seem more likely that he hired someone to do it. This text is reproduced from a copy in the library of Herman W. Liebert.

1   This story, taken from Hawkins (p. 2), is now considered apocryphal. See *Gleanings,* 3:14–17.

2   Joan Marklew.

3   See Hawkins, p. 3; *Anecdotes,* p. 10; Waingrow, pp. 64 and n. 2, 79–80.

4   We have been unable to identify the author's source for this version. Johnson's father wrote the last half of the epitaph. See Yale *Works,* 6:354 and *Gleanings,* 3:72–74.

5   For Johnson's juvenilia see Yale *Works,* 6:3–27.

6   William Butt was the grandfather of the Rev. George Butt.

7   A slight exaggeration. See Clifford, p. 130.

8   William Innys, whose generosity Johnson always remembered. See pp. 288–89 below.

9   The school was founded in the sixteenth century. Johnson's residence lasted from March to July.

10   Nathaniel had succeeded his father upon his death in 1731.

11 Hawkins, p. 15; *Letters,* 1:3–4.

12 See Hawkins, pp. 15–16, 280 n. 35. The "anonymous account" is either the *Account* in the *European Magazine* (pp. 45, 303 n. 13 above) or Cooke's *Life* (p. 94 above), for Hawkins apparently knew both. See Davis, pp. 46–47.

13 Mrs. Porter was not related to the Jarvis family with whom Johnson lodged. She had two sons and a daughter. Both errors are Hawkins's (p. 18).

14 *Letters,* 1:8–9.

15 See Hawkins, pp. 48–49.

16 Johnson went to Lichfield late in the summer of 1737 and returned to London with Tetty in late autumn. See Clifford, p. 183.

17 *Letters,* 1:9–10.

18 This is Hawkins's error (p. 34); Dodsley paid Johnson ten guineas.

19 Ll. 1–8; Yale *Works,* 6:47–48.

20 Hawkins states that "Johnson was well enough skilled in the Italian language for the undertaking" (pp. 36–37).

21 The translator was the Rev. John Johnson; this is Hawkins's error (p. 37).

22 Johnson translated the *Commentaire* of Crousaz (Hawkins's error, p. 37).

23 This account is taken from Hawkins (p. 41). Boswell "directed every possible search to be made in the records of the Treasury and Secretary of State's office but could find no trace of any warrant having been issued." See *Life,* 1:141–42. Even if no warrant was issued, Johnson may have heard rumors to that effect and taken the precaution of going into hiding. See Davis, pp. 100–02, and Hawkins, p. 284 n. 23.

24 Johnson served as editor from 1738 to 1745 (with some interruption), and performed editorial duties occasionally thereafter. Harrison probably confuses Johnson's tenure as editor with the alleged duration of his writing the *Parliamentary Debates.* There is no evidence that William Guthrie was an "assistant editor," though he was Cave's chief writer. See Bloom, *Samuel Johnson in Grub Street,* pp. 8, 52.

25 *Lives,* 3:187.

26 Hawkins, pp. 142, 294 n. 36.

27 Ibid., p. 77. Hawkins errs regarding the date of publication (p. 140).

28 On 22 February 1774, by a six to five margin, the judges in the House of Lords voted against perpetual copyright in the case of Donaldson vs. Becket. Alexander Donaldson was an Edinburgh bookseller, Thomas Becket, a London bookseller. See Sir Frank Mackinnon, "Notes on the History of English Copyright," *Oxford Companion to English Literature,* p. 886.

29   Hawkins, p. 142.

30   Ibid., p. 140. Boswell claims to have the true account. According to Boswell, it was a verbal exchange with the messenger who carried the last sheet to Millar. See *Life,* 1:287 and n. 2.

31   This imaginative account does not agree with Johnson's remarks on the transaction as recorded by Boswell in *Life,* 1:304–05.

32   Hawkins, p. 81. Johnson assured Boswell that there was not "the least foundation" for this story and that there was no particular incident which produced the quarrel. Because of Chesterfield's continued neglect "he resolved to have no connection with him." See *Life,* 1:257.

33   Sir Thomas Robinson, colonial governor. Chesterfield wrote two essays in the *World,* Nos. 100 and 101.

34   No evidence exists to suggest that Reynolds was involved in Chesterfield's efforts to apologize. Apparently Johnson and Reynolds did not meet until 1756. See *Portraits by Sir Joshua Reynolds,* ed. Frederick W. Hilles (New York, 1952), pp. 61–62.

35   *The Vanity of Human Wishes* was published 9 January and *Irene* was not produced until 6 February. Hawkins's chronology is misleading (p. 87).

36   John Payne, who published Lauder's pamphlet.

37   Yale *Works,* 1:43.

38   Yale *Works,* 5:320.

39   Hawkins, pp. 121–22. Hawkins may have misdated this celebration, which probably took place in the spring or autumn of 1750. See Duncan Isles, "Johnson and Charlotte Lennox," *New Rambler* (June 1967), p. 42 and n. 31.

40   This attribution requires further investigation. Isles (p. 45) does not accept it. The *Lady's Museum* ran for eleven numbers beginning in March 1760.

41   Hawkins states that Johnson received two guineas a paper (p. 127).

42   Hawkins, pp. 129–131.

43   Yale *Works,* 1:51. This quotation is from the "Prayer on Easter Day," 22 April 1753.

44   *Anecdotes,* p. 96.

45   Ibid., p. 98.

46   *Works,* 5:51.

47   Johnson's *Memoirs of Frederick III, King of Prussia* was reissued in 1786 "with notes and a continuation" by Harrison. See Courtney, p. 76.

48   Hawkins (2nd ed., 1787), p. 361.

49 John Newbery published the first collected edition in 1761. Johnson's original agreement was with John Payne.

50 Hawkins says Johnson borrowed six guineas from Allen (p. 294 n. 7). Most of this account of *Rasselas* does not appear in Hawkins; it is similar to that related by Shaw (see p. 170 above).

51 Johnson wrote three letters published in the *Daily Gazetteer* for 1, 8, 15 December. See *Works*, 5:303–10; *Letters*, 1:446–52; and Courtney, p. 98. As Hawkins points out (p. 158) Robert Mylne's elliptical design was used. The "rival architect" was John Gwynn, Johnson's friend.

52 Johnson did not move until August. See *Life*, 3:535.

53 Richard Bathurst, father of Johnson's friend, Dr. Richard Bathurst.

54 Yale *Works*, 7:105.

55 The interview with George III took place in February 1767. See *Life*, 2:33. This is Hawkins's error (p. 204).

56 See *Anecdotes*, p. 82.

57 See *Life*, 1:356 and n. 2. Harrison's source is *Anecdotes*, pp. 151–52.

58 Hawkins, p. 234. Johnson told Boswell he had been once in Dodd's company. See *Life*, 3:140.

59 *Anecdotes*, p. 159.

60 Hawkins, p. 261; *Letters*, 3:183.

61 Thurlow had offered to grant Johnson £500 or £600 as a mortgage on the pension. See *Life*, 4:348.

62 Hawkins, pp. 271–72.

Index

All page references are preceded by a chapter number in parentheses which identifies the biography in which the reference occurs. Works are usually cited by title with the author's name in parentheses, rather than under the author's listing. In all instances Samuel Johnson is abbreviated SJ. Italic reference numbers indicate that a document or long quotations from printed material appeared at that point in the text but have been deleted. A dagger following a reference number calls attention to a factual error in the text (the year of Johnson's birth, for example) which was corrected in a note only the first time it appeared. Every effort has been made in the index to correct and supplement the commentary. The index, compiled by Claudine Harris, was financed by a grant from the Graduate College of The University of Iowa.